W. H. Davenport Adams

Good Queen Anne

Or, men and manners, life and letters in England's Augustan age

W. H. Davenport Adams

Good Queen Anne
Or, men and manners, life and letters in England's Augustan age

ISBN/EAN: 9783337323714

Printed in Europe, USA, Canada, Australia, Japan

Cover: Foto ©ninafisch / pixelio.de

More available books at **www.hansebooks.com**

Good Queen Anne;

OR,

Men and Manners, Life and Letters

IN ENGLAND'S AUGUSTAN AGE.

BY

W. H. DAVENPORT ADAMS.

IN TWO VOLUMES.

London:
REMINGTON & CO., PUBLISHERS,
HENRIETTA STREET, COVENT GARDEN, W.C.
1886.

[All rights reserved.]

THESE VOLUMES,

DESIGNED TO FURNISH A COMPREHENSIVE VIEW OF

MEN AND MANNERS, LIFE AND LETTERS,

IN THE SO-CALLED AUGUSTAN AGE OF ENGLAND,

ARE, BY PERMISSION, INSCRIBED TO

SIR ALFRED SHERLOCK GOOCH, BART.,
of Benacre Hall, Suffolk,

WITH CORDIAL THANKS, BY HIS FAITHFUL SERVANT,

W. H. DAVENPORT ADAMS.

April 1886.

CONTENTS.

INTRODUCTION, ... PAGE xi

CHAPTER I.

THE STAGE IN QUEEN ANNE'S REIGN—I. THE DRAMATISTS—

Theatres in London — Their interior — Stage absurdities — Realism in Queen Anne's reign—Colley Cibber—Actor and manager—His quarrel with Pope—His plays—'She Would and She Would Not'—'The Careless Husband'—'The Nonjuror'—'The Provoked Husband'—Scene between Lord and Lady Townly—The Restoration Drama—George Farquhar—His qualities as a dramatist—'The Inconstant'—'The Recruiting Officer'—The opening scene—The plot described—The finale—Last days of Farquhar—Sir John Vanbrugh—'The Relapse'—'The Provoked Wife'—Daily life of a woman of fashion—'The Confederacy'—Sir Richard Steele as a dramatist—'The Tender Husband'—Steele as a moralist—'The Funeral'—Scene between Lady Harriet and Lady Charlotte—'The Conscious Lovers'—Dennis's attack—Plot of Steele's Comedy—Scene between Tom and Phillis—Scene between Bevil and Myrtle—Mrs Centlivre—Her life-story—Her dramatic compositions—'The Busybody'—'The Perplexed Lovers'—'The Cruel Gift'—'The Wonder'—A comedy of intrigue—Scene between Don Felix, Violante, Flora, and Don Pedro—'A Bold Stroke for a Wife'—The virtuoso—Aaron Hill—A life of activity—Hill's tragedies—Opera of 'Rinaldo'—Scenic effects—Hill as a speculator and projector—His tragedy of 'Zara'—Scene between Osman and Zara—Hill as a poet, ... 1·102

CHAPTER II.

THE STAGE IN QUEEN ANNE'S REIGN—II. THE PERFORMERS—

Barton Booth—Thomas Doggett—Robert Wilks—George Powell—Richard Estcourt—Cave Underhill—Verbruggen—Betterton—Edward Kynaston—'Jubilee Dicky,' and others—William Penkethman—Mrs Verbruggen or Mountford—Mrs Bracegirdle—Mrs Betterton—Mrs Elizabeth Barry—Mrs Anne Oldfield—Mrs Porter, . 103-146

CHAPTER III.

MUSIC AND MUSICIANS IN QUEEN ANNE'S REIGN—

Introduction of Operatic Representations—'Rosamond'—Italian Opera—'Hydaspes'—Nicolini and the Lion—'Rinaldo'—Various Operas—Operatic Airs—Handel's Operas—The Singers—John Abell—Richard Leveridge—Lawrence—Lewis Ramondon—Margarita de l'Epine—Mrs Tofts—The Cavaliere Nicolini—The Musical Composers—Congreve's Masque—The Competitors—John Weldon—John Eccles—Daniel Purcell—Godfrey Finger—Dr Blow—Dean Aldrich—Dr Croft—Jeremiah Clark—Maurice Greene—Charles King—Richard King—Nicolo Haym—Harry Carey—Thomas Britton—'The Musical Small-Coal Man'—Dr Pepusch—Galliard—Dr Tudway—Marshall—Dr Turner—Some celebrated Organists, . 147-202

CHAPTER IV.

ART AND ARCHITECTURE—

Characteristics of the 'Queen Anne' Architecture—Wood Carving and Grinling Gibbons—Francis Bud—Boit, the Painter in Enamel—Jervas—Howard—Cradock—Crowe—Jonathan Richardson—Wollaston—Dahl—Ricci—Pellegrini—John Closterman—Sir Godfrey Kneller—Anecdotes—Sir James Thornhill—Sir Christopher Wren—Sir John Vanbrugh—James Gibbs—Landscape Gardening—William Kent—Orlando Bridgman, . . . 203-233

CHAPTER V.

QUEEN ANNE'S SOLDIERS—

John, Duke of Marlborough—Early Life—Military Services—
In Ireland—William III.—Campaigns of the Great War
—Blenheim—Ramillies—Oudenarde—Malplaquet—Old
Age and Death—Charles Mordaunt, Earl of Peterborough
—His Romantic Career—His Exploits in Spain—His Last
Years—James Richmond Webb—Lord Cutts—Earl
Cadogan, ... 234-344

CHAPTER VI.

QUEEN ANNE'S SEAMEN—

Condition of the Navy—Our Seamen—The Press-gang—Our
Maritime Supremacy—Sir George Rooke—The Attack
upon Vigo—Capture of Gibraltar—Off Malaga—Memoir
of Rooke—Sir Cloudesley Shovel—His Career—His Shipwreck and Death—Strange Stories—His Monument—
Alexander Selkirk—His Solitary Life in Juan Fernandez
—Biographical Sketch, ... 345-367

GOOD QUEEN ANNE;

OR,

Men and Manners, Life and Letters in the Augustan Age.

INTRODUCTION.

THE reign of Queen Anne is one of the most interesting periods in our English history. It witnessed a remarkable development of intellectual activity, which permanently affected the tone and character of our literature. It witnessed the evolution of our constitutional system, and the greater definiteness of ministerial responsibility. It witnessed the foundation of our naval supremacy, and the origin of our military prestige. It witnessed the union of England and Scotland into a compact kingdom—a great and healing measure which both countries have long ago agreed to regard as a blessing. It was crowded with great or remarkable men and women, in politics, in letters, in art, in society—men and women who, through a variety of circumstances, are as familiar to us as, or even more familiar than, the famous personages of times much nearer to our own. For I think no one will dispute that Pope and Swift, Addison and Steele, are known to us as intimately as the writers of the first half of the present century. We trace with as much interest the fortunes of Harley and St John, Godolphin and Sunderland, as those of Bute and North and the Grenvilles, of Fox and Pitt. Marlborough is as grand a figure as Wellington; and Blenheim attracts us scarcely less than Waterloo; and I doubt whether any of Wellington's lieutenants has as strong a fascination for us as that knight-errant of the eighteenth century, Peterborough. Certainly, it was a brilliant, an illustrious period; a period not easily paralleled in the annals of any country; since it combined 'the victories of Marlborough with the researches of Newton—the statesmanship of Somers with the knight-errantry of Peterborough—the publication of Clarendon's History, with the composition of Burnet's— the eloquence of Bolingbroke in Parliament, and of Atterbury in the pulpit, with the writings in prose and verse of Swift and Addison, of Pope and Prior.' It was in this reign, too, that political writings acquired for the first time a direct influence on political events; and it was in this reign that political questions first began to evoke the eager attention of the public. Nor must we forget that from Defoe's *Review* and Steele's *Tatler*, sprung the various activities which have made our periodical literature so important a factor in our national progress. Ecclesiastically, too, the reign of Queen Anne is memorable; for it saw the beginning of that cleavage within the English Church, which has since had such injurious and lamentable effects. It is true that the causes of division had long been in existence; but the separation between High Church, Low Church, and Broad Church seems to me to show itself first with any distinctness in the reign of Queen Anne.

I am not sure that a comparison of the Queen Anne period with the present is of any practical advantage. Lord Stanhope makes it in some detail, and the principal points which he indicates may be put before the reader; but though he inclines the balance in favour of the past, I do not suppose that any person now living would care, if it were possible, to be relegated to it. We feel that, somehow or other, in spite of statistics, the present *is* better than the past; that larger views obtain and broader sympathies; that the national intellect has gained in energy and vigour; that moral questions are discussed from a higher standpoint; that a greater desire exists to do justice to the oppressed, to relieve the unfortunate, to promote the happiness of individuals and the welfare of the many. The old order has changed, giving place to the new; and we are satisfied that, on the whole, the new is a wiser and a purer and a better order than the old.

Lord Stanhope, however, while admitting the immense advance which has been made in knowledge and science, or their practical explanation; while recording the success of the great movements which have brought education within the reach of the poorest, and encouraged the growth of everything that lends grace and beauty to our daily life; is convinced in his own mind that the people of Queen Anne enjoyed a much larger measure of happiness than the subjects of Queen Victoria. But I fear it must have been a very sluggish and vulgar kind of happiness after all—the happiness, in a great degree, of apathy and indifference. 'How far more widely spread was, in those days,' he exclaims, 'the spirit of contentment! Men were willing to make the best of the present without a feverish anxiety for the past or for the future—without constantly longing that yesterday might come back, or that to-morrow might come on. The laws were not so good, but the people were better satisfied with them.' Or, shall we say, had not yet found the means or the opportunities of expressing their dissatisfaction? 'The Church was less efficient, but was more cheerfully maintained.' As a matter of fact, the great body of the people showed very little feeling either way; and it would be easy enough to prove that the Churchmanship of Victoria is a much more real and living force than that of Anne.

'If we look to the country districts,' he continues, 'we shall judge perhaps that in Queen Anne's time the harsh features of the feudal system had passed away, while some of the milder ones remained. In other words, there was no trace of serfdom or compulsory service, but there lingered the policy of protection due by the lord of the soil to his retainers in sickness or old age. Labour was then no mere contract of work done for value received. Service was still in some degree requited, even when it ceased to be performed. As between landlord and tenant also a more cordial spirit, a more intimate relation, appears to have prevailed.' The historian carries this roseate, and, I fear it must be said, fallacious view of things into the condition of the towns, where, he thinks, there was much less of wealth, but much less also of abject poverty. 'The contrasts were not so sharp, nor stood, as it were, so closely face to face with each other. Nevertheless, in that day also trade was not a little lucrative. As is stated by Budgell in the *Spectator*, "I have observed greater estates got about 'Change than at Whitehall or St James's." It would also seem, as far as negative evidence can show it, as if under Queen Anne the handicraftsman and the labourer had no difficulty in obtaining employment without dispute as to the hours of work or the rate of wages.'

I must ask the reader to look a little at the other side of the picture. In Queen Anne's reign there were one million three hundred and thirty thousand paupers in England, or nearly one in five of the whole population. The proportion now, perhaps, is about one in twenty-seven. And it may be added that that one is much better housed and fed than was his predecessor. As the value of money has considerably decreased since the opening years of the eighteenth century, the labourer probably had better wages then than he has now; when meat was about a penny a pound, tenpence a day would seem to be not inadequate payment, but unquestionably his life was much more sordid and monotonous. All the smaller comforts which the poorest now enjoy were wanting. He was lodged much worse; he had no chance of improving his condition through education: his thoughts and views were bounded by the village in which he lived.

From Gregory King's scheme we can gain some idea of the component parts and social condition of the rural population in Queen Anne's England. It was drawn up in 1688, but its main features held good for many years afterwards. King allows one hundred and sixty families as connected with and dependent upon the temporal lords; forty heads per family, or six thousand four hundred persons, with a yearly income per family of three thousand two hundred pounds. Twenty-six to the spiritual lords, twenty heads per family, or five hundred and twenty persons, with a yearly income of one thousand three hundred pounds per family. Eight hundred families are allotted to the baronets, sixteen heads per family, twelve thousand eight hundred persons, with a yearly income per family of eight hundred and eighty pounds. Six hundred knights. thirteen heads per family, seven thousand eight hundred persons, with a yearly income per family of six hundred and fifty pounds. Three thousand esquires, ten heads per family, thirty thousand persons, with a yearly income per family of four hundred and fifty pounds. We come next to twelve thousand gentlemen's families,[1] eight heads each,

---

[1] The gentry are painted in dark colours by contemporary writers. Bishop Berkeley speaks of the English gentleman as 'the most unsuccessful rake in the world. He is at variance with himself. He is neither brute enough to enjoy his appetites, nor man enough to govern them.' Says Burnet:—'They' (the gentry) 'are ill-taught and ill-bred; haughty and insolent: they have no love for their country, or of public liberty: they desire to return to tyranny, provided they might be the under-tyrants. In their marriages they look only for fortune.'

ninety-six thousand persons in all, with a yearly income
per family of two hundred and eighty pounds. Five
thousand families of persons in the greater offices and
places, with eight heads per family, forty thousand persons, and two hundred and forty pounds per family yearly.
Two thousand eminent merchants and traders by sea,
eight heads per family, sixteen thousand persons, and four
hundred pounds yearly income per family. Eight thousand lesser merchants and traders by sea, six heads each
family, forty-eight thousand persons, and two hundred
pounds yearly income per family. Ten thousand persons
in the law, seven heads per family, seventy thousand persons, a hundred and fifty-four pounds yearly income per
family. Two thousand families of eminent clergymen, six
heads, twelve thousand persons in all, seventy-two pounds
yearly income per family. Eight thousand lesser clergymen, five heads per family, forty thousand persons, fifty
pounds per annum each family. Forty thousand freeholders of the better sort,[1] seven heads per family, two
hundred and eighty thousand persons, average income
ninety-one pounds. A hundred and twenty thousand
freeholders of the lesser sort, with five and a half heads
per family, six hundred and sixty thousand persons in all,
average yearly income per family, fifty-five pounds. A
hundred and fifty thousand farmers, with five heads per
family, seven hundred and fifty thousand persons, average
yearly income forty-two pounds ten shillings. Fifteen
thousand families of persons engaged in the liberal professions, five heads per family, seventy-five thousand per-

---

[1] Addison describes this class in No. 122 of the *Spectator*:—'He is a yeoman of about an hundred pounds a year, an honest man : he is just within
the Game Act, and qualified to kill an hare or a pheasant : he knocks down a
dinner with his gun twice or thrice a week ; and by that means lives much
cheaper than those who have not so good an estate as himself. He would be
a good neighbour if he did not destroy so many partridges : in short, he is a
very sensible man ; shoots flying ; and has been several times foreman of the
petty jury.'

sons, and sixty pounds yearly income per family. Fifty thousand shopkeepers and tradesmen, with four and a half heads per family, two hundred and twenty-five thousand persons, and forty-five pounds average yearly income per family. Sixty thousand artisans and handicraftsmen, four heads per family, two hundred and forty thousand persons, and thirty-eight pounds average yearly income per family. Five thousand naval officers, four heads per family, twenty thousand persons, eighty pounds average income per family. Four thousand military officers, four heads per family, sixteen thousand persons, and sixty pounds average income per family. Here we have a total of five hundred thousand five hundred and eighty-six families, in twenty-one classes, which Gregory King calls accumulators, because, as a whole, they spent less than their income. We then come to fifty thousand common seamen, with three heads per family, a hundred and fifty thousand persons, and an average of twenty pounds yearly income per family. Three hundred and sixty-four thousand labouring people and out-servants, with three and a half heads per family, or one million two hundred and seventy-five thousand persons; average income per family, fifteen pounds. Four hundred thousand cottagers and paupers, with three and a quarter heads per family, or one million three hundred thousand persons: average income per family, six pounds ten shillings. Thirty-five thousand common soldiers, with two heads per family, or seventy thousand persons; average income per family, fourteen pounds. Add thirty thousand vagrants, such as gipsies, thieves, beggars, etc., acquiring in all sixty thousand pounds in the year. Total—one million three hundred and forty-nine thousand five hundred and eighty-six families, with an average of four and a half heads per family, and a yearly income on the average of thirty-two pounds five shillings. Five million five hundred thousand five hundred and twenty persons; and general yearly income, forty-three million four hundred and ninety-eight thousand eight hundred pounds. Gregory King founded his estimate on the returns of the collectors of the tax called hearth-money; but it agrees on the whole with the result attained by other methods of calculation.

The main produce of England in the reign of Anne was corn. A larger proportion of the population being then employed in agriculture, and the population being much smaller, England produced all the cereals that were required for her own use. Next in importance was wool, the manufacture of which had just begun to take root, and had already found in Leeds a busy and thriving centre. A considerable clothing trade, however, was carried on in the west, especially at Frome, Devizes, Bradford, and Trowbridge, whence the manufactured articles were removed to Bristol, then as a port inferior only to London, for exportation. Cotton was as yet in its infancy; the first ship with a cargo of the vegetable fibre from America arrived at Liverpool in 1700.[1] The chief manufactures of Manchester were fustian, ticking, girth web, and tapes. The great iron industry of England was yet to be developed; but Sheffield had already attained a reputation for its cutlery. Six iron furnaces, however, sufficed to supply its wants.

Our coal mines were being worked with some success, though as coal was used only for domestic purposes, the demand was not very considerable. Birmingham was famous for its hardware: 'Does not the small town of Birmingham,' says Bishop Berkeley, 'circulate every week, one way or other, to the value of fifty thousand pounds?' Its people, however, wrought scarcely anything else than iron tools and husbandry implements. Their blazing forges lay open to the public thoroughfares, by the side of the rude and homely shop where hung up for sale the spade and

---

[1] In this year the first dock was opened at Liverpool, which in nine years could boast of eighty-four ships, manned by nine hundred sailors.

the bag of nails. The now thriving district of the Potteries, thickly studded with populous towns, lay dormant in Queen Anne's reign, except that at Burslem flourished a manufacture of glazed brown earthenware, known as 'Butter Pottery,' from its property of keeping butter cool. The manufacture of glass had been crushed by an onerous excise duty until 1698. It lifted up its head a little under Queen Anne and George I., but the duty was re-imposed in 1746. The kinds of glass manufactured were green glass and common window-glass, and London and Bristol were the principal seats of trade. Defoe represents his boy-thief, Colonel Jack, as sleeping in winter time in 'the ash-holes and heating niches, in the glass-house in Rosemary Lane. or at another glass-house in Ratcliffe Highway.' The worsted stocking trade flourished at Nottingham, Derby, and Leicester. The lace trade, for which Nottingham is now celebrated, was in Queen Anne's time almost confined to the western and southern counties, where it furnished employment for men as well as women. Bishop Berkeley, addressing the Irish labourers in reproof of their idle ways, observes:—' In England, when the labour of the field is over, it is usual for men to betake themselves to some other labour of a different kind. In the northern parts of that industrious land, the inhabitants meet, a jolly crew, at one another's houses, where they merrily and frugally pass the long and dark winter evenings; several families, by the same light and the same fire, working at their different manufactures of wool, flax, or hemp, company meanwhile mutually cheering and provoking to labour. In certain other parts you may see, on a summer's evening, the common labourer sitting along the streets of a town or village, each at his own door, with a cushion before him. making bone lace, and earning more in an evening's pastime than an Irish family would in a whole day.'

London had already established its pre-eminence as

the capital of the empire. Its population was about six hundred thousand, or one-tenth of the whole English population. It's wealth was so great that in 1693 it was called upon to bear an assessment in aid six times as great as the united assessments of Bristol, Chester, Exeter, Norwich, Gloucester, and Worcester. In the first year of Queen Anne's reign the port of London owned five hundred and sixty vessels, with an aggregate burden of eighty-four thousand five hundred and sixty tons. The number of merchant-vessels in all our ports was three thousand two hundred and eighty-six, with an aggregate of two hundred and sixty-one thousand two hundred and twenty-two tons; so that London engrossed about one-third of the entire trade of the kingdom. Its municipal and social arrangements, however, were not in harmony with its wealth. Its streets were narrow and irregular; ill-paved, and lighted only by flickering lanterns. At night the security of the inhabitants was entrusted to the watch, which, as it was largely composed of old men, and numerically weak, could afford no efficient protection, and was frequently overpowered by young men of fashion, who banded together in clubs and companies, and with their wild revelry made night hideous for the peaceably-disposed citizens. The most notorious of these were the Mohawks, or Mohocks, who adopted their name from a tribe of American savages. It is probable enough, however, that the stories of their outrages are coloured by much romantic exaggeration.[1]

The fashionable district of London were then to be found in the neighbourhood of Queen's Square, Great Ormond Street, and Bloomsbury Square. High life made Covent Garden Square its headquarters. Soho and St James's Squares breathed a fine aroma of gentility, which continued, during Anne's reign, to stretch away westward

---

[1] The darker aspects of London life at this time are minutely described by Tom Brown and Ned Ward.

in the direction of Piccadilly. In 1708 Bolton Street marked the furthest limit which it had then reached.

Next to London, the chief English towns were Bristol, Norwich, York, Exeter, Shrewsbury, Derby, Nottingham, Canterbury, and Worcester.

From this rapid survey of Queen Anne's England, we must pass on to glance at the character of Queen Anne herself. It must be owned that she was not a *strong* woman; in scarcely any respect did she resemble England's first Queen regnant, the dauntless, energetic, and imperious Elizabeth. She was as much inferior to her in intellectual, as she was superior in the higher moral qualities. Her notions of state-craft were of the crudest: she had no faculty of foresight, no clearness of judgment, no strength of will. She had not been trained for the lofty position to which circumstances had raised her; and her consciousness of incapacity induced her to rely upon the first vigorous mind that offered its support. As no such mind could be found in her own family, she threw herself unreservedly into the arms of Sarah, Duchess of Marlborough, and for many years endured the infliction of her irritable and imperious temper, chiefly because she knew in her heart of hearts that she could not stand alone. Nor did she break away from the thraldom that cost her so much pain, until the tactics of Harley had provided her with a substitute in Abigail Hill, afterwards Lady Masham. History presents few examples of a dependence so servile, so complete. The sovereign forgot her rank, her dignity, almost her self-respect, in order to draw closer the ties of intimacy with her 'guide, philosopher, and friend.' She condescended to become Mrs Morley, and her husband Mr Morley; while the Duchess assumed the name of Mrs Freeman, and the great Duke of Mr Freeman. They formed a *partie carrée* of the most curious description,—the members of which made a pretence of putting aside the restraints of rank in order to gratify the sweet obligations of an absorbing friendship.

It is certain that the vast intellectual movement which invests her reign with so powerful an attraction owed nothing to her inspiration or her sympathy; and that she was unable even to understand it—to fathom its significance, or to appreciate the genius of the men who were the authors of it. She seems to have ignored the greatness of Sir Isaac Newton; and of Swift she knew nothing except that he had written an improper book. Of all the men of the time, I suspect that Dr Sacheverel was, to her mind, the most heroic. But though she was unquestionably a weak woman of the ordinary type, she was also, what such women very often fail to be, a *good* woman. She was a devout Churchwoman, and received the Sacrament monthly, according to the rites of the Church of England. The attempts at her perversion made in her father's reign she had steadily resisted. As wife and mother her conduct was irreproachable. On the purity of her wedded life not the shadow of a shade darkens, though she had not been fortunate in the choice of a husband. Prince George of Denmark was a man of coarse tastes and limited understanding. 'I have tried him drunk, and I have tried him sober,' said Charles II., 'and there is nothing in him.' A pathetic destiny pursued her with regard to her children. One after another they came into the world—seventeen in all—some perishing prematurely, others dying in their infancy. At length, there seemed reason to hope that the brightest, Prince William. Duke of Gloucester,—a boy of sweet nature and abundant promise—would escape the general doom. He reached the age of eleven, and then was seized with a malignant fever, of which he died after an illness of only four days. This was a terrible blow to the unfortunate Queen, but she bore it in a spirit of pious resignation.

A warm and faithful friend; with a genial temper and

a heart full of kindly feelings ; liberal, even to lavishness, in her charities ; she honestly deserved—and this is no light praise—the fond epithet which her subjects spontaneously attached to her name, and is still remembered in history as

'GOOD QUEEN ANNE.'

The volumes now submitted to the public are the result of considerable labour, and have occupied me at intervals for several years. They are designed to provide the general reader with a comprehensive and readable survey of some of the more interesting aspects of England's Augustan Age ; and will be found to deal with its art, literature, and its society, its actors and actresses, dramatists and poets, men of letters, seamen, and soldiers, musicians and architects,—not, indeed, with any attempt at exhaustive criticisms, which, within the limits I have laid down, would be impossible, but in such a manner as to present, I trust, their leading characteristics, and to illustrate the abounding intellectual activity of a remarkable and interesting period. I hope hereafter to complete the survey, and in future volumes to glance at its Science, its Politics, its Law, and its Religion. Its social life has been so fully treated by Mr Ashton, that little in that direction remains to be done. The field, however, is one of vast extent, and in some parts has been cultivated by men in whose footsteps I follow with diffidence ; but I do not think that any general picture of it, such as I have here essayed to draw, has hitherto been attempted. At all events, it is very possible that these volumes contain enough to interest and entertain the reader, and that they will prove acceptable as a companion to the histories, and as an introduction to the study of Men and Manners, Life and Letters, in England's Augustan Age. W. H. D. A.

CHAPTER I.

THE STAGE IN QUEEN ANNE'S REIGN.

I. THE DRAMATISTS.

Theatres in London—Their interior—Stage absurdities—Realism in Queen Anne's reign—Colley Cibber—Actor and manager—His quarrel with Pope—His plays—'She Would and She Would Not'—'The Careless Husband'—'The Nonjuror'—'The Provoked Husband'—Scene between Lord and Lady Townly—The Restoration Drama—George Farquhar—His qualities as a dramatist—'The Inconstant'—'The Recruiting Officer'—The opening scene—The plot described—The finale—Last days of Farquhar—Sir John Vanbrugh—'The Relapse'—'The Provoked Wife'—Daily life of a woman of fashion—'The Confederacy'—Sir Richard Steele as a dramatist—'The Tender Husband'—Steele as a Moralist—'The Funeral'—Scene between Lady Harriet and Lady Charlotte—'The Conscious Lovers'—Dennis's attack—Plot of Steele's Comedy—Scene between Tom and Phillis—Scene between Bevil and Myrtle—Mrs Centlivre—Her life-story—Her dramatic compositions—'The Busybody'—'The Perplexed Lovers'—'The Cruel Gift'—'The Wonder'—A comedy of intrigue—Scene between Don Felix, Violante, Flora, and Don Pedro—'A Bold Stroke for a Wife'—The virtuoso—Aaron Hill—A life of activity—Hill's tragedies—Opera of 'Rinaldo'—Scenic effects—Hill as a speculator and projector—His tragedy of 'Zara'—Scene between Osman and Zara—Hill as a poet.

IN the London of Queen Anne's time, and among the higher classes and the well-to-do citizens, the Stage was a sufficiently popular institution. Yet the public to which it appealed was limited in numbers; and of the four theatres which the metropolis then possessed, only two were really successful—Drury Lane, and the Queen's Theatre, Haymarket. The Dorset Gardens Theatre, in Salisbury Court, Fleet Street, erected from Sir Christopher Wren's designs, was open at intervals down to the close of 1706, but nothing flourished there, and in

VOL. I. A

1709 it was pulled down. Lincoln's Inn Fields Theatre, associated with so many successes in the reign of Charles II., was rebuilt by Christopher Rich about 1707, but closed during the remainder of Queen Anne's reign.

A fairer fortune attended Drury Lane, where 'Her Majesty's Servants,' as they had the right to call themselves, presented a great variety of entertainments, in order to retain their hold upon the public. Tragedy, comedy, farce, concert, ballet, and pantomime—each in its turn appeared on the boards of 'Old Drury,' under the management of the energetic Rich, and afterwards of Wilks, and Cibber. Its interior is thus described by Misson :—' The pit is an amphitheatre, filled with benches without backboards, and adorned and covered with green cloth. Men of quality, particularly the younger sort, some ladies of reputation and virtue, and abundance of damsels that hunt for prey, sit all together in their place, higgledy-piggledy, chatter, toy, play, hear, hear not. Further up, against the wall, under the first gallery, and just opposite to the stage, rises another amphitheatre, which is taken up by persons of the best quality, among whom are generally very few men. The galleries, whereof there are only two rows, are filled with none but ordinary people, particularly the upper one.' The upper gallery was free to the footmen whose masters or mistresses were seated in other parts of the theatre. Frequently their noisy and irregular behaviour gave great offence. Mr Ashton quotes a satirical notice from *The Female Tatler*, December 9, 1719, which bears upon this subject :—' Dropped, near the Playhouse, a bundle of horsewhips, designed to belabour the footmen in the Upper Gallery, who almost every night this winter have made such an intolerable disturbance that the players could not be heard, and their masters were obliged to hiss them into silence. Whoever has taken up the said whips, is desired to leave 'em with my Lord Rake's porter, several noblemen resolving to exercise 'em on their backs, the next frosty morning.'

The inimitable pen of Addison has furnished us with some touches illustrative of things as they were in the theatres of his time. He quotes the observation of Aristotle, that ordinary writers of tragedy endeavour to raise terror and pity in their audience, not by the force and dignity of their language, but by the dresses and decorations of the stage. 'There is something of this kind,' he says, 'very ridiculous in the English theatre. When the author has a mind to terrify us, it thunders; when he would make us melancholy, the stage is darkened. But among all our tragic artifices, I am the most offended at those which are made use of to inspire us with magnificent ideas of the persons that speak. The ordinary method of making an hero. is to clap a large plume of feathers upon his head, which rises so very high, that there is often a greater length from his chin to the top of his head, than to the sole of his foot. One would believe that we thought a great man and a tall man the same thing. This very much embarrasses the actor, who is forced to hold his neck extremely stiff and steady all the while he speaks; and, notwithstanding any anxieties which he pretends for his mistress, his country, or his friends, one may see by his action that his greatest care and concern is to keep the plume of feathers from falling off his head. . . . As these superfluous ornaments upon the head make a great man, a princess generally receives her grandeur from those additional encumbrances that fall into her tail: I mean the broad sweeping train that follows her in all her motions, and finds constant employment for a boy who stands behind her to open and spread it to advantage. I do not know how others are affected at this sight, but I must confess, my eyes are wholly taken up with the page's part; and as for the queen, I am not so attentive to anything she speaks, as to the right adjusting of her train, lest it should chance to trip up her heels, or incommode her, as she walks to and fro upon the stage.'

The following paragraph might be studied with advantage by living creators of the realistic drama. 'Another mechanical method of making great men,' continues our humorist, 'and adding dignity to kings and queens, is to accompany them with halberts and battle-axes. Two or three shifters of scenes, with the two candle-snuffers, make up a complete body of guards upon the English stage; and, by the addition of a few porters dressed in red coats, can represent above a dozen legions. I have sometimes seen a couple of armies drawn up together upon the stage, when the first has been disposed to do honour to his generals. It is impossible for the reader's imagination to multiply twenty men into such prodigious multitudes, or to fancy that two or three hundred thousand soldiers are fighting in a room of forty or fifty yards in compass. Incidents of such nature should be told, not represented.' But if this maxim of Addison's were generally accepted, what would become of the modern melodrama, which loves to put upon the stage a London mob or an Anglo-Egyptian army?

The behaviour of the audience, even in the better parts of the house, was not such as would now-a-days find toleration. 'I was at the tragedy of Macbeth,' says Addison, 'and unfortunately placed myself under a woman of quality, that is since dead, who, as I found by the noise she made, was newly returned from France. A little before the rising of the curtain, she broke out into a loud soliloquy, "When will the dear witches enter?" and immediately upon their first appearance, asked a lady that sat three boxes from her, on her right hand, if those witches were not charming creatures. A little after, as Betterton was in one of the finest speeches of the play, she shook her fan at another lady, who sat as far on the left hand, and told her with a whisper, that might be heard all over the pit, we must not expect to see Baloon tonight. Not long after, calling out to a young baronet by his name, who sat three seats before me, she asked him whether Macbeth's wife was still alive? and before he would give an answer, fell a-talking of the ghost of Banquo. She had by this time formed a little audience to herself, and fixed the attention of all about her. But as I had a mind to hear the play, I got out of the sphere of her impertinence, and planted myself in one of the remotest corners of the pit.'

Among the playwrights who ministered to the entertainment—we can hardly say to the edification—of the theatre-going public in the early years of the eighteenth century, a conspicuous place was held by COLLEY CIBBER. He resembled, by the way, Mrs Malaprop's Cerberus, or Colman's 'three single gentlemen rolled into one,' for he filled three important positions—he was dramatist, actor, and manager. Though Pope, in a fit of spleen, pilloried him in *The Dunciad*, he was a man of very considerable and versatile talents: the author of bright and diverting comedies which are not yet forgotten—an actor almost unequalled in some of the characters he assumed—and the sparkling historiographer of the stage, during a long and important period. From his contemporaries he scarcely received a full measure of justice: partly because the age in which he lived was specially notorious for the prevalence of an exceptional jealousy and spitefulness among its literary men; and partly, because his abundant egotism and candid indiscreetness surrounded him with a host of foes, whose animosity his imperturbable good temper failed to disarm. But I think no one can read his *Apology for My Own Life* without a conviction that he was gifted with some rare and excellent qualities; that he was, in short, a *likeable* man,—a man who might not always command our respect, but would never cease to hold our regard. There was a certain instability in his disposition ; sometimes his animal spirits got the better of his judgment ; and he had an unlucky knack of saying the right thing at the wrong time. Perhaps few men have made more enemies while deserving less enmity ; for it is safer to stab your adversary in the back, than, like Cibber, to tread on his corns! But against these foibles and failings I find more than a sufficient set-off in his inexhaustible good nature, his loyalty to his friends, his generosity, his readiness to join in the laugh against himself, in the humility which really lay at the bottom of his surface vanity. In his quarrel with Pope, who will not admire his unaffected amiability as well as his quick and pungent wit ? Who does not own that he bore himself in it and came out of it with a much better grace than his formidable opponent ? On the whole, there are many greater men than Colley Cibber, whose acquaintance, if one had the alternative, one would rather give up than that of the bright, witty, talkative, observant, and kindly-hearted author of ' The Careless Husband.'

Colley Cibber was born on the 6th of November, Old Style, 1671, in Southampton Street, Covent Garden. His father, Caius Gabriel Cibber, a native of Holstein, settled in England during the Commonwealth period, and rose to distinction as a sculptor. His fame was long preserved by the two images of ' Melancholy' and 'Raging Madness' with which he adorned the great gates of Bethlehem Hospital, and the bassi-rilievi attached to the pedestal of the Monument. In 1682 he sent his son to the free grammar school of Grantham, in Lincolnshire. He had made up his mind that the young fellow should go to Cambridge and follow out the usual University course, when William of Orange landed at Torbay, and the elder Cibber joined the forces with which his patron, the Earl of Devonshire, hastened to the great Dutchman's assistance. At Nottingham father and son met, and the younger Cibber took the elder's place among the ranks. No doubt his martial ardour was genuine enough; but he had no opportunity of displaying it. Public tranquillity was quickly restored; the Earl of Devonshire's levies marched back to Nottingham; and Cibber obtained his discharge, with some promises of patronage from the Earl. Of these he did not wait to avail himself, but gratified an early bias by taking up the life of an actor.

It seems to have been in February 1689 that Cibber came to this determination. At first, and for some time, we are told, he considered the privilege of seeing plays daily a sufficient remuneration for his services; and it was fully nine months before he was rewarded with a salary of ten shillings a week. He had to contend against the disadvantages of a feeble voice and a weak and unformed person; and only trivial parts being assigned to him, it was necessarily long before he attracted favourable notice. As the Chaplain in Otway's tragedy of 'The Orphan,' he was commended by the veteran Goodman, who exclaimed, 'If he does not make a good actor, I will be d—;' a circumstance which so delighted him that he doubts 'whether Alexander himself, or Charles XII. of Sweden, when at the head of their first victorious armies, could feel a greater transport in their bosoms than I did then in mine.' It was about this time, when his whole fortune consisted of twenty pounds a year granted to him by his father, and of ten shillings a week from the theatre, that he plunged into matrimony with the sister of 'John Shore, Esq., who was for many years serjeant-trumpet of England,' a lady of great sprightliness of disposition and rare personal charms, who made him an admirable wife, and eventually, her father's resentment at the imprudent match having subsided, brought him a small fortune.

The young actor's next step to fame was taken through the illness of Kynaston, who was therefore unable to appear as Lord Touchwood when Queen Mary, on one occasion, commanded the play of 'The Double Dealer.' On the recommendation of Congreve, the part was given to Cibber, who acquitted himself in it with so much ability, that he was warmly complimented by Congreve, and rewarded by the advance of his salary to twenty shillings a week. His progress, however, was very slow and laborious; and a less gaily intrepid and persevering spirit might well have been discouraged. When the Drury Lane company broke up in 1695, through the revolt of Betterton and some of the leading performers, who went over to the theatre in Lincoln's Inn Fields, Cibber adhered to the old house, and on its re-opening in April, supplied a new 'occasional prologue.' In such low estimation, however, was still held his capacity as an actor, that he was not allowed to deliver it; but the management insisted on entrusting it to Powell, and Colley had to be content with a fee of two guineas, and the manager's declaration, that he was 'a very ingenious young man.'

A furious opposition arose between the two companies, and both having announced the production of 'Hamlet' on the same evening. the Drury Lane managers suddenly changed their bill, and substituted 'The Old Bachelor.' To give the undertaking a certain novelty, it was duly proclaimed that the part of the Old Bachelor would be played by Powell in imitation of the original—the celebrated Betterton. Cibber was cast for Alderman Fondlewife, and followed up the idea by mimicking Doggett, its creator; and this with such ingenuity and cleverness, that he won the almost unbounded applause of the audience. Even then the managers do seem to have been unconvinced of his talents, or to have supposed that they were limited to eccentric characters; nor did the approval which he obtained, both as author and actor, by his first comedy, called 'Love's Last Shift; or The Fool in Fashion,' lift him to the position to which his abilities entitled him. Yet the accomplished Dorset, then Lord Chamberlain, asserted that it was the best first play which any author, in his memory, had produced; 'and that for a young fellow to show himself such an actor, and such a writer, in one day, was something extraordinary.' With singular patience, good humour, and perseverance he bided his time; and in 1697, was fully rewarded, when Sir John Vanbrugh founded his comedy of 'The Relapse' on a suggestion from Cibber's play, and fixed upon Cibber to perform in it the arduous character of Lord Foppington. He made a complete success, stepping at once into the front rank of his profession; so that in 1707 Mr Rich, the patentee of Drury Lane, refused to include him among the performers whom he permitted the new manager of the Haymarket to draft from his company. Cibber, however, disregarded the exemption, and went over to Swiney, returning in the following year when the actors entered into a kind of commonwealth. The patent fell through in 1709, and Cibber again enlisted under Swiney, together with Wilks, Doggett, and Mrs Oldfield. But, two years later, he, Collier, Wilks, and Doggett united, as joint-patentees, in the management of Drury Lane; at a later date joining in a similar partnership with Booth, Wilks, and Sir Richard Steele. During the latter period, which did not terminate until 1731, the English stage was graced by an extraordinary number of first-rate artists; but when Booth and Wilks, Mrs Oldfield and Mrs Porter, had passed from the scene of their glories, Cibber felt that the time had come for his retirement also, and selling his share of the patent, he withdrew into private life. Occasionally he re-appeared, and when he did so, commanded a payment of fifty guineas per night. As late as 1745, when he was in his seventy-sixth year, he performed—and, it is said, with surprising vigour—the part of Pandulph in his own tragedy of 'Papal Tyranny.'

In 1730, on the death of Mr Eusden, Colley Cibber was appointed poet laureate; though it is certain that the gods, in granting him many gifts, had denied him the poetical faculty. All that can be said is that he did not write worse verses than his predecessor, to whom, in intellectual acquirements and general culture, he was vastly superior. The immediate cause of his preferment was, no doubt, his play of 'The Nonjuror,'—a satire upon the Roman Catholics and Nonjurors, whose sympathies had been excited by the abortive Jacobite Rebellion of 1715. At the same time, the savage tone of this dramatic invective drew upon him the formidable resentment of Pope, and procured him that conspicuous place in *The Dunciad* in which he succeeded Theobald. To Pope's hostility, which had already shown itself, Cibber had referred in the *Apology for his Life*, published in 1740; and attributed it to a purely personal cause—the poet's annoyance at a bit of ridicule of which Cibber, when playing Bayes in 'The Rehearsal,' had made him the object;—but at the bottom of it lay religious as well as personal feeling. Cibber, in his brisk, airy way, laughed down his petulant adversary. He observed, with gay indifference, that the wits might call him light or flippant, or what they pleased, but, thank Heaven, they could not call him *dull*. And the public were of the same opinion. He did not hesitate to cross swords with the irascible little satirist of Twickenham, and published two lively and good-humoured replies to his attacks —'A Letter from Mr Cibber to Mr Pope, inquiring into the Motives that might Induce him in his Satirical Works to be so frequently fond of Mr Cibber's name;' and, secondly, 'Another Occasional Letter from Mr Cibber to Mr Pope, wherein the New Hero's Preferment to his Throne in the *Dunciad* seems not to be Accepted, and the Author of that Poem his lightful Claim to it is Asserted ; with an Expostulatory Address to the Rev. Mr W. W―――on (Warburton), Author of the New Preface, and Adviser in the Curious Improvements in that Satire.'

Born midway in the reign of Charles II., Cibber lived into the closing years of the reign of George II. His death took place suddenly on the 12th of December 1757, in Berkeley Square. His man-servant, with whom he had chatted gaily at six in the evening, found him dead, three hours later, with his face calmly reclining on his pillow.

Cibber is seen to most advantage in his *Apology*, which even Johnson surlily owned was 'very well done,' and so interested Swift that he sat up all night to finish it. As Hazlitt says, ' He is a most amusing biographer; happy in his own opinion, the best of all others ; teeming with animal spirits, and uniting the self-sufficiency of youth with the garrulity of old age. He brings down the history of the stage, either by the help of observation or tradition, from the time of Shakespeare to his own, and quite dazzles the reader with a constellation of male and female, of tragic and comic, of past and present excellence. His sketches of Betterton, Mountford, Mrs Bracegirdle, Wilks, Mrs Oldfield, are drawn with wonderful *verve*, and, on the whole, in a fair and even kindly spirit.

His dramatic compositions are thirty in number. I shall glance at them in order of publication :—

To 'Love's Last Shift' (1696), allusion has already been made. The hero, Sir Novelty Fashion, is a distinct creation, and Vanbrugh adopted it in his 'Relapse,' raising him to the peerage as Lord Foppington.

In 'Woman's Wit ; or, The Lady in Fashion' (1697), Cibber is seen to be clearly indebted to Mountford's 'Greenwich Park.' He is much duller in this piece than is his wont, and there are evident signs of haste and carelessness.

But duller still is the tragedy of 'Xerxes' (1699), so dull as to fully justify the pitiless condemnation it received on the first and only night it was acted. In Steele's amusing catalogue of theatrical properties to be sold by auction (See *The Tatler*, No. 42), reference is made to its ill-fortune. 'The Imperial Robes of Xerxes, *never worn but once.*'

In 1700, Cibber boldly produced an alteration of Shakespeare's 'Richard the Third,' which held the stage until a very recent period, and was the 'Richard the Third' illustrated by the genius of Garrick, Edmund Kean, George Frederick Cooke, and other famous actors. To Cibber belongs the well known line, which always provoked a loud outburst of applause—

'Off with his head—so much for Buckingham!'

The comedy of 'Love makes a Man; or, The Fop's Fortune' (1701), was produced at Drury Lane with great success, and deserved it by the sprightliness of the writing and the effective contrast of the characters. The plot, however, is taken partly from Beaumont and Fletcher's 'Custom of the Country,' and partly from their play of 'The Elder Brother.' It may be hinted that Cibber does not always write in a style adapted to *pueris virginibusque*.

A much higher level of attainment is reached in 'She Would and She Would Not; or, The Kind Impostor' (1703). The dramatist has obtained a more complete command of his resources; his style is as lively as before but terser and more correct; his story is told with greater conciseness; and the situations are put together with more dexterity. The plot seems to be borrowed from Leonard's 'Counterfeits,' but is worked out by Cibber in his own vivacious manner.

The shifts of impoverished innkeepers, when their larder is empty, now prove a stock subject with our dramatists. Cibber, in the following amusing scene, was, I think, one of the first to deal with it. Hypolita and

Flora, who, to carry out a love adventure, have disguised themselves in men's habits, come to an inn, and are received by a certain Trappanto:—

Trap. Servant, gentlemen; I have taken nice care of your nags; good cattle they are, by my troth! right and sound, I warrant them; they deserve care, and they have had it, and shall have it, if they stay in this house. I always stand by, sir; see them rubbed down with my own eyes. Catch me trusting an ostler. I'll give you leave to fill for me, and drink for me, too.

Flo. I have seen this fellow somewhere.

Trap. Hey-day! what, no cloth laid? was ever such attendance! Hey, house! tapster! landlord, hey! [*Knocks.*] What was it you bespoke, gentlemen?

Hyp. Really, sir, I ask your pardon; I have almost forgot you.

Trap. Pshaw, dear sir, never talk of it; I live here hard by. I have a lodging. I cannot call it a lodging, neither—that is, I have a— Sometimes I am here, and sometimes I am there; and so, here and there, one makes shift, you know. Hey! will these people never come? [*Knocks.*

Hyp. You give a very good account of yourself, sir.

Trap. Oh, nothing at all, sir. Lord, sir—was it fish or flesh, sir?

Flo. Really, sir, we have bespoke nothing yet.

Trap. Nothing! for shame! It's a sign you are young travellers. You don't know this house, sir; why, they'll let you starve if you don't stir and call, and that like thunder, too. Hey! [*Knocks.*

Hyp. Ha! you eat here sometimes, I presume, sir?

Trap. Humph! Ay, sir, that's as it happens. I seldom eat at home, indeed—things are generally, you know, so out of order there, that— Did you hear any fresh news upon the road, sir?

Hyp. Only, sir, that the King of France lost a great horse-match upon the Alps t'other day.

Trap. Ha! a very odd place for a horse-race—but the King of France may do anything— Did you come that way, gentlemen? or— Hey! [*Knocks.*

Enter HOST.

Host. Did you call, gentlemen?

Trap. Yes, and bawl, too, sir. Here, the gentlemen are almost famished, and nobody comes near them. What have you in the house, now, that will be ready presently?

Host. You may have what you please, sir?

Hyp. Can you give us a partridge?

Host. Sir, we have no partridges; but we'll get you what you please in a moment. We have a very good neck of mutton, sir; if you please, it shall be clapped down in a moment.

Hyp. Have you no pigeons or chickens?

Host. Truly, sir, we have no fowl in the house at present; if you please, you may have anything else in a moment.

Hyp. Then, prithee, get us some young rabbits.

Host. Upon my word, sir, rabbits are so scarce, they are not to be had for money.

Flo. Have you any fish?

Host. Fish, sir! I drest yesterday the finest dish that ever came upon a table; I am sorry we have none left, sir; but if you please, you may have anything else in a moment.

Trap. Plague on thee! hast thou nothing but anything else in the house?

Host. Very good mutton, sir.

Hyp. Prithee get us a breast, then.

Host. Breast! Don't you like the neck, sir?

Hyp. Have ye nothing in the house but the neck?

Host. Really, sir, we don't use to be so unprovided; but at present we have nothing else left.

Trap. Faith, sir, I don't know but a nothing else may be very good meat, when anything else is not to be had.

Hyp. Then, prithee, friend, let's have thy neck of mutton before that is gone, too.

Trap. Sir, we shall lay it down this minute; I'll see it done, gentlemen; I'll wait upon ye presently; for a minute I must beg your pardon, and leave to lay the cloth myself.

Hyp. By no means, sir.

Trap. No ceremony, dear sir! Indeed I'll do it."

Cibber's best dramatic composition is, undoubtedly, 'The Careless Husband' (1704). The plot is ingenious and skilfully developed; and the dialogue is brisk, airy, and spontaneous.[1] The characters do not commend themselves to our sympathies; for Sir Charles Easy, though

---

[1] The effective situation, where Lady Easy finds her husband and her maid asleep in two chairs, and throws her lace handkerchief over her husband's face, was adapted from a real incident in the married life of Colonel and Mrs Brett.

agreeable, cheerful, and lively, is by no means a model husband; Lady Easy forgives too readily; and Lady Betty Modish is too flippant in her coquetry; but they seem to have been drawn from life, and are finished portraits, in which each touch heightens their effectiveness, and no detail is wanting that can make them real and forcible. The author tells us that when he had written two acts of this play, he threw them aside in despair of finding a performer capable of doing justice to the character of Lady Betty Modish—Mrs Verbruggen being ill, and Mrs Bracegirdle engaged at the other theatre. But while he was in this condition of suspense, Mrs Oldfield came to the front as an actress of unusual grace, charm, and intelligence; and perceiving in her the very embodiment of his heroine, he finished his play. Lady Betty Modish became one of Mrs Oldfield's most successful impersonations. In his *Apology*, Cibber says, in reference to his *chef d'œuvre*, 'Whatever favourable reception it met with, it would be unjust in me not to place a large share of it to the account of Mrs Oldfield; not only from the uncommon excellence of her action, but even from her personal manner of conversing. There are many sentiments in the character of Lady Betty Modish that I may almost say were originally her own, or only dressed with a little more care than when they negligently fell from her lively humour: had her birth placed her in a higher rank of life, she had certainly appeared in reality what in this play she only excellently acted—an agreeable gay woman of quality, a little too conscious of her natural attractions.'

'The Double Gallant; or, the Sick Lady's Cure' (1707), when first produced at the Haymarket, met with a very unfavourable reception; but, two years later, when revived, attained a complete success. It is founded to some extent on the French comedy of '*Le Gallant Double*,' and in parts, is too broad for the taste of the present day. 'It abounds,' says Hazlitt, 'in character, bustle, and stage effect, and very happily mixes up the comedy of intrigue, such as we see it in Mrs Centlivre's Spanish plots, with a tolerable share of the wit and spirit of Congreve and Vanbrugh.'

Not without merit is the comedy of 'The Lady's Last Stake; or, The Wife's Resentment' (1708). Some of the incidents are amusing, and the style is marked by Cibber's easy elegance. The subject may have suggested a famous picture in Hogarth's '*Marriage à la Mode.*'

The plot of 'The Rival Fools' (1707) is partly borrowed from Fletcher's 'Wit at Several Weapons.' It is not a successful effort. 'There happened to be a circumstance in it which, being in itself somewhat ridiculous, gave a part of the audience a favourable opportunity of venting their spleen on the author—viz., a man in one of the earlier scenes on the stage, with a long angling-rod in his hand, going to fish for miller's thumbs:' on which account some of the spectators took occasion, whenever Mr Cibber appeared, who himself played the character, to cry out continually, 'Miller's thumbs'—a satirical allusion, we presume, to the fine faculty of appropriation possessed, according to popular belief, by the human miller's thumbs, and by so many English playwrights. The cry of 'Miller's thumbs,' if raised by audiences now-a-days, would overwhelm with confusion not a few of our 'adaptors from the French.'

'Hob; or, The Country Wake' (1715), is Doggett's comedy of 'The Country Wake,' compressed into the dimensions of a farce.

The pastoral interlude of 'Myrtillo' (1716) was performed with indifferent success at Drury Lane. The music was composed by Dr Pepusch.

'Venus and Adonis' is a masque (1716), performed at Drury Lane, with music composed by Dr Pepusch.

Cibber always failed in this kind of composition: Nature had not made him poetical, and a masque without poetry is a very dull thing indeed.

In 'The Nonjuror' (1718) Cibber regained his laurels; for though the general idea was borrowed from Molière's '*Tartuffe*,' as well as the character of the hypocrite, Dr Wolf, yet the conduct of the piece was his own, his was the forcible and often witty dialogue, and his some of the most effective situations. The coquettish Maria is also Cibber's invention, and a happy one.

Here is what Cibber himself has to say about that one of his comedies which probably made the greatest impression upon contemporary opinion, owing to its strong political bias:—

'About this time Jacobitism had lately exerted itself, by the most unprovoked rebellion that our histories have handed down to us since the Norman Conquest. I therefore thought, that to set the authors and principles of that desperate folly in a fair light, by allowing the mistaken consciences of some their best excuse, and by making the artful pretenders to conscience as ridiculous as they were ungratefully wicked, was a subject fit for the honest satire of comedy, and what might, if it succeeded, do honour to the stage, by showing the valuable use of it. And considering what numbers at that time might come to it as prejudiced spectators, it may be allowed that the undertaking was not less hazardous than laudable.

'To give life, therefore, to this design, I borrowed the "*Tartuffe*" of Molière, and turned him into a modern "Nonjuror"; upon the hypocrisy of the French character I ingrafted a stronger wickedness, that of an English Popish priest, lurking under the doctrine of our own Church to raise his fortune upon the ruin of a worthy gentleman, whom his dissembled sanctity had seduced into the treasonable cause of a Roman Catholic outlaw.

How this design in the play was executed, I refer to the readers of it; it cannot be mended by any critical remarks I can make in its favour; let it speak for itself. All the reason I had to think it no bad performance was, that it was acted eighteen days running, and that the party that were hurt by it (as I have been told) have not been the smallest number of my back friends ever since.'

'The Nonjuror' was dedicated to George I., who rewarded its author with a present of two hundred pounds, and afterwards made him poet-laureate.

For obvious reasons, Cibber always failed in tragedy; and his 'Ximena; or, The Heroic Daughter' (1719), was no exception to the rule, though the plot and much of the language were borrowed from the '*Cid*' of Corneille. When it was first printed, it was dedicated to Sir Richard Steele; but the dedication containing an ungenerous allusion to Addison, who was represented as a wren mounted aloft on Steele's 'eagle back,' Cibber afterwards suppressed it.

Our indefatigable dramatist's next production was the comedy of 'The Refusal; or, The Ladies' Philosophy,' founded upon Molière's '*Les Femmes Savantes.*' The underplot, suggested by the catastrophe of the South Sea Bubble, is Cibber's own; and in the South Sea Company's director, Sir Gilbert Wrangle, he put upon the stage a new type of character, which later dramatists have extensively adopted. The prejudice which Cibber had excited against himself among a portion of the public by his play of 'The Nonjuror' proved fatal to the success of 'The Refusal.' An organised opposition raised disturbances every night, and at the end of a week it was withdrawn.

From Corneille's '*Pompée*' Cibber borrowed the plot of his 'Cæsar in Egypt' (1726); but he borrowed nothing else.

'The Provoked Husband' (1726) is one of his best

compositions, but it had at first to encounter the violent hostility to which I have already alluded. 'On the first day of the "Provoked Husband,"' says Cibber, 'two years after the "Nonjuror" had appeared, a powerful party, not having the fear of public offence or private injury before their eyes, appeared most impetuously concerned for the demolition of it, in which they so far succeeded, that for some time I gave it up for lost; and, to follow their blows, in the public papers of the next day it was attacked and triumphed over as a dead and damned piece; a swinging criticism was made upon it in general invective terms, for they disdained to trouble the world with particulars; their sentence, it seems, was proof enough of its deserving the fate it had met with. But this damned play was, notwithstanding, acted twenty-eight nights together, and left off at a receipt of upwards of a hundred and forty pounds, which happened to be more than in fifty years before could then be said of any play whatsoever.'

The first portion of this play—the 'Journey to London' part—was written by Sir John Vanbrugh, at whose death Cibber took it up, and completed it in admirable style. It contains some of his most finished dialogue, and the recriminatory scenes between Lord and Lady Townly are worked up with a point and finish worthy of Sheridan.

Enter LADY TOWNLY, LORD TOWNLY *following*.

Lady Town. Well, look you, my lord, I can bear it no longer; nothing still but about my faults, my faults: an agreeable subject, truly.

Lord Town. Why, madam, if you won't hear of them, how can I ever hope to see you mend them?

Lady Town. Why, I don't intend to mend them—I won't mend them—you know I have tried to do it a hundred times—and—it hurts me so—I can't bear it.

Lord Town. And I, madam, can't bear this daily licentious abuse of your time and character.

Lady Town. Abuse! astonishing! when the universe knows I am never better company than when I am doing what I have a mind to! But to see this world! that men can never get over that silly spirit of contradiction. Why, but last Thursday, now, there you wisely amended one of my faults, as you call them; you insisted upon my not going to the masquerade—and, pray, what was the consequence? Was not I as cross as the devil all the night after? Was not I forced to get company at home? And was it not almost three o'clock in the morning before I was able to come to myself again? And then the fault is not mended neither—for next time I shall only have twice the inclination to go: so that all this mending and mending, you see, is but darning an old ruffle, to make it worse than it was before.

Lord Town. Well, the manner of women's living of late is insupportable; and one way or other—

Lady Town. It's to be mended, I suppose? Why so it may; but, there, my dear lord, you must give one time—and when things are at worst, you know, they may mend themselves, ha, ha!

Lord Town. Madam, I am not in a humour now to trifle.

Lady Town. Why, then, my lord, one word of fair argument—to talk with you in your own way, now. You complain of my late hours, and I of your early ones. So far we are even, you'll allow. But pray, which gives us the best figure in the eye of the polite world? my active, spirited three in the morning, or your dull, dreary eleven at night? Now, I think, one has the air of a woman of quality, and t'other of a plodding mechanic, that goes to bed betimes, that he may rise early to open his shop. Faugh!

Lord Town. Fy, fy, madam! is this your way of reasoning? 'Tis time to awake you, then. 'Tis not your ill hours alone that disturb me, but as often the ill company that occasion those ill hours.

Lady Town. Sure I don't understand you now, my lord; what ill company do I keep?

Lord Town. Why, at best, women that lose their money, and men that win it; or, perhaps, men that are voluntary bubbles at one game, in hopes a lady will give them fair play at another. Then that unavoidable mixture with known rakes, concealed thieves, and sharpers in embroidery—or, what to me is still more shocking, that herd of familiar, chattering, crop-eared coxcombs, who are so often like monkeys, there would be no knowing them asunder, but that their tails hang from their heads, and the monkey's grows where it should do.

Lady Town. And a husband must give eminent proof of his sense, that thinks these powder-puffs dangerous.

Lord Town. Their being fools, madam, is not always the husband's security; or, if it were, fortune sometimes gives them advantages that might make a thinking woman tremble.

Lady Town. What do you mean?

Lord Town. That women sometimes lose more than they are able to pay: and if a creditor be a little pressing, the lady may be reduced to try if, instead of gold, the gentleman will accept of a trinket.

Lady Town. My lord, you grow scurrilous; you'll make me hate you. I'll have you to know I keep company with the politest people in town, and the assemblies I frequent are full of such.

Lord Town. So are the churches—now and then.

Lady Town. My friends frequent them, too, as well as the assemblies.

Lord Town. Yes, and would do it oftener, if a groom of the chambers were there allowed to furnish cards to the company.

Lady Town. I see what you drive at all this while. You would lay an imputation on my fame, to cover your own avarice. I might take any pleasures, I find, that were not expensive.

Lord Town. Have a care, madam; don't let me think you only value your chastity to make me reproachable for not indulging you in everything else that's vicious. I, madam, have a reputation, too, to guard, that's dear to me as yours. The follies of an ungoverned wife may make the wisest man uneasy, but 'tis his own fault, if ever they make him contemptible.

Lady Town. My lord, you would make a woman mad.

Lord Town. You'd make a man a fool!

Lady Town. If Heaven has made you otherwise, that won't be in my power.

Lord Town. Whatever may be in your inclination, madam, I'll prevent you making me a beggar, at least.

Lady Town. A beggar! Crœsus! I'm out of patience. I won't come home till four to-morrow morning.

Lord Town. That may be, madam; but I'll order the doors to be locked at twelve.

Lady Town. Then I won't come home till to-morrow night.

Lord Town. Then, madam, you shall never come home again.

[*Exit* Lord Town.

Nothing so good as this was ever written by Cibber again: his later work being all of indifferent quality. My censure does not apply to his burlesque 'The Rival Queans, with the Humours of Alexander the Great,' which parodied pretty closely Nat Lee's once popular tragedy of 'The Rival Queens; or, The Death of Alexander the Great;' for though not printed until 1729, it had been acted at least thirty years before, and belonged to Cibber's early period. It contains a good deal of *rococo* humour, scarcely to be appreciated by readers of to-day. The pastoral of 'Love in a Riddle,' suggested by Gay's 'Beggar's Opera,' was produced in 1729. Baker says it met with a most severe and undeserved reception. A general disturbance prevailed throughout the whole representation, except while Miss Rafter (afterwards Mrs Clive) was singing. 'On the second night the riot was still greater, notwithstanding the late Frederick, Prince of Wales, was present, and that for the first time after his arrival in these kingdoms; nor would it have been appeased had not Mr Cibber himself come forward and assured the audience that if they would suffer the performance to go on quietly for that night, out of respect to the royal presence, he would not insist on the piece being acted any more, although the ensuing night should in right have been his benefit; which promise he faithfully kept. Yet, as a proof that it was party prejudice against the author, and not want of merit in the piece itself, which was the occasion of all this violent opposition, when some time afterwards the farce of "Damon and Phyllida," taken entirely from this play, was brought on the stage as a novelty, and not known to be Cibber's, it was very favourably received, and till of late years continued to be acted, and constantly with great applause.'

The tragedy of 'Papal Tyranny in the Reign of King John' (1745), a cumbrous and unattractive title, is sufficiently prosaic. The most notable incident connected with its production was the appearance of Cibber, then seventy-three years of age, in the character of Cardinal Pandulph, which, it is said, he played with much dignity.

'The Lady's Lectures,' a dramatic dialogue between Sir Charles Easy and his marriageable daughter, bears the date of 1748. To Cibber's pen have also been ascribed the opera of 'Chuck' (1736), the tragedy of 'Cinna's Conspiracy' (1756), the comic opera of 'The Temple of Dulness,' and the musical entertainment of 'Capochio and Doriana.'

Speaking of the dramatic literature of the Restoration period, the forty years subsequent to the accession of Charles II. to the throne, Lord Macaulay says, with emphasis strong, but not too strong, it is a disgrace to our language and our national character. 'It is clever,' he continues, 'and very entertaining; but it is, in the most emphatic sense of the words, "earthly, sensual, devilish." Its indecency, though perpetually such as is condemned not less by the rules of good taste than by those of morality, is not, in our opinion, so disgraceful a fault as its singularly inhuman spirit. We have here Belial, not as when he inspired Ovid and Ariosto, "graceful and humane," but with the iron eye and cruel smile of Mephistopheles. We find ourselves in a world in which the ladies are like very profligate, impudent, and unfeeling men, and in which the men are too bad for any place but Pandemonium or Norfolk Island. We are surrounded by foreheads of bronze, hearts like the nether millstone, and tongues set on fire of hell.'

The four principal dramatists, arranged in chronological order, are William Wycherley, born 1640, died 1715; Sir George Vanbrugh, born 1666, died 1726; William Congreve, born 1669, died 1729; and George Farquhar, born 1678, died 1707. In order of merit, we should probably place Congreve first, Wycherley second, Farquhar third, and Vanbrugh fourth; and in order of indecency, Wycherley, Congreve, Farquhar, and Vanbrugh. As we approach the Queen Anne era we find that the improved tone of society makes itself felt upon the stage ; and that neither Farquhar nor Vanbrugh durst venture to the extremes of licence permitted to their predecessors. 'The Beaux' Stratagem' is not always decent ; but it is purity itself compared with 'The Plain Dealer' or 'Love for Love.' But if their morals improved, their wit deteriorated, and the animal spirits and lively humour of Farquhar are far inferior to the epigrammatic sparkle and radiant airy satire of Congreve.

Though Wycherley lived into the reign of George I., his latest dramatic composition, and his best, 'The Plain Dealer,' appeared as remotely as 1667. His plays, therefore, belong to the time of Charles II., and call for no further mention here. Congreve's dramatic fame was made under William III., and the only thing which he produced *temp.* Anne, was his very dull and extravagant opera 'Semele'[1] (1707), founded upon a myth which is utterly unsuitable for dramatic representation. 'It seems strange,' says Dr Warton, 'that a writer of Mr Congreve's good and classical taste should choose "Semele" for the subject of a drama, when the catastrophe is so very absurd. The stage direction in the last act is, "As the cloud which contains Jupiter is arrived just over the canopy of Semele, a sudden and great flash of lightning breaks forth, and a clap of thunder is heard ; when, at one instant, Semele, with the palace and the whole scene, disappears, and Jupiter reascends swiftly."' With these two dramatists, however, we shall not concern ourselves ; but shall continue our review of the Dramatists of the reign of Queen Anne with—

GEORGE FARQUHAR, who came of a respectable family in the north of Ireland ; his father, according to some authorities, being Dean of Armagh. This, however, seems

---

[1] The music was composed by John Eccles.

doubtful. The future dramatist was born at Londonderry in 1678, and educated in 'the loyal city' until he was old enough and qualified enough to enter Trinity College, Dublin (1694). His gay and volatile temper took no pleasure in serious studies ; and in the following year he quitted college, obtained an engagement from Mr Ashbury, the manager of the Drury Lane Theatre, and appeared on the stage in no less formidable a part than that of Othello. He who aims too high will always miss the mark ; and Farquhar in his new vocation failed to secure the public suffrages. His person was good, his deportment easy and graceful, his delivery clear and judicious ; but these good qualities were neutralised by an excessive timidity as well as by a serious vocal deficiency. An unusual accident hastened his retirement from the stage. Playing the part of Guyomar in Dryden's 'Indian Emperor,' who has to kill Vasquez, one of the Spanish generals, he took up a real sword, by mistake, instead of a foil, and in the heat of combat so dangerously wounded the tragedian who personated Vasquez that at first his life was despaired of. This occurrence so deeply affected Farquhar that he abandoned the stage for ever.

In the following year young Farquhar accompanied the actor Wilks, who had been engaged at Drury Lane, to London, and moving freely in theatrical circles, won a certain amount of distinction by the graceful gaiety of his manners and the sparkle of his conversation. The Earl of Orrery was so pleased with him that he gave him a lieutenant's commission in his own regiment, then in Ireland ; and the brilliant young man held it for some years without reproach, showing himself possessed both of conduct and courage. Wilks, however, had detected in his friend the qualifications which constitute a successful playwright—wit, a knowledge of stagecraft, a quick faculty of observation, invention, and animal spirits. He urged him

to write a comedy; and Farquhar at length consented.
In 1698, at the age of twenty, he produced his first play,
'Love and a Bottle,' a wonderfully clever piece of work
for so young a man, and impossible for any young man
whose experience of the world had not been unusually
extensive. The too frequent licentiousness of dialogue is
an unfortunate proof that this experience had included
much intercourse with vice and the vicious.

The success of his first effort encouraged Captain
Farquhar to persevere in his new avocation; and in the
winter season of the jubilee year he gave the public his
favourite comedy of 'The Constant Couple; or, A Trip
to the Jubilee,' in which Mr Wilks gained the applause of
the town by his brisk and airy impersonation of Sir Harry
Wildair, afterwards one of Mrs Oldfield's most successful
characters. The sprightly dialogue, the humorous incidents, and the well-defined characters in this brilliant play
so delighted the public that in its first season it ran for
the then extraordinary number of fifty-three nights. Its
author, for two of his *dramatis personæ*, Lady Lurewell
and Colonel Standard, and for the incidents of Beau Clincher and Tom Errand's change of clothes, seems to have
been indebted to a small volume, published in 1699, '*The
Adventures of Covent Garden*.' The treatment, however,
is unquestionably Farquhar's own. It is needless to say
that the low estimate of women common to the Restoration
dramas—the glorification of adultery—and the apparent
incapacity to appreciate or understand the moral law, are
all found in this clever comedy, which glitters with the
phosphorescence of its own corruption.

Farquhar was so well pleased with his Sir Harry
Wildair that he brought him on the stage again in the
following year, surrounding him with several of the characters in 'The Constant Couple.' But like most continuations, the comedy of 'Sir Harry Wildair' is but an

indifferent composition. In 'The Inconstant,' which this prolific dramatist brought out in 1702, we recognise, however, his characteristic merits. The writing is always smart, and scene follows scene with admirable care and unfailing liveliness. In this, as in his other plays, Farquhar makes good use of his knowledge of military men and manners, and the gay, dashing, drinking, marching, jesting, fighting officer of his time is reproduced with a freshness that seems never to fail. In the lines which our witty captain puts into the mouth of Mirabell, he may be assumed to draw a portrait of himself:—

> 'I hate the man who makes acquaintance nice,
> And still discreetly plagues me with advice;
> Who moves by caution and mature delays,
> And must give reasons for whate'er he says.
> The man, indeed, whose converse is so full,
> Makes me attentive, but it makes me dull:
> Give me the careless rogue who never thinks,
> That plays the fool as freely as he drinks.
> Not a buffoon, who is buffoon by trade,
> But one that nature not his wants have made;
> Who still is merry, but does ne'er design it;
> And still is ridiculed, but ne'er can find it:
> Who, when he's most in earnest, is the best,
> And his most grave expression is a jest.'

A bright passage which throws a side-light on the theatre of the time will entertain the reader:—

Duretête. How d'ye like this play?

Mirabell. I liked the company; the lady, the rich beauty in the front box, had my attention: these impudent poets bring the ladies together to support them, and kill everybody else.

> For death's upon the stage the ladies cry,
> But ne'er mind us that in the audience die;
> The poet's hero should not move their pain,
> But they should weep for those their eyes have slain.

Dur. Hoyty, toyty! did Phillis inspire you with all this?

Mir. Ten times more; the playhouse is the element of poetry because the region of beauty: the ladies, methinks, have a more inspiring, triumphant air in the boxes, than anywhere else; they sit commanding in their thrones with all their subject slaves about them. Their best clothes, best looks, shining jewels, sparkling eyes, the treasure of the world in a ring. Then there's such a hurry of pleasure to transport us; the bustle, noise, gallantry, equipage, garters, feathers, wigs, bows, smiles, ogles, love, music, and applause; I could wish that my whole life long were the first night of a new play.

In the Restoration dramas nothing is more extraordinary than the dramatist's sudden plunge into morality at the finale. After ridiculing matrimony all through five acts, after extolling illicit love, and laughing at cuckolded husbands and wanton wives, he makes a kind of well-bred, good-natured concession to the decencies, and just before the curtain drops marries off his hero and heroine with a dull tag, in sorry rhymes, about the bliss of wedded love. A conversion such as this imposes upon no one. We feel that the rake remains a rake in spite of his sugared speeches. In this play of 'The Inconstant,' Mirabell is represented to be as ardent in his hatred of marriage as he is incessant in the pursuit of lewd women. He is a monster of lust, though disguised with a fascinating air of polish, wit, and nonchalance. The lady to whom he is betrothed—whose charms he acknowledges, while flying from them because he cannot make them his own without the obligation of matrimony—follows him everywhere, and at last, in the disguise of a page, becomes the instrument of saving his life when threatened by bravos in a courtesan's chamber. Up to this point the railing against marriage, and wives, and chastity has flowed on merrily in a continuous strain; but all at once it ceases. The prompter is about to ring down the curtain, and custom requires that after the luscious draught of immorality the audience shall taste a cup of bitters. Thus ends the play:—

Enter ORIANA (in her page's disguise).

Mir. Ha! (*runs and embraces her*). My dear preserver! what shall I do to recompense your trust? Father, friends, gentlemen, behold the youth, that has relieved me from the most ignominious death—from the scandalous poniards of these bloody ruffians, when to have fallen would have defamed my memory with vile reproach. My life, estate, my all, is due to such a favour—command me, child ; before you all, before my late so kind, indulgent stars, I swear to grant whate'er you ask.

Ori. To the same stars, indulgent now to me, I will appeal as to the justice of my claim : I shall demand but what was mine before— the just performance of your contract to Oriana.

[*Discovering herself.*

Omnes. Oriana !

Ori. In this disguise I resolved to follow you abroad ; counterfeited that letter that got me into your service ; and, so by this strange turn of fate, I became the instrument of your preservation. Few common servants would have had such cunning.

Duretête. Mirabell, you're caught.

Mir. Caught ! I scorn the thought of imposition ; the tricks and artful cunning of the sex I have despised, and broke through all contrivance. Caught ! no, 'tis my voluntary act ; this was no human stratagem ; but by my providential stars designed to show the dangers wandering youth incurs by the pursuit of an unlawful love, to plunge me headlong in the snares of vice, and then to free me by the hands of virtue : here, on my knees, I humbly beg my fair preserver's pardon ; my thanks are needless, for myself I owe. And now, for ever, do protest me yours.

Old Mir. Tall all di dall—[*sings*]. Kiss me, daughter—no, you shall kiss me first [*to* LAMORCE], for you're the cause on't. Well, Bisarre, what say you to the Captain ?

Bis. I like the beast well enough, but I don't understand his paces so well, as to endanger him in a strange road.

Old Mir. But marriage is so beaten a path that you can't go wrong.

Bis. Ay, 'tis so beaten that the way is spoiled.

Dur. There is but one thing should make me thy husband. I could marry thee to-day, for the privilege of beating thee to-morrow.

Old Mir. Come, come, you may agree for all this. Mr Dugard, are not you pleased with this ?

Dug. So pleased, that if I thought it might secure your son's affection to my sister, I would double her fortune.

Mir. Fortune ! has she not given me mine ? my life, estate, my all, and, what is more, her virtuous self! Virtue, in this so advantageous life, has her own sparkling charms, more tempting far than glittering gold or glory. Behold the foil [*pointing to* LAMORCE] that sets this brightness off! [*to* ORIANA]. Here view the pride [*to* ORIANA] and scandal of the sex [*to* LAMORCE]. There the false meteor, whose deluding light leads mankind to destruction; here, the bright shining star that guides to a variety of happiness. A garden and a single she—[*to* ORIANA]—was our first father's bliss; the tempter [*to* LAMORCE] and to wander was his curse.

> What liberty can be so tempting there [*to* LAMORCE]
> As a soft, virtuous, am'rous bondage here? [*to* ORIANA].

Admirable sentiments! But what are we to think of them when they fall from the lips of a man who, five minutes before, sought the embraces of a harlot? Or rather, what are we to think of *him* or of his sincerity? One might as readily believe in a Red Republican if he suddenly broke out into a panegyric upon the blessings of law and order. As for the effect of this highly moral conclusion upon an audience which, for five long acts, has been deliberately debauched by an insidious sensuality, I doubt if it can be represented by any known quantity. The dramatist resembles the poisoner who, after bringing his victim to the brink of the grave by a long series of subtle doses, should suddenly attempt to avert a catastrophe by administering a single draught of rose-water. This was keenly felt by all women of the age who preserved a sense of true modesty and a feeling of genuine refinement; and they absented themselves from the theatre when the comedies of Wycherley and his school were performed. It was no place for them where love was degraded into lust, and their sex represented as existing only to serve the baser passions of man. In Crowne's famous comedy, Sir Courtly Nice, addressing Leonora, remarks that, 'Comedies are always crammed with an odious sex —that have not always the most inviting smell—madam, you'll pardon me. Now at tragedies the house is all lined with beauty, and then a gentleman may endure it.'

In 1705 Captain Farquhar produced 'The Twin Rivals,' which, by some critics, is considered the most regular and complete of all his dramas. The improbabilities of the plot, however, and the extravagance of such characters as Teague and Mrs Midnight, will account for the comparative oblivion into which it has fallen; and from which there are good reasons for making no attempt to rescue it.

'The Recruiting Officer' (1706) is one of his liveliest compositions; and, we may add, one of the most decent and least immoral. It has an historical value, as furnishing an undeniably authentic picture of the conditions under which a British army was formed in the days of Marlborough. This play was written on the very spot—Shrewsbury—which the author has made his scene of action, and at a time when he himself was engaged in the work of recruiting. Captain Plume is Captain Farquhar under another name; Justice Balance was designed as a compliment to be then Recorder of Shrewsbury, Mr Berkely; Sylvia was his daughter; Worthy, a Mr Owen, of Russason; and Melinda, as Miss Hamage, of Balsadine. The play is dedicated with familiarity and gratitude to 'all friends round the Wrekin'; and ends with an *à propos* epilogue, ushered in by beat of drum with the Grenadier's March, which commemorates the victories of Marlborough. There are few livelier comedies in our British Theatre than 'The Recruiting Officer': the dialogue sparkles with a natural and spontaneous wit; the characters are forcibly drawn; and the scenes move onward easily to the music of drum and fife. What Farquhar has done in this strong and capable drama no other of our playwrights could have done as well.

But confessedly his best work was his last, 'The Beaux' Stratagem' (1707), which he wrote in six weeks

under high pressure; beset with difficulties, with sickness
and poverty, as if the most unfavourable conditions were
necessary to the full development of his rare dramatic
powers. While engaged in the task of composition, he
was quite sensible of the close approach of death, and
foretold that he would die before the run of his play was
over. These circumstances must increase our admiration
of the rare animal spirits which pervade from beginning
to end; so that there is not a dull scene, scarcely a dull
line; and the interest throughout is vigorously maintained.
Of wit there is enough and to spare: it may lack Congreve's
polish, but it has an effervescence which is Farquhar's
own. The characters, too, are not without individuality;
and the airy and attractive Archer, Mrs Sullen, the lively
Cherry, and Scrub, the country servant, are real persons,
with a vitality in them which has defied the vicissitudes of
public taste. As for Boniface and Lady Bountiful, it is
no exaggeration to speak of them as types which have
obtained general acceptance among our dramatists, while
their names, as representing two well-marked classes of
society, have entered into our daily speech. To this day
the ruddy-cheeked host of 'mine inn' is a Boniface; and
the charitable dame of the village, who dispenses soups
and medicines with equal liberality, is still known as Lady
Bountiful.

Aimwell and Archer are two young gentlemen who
have dissipated their fortunes in the follies of the town;
and with two hundred pounds, the residue, their horses,
clothes, and jewellery, they set out from London in search
of a couple of heiresses,—the understanding between them
being that as they go from place to place they shall alternately exchange the parts of master and servant. They
arrive at Lichfield when it is Aimwell's turn to appear as
master. The opening scene—at Boniface's inn—prepares
the reader for what is to follow:—

Bon. I'll show you such ale! Here, tapster, broach number 1706, as the saying is. Sir, you shall taste my *Anno Domini*. I have lived in Lichfield, man and boy, above eight-and-fifty years, and I believe have not consumed eight-and-fifty ounces of meat.

Aim. At a meal, you mean, if one may guess your sense by your bulk.

Bon. Not in my life, sir: I have fed purely upon ale; I have ate my ale, drank my ale, and I always sleep upon ale.

Enter TAPSTER *with a bottle and glass, and exit.*

Now, sir, you shall see!—[*pours out a glass*]. Your worship's health. Ha! delicious, delicious! fancy it burgundy, only fancy it, and 'tis worth ten shillings a quart.

Aim. [*drinks*]. 'Tis confounded strong!

Bon. Strong! it must be so, or how shall we be strong that drink it?

Aim. And have you lived so long upon this ale, landlord?

Bon. Eight-and-fifty years, upon my credit, sir—but it killed my wife, poor woman, as the saying is.

Aim. How came that to pass?

Bon. I don't know how, sir. She would not let the ale take its natural course, sir; she was for qualifying it every now and then with a dram, as the saying is; and an honest gentleman that came this way from Ireland, made her a present of a dozen bottles of usquebaugh—but the poor woman was never well after; but, however, I was obliged to the gentleman, you know.

Aim. Why, was it the usquebaugh that killed her?

Bon. My Lady Bountiful said so. She, good lady, did what could be done; she cured her of three tympanies, but the fourth carried her off. But she's happy, and I'm contented, as the saying is.

Aim. Who's that Lady Bountiful you mentioned?

Bon. Ods my life! sir, we'll drink her health—[*drinks*]. My Lady Bountiful is one of the best of women. Her last husband, Sir Charles Bountiful, left her with a thousand pound a year; and, I believe, she lays out one-half on't in charitable uses for the good of her neighbours. She cures rheumatisms, ruptures, and broken shins, in men; green-sickness, obstructions, and fits of the mother, in women; the king's evil, chincough, and chilblains, in children: in short, she has cured more people in and about Lichfield within ten years than the doctors have killed in twenty; and that's a bold word.

Aim. Has the lady been any other way useful in her generation?

Bon. Yes, sir, she has a daughter by Sir Charles, the finest woman in all our country, and the greatest fortune. She has a son too, by her first husband, Squire Sullen, who married a fine lady from London t'other day; if you please, sir, we'll drink his health.

Aim. What sort of a man is he?

Bon. Why, sir, the man's well enough; says little, thinks less, and does—nothing at all, faith. But he's a man of great estate, and values nobody.

Aim. A sportsman, I suppose?

Bon. Yes, sir, he's a man of pleasure; he plays at wisk and smokes his pipe eight-and-forty hours together sometimes.

Aim. And married, you say!

Bon. Ay, and to a curious woman, sir. But he's a—he wants it—here, sir—[*pointing to his forehead*].

Aim. He has it there, you mean?

Bon. That's none of my business: he's my landlord, and so a man, you know—would not. But—and, he's no better than— Sir, my humble service to you—[*drinks*]. Though I value not a farthing what he can do to me; I pay him his rent at quarter-day; I have a good running trade; I have but one daughter, and I can give her—but no matter for that.

Aim. You're very happy, Mr Boniface. Pray, what other company have you in town?

Bon. A power of fine ladies; and then we have the French officers.

Aim. Oh, that's right, you have a good many of those gentlemen: pray, how do you like their company?

Bon. So well, as the saying is, that I could wish we had as many more of 'em: they're full of money, and pay double for everything they have. They know, sir, that we paid good round taxes for the taking of 'em, and so they are willing to reimburse us a little. One of 'em lodges in my house.

The innkeeper goes out, and Archer enters. A dialogue between Archer and Aimwell explains their plans, and Boniface then returns.

Bon. What will your worship please to have for supper?

Aim. What have you got?

Bon. Sir, we have a delicate piece of beef in the pot, and a pig at the fire.

Aim. Good supper-meat, I must confess. I can't eat beef, landlord.
Arch. And I hate pig.
Aim. Hold your prating, sirrah; do you know who you are?
Bon. Please to bespeak something else; I have everything in the house.
Aim. Have you any veal?
Bon. Veal! sir, we had a delicate loin of veal on Wednesday last.
Aim. Have you got any fish or wild fowl?
Bon. As for fish, truly, sir, we are an inland town, and indifferently provided with fish, that's the truth on't; and then for wild fowl—we have a delicate couple of rabbits.
Aim. Get me the rabbits fricasseed.
Bon. Friscasseed! Lord, sir, they'll eat much better smothered with onions.
Arch. Psha, damn your onions![1]
Aim. Again, sirrah. Well, landlord, what you please.

Aimwell, in order to impress the landlord with a sense of their good position, places in his hand for safe custody, a box containing, as he says, above two hundred pounds. Afterwards, in conversing with his daughter Cherry, Boniface comes to believe they are highwaymen, and meditates betraying them; but first he sets Cherry to worm out the traveller's secret from his footman. Cherry is disposed to look down upon footmen; but Archer makes love to her so boldly, and with the natural manners of a gentleman, that she is more than half inclined to smile upon him.

In the second act, Dorinda, Lady Bountiful's unmarried daughter, and Mrs Sullen, her sister-in-law, hold unreserved talk together, and Mrs Sullen expatiates on the miseries of matrimony, judging from her own unhappy experience. 'Oh, sister, sister, sister!' she exclaims, 'if ever you marry, beware of a sullen, silent sot; one that's always musing, but never thinks. There's some diversion in a

---

[1] Goldsmith, in the scene in 'She Stoops to Conquer,' between Marlow Hastings, and Hardcastle, seems to have imitated this.

talking blockhead; and since a woman must wear chains, I would have the pleasure of hearing them rattle a little. Now you shall see; but take this, by the way: he came home this morning at his usual hour of four, wakened me out of a sweet dream of something else, by tumbling over the tea-table, which he broke all to pieces. After his man and he had rolled about the room, like sick passengers in a storm, he comes flounce into bed, dead as a salmon into a fishmonger's basket; his feet cold as ice; his breath hot as a furnace; and his hands and his face as greasy as his flannel night-cap. Oh, matrimony! matrimony! He turns up the clothes with a barbarous swing over his shoulders, disorders the whole economy of my bed, leaves me half naked, and my whole night's comfort is the tuneable serenade of that wakeful nightingale, his nose. Oh, the pleasure of counting the melancholy clock by a snoring husband!' It is soon evident that Mr and Mrs Sullen are bound together by no ties of sympathy or affection: and Mrs Sullen, a young, handsome, and susceptible woman, is disposed to avenge herself or her sottish husband, by awakening his jealousy. A certain French Count, one of the prisoners of war in Lichfield, is no less disposed to assist her in this direction. Changing the scene, we find that Aimwell resolves to go to church to hunt up an heiress, in which resolution he is encouraged by Archer, who afterwards has a conversation with Cherry, and so impresses her with his good looks and good manners, that she offers herself, with two thousand pounds, if he will marry her before he sleeps. 'And have you actually two thousand pounds?' *Cherry.* 'Sir, I have my secrets as well as you—when you please to be more open, I shall be more free; and be assured, that I have discoveries that will match yours, be they what they will. In the meanwhile, be satisfied that no discovery I make shall ever hurt you; but, beware of my father!'

'So,' says Archer, when she has retired, 'we're likely to have as many adventures in our inn, as Don Quixote had in his. Let me see—two thousand pounds! If the wench would promise to die when the money were spent, egad, one would marry her, but the fortune may go off in a year or two, and the wife may live—Lord knows how long! Then an innkeeper's daughter! Ay, that's the devil—there my pride brings me off.'

The third act brings before us Dorinda and Mrs Sullen, who have been to church, and have seen Aimwell there, and it is clear that Dorinda regards him with no unfavourable eyes. They employ the country servant, Scrub, who acts as butler on Sundays, to scrape acquaintance with the stranger's brilliant footman, and find out who his master is. The scene changes to the inn. Aimwell has fallen in love with Dorinda; Archer, as the footman, is invited by Scrub to see Lady Bountiful's cellar, and Aimwell whiles away his time with one Gibbet, who is by profession a highwayman, and believes Aimwell and his friend to be of the same calling. Another visitor appears —'a downright Teague'—who pretends to be a Frenchman, calls himself Foigard, and is engaged as chaplain to the French prisoners of war in Lichfield. The three go to dinner; while Archer and Scrub make merry over Lady Bountiful's wine. Scrub confides to his new-found friend that he is consumedly in love with Gipsy, his mistress's maid, but has a dangerous rival in the priest Foigard, and that the French Count is pursuing Mrs Sullen with dishonourable designs. He has also something to say about his heavy labours. 'What d'ye think,' he asks, 'is my place in this family?' 'Butler, I suppose,' answers Archer. 'Ah, Lord help your silly head! I'll tell you. Of a Monday, I drive the coach; of a Tuesday, I drive the plough; on Wednesday, I follow the hounds; on Thursday, I dun the tenants; on Friday, I go to market;

on Saturday, I draw warrants; and on Sunday, I draw beer.' The ladies, who have already learned through Gipsy that the stranger is Lord Viscount Aimwell—in truth, he is the Viscount's brother—here enter, as if by accident, and speedily engage Archer in conversation; an opportunity of which he makes such good use that Mrs Sullen finds him very much to her liking, and regrets that he wears the livery. She is vastly relieved when Dorinda suggests that he is a gentleman who, out of friendship and loyalty to Lord Aimwell, accompanies him in a servant's disguise, and shares all his adventures. 'It is so,' she exclaims; 'it must be so, and it shall be so! for I like him.'

The act closes with a device of Mrs Sullen's to stir up some kind of feeling in her boorish husband. She persuades his sister Dorinda to hide himself where he may overhear a conversation between his wife and Count Bellair. Mrs Sullen rejects the Count's suit as becomes an English gentlewoman; but her husband simply behaves with even greater brutality than before.

The fourth act opens with the Beaux' stratagem to gain admission to Lady Bountiful's house and to Dorinda's presence. Trading upon her mania for acting as an amateur physician, Aimwell pretends to be taken in a fit just at the good lady's gate. Archer, still disguised as Mr Martin, rushes in to seek assistance, and Lady Bountiful, entirely in her element, has him brought into the gallery, where she prescribes for him, and makes a great fuss about him. Aimwell finds an opportunity for pressing his suit upon the nowise reluctant Dorinda, and Archer improves the good understanding already existing between him and Mrs Sullen. The complexity of the plot now increases. Scrub, whom jealousy makes vigilant, overhears an agreement between Foigard and Gipsy, by which the latter is bribed into promising to conceal the

French Count in a closet beside Mrs Sullen's chamber. He makes it known to Archer, who convicts Foigard of being an Irishman, threatens to bring him to the gallows as a British subject in the pay of the enemy; and spares him only on condition that he admits Archer into the closet instead of the Count. On this same night Boniface, Gibbet, and some highwaymen have resolved to break into and plunder Lady Bountiful's house.

At the opening of the fifth act Sir Charles Freeman arrives at Boniface's inn. He is Mrs Sullen's brother, and his errand is to effect a separation between her and her husband. The squire, who visits the tavern every night, enters drunk, and unconsciously reveals his character and his wife's unhappy position to Sir Charles. Then Cherry, who has been looking for Archer, and failed to find him, calls upon Aimwell, and informs him that a gang of rogues have set out to rob Lady Bountiful's house. Aimwell hastens at once to the rescue of his Dorinda.

But inside the house, and inside Mrs Sullen's bed-chamber, is the audacious Archer, who is on the point of carrying her off, when Scrub, in an agony of fear, breaks into the room. Thieves are in the house! 'Thieves, thieves,' he cries, 'murder and Popery!' At first he mistakes Archer for one of them, and throwing himself on his knees, exclaims, 'O pray, sir, spare all I have, and take my life!' By degrees he is able to tell his tale. But Captain Gibbet approaches; Archer and Scrub conceal themselves behind the bed; Gibbet lays hands upon Mrs Sullen, and is stripping her of her jewellery, when Archer suddenly throws himself upon him, trips him up, and claps the highwayman's own pistol to his breast. Scrub brings in Foigard, and the two are directed to convey Gibbet into the cellar, and there bind him; while Archer and Mrs Sullen, attracted by shrieks in another part of the house, are in time to assist Aimwell in disposing of the other robbers. Sir Charles Freeman arrives. It is evident that a man of his social position will know the real Lord Aimwell, and that the suitor of Dorinda is only his younger brother. By the help of Foigard as chaplain, Dorinda must be married before Sir Charles can interfere. She is ready; but puts such simple faith in her lover's honesty, that he can no longer carry on the deception,— he explains who he is, and what he intended. The confession increases Dorinda's love and admiration, and meanwhile the news arrives of Lord Aimwell's death, and that Aimwell has succeeded to the title he had previously assumed. His happiness and Dorinda's is therefore complete. As for the fate of the other characters, we need concern ourselves only with that of Mrs Sullen, whose separation from her husband Sir Charles endeavours to arrange. The sequel is in Farquhar's airiest manner, and I shall therefore quote it :—

Enter SULLEN.

Sul. What's all this? They tell me, spouse, that you had like to have been robbed.

Mrs Sul. Truly, spouse, I was pretty near it, had not these two gentlemen interposed.

Sul. How came these gentlemen here?

Mrs Sul. That's his way of returning thanks, you must know.

Forg. Ay; but, upon my conscience, de question be *apropos* for all dat.

Sir Chas. You promised last night, sir, that you would deliver your lady to me this morning.

Sul. Humph.

Arch. Humph! What do you mean by humph? Sir, you shall deliver her. In short, sir, we have saved you and your family; and, if you are not civil, we'll unbind the rogues, join with them, and set fire to your house. What does the man mean? Not part with his wife?

Forg. Arra, not part wid your wife! Upon my shoul, de man doth not understand common shivility.

The Stage in Queen Anne's Reign.   41

Mrs Sul. Hold, gentlemen; all things here must move by consent. Compulsion would spoil us. Let my dear and I talk the matter over, and you shall judge it between us.

Sul. Let me know first who are to be our judges. Pray, sir, who are you?

Sir Chas. I am Sir Charles Freeman, come to take away your wife.

Sul. And you, good sir?

Aim. Thomas, Viscount Aimwell, come to take away your sister.

Sul. And you, pray, sir?

Arch. Francis Archer, Esquire, come—

Sul. To take away my mother, I hope. Gentlemen, you're heartily welcome. I never met with three more obliging people since I was born. And now, my dear, if you please, you shall have the first word.

Arch. And the last, for five pounds. [*Aside.*]

Mrs Sul. Spouse.

Sul. Rib.

Mrs Sul. How long have you been married?

Sul. By the almanack, fourteen months; but, by my account, fourteen years.

Mrs Sul. 'Tis thereabouts, by my reckoning.

Forg. Upon my conshience, dere accounts vil agree.

Mrs Sul. Pray, spouse, what did you marry for?

Sul. To get an heir to my estate.

Sir Chas. And have you succeeded?

Sul. No.

Arch. The condition fails of his side. Pray, madam, what did you marry for?

Mrs Sul. To support the weakness of my sex, by the strength of his, and to enjoy the pleasures of an agreeable society.

Sir Chas. Are your expectations answered?

Mrs Sul. No.

Forg. Arra, honey! a clear cause, a clear cause!

Sir Chas. What are the bars to your mutual contentment?

Mrs Sul. In the first place, I can't drink ale with him.

Sul. Nor can I drink tea with her.

Mrs Sul. I can't hunt with you.

Sul. Nor can I dance with you.

Mrs Sul. I hate cocking and racing.

Sul. I abhor ombre and piquet.

Mrs Sul. Your silence is intolerable.
Sul. Your prating is worse.
Mrs Sul. Have we not been a perpetual offence to each other—a gnawing vulture at the heart?
Sul. A frightful goblin to the sight?
Mrs Sul. A porcupine to the feeling?
Sul. Perpetual wormwood to the taste?
Mrs Sul. Is there on earth a thing we can agree in?
Sul. Yes—to part.
Mrs Sul. With all my heart.
Sul. Your hand.
Mrs Sul. Here.
Sul. These hands joined us, these shall part us—away.
Mrs Sul. East.
Sul. West.
Mrs Sul. North.
Sul. South; far as the Poles asunder.
Forg. Upon my shoul, a very pretty sheremony!

Eventually Sullen surrenders the lady's portion, and the play comes to an end:—

Sul. My head aches consumedly. Well, gentlemen, you shall have her fortune, but I can't talk. If you have a mind, Sir Charles, to be merry, and celebrate my sister's wedding, and my divorce, you may command my house; but my head aches consumedly. Scrub, bring me a dram.

Arch. 'Twould be hard to guess which of these parties is the better pleased, the couple joined, or the couple parted; the one rejoicing in hopes of an untasted happiness, and the other in their deliverance from an experienced misery.

> Both happy in their several states we find;
> These parted by consent, and those conjoined.
> Consent, if mutual, saves the lawyer's fee;
> Consent is law enough to set you free.

The wit, the humour, the high spirits, the drollery of the situations, the admirable drawing of the principal characters, render 'The Beaux' Stratagem,' in my opinion, one of the best specimens of the so-called Comedy of Manners which the English stage has produced. Its lax moral tone I do not pretend to excuse; though it is infinitely less objectionable than the majority of the plays of the period. Whether it accurately represents the habits and ways of English gentlemen and gentlewomen in the reign of Anne, I very much doubt. Whether it fairly represents those of the reign of Charles II., is also doubtful. Were it so, we must believe that Society was rotten to the core; that every man was at heart a rake, and every woman a harlot; and that their sole occupation was intrigue—their sole pleasure debauchery. If this were true of the Court in the evil time of the second Charles, it was not true of the Court in the more decorous age of Anne; and I do not think it was true of Society at large, either in the one or the other period. I have always been disposed, in spite of Lord Macaulay's adverse criticism, to agree with Charles Lamb that, at all events to a great extent, the Restoration drama dealt with a conventional and unreal world, and did not accurately represent the *actual* world—the England of the latter part of the seventeenth century. But this is no excuse for its immorality, while it deprives it of half its value. It takes away from it all historical importance, and leaves behind only its literary merit; and however highly we may rate its wit and humour, its fun and satire, we cannot accept them as condonation for its gross licence.

To return to Farquhar. He seems to have been himself the model from which he sketched his brisk and joyous sparks, with all their blithesomeness and ease of manner and gaiety of spirit. He made love readily, and his attachments were as numerous as they were transitory. At one time he appears to have devoted himself with more fervency than usual to his 'dear Penelope,' the charming Mrs Oldfield, whose genius as an actress he was the first to recognise and develop. Dining one day at the Mitre Tavern, in St James's Market, which was kept by her aunt, a Mrs

Voss, he heard Miss Nancy, then a girl of sixteen, handsome, tall, and slender, with fine eyes, and a musical voice, reading a play behind the bar, and was so pleased with the mellow sweetness of her tones, the justness of her emphasis, and 'the agreeable turn she gave to each character,' that he declared she was born to shine upon the stage. As this was her own inclination, her mother, the next time she saw Captain Vanbrugh, who was acquainted with the family, made known to him Farquhar's opinion, whereupon Vanbrugh inquired whether her bent was most to tragedy or comedy. Miss Nancy, on being interrogated, expressed her preference for the latter. She had read all Beaumont and Fletcher's comedies, she said, and the play which Captain Farquhar had overheard her reading was their 'Scornful Lady.' She was accordingly introduced to Mr Christopher Rich, of Drury Lane, who gave her an engagement at fifteen shillings a week, which was almost immediately increased to twenty shillings. In Farquhar's comedies she generally played the heroine, and it is a moot point whether the dramatist was more indebted to the actress or the actress to the dramatist. If she was fortunate in the opportunities he gave her of displaying her fine qualities as an actress, he was not less fortunate in finding an actress so well able to do justice to the creatures of his invention.

Whether Captain Farquhar's relation to this charming woman was wholly platonic, we need not inquire. What is certain is, that in 1703 he was married to a lady who was supposed to enjoy a very considerable fortune. But it afterwards appeared that no such fortune existed, and that she had spread a report of her wealth abroad in order to draw the attention of Captain Farquhar, with whom she was passionately in love. She allowed him to discover her affection; and thus, flattered in his vanity and attracted by a prospect of competency, he was induced to surrender his bachelorhood, and offer the lady his hand. After marriage he learned the truth; and one of his biographers oddly records it as to his 'immortal honour' that, though he found himself deceived, he never reproached his wife with it, but always behaved towards her with the delicacy of an indulgent husband. Possibly he may have felt that there had been deception on both sides; that if the lady had imposed on him by pretending to be wealthy, he had imposed on her by pretending a disinterested attachment.

The closing years of his brief life were spent under a cloud. His pay as an officer was small; and though the profits from his dramas must have been considerable, his entire income was inadequate to the payment of his debts and the support of an increasing family. As difficulties grew upon him, he applied to 'a certain noble courtier' who had made many warm professions of friendship, and given frequent assurances of his readiness to help him. This pretended patron repeated his declarations; but, expressing deep regret that he could not at the moment assist him, advised him to raise some ready money by the sale of his commission, pledging himself to procure another for him with very little delay. Farquhar acted on the advice; but when he applied for a fulfilment of the promise, could obtain no satisfaction. The disappointment proved too much for Farquhar's light, easy temper; he fell into a condition of debility which no skill of the physicians could repair; and at the early age of twenty-nine, and towards the end of April 1707, terminated his chequered career.

As already hinted, 'The Beaux' Stratagem' was written in about six weeks during his last illness. Of the good humour with which he bore his sufferings, an anecdote is told in connection with this play. While it was in rehearsal, Mr Wilks, who frequently visited him, told him one day that Mrs Oldfield thought he had dealt too freely with the character of Mrs Sullen, in giving her to Archer, without such a proper divorce as might be a security for her honour. 'Oh,' replied Farquhar, with his usual careless vivacity, 'tell her I will, if she pleases, salve that immediately by getting a real divorce, marrying her myself, and giving her my bond that she shall be a real widow in less than a fortnight.'

The following letter—very pathetic in its dreadful brevity—was found among Farquhar's papers, addressed to Mr Wilks, who, so far as his means allowed, acted upon it :—

'DEAR BOB,—I have not anything to leave thee to perpetuate my memory but two helpless girls; look upon them sometimes, and think of him that was, to the last moment of his life, thine, GEORGE FARQUHAR.'

The moralist may do what he pleases with this story of a wasted life and a prematurely ended career. I do not deny the possibility of deducing from it a useful lesson. I am sure that it is suggestive of many painful reflections. But with this brilliant young wit and dramatist, the author of seven first-rate comedies before he was thirty, the reader and I would wish to part on good terms; and, therefore, I adopt as an epilogue, and in the place of the inevitable moral, the lively sketch of his own character, called *The Picture*, which he drew in bold outlines for an anonymous lady :—

My outside is neither better nor worse than my Creator made it; and the piece being drawn by so great an artist, it were presumption to say there were many strokes amiss. I have a body qualified to answer all the ends of its creation, and that is sufficient.

As to the mind, which in most men wears as many changes as their body, so in me it is generally dressed like my person, in black. Melancholy is its every-day apparel; and it has hitherto found few holidays to make it change its clothes. In short, my constitution is very splenetic, and yet very amorous; both which I endeavour to hide, lest the former should offend others, and the latter incommode myself. And my reason is so vigilant in restraining these two failings, that I am taken for an easy-natured man with my own sex, and an ill-natured clown by yours. . . .

I have very little estate, but what lies under the circumference of my hat; and should I by mischance come to lose my head, I should not be worth a groat; but I ought to thank Providence that I can by three hours' study live one and twenty with satisfaction to myself, and contribute to the maintenance of more families than some who have thousands a year.

I have something in my outward behaviour which gives strangers a worse opinion of me than I deserve; but I am more than recompensed by the opinion of my acquaintance, which is so much above my desert.

I have many acquaintances, very few intimates, but no friends—I mean in the old romantic way; I have no secret so weighty but what I can bear in my own breast, nor any duels to fight but what I may engage in without a second; nor can I love after the old romantic discipline. I would have my passion, if not led, yet at least waited on, by my reason; and the greatest proof of my affection that a lady must expect is this: I would run any hazard to make us both happy; but would not for any transitory pleasure make either of us miserable.

If ever, madam, you come to know the life of this piece as well as he that drew it, you will conclude that I need not subscribe the name to the picture.

Leigh Hunt's criticism is, as usual, not less genial than felicitous. It is just without being rigorous, and generous without being partial:—

'Farquhar,' he says, 'was a good-natured, sensitive, reflecting man, of so high an order of what may be called the *town* class of genius as to sympathise with mankind at large upon the strength of what he saw of them in little, and to extract from a quintessence of good sense an inspiration just short of the romantic and imaginative; that is to say, he could turn what he had experienced in common life to the best account, but required in all cases the support of its ordinary associations, and could not project his spirit beyond them. He felt the little world too much, and the universal too little. He saw into all false pretensions, but not into all true ones; and if he had had a larger sphere of nature to fall back upon in his adversity, would probably not have died of it. The wings of his fancy were too common, and grown in too artificial an air, to support him in the sudden gulfs and aching voids of that new region, and enable him to beat his way to their green islands. His genius was so entirely social that, notwithstanding what appeared to the contrary in his personal manners, and what he took for his own superiority to it, it compelled him to assume in his writings all the airs of the most received town ascendancy; and when it had once warmed itself in this way, it would seem that it had attained the healthiness natural to its best condition, and could have gone on for ever, increasing both in enjoyment and in power, had external circumstances been favourable. He was becoming gayer and gayer, when death, in the shape of a sore anxiety, called him away as if from a pleasant party, and left the house ringing with his jest.' The jest, however, scarcely hid the tear, and was the last utterance of a breaking heart.

Sir John Vanbrugh was descended, it is said, from an old and respectable family, which came originally from France, though the name would seem to indicate a Dutch origin. His father was a successful sugar-baker, who, flourishing greatly in the world, rose to the rank of an esquire, and became Comptroller of the Treasury Chamber. He married the daughter of Sir Dudley Carleton, by whom he had this distinguished son, born about 1666 in the French Bastile, or, as some authorities record, in the parish of St Stephen's, Walbrook. Of his early life and education I can gather no particulars; but it is known that he was in France at the age of nineteen, and that he remained there some years. It is conjectured that he made his architectural studies at this period. Returning to England, he was appointed, in 1695, secretary to the

Commission for the Administration of Greenwich Hospital; an official position which brought him into social contact with the men of fashion and of letters of the day: and under their influence his dramatic ability rapidly developed. That he had acquired a wide knowledge of society—an intimate acquaintance with the habits and follies of fashionable life—is evident from his comedy of 'The Relapse,' which he produced with considerable success in 1697. In this he adopted the characters of Cibber's 'Love's Last Shift,' and with much dexterity kept up their distinctive traits, though with a certain process of inversion. It was a hastily-written performance: like Farquhar's 'Beaux' Stratagem,' it was begun and finished in six weeks, but it abounds in a rough, vigorous animation, and is profuse in wit and high spirits. Its licentiousness is deplorable; and two or three of the scenes are so pre-eminently suggestive, and so highly coloured, that one wonders how a respectable audience could tolerate them.[1] 'Cibber, in his play, had laudably endeavoured to fashion the stage into something like decency by bringing back a rakish husband to reason, to happiness, and to his family. Vanbrugh, seeming to think it a scandal to polite manners to leave him there, makes him *relapse*, as if it were disgraceful to a man of the world to be honourable. The taste, however, of the age Sir John Vanbrugh lived in, alone could justify his committing such violence on the chastity of the Comic Muse; and whoever will peruse Cibber's prologue to "The Provoked Husband" will be satisfied, from the testimony of one who was certainly well acquainted with this gentleman's sentiments, that he was before his death not only

---

[1] Yet Vanbrugh, in his Preface, could say,—'There is not one woman of real reputation in town but, when she has read the play impartially over in her closet, will find it so innocent she will think it *no affront to her Prayer-Book* to lay it upon the same shelf.'

convinced of, but determined to reform, this error of taste.'

In 1777 Sheridan 'bowdlerised' 'The Relapse,' purging it of much of its wit as well as of its indecency, and bringing it out in an abridged form under the title of 'A Trip to Scarborough.'

Encouraged by the success of 'The Relapse,' Vanbrugh again sought the suffrages of the playgoing public, and within a few months of the production of his first comedy put on the stage his best—a masterpiece of the comic drama—'The Provoked Wife.' The wit is ripe and easy, the characters are drawn with a strong hand, the situations, though broad, are conceived in a spirit of the richest humour; but, unfortunately, 'the trail of the serpent is over it all;' there is an undisguised libertinism in the conduct of the play as well as in the language. No modern audience would permit it to be put before them. He starts with a false motive; that the bad behaviour of a brutal husband justifies the aggrieved wife in avenging herself by the commission of adultery. But the dramatist does not keep even to this flimsy argument, for Lady Brute is disposed to sin quite as much from the warmth of her inclinations as from any feeling of resentment against her husband. Jeremy Collier was fully warranted in the severe censure he passed upon this play, which is one of the most thoroughly immoral in our dramatic literature. It is impossible not to regret that so much wit, and invention, and humorous force should be expended on a subject so unsavoury. 'The licence of the times,' says Leigh Hunt, 'allowed Vanbrugh to be plain-spoken to an extent which was perilous to his animal spirits;' but he is something more than plain-spoken. He does not call a spade a spade, but uses any uglier word in his teeming vocabulary. Besides, it is not only the indecorum of his language, but the suggestiveness of his situations, which shock and confuse us.

For illustrations of contemporary manners Vanbrugh may be consulted with even more advantage than any of his dramatic contemporaries. How excellent is the description of the daily life of a fine lady which he puts into the mouth of Sir John Brute,[1] when disguised as a woman of quality. He makes him say,—

I wake about two o'clock in the afternoon—I stretch—and make a sign for my chocolate. When I have drunk three cups, I slide down again upon my back, with my arms over my head, while my two maids put on my stockings. Then, hanging upon their shoulders, I am trailed to my great chair, where I sit—and yawn for my breakfast. If it don't come presently, I lie down upon my couch to say my prayers, while my maid reads me the play-bills.

When the tea is brought in, I drink twelve regular dishes, with eight slices of bread and butter. And half-an-hour after, I send to the cook to know if the dinner is almost ready . . . By that time my head is half drest. I hear my husband swearing himself into a state of perdition that the meat's all cold upon the table, to amend which, I come down in an hour more, and have it sent back to the kitchen to be all dressed over again.

When I have dined, and my idle servants are presumptuously set down at their ease to do so too, I call for my coach to go visit dear friends, of whom I hope I never shall find one at home while I shall live . . .

---

[1] Says Pope:—'Here Van wants grace, he never wanted wit.' The character of Sir John Brute is not only without grace, but without proportion. He is painted in such heavy colour that one feels it to be impossible he could ever have obtained so fair, so young, and so witty a wife as Lady Brute is represented. 'Sir John Brute,' says Hazlitt, 'is an animal of English growth, and of a cross-grained breed. He has a spice of the demon mixed up with the brute; is mischievous as well as stupid; has improved his natural parts by a town education and example; opposes the fine lady airs and graces of his wife, by brawling oaths, impenetrable surliness, and pot-house valour: overpowers any tendency she might have to vapours or hysterics by the fumes of tobacco and strong beer; and thinks to be master in his own house, by roaring in taverns, reeling home drunk every night, breaking lamps, and beating the watch.' He is closely related to Farquhar's Sullen, but ten times more odious.

To the question,—'Pray, madam, how do you pass your evenings?' she replies,—

Like a woman of spirit, and great spirit. Give me a box and dice—Seven. The main wins! Sir, I set you a hundred pounds! Why, do you think women are married now-a-days to sit at home and mend napkins? We have nobler ways of passing time.

In *The English Lady's Catechism* (1703), quoted by Mr Ashton, a fine lady sums up her daily occupations in the tersest phrase. 'I lie in bed till noon, dress all the afternoon, dine in the evening, and play at cards till midnight.' In *The Spectator* (No. 323) they are set forth with more detail, as thus :—

From 8 *till* 10. Drunk two dishes of chocolate in bed, and fell asleep after 'em.

From 10 *to* 11. Ate a slice of bread and butter, drank a dish of bohea, read the *Spectator*.

From 11 *to* 1. At my toilet, tried a new head. Gave orders for Knay to be combed and washed. *Mem.* I look best in blue.

From 1 *till half-past* 2. Drove to the 'Change. Cheapened a couple of fans.

Till 4. At dinner. *Mem.* Mr Fisk passed by in his new liveries.

From 4 *to* 6. Dressed, paid a visit to old Lady Blithe and her sister, having heard they were gone out of town that day.

From 6 *to* 11. At basset.¹ *Mem.* Never set again upon the ace of diamonds.'

It was a gambling age, and women—it is evident from the numerous allusions in contemporary dramas—gambled as much as or even more than men. Their unfortunate mania for play frequently beggared and disgraced themselves and their husbands. Everybody knows Hogarth's famous picture of the lady and her suitor, and the last stake they play for. It was a stake too frequently ven-

---

¹ A game of cards resembling *pharaoh*. See Pope's poem of *The Basset Table* in *Town Eclogues* (1716).

tured by infatuated women in the reign of Anne. In the Epilogue to Mrs Centlivre's 'Gamester' we read,—

> 'This itch for play has likewise fatal been,
> And more than Cupid draws the ladies in.
> A thousand guineas for basset prevails,
> A bait when cash runs low, that seldom fails;
> And when the fair one can't the debt defray
> In sterling coin, does sterling beauty pay.'

Vanbrugh's next dramatic venture was his comedy of 'Esop' (in two parts), acted at Drury Lane in 1697. The main plot was borrowed from a play by Boursault, written about six years before; but the scenes between Sir Polidorus Hogstye, the Players, the Senator, and the Beau, in the fourth and fifth acts, are entirely Vanbrugh's own. This comedy is not wanting in the *vis comica*, but it has never been a favourite on the stage. The construction is awkward, and the characters are not such as any audience can sympathise with.

'The Pilgrim,' produced in 1700, with Mrs Oldfield as Alinda, was adapted from Beaumont and Fletcher, and furnished with a prologue, epilogue, and secular masque by Dryden, which he wrote but very shortly before his death. The prologue contains a severe attack upon that unlucky versifier, Sir Richard Blackmore.

The reputation which Vanbrugh had acquired by his dramatic work benefited him in his profession as an architect, and led to his being employed to raise the stately piles of Castle Howard, Claremont, and Blenheim. He also built the Opera House in the Haymarket. His structures are distinguished by grandiosity rather than grandeur. They are boldly conceived, however, and solidly executed; and though ponderous in outline and frigid in detail, produce an impressive effect by their general massiveness. The characteristic of his style is indicated in the epigrammatic epitaph which witty Dr Evans suggested for him :—

> 'Under this stone, reader, survey
> Dead Sir John Vanbrugh's house of clay.
> Lie heavy on him, earth ! for he
> Laid many heavy loads on thee.'

In his time he was without a rival, and well deserved the preferments heaped upon him—Surveyor of the Works at Greenwich Hospital, Comptroller-General of Works, and Surveyor of the Royal Gardens and Waters.

Vanbrugh died of a quinsy, at his house in Whitehall, in 1726. He was the friend of Congreve, whom in his comedies he seems to have imitated. In wit he was considerably his inferior, but he had a greater command of animal spirits, and moved his audiences to laughter by the irresistble fun of his situations. It is sad to confess that he was not far behind him in indecency ; and Jeremy Collier in his well-known attack on the immorality of the stage, joins him with Congreve in his fierce denunciations.

In addition to the comedies already mentioned, Vanbrugh wrote 'The False Friend' (1702); 'The Confederacy' (1706) ; ' The Mistake' (1706) ; 'The Cuckold in Conceit' (1706—never printed) ; 'The Country House,' a farce (about 1715) ; and ' A Journey to London,' which was finished by Colley Cibber.

On 'The Confederacy' Lord Gardenstone passes a severe judgment. He speaks of it as one of those plays which throw infamy on the English stage, and general taste ; though he admits that it is not deficient in wit and humour. And he thinks that a people must be in the last degree depraved, among whom such public enterments are produced and encouraged. 'The Confederacy' is largely founded on D'Ancourt's '*Les Bourgeoises à la Mode.*'

In like manner, 'The Mistake' is little more than a

free and concise version of Molière's '*Le Dépét Amoureux*.' When this play was first brought out at the Haymarket, it was furnished with an epilogue by Motteux, and a prologue by Steele.

'The Cuckold in Conceit' was translated from Molière's '*Le Cocu Imaginaire*'; and the amusing farce of 'The Country House,' from D'Ancourt's '*Maison de Campagne*.'

While we condemn the low moral tone of Vanbrugh's dramatic work, the licence which he allows himself in plot and situation, the brutal husbands and liberal wives and loose gallants whom he loved to draw, we may remember to his credit that he is not easy in his own mind while thus degrading his art, and that he shrinks from the excess of immorality into which Wycherly and Congreve plunged. We rescue two passages from the grossness of his dialogue:—' Though marriage be a lottery in which there are a wondrous many blanks, yet is there one inestimable lot, in which the only heaven upon earth is written.' . . . ' To be capable of loving one, doubtless, is better than to possess a thousand.'

'The Relapse,' as we have seen, and 'The Provoked Wife,' were brought before the public in 1697, and received with considerable favour. Steele's 'Tender Husband' appeared in 1703,—only six years later in point of time—but in point of morality one might almost say a century. No doubt Steele was actuated by a sincere desire to elevate the standard of the drama, and to purge the atmosphere of the stage; but he would hardly have made such an attempt without some certain knowledge that the public were prepared to support it, and from this fact we may understand the greatness of the change which had come over society, the sudden moral transformation which had been brought about by the civil and religious freedom due to the constitutional revolution of 1688. Turn to 'The Relapse,' and glance for a moment at the characters which rant and storm through its bustling scenes. Sir Tombelly Fashion, a coarse country squire; Tom Fashion, an ignorant, brutal rake; Miss Hoyden, a forward young hussy, whose *naïve* animalism almost makes one sick. 'It's well I have a husband a-coming,' she cries, 'or, ecod, I'd marry the baker; I would so! Nobody can knock at the gate, but presently I must be locked up; and here's the young greyhound bitch can run loose about the house all the day long; she can; 'tis very well.' Turn to the 'Provoked Wife.' What a gallery of odious pictures! Sir John Brute, so aptly named, for the brutishness of his nature is unrelieved by a single gleam of intellect or virtue; Mademoiselle, the French chambermaid, with her leers, her lewd talk, and lewder gestures; Belinda, with her easy ideas of matrimonial duty; and Lady Brute, always hesitating on the brink of adultery, though, to do her justice, not wholly unconscious of better things. She has a fine sense of the wickedness of women of quality like herself. 'We are as wicked as men,' she says, 'but our vices lie another way. Men have more courage than we, so they commit more bold, impudent sins. They quarrel, fight, swear, drink, blaspheme, and the like; whereas we being cowards, only backbite, tell lies, cheat at cards, and so forth.' What a relief to pass from such company as this into the purer theatre which Steele provides! So a man who has been exposed to the furnace-breath must feel when he is carried into the fresh cool air of breezy uplands, where he sees once more the blue azure skies; and listens once more to the songs of birds.

SIR RICHARD STEELE made his first appearance as a dramatist in 1702, when his light and lively comedy—not very happily named—of 'The Funeral; or, Grief à la Mode,' was acted with some success at Drury Lane. He wrote it, according to his own statement, from a necessity of enlivening his character, which had been elevated into too decorous a respectability by his manual of *The Christian Hero*. And there is a good deal of amusing matter in the satire directed against the dishonesties of lawyers and the impositions of undertakers—those who fleece us while alive, and those who rob our kith and kin when we die. The plot turns on the circumstance of a nobleman, Lord Brumpton, who is supposed to be dead, having fallen simply into a lethargy. From this he awakes, but, in order to test his wife's disposition, and to observe what goes on in his household, he pretends for a while to the character of a defunct. There is a certain improbability in the device of conveying Lady Charlotte away in a coffin, but, on the other hand, it is skilfully made the means of bestowing a due reward on the filial piety of Lord Hardy, the Earl of Brumpton's son and heir. In this diverting comedy Steele's dramatic abilities are seen to advantage; the characters are forcibly presented, the language is full of wit and sprightliness, and the story is developed with much ingenuity. We quote one of the brightest passages :—

[*Scene draws and discovers* LADY CHARLOTTE *reading at a table*—LADY HARRIET, *playing at a glass, to and fro, and viewing herself.*]

Lady Har. Nay, good sister, you may as well talk to me [*looking at herself as she speaks*] as sit staring at a book which I know you can't attend. Good Dr Lucas may have writ there what he pleases, but there's no putting Francis, Lord Hardy, now Earl of Brumpton, out of your head, or making him absent from your eyes. Do but look on me, now, and deny it if you can.

Lady Char. You are the maddest girl [*smiling*].

Lady Har. Look ye, I knew you could not say it, and forbear laughing. [*Looking over Charlotte.*] Oh, I see his name as plain as you do—F-r-a-n, Fran, c-i-s, cis, Francis ; 'tis on every line of the book.

Lady Char. [*rising.*] It's in vain, I see, to mind anything in such impertinent company—but, granting 'twere as you say, as to my Lord Hardy—'tis more excusable to admire another than oneself.

Lady Har. No, I think not—yes, I grant you, than really to be vain of one's person; but I don't admire myself. Pish! I don't believe my eyes to have that softness. [*Looking in the glass.*] They a'n't so piercing: no, 'tis only stuff. The men will be talking. Some people are such admirers of teeth. Lord, what signifies teeth! [*Showing her teeth.*] A very black-a-moor has as white a set of teeth as I. No, sister, I don't admire myself, but I've a spirit of contradiction in me. I don't know I'm in love with myself, only to rival the men.

Lady Char. Ay, but Mr Campley will gain ground even of that rival of his, your dear self.

Lady Har. Oh, what have I done to you that you should name that insolent intruder? A confident, opinionative fop. No, indeed, if I am, as a poetic lover of mine sighed and sang, of both sexes—

The public envy and the public care,

I sha'n't be so easily catched. I thank him. I want but to be sure I should heartily torment him by banishing him, and then consider whether he should depart this life or not.

Lady Char. Indeed, sis, to be serious with you, this vanity in your humour does not at all become you.

Lady Har. Vanity! All the matter is, we gay people are more sincere than you wise folks. All your life's an act. Speak your soul. Look you there. [*Handing her to the glass.*] Are you not struck with a sweet pleasure when you view that bloom in your look, that harmony in your shape, that promptitude in your mien?

Lady Char. Well, simpleton, if I am at first so simple as to be a little taken with myself, I know it's a fault, and take pains to correct it.

Lady Har. Pshaw! Pshaw! Talk this musty tale to old Mrs Fardingale. 'Tis too soon for me to think at that rate.

Lady Char. They that think it too soon to understand themselves, will very soon find it too late. But tell me honestly, don't you like Campley?

Lady Har. The fellow is not to be abhorred, if the forward thing did not think of getting me so easily. Oh, I hate a heart I can't break when I please! What makes the value of dear china, but that 'tis so brittle? Were it not for that, you might as well have stone mugs in your closet.

In 1703 Steele came on the town with a second comedy, 'The Lying Lover; or, The Ladies' Friendship,' which was very straightforwardly damned—on account of its piety, said Steele—on account of its dulness, said the critics. It is not dull, however, though inferior to his other dramatic work; but Steele's conscientiousness insisted on punishing the hero for his follies, and the last act shows him in Newgate, where the audience, much disgusted, were content to leave him. For his plot Steele was largely indebted to Corneille's '*Le Menteur*'; and he adapted the characters of Old and Young Bookwit from the Geronte and Dorante of the French dramatist. He borrowed, however, with a lordly air; and the appropriated livery becomes him so well, that the unsuspicious spectator takes it to be his own.

Steele's third dramatic venture was 'The Tender Husband; or, The Accomplished Fools,' produced in 1705, and written during the early part of his intimacy with Addison. 'I remember,' wrote Steele, at a later time 'when I finished "The Tender Husband," I told him there was nothing I so ardently wished as that we might some time or other publish a work written by us both, which should bear the name of the "Monument," in memory of our friendship.' There is, as Thackeray says, 'some delightful farcical writing,' in it, and 'many applauded strokes' came from Addison's graceful pen. Is it not a pleasant partnership to remember? Can't one fancy Steele, full of spirits and youth, leaving his gay company to go to Addison's lodging, where his friend sits in the shabby sitting-room, quite serene, and cheerful, and poor?' For this literary partnership belonged to the day of Addison's poverty, before he had written 'The Campaign,' and begun to ascend the ladder of political preferment. The prologue was composed by Addison.

The characters in 'The Tender Husband' are well conceived and consistently defined. The incidents are mostly of Steele's invention, except that of Clerimont's disguising himself and painting his mistress's picture, which seems to have been derived from Molière's '*Sicilien, ou l'Amour Peintre.*'

In his *Apology for Himself and His Writings*, he alludes to his unfortunate comedy at length. 'I have carried,' he says, 'my inclination to the advancement of virtue so far as to pursue it even in things the most indifferent, and which, perhaps, have been thought foreign to it. To give you an instance of this, I must mention a comedy called "The Lying Lover," which I writ some years ago, the preface to which says,—

> Though it ought to be the care of all governments that public representations should have nothing in them but what is agreeable to the manners, laws, religion, and policy of the place or nation wherein they are exhibited, yet it is the general complaint of the more learned and virtuous amongst us, that the English stage has extremely offended in this kind. I thought, therefore, it would be an honest ambition to attempt a comedy which might be no improper entertainment in a Christian commonwealth.

'Mr Collier had, about the time wherein this was published, written against the immorality of the stage. I was (as far as I durst for witty men, upon whom he had been too severe) a great admirer of his work, and took it into my head to write a comedy in the severity he required. In this play I make the spark or hero kill a man in his drink; and finding himself in prison the next morning, I give him the contrition which he ought to have on that occasion. It is in allusion to that circumstance that the preface further says as follows:—

> The anguish he there expresses, and the mutual sorrow between an only child and a tender father in that distress, are perhaps an injury to the rules of comedy, but I am sure they are a justice to those of morality; and passages of such a nature being so frequently applauded on the stage, it is high time that we should no longer draw

occasions of mirth from those images which the religion of our country tells us we ought to tremble at with horror.

But Her Most Excellent Majesty has taken the stage into her consideration; and we may hope, from her gracious influence on the Muses, that wit will recover from its apostacy, and that, by being encouraged in the interests of virtue, it will strip vice of the gay habit in which it has too long appeared, and clothe it in its native dress of shame, contempt, and dishonour.

I cannot tell, sir, what they would have me do to prove me a Churchman; but I think I have appeared one even in so trifling a thing as a comedy: and considering me as a comic poet, I have been a martyr and confessor for the Church; for this play was damned for its piety.'

No one can dispute the claim which Steele here puts forward. His plays are excellent in tone and motive, and are 'no improper entertainment in a Christian commonwealth.' But then decency is not an excuse for dulness; and it is true enough that Steele's comedies are not so rapid in movement and sprightly in tone as one could wish. His characters sermonise too much. Here is a passage which he puts into the mouth of a young lover:—'If pleasure be worth purchasing, how great a pleasure it is to him who has a true taste of life to ease an aching heart; to see the human countenance lighted up into smiles of joy, on the receipt of a bit of ore, which is superfluous and otherwise useless in a man's own pocket! What could a man do better,' etc., etc. It reads like an extract from a moral essay!

We pass on to our author's last dramatic effort.

The comedy of 'The Conscious Lovers,' which Fielding's Parson Adams declares to be the only play fit for a Christian to see, and as good as a sermon, remained in manuscript for some years before Steele could obtain its production on the stage. It was acted at Drury Lane in 1722, and with so much success, that it enjoyed the then extraordinary run of twenty-six nights. Originally it was entitled 'The Unfashionable Lovers,' or, according to some authorities, 'The Fine Gentleman.' Steele's motive in writing it seems to have been to exhibit the folly of duelling, and to ridicule the fashionable fetish of the fine gentlemen of his day—the so-called 'point of honour.' For the suggestion of his plot he has been indebted to the Andria of Terence.

While it was in rehearsal, cross-grained John Dennis —sourest of critics!—attacked it and its author in a pamphlet which, in allusion to Steele's sharp censure of Etherege's 'Man of Mode' (in the *Spectator*, No. 65), he entitled, 'A Defence of Sir Fopling Flutter, written by Sir George Etherege: in which Defence is shown that Sir Fopling, that merry knight, was rightly composed by the Knight, his Father, to answer the Ends of Comedy; and that he has been barbarously and scurrilously attacked by the Knight, his Brother, in the 65th *Spectator;* by which it appears that the Knight knows nothing of the nature of Comedy.' The scurrilous pamphleteer not only attacks Steele on the score of his nationality, but ridicules him as a twopenny author, because he produced the *Tatlers*, *Spectators*, and *Guardians*. He promised a criticism on 'The Conscious Lovers' as soon as it appeared on the stage, and kept his word; but, for a wonder! it was decently written, and, therefore, very dull.

The characters introduced in Steele's comedy are:— Sir John Bevil, Mr Sealand, the younger Bevil (who is in love with Indiana, Sealand's daughter by his first wife), and Myrtle (who is in love with Lucinda, Indiana's half-sister), a coxcomb named Cimberton, and Humphrey, Sir John Bevil's old and faithful servant. There are also Mrs Sealand (Mr Sealand's second wife), Isabella (Mr Sealand's sister), Indiana and Lucinda, and Phillis (Lucinda's maid). A synopsis of the play may interest my readers.

Act I. The first scene opens with a confidential colloquy

between Sir John Bevil and Old Humphrey from which we learn that the younger Bevil is endowed with all the virtues, as well as with a large estate bequeathed to him by his mother—and has therefore been selected by Sealand, the great India merchant, as a suitable husband for his daughter and heiress. But at the masquerade an incident has occurred which has awakened Mr Sealand's suspicions, and to dispel these, Sir John announces his intention of insisting upon the immediate performance of the marriage ceremony. Exit Sir John; and enter Tom, the younger Bevil's servant, one of those lively sparks so common in our older comedies—amusing enough on the stage, but in actual life, one would suppose, intolerable from their impudence. Tom comments on his young master's secret anxiety: he is dressed for the marriage, but carries a very heavy heart under all his bravery. He adds, to old Humphrey's astonishment, that Mrs Sealand is averse to the match, and has provided a relation of hers, 'a stiff starched philosopher, and a wise fool,' for her daughter. Old Humphrey departs, and Phillis, Lucinda's maid, appears. She and Tom flirt in the traditional fashion, and he in the end bribes her to carry a letter from young Bevil to her mistress.

In the second scene young Bevil seeks Humphrey's assistance to extricate him from a marriage he loathes, and to further his union with the lady he secretly loves—a lady of the name of Danvers, who has experienced more than the ordinary misfortunes reserved by romancists for their heroines. Humphrey consents, and hints at his knowledge of a secret which may by-and-by release his young master from his engagement to Lucinda.

Act II. The first scene passes between the younger Bevil and his friend Myrtle, who, it appears, is in love with Lucinda. The dialogue here is skilfully and pleasantly managed :—

Myr. I am told that you are this very day (and your dress confirms me in it) to be married to Lucinda.

Bev. You are not misinformed. Nay, put not on the terms of a rival, till you hear me out. I shall disoblige the best of fathers, if I don't seem ready to marry Lucinda; and you know I have ever told you, you might make use of my secret resolution never to marry her, for your own service as you please, but I am now driven to the extremity of immediately refusing or complying, unless you help me to escape the match.

Myr. Escape, sir! neither her conceit nor her fortune are below your acceptance. Escaping, do you call it?

Bev. Dear sir, do you wish I should desire the match?

Myr. No. But such is my humorous and sickly state of mind, since it has been able to relish nothing but Lucinda, that, though I must owe my happiness to your aversion to this marriage, I cannot bear to hear her spoken of with levity or unconcern.

Bev. Pardon me, sir; I shall transgress that way no more. She has understanding, beauty, shape, complexion, wit.

Myr. Nay, dear Bevil! Don't speak of her as if you loved her neither.

Bev. Why, then, to give you ease at once, though I allow Lucinda to have good sense, wit, beauty, and virtue, I know another in whom these qualities appear to me more amiable than in her.

Myr. There you spoke like a reasonable and good-natured friend. When you acknowledge grace, merit, and own your prepossession for another, at once you gratify my fondness, and cure my jealousy.

Bevil has promised his father not to marry without his consent. This restrains him from offering his hand to the fair lady of his love, Indiana, and leads to injurious suspicions of his intentions in the mind of Indiana's aunt, Sabella. In an interview which he has with Indiana (Scene 2), she indirectly seeks from him an explanation, which he does not give, though he furnishes fresh proof of his respect and regard.

Act III. In Scene 1 we are again introduced to Tom and Phillis. There is some humour in Tom's account of how and where he fell in love with this pert handmaid:—

Tom. Ah, Phillis! can you doubt, after what you have seen?

Phil. I know not what I have seen, nor what I have heard; but, since I am at leisure, you may tell me where you fell in love with me, how you fell in love with me, and what you have suffered, or are ready to suffer for me.

Tom. Ah, too well I remember where, and how, and on what occasion I was first surprised. It was on the first of April, one thousand seven hundred and fifteen, I came into Mr Sealand's service. I was then a hobble-de-hoy, and you a pretty little tight girl, a favourite handmaid of the housekeeper. At that time, we neither of us knew what was in us. I remember, I was ordered to get out of the window, one pair of stairs, to rub the sashes clean—the person employed on the inner side was your charming self, whom I had never seen before.

Phil. I think I remember the silly accident. What made ye, you oaf, ready to fall down into the street?

Tom. You know not, I warrant you—you could not guess what surprised me—you took no delight when you immediately grew wanton in your conquest, and put your lips close, and breathed upon the glass; and, when my lips approached, a dirty cloth you rubbed against my face, and hid your beauteous form; when I again drew near, you spit, and rubbed, and smiled, at my undoing.

Phil. What silly thoughts you men have!

Tom. We were Pyramus and Thisbe—but ten times harder was my fate: Pyramus could peep only through a wall; I saw her, saw my Thisbe in all her beauty, but as much kept from her as if a hundred walls between; for there was more, there was her will against me. Would she but relent! Oh, Phillis! Phillis! shorten my torment, and declare you pity me.

Phil. I believe 'tis very sufferable. The pain is not so exquisite but that you may bear it a little longer.

Tom. Oh, my charming Phillis! if all depended on my fair one's will, I could with glory suffer—but, dearest creature! consider our miserable state.

Phil. How! miserable!

Tom. We are miserable to be in love, and under the command of others than those we love—with that generous passion in the heart to be sent to and fro on errands, called, checked, and rated for the meanest trifles. Oh, Phillis! you don't know how many china cups and glasses my passion for you has made me break. You have broken my fortune as well as my heart.

Phillis informs her lover that Mrs Sealand is arranging with Cimberton to marry her daughter Lucinda, though her husband, as we have seen, has selected young Bevil, and it appears that the lady herself is in love with Bevil's friend, Mr Myrtle. Mrs Sealand, Cimberton, and Lucinda next appear, and a scene ensues which is not without cleverness, though it is too indecorous for the modern stage:—Cimberton appraising the various 'points' of the young lady with an offensive sensuality, while professing an exceptional degree of refinement and an austere philosophy. Lucinda retires indignant, and her mother and Cimberton remain to meet the lawyers engaged to draw up the marriage settlements. These are Mr Myrtle and Bevil's servant Tom, disguised as Bramble and Target, who contrive so to obscure the matter as to secure a further delay.

Meanwhile, Myrtle's suspicions have been awakened. Letters have passed between Bevil and Lucinda, the former expressing his desire to withdraw from an engagement which is unacceptable to both of them, and the latter accepting his withdrawal, but candidly confessing that she may be forced into another alliance, unless his friend Myrtle exerts himself for their common safety and happiness. Of the purport of these letters Myrtle is ignorant; but he knows they have been sent, and his jealous temper flaming up into a passion of wrath, he sends Bevil a challenge. This leads to a scene between the two friends, which is the best in the comedy, and one of the best Steele ever wrote:—

Bevil. Well, Mr Myrtle, your commands with me?

Myrtle. The time, the place, our long acquaintance, and many other circumstances which affect me on this occasion, oblige me, without further ceremony or conference, to desire you would not only, as you already have, acknowledge the receipt of my letter, but also comply with the request in it. I must have further notice taken of my message than these half lines—'I have yours'—'I shall be at home.'

Bev. Sir, I own I have received a letter from you in a very unusual style; but, as I design everything in this matter shall be your own action, your own seeking, I shall understand nothing but what you are pleased to confirm face to face; and I have already forgot the contents of your epistle.

Myr. This cool manner is very agreeable to the abuse you have already made of my simplicity and frankness, and I see your moderation tends to your own advantage, and not mine; to your own safety, not consideration of your friend.

Bev. My own safety, Mr Myrtle.

Myr. Your own safety, Mr Bevil.

Bev. Look you, Mr Myrtle, there's no disguising that; I understand what you would be at; but, sir, you know I have often dared to disapprove of the decisions a tyrant custom has introduced, to the breach of all laws, both divine and human.

Myr. Mr Bevil, Mr Bevil! it would be a good first principle in those who have so tender a conscience that way, to have as much abhorrence of doing injuries as—

Bev. As what?

Myr. As fear of answering for them.

Bev. As fear of answering for them! But that apprehension is just or blameable according to the object of that fear. I have often told you, in confidence of heart, I abhorred the daring to offend the Author of life, and rushing into His presence. I say, by the very same act, to commit the crime against Him, and immediately to urge on to His tribunal.

Myr. Mr Bevil, I must tell you, this coolness, this gravity, this show of conscience, shall never cheat me of my mistress. You have, indeed, the best excuse for life, the hopes of possessing Lucinda; but consider, sir, I have as much reason to be weary of it, if I am to lose her, and my first attempt to recover her shall be to let her see the dauntless man who is to be her guardian and protector.

Bev. Sir, show me but the least glimpse of argument that I am authorised, by my own hand, to vindicate any lawless insult of this nature, and I will show thee [that] to chastise thee hardly deserves the name of courage. Slight, inconsiderate man! There is, Mr Myrtle, no such terror in quick anger, and you shall, you know not why, be cool, as you have, you know not why, been warm.

Myr. Is the woman one loves so little an occasion of anger? You, perhaps, who know not what it is to love, who have your ready, your commodious, your foreign trinket, for your loose hours, and, from your fortune, your specious outward carriage, and other lucky circumstances, as easy a way to the possession of a woman of honour ; you know nothing of what it is to be alarmed, to be distracted, with anxiety, and terror of losing more than life. Your marriage, happy man ! goes on like common business ; and, in the interim, you have your rambling captive, your Indian princess, for your soft moments of dalliance ; your convenient, your ready Indiana.

Bev. You have touched me beyond the patience of a man, and I'm excusable, in the guard of innocence, or from the infirmity of human nature, which can bear no more, to accept your invitation, and observe your letter. Sir, I'll attend you.

[*Enter* TOM.

Tom. Did you call, sir? I thought you did ; I heard you speak loud.

Bev. Yes ; go call a coach.

Tom. Sir—Master—Mr Myrtle—friends—gentlemen—what d'ye you mean ? I'm but a servant, or—

Bev. Call a coach.

[*Exit* TOM.

[*A long pause, walking sullenly by each other.*

Bev. [*aside.*] Shall I, though provoked to the uttermost, recover myself at the instance of a third person, and that my servant, too, and not have respect enough to all I have ever been receiving from infancy, the obligation to the best of fathers, to an unhappy virgin, too, whose life depends on mine ? [*Shutting the door.*

[*To* MYRTLE.] I have, thank Heaven, time to recollect myself, and shall not, for fear of what such a rash man as you think of me, keep longer unexplained the false appearances under which your infirmity of temper makes you suffer, when, perhaps, too much regard to a false point of honour makes me prolong that suffering.

Myr. I am sure Mr Bevil cannot doubt but I had rather have satisfaction from his innocence than his sword.

Bev. Why, then, would you ask it first that way ?

Myr. Consider ; you kept your temper yourself no longer than till I spoke to the disadvantage of her you loved.

Bev. True. But let me tell you, I have saved you from the most exquisite distress, even though you had succeeded in the dispute. I know you so well that, I am sure, to have found this letter about a man you had killed, would have been worse than death to yourself. Read it. When he is thoroughly mortified, and shame has got the better of jealousy, he will deserve to be assisted towards obtaining Lucinda—[*aside*].

Myr. With what a superiority has he turned the injury upon me as the aggressor! I begin to fear I have been too far transported. ... With what face can I see my benefactor, my advocate, whom I have treated like a betrayer! Oh, Bevil! with what words shall I—

Bev. Three words more; to convince is much more than to conquer.

Myr. But can you—

Bev. You have overpaid the inquietude you gave me in the change I see in you towards me! Alas! what machines we are! Thy face is altered to that of another man, to that of my companion—my friend.

Myr. That I could be such a precipitate wretch!

Bev. Pray, no more.

Myr. Let me reflect, how many friends have died by the hands of friends for want of temper; and you must give me leave to say, again and again, how much I am beholden to that superior spirit you have subdued me with. What had become of one of us, or perhaps both, had you been as weak as I was, and as incapable of reason?

Bev. I congratulate to us both the escape from ourselves, and hope the memory of it will make us dearer friends than ever.

Myr. Dear Bevil! your friendly conduct has convinced me, that there is nothing manly but what is conducted by reason, and agreeable to the practice of virtue and justice; and yet, how many have been sacrificed to that idol, the unreasonable opinion of men! Nay, they are so ridiculous in it, that they often use their swords against each other with dissembled anger and real fear.

> Betrayed by honour, and compelled by shame,
> They hazard being to preserve a name,
> Nor dare inquire into the dread mistake,
> Till, plunged in sad eternity they wake!

[*Exuent.*

It must be admitted that this is a dramatically effective scene, with a good deal of subdued passion in it, while as a protest against the duelling habits of the age, it is bold, direct, and plain-spoken. Evidently Steele was disposed to employ the stage as an agent in the elevation of the moral standard of society, and, while ministering to the public entertainment, was anxious to purge and purify the public conscience. Compare 'The Conscious Lovers' with any one of the dramatic compositions of the Restoration dramatists, and you see at once the enormous progress which had been made in a few years in the reformation of the drama.

The various perplexities into which the dramatist has plunged his characters are solved, of course, in the fifth act. The relationship of Indiana to Mr Sealand is discovered through a bracelet she wears. He had formerly borne the name of Danvers, but for various unspecified reasons, had changed it to that of Sealand; had gone privately to India to make his fortune; had sent for his wife and daughter, who on the voyage out were captured by a French privateer, and having been no more heard of, were concluded to be dead. Sir John Bevil consents, of course, to his son's marriage; and Mr Sealand bestows the hand of Lucinda on Mr Myrtle. Thus, 'The Conscious Lovers' are made happy; and, in the dramatist's opinion, the 'several difficulties they have struggled with,' evidently demonstrate that

> Whate'er the generous mind itself desires,
> The secret care of Providence supplies.

MRS CENTLIVRE was one of the most popular dramatists of Queen Anne's reign. According to the writer of a biographical notice prefixed to the first collected edition of her works in 1761, she was a woman of extraordinary gifts, and he professes a very warm indignation because 'neither the nobility nor the commonalty of the year 1726 had spirit enough to erect in Westminster Abbey a monument justly due to the manes of the never-to-be-forgotten Mrs Centlivre, whose works are full of lively incidents, genteel language, and humorous descriptions of real life.' It may be admitted that there are many sepultured in the famous Abbey less deserving of monumental commemoration than Mrs Centlivre, without acknowledging, however, that 'the lively incidents, genteel language, and humorous descriptions' of her works would really entitle her to such an honour. And we may hint that those incidents and descriptions have a little too much of the rank flavour of the Restoration Drama about them to secure our unrestricted suffrages. Compared with Congreve and Farquhar and Wycherley she is purity itself; but from the point of view of the strict moralist, there is plenty of room for excision and omission, without destroying or impairing the vivacity which is, I think, their principal attraction.

Mrs Centlivre was the daughter of a Mr Freeman, of Holbeach, in Lincolnshire, who, as a Puritan and 'a zealous Parliamentarian,' had suffered considerably in his fortune at the time of the Restoration. She was born in 1677. Her father died when she was three years of age, and her mother nine years later. The little orphan had already given signs of the possession of exceptional talents, and when only seven years old, had written a pretty song and adapted it to a tune of her own composition, which afterwards became a popular country dance. Before she was fifteen she had acquired a very considerable knowledge of the Latin, French, Italian, and Spanish languages. In her social relations, as in her educational achievements, her precocity was remarkable. She was twice a widow before she was out of her teens. Her first husband, whom she married in 1693, was a nephew of Sir Stephen Fox; but he died in less than a twelvemonth. Her wit and beauty soon secured her a second husband, one Captain Lamb, who, within a year and a half of their marriage, was killed in a duel. She is said to have regretted him deeply; and it was partly to divert her melancholy, and partly, perhaps, to gain a livelihood, that she began to write—as most people with literary proclivities then wrote—for the stage.

Her first dramatic essay was a tragedy, entitled 'The Perjured Husband; or, The Adventures of Venice.' The scene is Venice in the carnival-time, and the chief motive is the unhappy loves of Count Bassino and Aurelia—a story not without spirit and vigour in itself, but made wearisome by being involved with various episodes, until the whole forms a tangled skein by no means capable of being easily unravelled. The *dénouement* is not deficient in dramatic force: Placentia, the wife of Bassino, assassinates Aurelia, and is herself slain, while in disguise, by her inconstant husband, who in his turn is punished for his frailties by the dagger of Alonzo, Aurelia's lover. The moral of the piece is conveyed in the following 'tag':—

> The gods are just in all their punishments:
> And by this single act we plainly see
> That vengeance always treads on perjury;
> And tho' sometimes no bolts be at us hurled,
> Whilst we enjoy the pleasures of this world;
> Yet a day awaits, a day of general doom,
> When guilty souls must to an audit come;
> Then that we may not tremble, blush, or fear,
> Let our desires be just, our lives unsullied here.

The style is fairly smooth and correct, with slight reminiscences of Dryden's manner; and the drama, as the production of a young lady of nineteen, deserves consideration.

At Drury Lane, a year or two later, was acted the comedy of 'Love's Contrivance; or, *Le Médecin malgré Lui*,' which is simply an expanded version of Molière's well-known play.

Mrs Centlivre was about twenty-four when she wrote her comedy of 'The Beau's Duel; or, A Soldier for the Ladies,' in which the leading idea is that of a coward, like Parolles, compelled to assume the attitude of a fire-eater, while trembling all the time at the prospect of being summarily called to account. It is possible to follow the story with some amount of interest; but the characters, with the exception of Sir William Mode, the fop, and Colonel Manly, the hero, a frank and honest soldier, are mere stage-puppets, possessing no definite individuality.

In all her plays Mrs Centlivre shows herself well versed in stage-business; they are invariably put together with a good deal of constructive skill. She profited, no doubt, by her experience as an actress, though it extended over a few years only, and was confined to provincial theatres. While at Windsor in 1706, and personating Alexander the Great in Nat Lee's 'Rival Queens,' she won the affections of Mr Joseph Centlivre, who occupied the position of yeoman of the mouth (that is, principal cook) to Her Majesty, and soon afterwards he offered her his hand. They spent together several years of happy wedded life; but at the comparatively early age of forty-six she died of fever, at his house in Spring Garden, Charing Cross, on the 1st of December 1723, and was buried in the parish church of St Martin's-in-the-Fields.

'Thus did she at length happily close a life,' says one of her biographers, 'which at its first setting-out was overclouded with difficulty and misfortune. She for many years enjoyed the intimacy and esteem of the most eminent wits of the time, viz., Sir Richard Steele, Mr Rowe, Budgell, Farquhar, Dr Sewell; and very few authors received more tokens of esteem and patronage from the great; to which, however, the consideration of her sex, and the power of her beauty, of which she possessed a considerable share, might in some degree contribute.

'Her disposition was good-natured, benevolent, and friendly; and her conversation, if not what could be called witty, was at least sprightly and entertaining. Her family had been warm party-folks; and she seemed to inherit the same disposition from them, maintaining the strictest attachment to Whig principles, even in the most dangerous times, and a most zealous regard for the illustrious House of Hanover. This party-spirit, however, which breathes even in many of her dramatic pieces, procured her some friends and many enemies.'

What has just been said of her conversation is true also of her dramatic writing; it cannot be called witty, but it is brisk, gay, and entertaining. These qualities are scarcely present, however, in 'The Stolen Heiress; or, the Salamanca Doctor Outplotted,' which is little more than a succession of intrigues and disguises, borrowed, apparently, from some Spanish source: but they attract our attention in 'The Basset Table,' a well-written and well-contrived comedy, in which the miseries of gambling are forcibly put forward, and we have in the character of Valeria a distinct anticipation of the typical Girton Girl. Here is part of a scene between Valeria and her cousin, Lady Reveller:—

Val. Oh, dear cousin, don't stop me! I shall lose the finest insect for dissection—a huge flesh fly, which Mr Lively sent me just now, and opening the box to try the experiment, away it flew.

Lady. I am glad the poor fly escaped. Will you never be weary of those whimsies?

Val. Whimsies! Natural philosophy a whimsy! Oh, the unlearned world!

Lady. Ridiculous learning!

Alpein. Ridiculous, indeed, for women; philosophy suits our sex as jack-boots would do.

Val. Custom would bring them as much in fashion as furbelows, and practice would make us as valiant as e'er a hero of them all. The resolution is in the mind; nothing can enslave that.

Lady. My stars! this girl will be mad, that's certain.

Val. Mad! So Nero banished philosophers from Rome, and the first discoverer of the Antipodes was condemned for a heretic.

Lady. In my conscience, Alpein, this pretty creature's spoilt. Well, cousin, might I advise: You should bestow your fortune in founding a college for the study of philosophy, where none but women should be admitted ; and to immortalise your name, they should be called Valerians.

A much inferior effort is 'Love at a Venture' (1706), which was acted at Bath by the Duke of Grafton's servants, but, so far as we can learn, never in London. It is adapted from a French comedy, '*Le Galant Double*,' which Cibber afterwards brought out as 'The Double Gallant.' There is little in it of Mrs Centlivre's habitual liveliness, while its sentimentality is mawkish, and the characters and incidents never rise out of the commonplace.

We come to much of Mrs Centlivre's best work in the 'Busybody' (1709). When it was first offered to the Drury Lane authorities, it was coldly received ; nor could they be persuaded to produce it until very late in the season. At its rehearsal, Wilks, who was cast for Sir George Airy, conceived such a disgust at his part that he threw his copy one morning into the pit, and emphatically swore that nobody would listen to such stuff. With tears, Mrs Centlivre begged and prayed him to take it up again, and he at last consented, but with obvious reluctance. Towards the end of April it was performed. No flourish of trumpets, no shower of puffs, heralded it. If any mention had been made of it, the inquirer was told that it was a silly thing, written by a woman. So it happened that on the first night the theatre was half empty, and the audience very cold. They expected nothing, and received the opening scenes with yawns and listless faces. But quickly the aspect of the house changed. Every face brightened ; laughter and applause became frequent and hearty, and the curtain fell amid a tumult of applause. For thirteen successive nights 'The Busybody' filled the theatre ; and in the following year it was acted for six nights running both at Drury Lane and the Haymarket, Park playing Marplot at the former, and Doggett at the latter house. It has since taken rank as a stock piece, and in the writer's young days was frequently performed. There is so much bustle in the play, so much humour in the situations, and such a naturalness in the principal character, whose name has become a synonym for meddlesomeness, inquisitiveness, and ill-timed interference, that I fancy it would be found acceptable even now by some of our audiences. 'The plot and the incidents,' says Sir Richard Steele, who was no bad judge of a play, 'are laid with that subtlety of spirit which is peculiar to females of wit, and is very seldom well performed by those of the other sex, in whom craft in love is an act of invention, and not, as in women, the effect of nature and instinct.'

The success of 'The Busybody' induced its author to adventure a second part, under the title of 'Marplot' (1711), or, as it was afterwards known, 'Marplot in Lisbon;' but it met with the usual fate of second parts, and is now forgotten. It was tolerably well received on its first production, and the Duke of Portland, to whom it was dedicated, presented Mrs Centlivre with fifty guineas—a good deal more than anybody would give for a dedication now-a-days.

'The Platonic Lady' (1707) is not one of Mrs Centlivre's best productions. In some parts it is undoubtedly vulgar; and all the scenes in which Mrs Dowly, the ill-bred Somersetshire widow, appears, must be pronounced objectionable.

'The Perplexed Lovers' (1712), produced at Drury Lane, is full of truth and movement. For the plot its author acknowledges that she was largely indebted to a Spanish original—one of those comedies of intrigue so numerous on the Spanish stage. The scene lies in London, and the action occupies from five in the evening to eight in the morning. To this play was appended a poem inscribed to Prince Eugene, the illustrious companion-in-arms of Marlborough; in return for which the prince sent the author a very handsome and weighty gold snuff-box—how a lady would stare now-a-days at such a gift! The epilogue, as originally written, celebrated the elevated character and achievements of the great Duke; but Mrs Oldfield, who was to have spoken it, was warned that she would be ill received, as a powerful party was being formed to punish the author's Whig proclivities by damning her piece. In her preface, Mrs Centlivre says, with the frankness of a true woman :—' The sinking of my play cut me not half so deep as the notion I had that there could be people of this nation so ungrateful as not to allow a single compliment to a man that has done such wonders for it. I am not prompted by any private sinister end, having never been obliged to the Duke of Marlborough otherwise than as I shared in common with my country ; as I am an Englishwoman, I think myself obliged to acknowledge my obligation to his Grace for the many glorious conquests he has obtained, and the many hazards he has run, to establish us a nation free from the insults of a foreign power.'

In the composition of the tragedy of 'The Cruel Gift,' she was assisted by Nicholas Rowe, the poet-laureate, who also wrote the epilogue to it. His ponderous want of style is apparent in many of the scenes. As for the plot, it is founded on Boccacio's 'Sigismund and Guiscardo,' which Dryden has made familiar to us by his spirited poetical version. I should say that its not unskilful development is the work of Mrs Centlivre, and that the set speeches are due to Rowe. The Princess Leonora, daughter of the King of Lombardy, is secretly married to the king's general, Lorenzo, a man of nobly heroic type of character, who has provoked the enmity of Antonio, the prime minister. The latter acquires a knowledge of the secret interviews between Lorenzo and Leonora, held within a remote grotto,—betrays them to the king, and conveys him there one night to satisfy himself of the truth of his informant. In a great storm of passion the king orders the arrest of Lorenzo, and he is thrown into prison. The princess then confesses their marriage ; but the king is only the more determined to be revenged on his general, and being skilfully stimulated by Antonio, declares for his immediate execution. A messenger is sent to the princess, with a cup, which is alleged to contain her husband's heart. She attempts to slay herself, but is prevented. At this conjuncture, an aged hermit appears with a packet, which Lorenzo had placed in his hands, to be delivered to the king ; and it is then and there discovered that the supposed hermit is the king's uncle, who has wandered abroad in disguise for twenty years, and that Lorenzo is his son. The reader can imagine the grief of the king when he discovers the treachery of Antonio, and reflects on the excesses into which he has been impelled. The reader's imagination may also be credited with power to understand the aged monarch's gratification when he finds that his order has been unfulfilled, and that Lorenzo is still alive. General happiness all round ! except that poetical justice is done to the traitor, whose death, in a popular outbreak, draws from the king a very obvious moral :—

> Be warned by his unhappy fate,
> What dangers on the doubling statesman wait !
> Had he preferred his king's and country's good,
> This public vengeance had not sought his blood ;
> But while the secret paths of guilt he treads,
> Where lust of power, revenge, or envy leads ;
> While to ambition's lawless height he flies,
> Hated he lives, and unlamented dies.

Some of my readers are old enough, perhaps, to remember the dashing way in which the late James Wallack played the part of Don Felix in Mrs Centlivre's second best comedy, 'The Wonder : A Woman Keeps a Secret.' Mercurial—vivacious—picturesque—he was just the cavalier to win and keep a lady's love; and so long as such a Don Felix trod the stage, there was no fear that Mrs Centlivre's rattling comedy would lose its popularity. When first produced, Wilks was Don Felix, and the ever-charming Mrs Oldfield the Donna Violante. As an acting play, 'The Wonder' has conspicuous merits. The interest never flags; the situations are highly diverting; the plot, though intricate, is worked out with great clearness and dexterity; and if the characters are not very original, they are drawn with a good deal of boldness. The scene is laid at Lisbon. A Portuguese grandee, Don Lopez, has a son, Don Felix, who is passionately attached to Donna Violante; but as her father, Don Pedro, intends her to be a nun, it is evident that in their case the course of true love will be obstructed by many difficulties. Again, Donna Isabella, sister to Don Felix, is destined by *her* father—in these old comedies the fathers always want to marry their daughters to the wrong men!—to become the unwilling bride of a Dutch gentleman. The projected union is so unwelcome to the lady, that she escapes from her father's house by jumping from a window—is caught by Colonel Britton—and conveyed by him (at her earnest request) to her friend Donna Violante, with whom she obtains shelter. What more natural than that the colonel should call next day to inquire after her well-being, and should call when Don Felix is present?—that Don Felix, as he is ignorant of Donna Isabella's concealment in the house, should suppose him to be attracted by Violante? He breaks from the latter in a storm of jealous rage, and a series of misunderstandings follow, which the dramatist knots up and unravels with much animation, until a double marriage brings down the curtain with applause. The secret is, of course, the hiding of Isabella in Donna Violante's house, and Donna Violante keeps it in spite of prolonged unhappiness.

The following scene is a fair specimen of Mrs Centlivre's dramatic manner (Act IV. Scene 1, Violante's Lodgings) :—

Enter FELIX.

Fel. I wonder where this dog of a servant is all this while.—But she is at home, I find. How coldly she regards me !—You look, Violante, as if the sight of me were troublesome to you.

Viol. Can I do otherwise, when you have the assurance to approach me after what I saw to-day?

Fel. Assurance! rather call it good nature, after what I heard last night. But such regard to honour have I in my love to you, I cannot bear to be suspected, nor suffer you to entertain false notions of my truth, without endeavouring to convince you of my innocence— so much good-nature have I more than you, Violante. Pray, give me leave to ask your woman one question ? My man assures me she was the person you saw at my lodgings.

Flo. I confess it, madam, and ask your pardon.

Viol. Impudent baggage! not to undeceive me sooner; what business could you have there ?

Fel. Lissardo and she, it seems, imitate you and I.

Flo. I love to follow the example of my betters.

Fel. I hope I am justified.

Viol. Since we are to part, Felix, there needs no justification.

Fel. Methinks you talk of parting as a thing indifferent to you. Can you forget how I have loved ?

Viol. I wish I could forget my own passion, I should with less concern remember yours. But for Mistress Flora—

Fel. You must forgive her—must, did I say ? I fear I have no power to impose, though the injury was done to me.

Viol. 'Tis harder to pardon an injury done to what we love, than to ourselves ; but, at your request, Felix, I do forgive her. Go, watch my father, Flora, lest he should awake and surprise us.

Flo. Yes, madam. [*Exit* FLORA.

Fel. Dost thou, then, love me, Violante ?

Viol. What need of repetition from my tongue, when every look confesses what you ask ?

Fel. Oh, let no man judge of love but those who feel it : what wondrous magic lies in one kind look ! One tender word destroys a lover's rage, and melts his fiercest passion into soft complaint. Oh, the window, Violante ! wouldst thou but clear that one suspicion !

Viol. Prithee, no more of that, my Felix; a little time shall bring thee perfect satisfaction.

Fel. Well, Violante, on condition you think no more of a monastery, I'll wait with patience for this weighty secret.

Viol. Ah, Felix! Love generally gets the better of religion in us women. Resolutions, made in the heat of passion, ever dissolve upon reconciliation.

Enter FLORA, *hastily.*

Flo. Oh! madam, madam, madam! my lord, your father, has been in the garden, and locked the back door, and comes muttering to himself this way.

Viol. Then we are caught! Now, Felix, we are undone!

Fel. Heavens forbid! This is most unlucky! Let me step into your bed-chamber; he won't look under the bed; there I may conceal myself. [*Runs to the door, and pushes it open a little.*

Viol. My stars! if he goes in there, he'll find the colonel! No no, Felix, that's no safe place: my father often goes thither, and should you cough or sneeze, we are lost.

Fel. Either my eye deceived me, or I saw a man within; I'll watch him close.

Flo. Oh, invention! invention! I have it, madam. Here, here, sir; off with your sword, and I'll fetch you a disguise. [*Exit.*

Fel. [*aside*]. She shall deal with the devil, if she conveys him out without my knowledge.

Viol. Bless me, how I tremble!

Enter FLORA *with a riding-hood.*

Flo. Here, sir, put on this.

Fel. Ay, ay; anything to avoid Don Pedro. [*She puts it on.*

Viol. Oh, quick, quick! I shall die with apprehension.

Flo. Be sure you don't speak a word.

Fel. Not for the Indies—but I shall observe you closer than you imagine—[*Aside*].

Pedro [*within*]. Violante, where are you, child?

Enter DON PEDRO.

Ped. Why, how came the garden-door open? Ha! how now, who have we here?

Viol. Humph! he'll certainly discover him—[*Aside*].

Flo. 'Tis my mother, an't please you, sir?

SHE *and* FELIX *both courtesy.*

Ped. Your mother! by St Andrew, she's a strapper! Why, you are a dwarf to her. How many children have you, good woman?

Viol. Oh, if he speaks we are lost—[*Aside*].

Flo. Oh, dear signior, she cannot hear you; she has been deaf those twenty years.

Ped. Alas, poor woman! Why, you muffle her up as if she were blind, too.

Fel. Would I were fairly off—[*Aside*].

Ped. Turn up her hood.

Viol. Undone for ever! St Anthony forbid! Oh, sir, she has the dreadfullest unlucky eyes. Pray, don't look upon them; I made her keep her hood shut on purpose. Oh, oh, oh, oh!

Ped. Eyes! Why, what's the matter with her eyes?

Flo. My poor mother, sir, is much afflicted with the colic; and, about two months ago, she had it grievously in her stomach, and was over-persuaded to take a dram of filthy English Geneva, which immediately flew up into her head, and caused such a defluxion in her eyes, that she could never since bear the daylight.

Ped. Say you so? Poor woman! Well, make her sit down, Violante, and give her a glass of wine.

Viol. Let her daughter give her a glass below, sir. For my part, she has frightened me so. I sha'n't be myself these two hours. I am sure her eyes are evil eyes.

Fel. [*aside*]. Well hinted.

Ped. Well, well; do so. Evil eyes! there are no evil eyes, child.

Flo. Come along, mother—[*Speaks loud*].

[*Exeunt* FELIX *and* FLORA.

Viol. I am glad he's gone—[*Aside*].

Ped. Hast thou heard the news, Violante?

Viol. What news, sir?

Ped. Why, Vasquez tells me that Don Lopez' daughter, Isabella, is run away from her father! That lord has very ill fortune with his children. Well, I'm glad my daughter has no inclination to mankind, —that my house is plagued with no suitors—[*Aside*].

Viol. This is the first word ever I heard of it! I pity her frailty.

Ped. Well said, Violante.

Shortly afterwards, Don Pedro withdraws, accompanied by Violante, and Flora calls the colonel from his retirement.

Flo. So, now for the Colonel! Hist, hist, Colonel!

Enter COLONEL BRITTON.

Col. Is the coast clear?

Flo. Yes, if you can climb; for you must get over the wash-house, and jump from the garden-wall into the street.

Col. Nay, nay; I don't value my neck, if my incognito answers but thy lady's promise.

[*Exeunt* COLONEL *and* FLORA.

Enter FELIX.

Fel. I have lain perdue under the stairs till I watched the old man out—[VIOLANTE *opens the door*].—S'death! I am prevented.

[*Exit* FELIX.

Enter VIOLANTE.

Viol. Now to set my prisoner at liberty—[*Goes to the door where the Colonel is hid*].—Sir, sir, you may appear.

Enter FELIX, *following her.*

Fel. May be so, madam? I had cause for my suspicion, I find. Treacherous woman!

Viol. Ha, Felix here! Nay, then, all is discovered.

Fel. [*Draws*]. Villain! whoever thou art, come out I charge thee, and take the reward of thy adulterous errand.

Viol. What shall I say? Nothing but the secret, which I have sworn to keep, can reconcile this quarrel—[*Aside*].

Fel. A coward! Nay, then, I'll fetch you out. Think not to hide thyself: no, by St Anthony, an altar should not protect thee; even there, I'd reach thy heart, though all the saints were armed in thy defence. [*Exit* FELIX.

Viol. Defend me, Heaven! what shall I do? I must discover Isabella, or here will be murder.

Enter FLORA.

Flo. I have helped the Colonel off clear, madam.

Viol. Sayest thou so, my girl? Then, I am armed.

Re-enter FELIX.

Fel. Where has the devil, in compliance to your sex, conveyed him from my resentment?

Viol. Him! whom do you mean, my dear inquisitive spark? Ha, ha, ha, ha! you will never leave these jealous whims.

Fel. Will you never cease to impose upon me?

Viol. You impose upon yourself, my dear. Do you think I did not see you? Yes, I did, and resolved to put this trick upon you.

Fel. Trick?

Viol. Yes, trick! I knew you'd take the hint, and soon relapse into your wonted error. How easily your jealousy is fired! I shall have a blessed life with you.

Fel. Was there nothing in it then, but only to try me?

Viol. Won't you believe your eyes?

Fel. My eyes! No, nor my ears, nor any of my senses, for they have all deceived me. Well, I am convinced that faith is as necessary in love as in religion: for, the moment a man lets a woman know her conquest, he resigns his senses, and sees nothing but what she would have him.

Viol. And as soon as that man finds his love returned, she becomes as arrant a slave, as if she had already said after the priest.

Fel. The priest, Violante, would dissipate those fears which cause these quarrels. When wilt thou make me happy?

Viol. To-morrow I will tell thee: my father is going for two or three days to my uncle's; we have time enough to finish our affairs. But, prithee, leave me now, lest some accident should bring my father.

Fel. To-morrow, then—
    Fly swift, ye hours, and bring to-morrow on!
    But I must leave you now, my Violante.

Viol. You must, my Felix. We soon shall meet to part no more!

Fel. Oh, rapturous sounds! Charming woman!
    Thy words and looks have filled my heart
    With joy, and left no room for jealousy.
    Do thou, like me, each doubt and fear remove,
    And all to come be confidence and love.'

It will be seen that Mrs Centlivre attempts no local colouring. She lays the scene at Lisbon, but it might be at Vienna, or Paris, or Buda-Pesth, or anywhere else, so far as the dramatic atmosphere is concerned. She introduces us, indeed, to an unreal world, and our perception of its unreality leads us to regard indifferently the dubious moral tone of such plays as 'The Wonder,' in which young ladies unhesitatingly pledge their troth to unknown cavaliers, and calmly hide their friends' lovers in their bedrooms! We are conscious that these are not the habits of 'civilised society,' and, therefore, when they are put before us on the mimic scene, are not at all afraid that they will exercise any injurious influence on the morals or manners of our daughters or our sons. It is all artificial and impracticable,—a comedy of surprises, intrigues, and contrivances; a drama of deception—for everybody is engaged in deceiving somebody—the daughter deceives the father, and the maiden her lover, and the wife her husband—yet no one thinks of being shocked at the moving panorama; the life which revolves upon the stage is so absolutely fictitious.

But, to my thinking, the best of Mrs Centlivre's dramatic compositions is 'A Bold Stroke for a Wife.' I admit that the dialogue has small flavour of wit,—that the characters, with the exception, perhaps, of Periwinkle, the foolish virtuoso, are mainly conventional; but there is a truth and a liveliness and an easy humour throughout the comedy—the situations are so ingenious—the intrigue is so skilfully developed—that one never fails to be diverted by it. The plot turns on the adventures of one Colonel Fainwell, who is in love (and not unsuccessfully) with Mrs Lovely, 'a fortune of thirty thousand pounds,' and wins her at length by outwitting her four guardians, 'as opposite to each other as the four elements.' She is subject to each for three months at a time. 'One is a kind of virtuoso; a silly, half-witted fellow, but positive and surly; fond of everything antique and foreign, and wears his clothes of the fashion of the last century; doats upon travellers, and believes more of Sir John Mandeville than he does of the Bible.' . . . 'Another is a 'Change broker; a fellow that will outlie the devil for the advantage of stock, and cheat his father that got him, in a bargain: he is a great stickler for trade, and hates every man that wears a sword.' . . . 'The third is an old beau, that has May in his fancy and dress, and December in his face and his heels: he admires all the new fashions, and those must be French; loves operas, balls, masquerades, and is always the most tawdry of the whole company on a birthday.' ... 'And the fourth is a very rigid Quaker.' Much ingenuity is shown by Mrs Centlivre in Colonel Fainwell's contrivances for cheating the guardians out of their consent. They succeed each other with an unforced animation, which irresistibly compels the spectator's attention. As an illustration of their humour, I shall quote the scene in which Fainwell, in the character of a great traveller, who has collected many valuable curiosities, waits upon Periwinkle :—

Per. A person of your curiosity must have collected many rarities.

Col. I have some, sir, which are not yet come ashore; as, an Egyptian idol.

Per. Pray, what may that be?

Col. It is, sir, a kind of ape, which they formerly worshipped in that country; I took it from the breast of a female mummy.

Per. Ha, ha! Our women retain part of their idolatry to this day; for many an ape lies upon a lady's bosom; ha, ha!

Col. Two tusks of an hippopotamus, two pair of Chinese nut-crackers, and one Egyptian mummy.

Per. Pray, sir, have you never a crocodile?

Col. Humph! The boatswain brought one with a design to show it; but touching at Rotterdam, and hearing it was no rarity in England, he sold it to a Dutch poet.

Per. I should have been very glad to have seen a living crocodile.

Col. My genius led me to things more worthy of regard. Sir, I have seen the utmost limits of this globular world; I have seen the sun rise and set; know in what degree of heat he is at noon, to the breadth of a hair; and what quantity of combustibles he burns in a day; and how much of it turns to ashes, and how much to cinders.

Per. To cinders! You amaze me, sir! I never heard that the sun consumed anything. Descartes tells us—

Col. Descartes, with the rest of his brethren, both ancient and modern, knew nothing of the matter. I tell you, sir, that nature admits of an annual decay, though imperceptible to vulgar eyes. Sometimes his rays destroy below, sometimes above. You have heard of blazing comets, I suppose?

So the fun goes on, until the Colonel produces the greatest rarity in his collection, *Zona*, or *Mores Mecsphonon*, a girdle which has carried him all over the world.

Per. You have carried *it*, you mean.

Col. I mean as I say, sir. Whenever I am girded with this, I am invisible; and, by turning this little screw, can be in the court of the Grand Mogul, the Grand Signior, and King George, in as little time as your cook can poach an egg.

Per. You must pardon me, sir; I cannot believe it.

Col. If my landlord pleases, he shall try the experiment immediately.

Sackbut. I thank you kindly, sir; but I have no inclination to ride post to the devil.

Col. No, no, you sha'n't stir a foot; I'll only make you invisible.

Sack. But if you could not make me visible again?

Per. Come, try it upon me, sir; I am not afraid of the devil, nor all his tricks. 'Sdeath, I'll stand them all.

Col. There, sir; put it on. Come, landlord, you and I must face to the east—[*They turn about*].—Is it on, sir?

Per. 'Tis on—[*They turn about again*].

Sack. Heaven protect me! Where is it?

Per. Why here, just where I was.

Sack. Where, where, in the name of virtue? Ah, poor Mr Periwinkle! Egad, look to't, you had best, sir; and let him be seen again, or I shall have you burnt for a wizard.

Col. Have patience, landlord.

Per. But, really, don't you see me now?

Sack. No more than I see my grandmother that died forty years ago.

Per. Are you sure you don't lie? Methinks I stand just where I did, and see you as plain as I did before.

Sack. Ah, I wish I could see you once again.

Col. Take off the girdle, sir.   [*He takes it off.*

Sack. Ah, sir, I am glad to see you with all my heart.
       [*Embraces him.*

Per. This is very odd; certainly there must be some trick in't. Pray, sir, will you do me the favour to put it on yourself?

Col. With all my heart.

Per. But, first, I'll secure the door.

Col. [*aside*]. You know how to turn the screw, Mr Sackbut?

Sack. Yes, yes. Come Mr Periwinkle, we must turn full east.

[*They turn, the Colonel sinks down the trap-door.*]

Col. 'Tis done ; now turn. [*They turn.*]

Per. Ha ! Mercy upon me ! my flesh creeps upon my bones. This must be a conjurer, Mr Sackbut.

Sack. He is the devil, I think.

Per. Oh, Mr Sackbut, why do you name the devil, when, perhaps, he may be at your elbow ?

Sack. At my elbow ? marry, Heaven forbid !

Col. Are you satisfied ? [*From under the stage.*]

Per. Yes, sir, yes. How hollow his voice sounds !

Sack. Yours seemed just the same. Faith, I wish this girdle were mine. I'd sell wine no more. Hark ye, Mr Periwinkle—[*Takes him aside till the Colonel rises again*]—if he would sell this girdle, you might travel with great expedition.

Col. But it is not to be parted with for money.

Per. I'm sorry for't, sir, because I think it the greatest curiosity I ever heard of.

Col. By the advice of a learned physiognomist in Grand Cairo, who consulted the lines in my face, I returned to England, where he told me I should find a rarity in the keeping of four men, which I was born to possess for the benefit of mankind ; and the first of the four that gave me his consent, I should present him with this girdle.

Eventually, as the reader will anticipate, the girdle is promised to Mr Periwinkle ; but at this point a Mr Staytape, the Colonel's tailor, is announced, and Periwinkle discovers the imposition practised upon him. The Colonel is constrained, therefore, to resort to another stratagem.

Mrs Centlivre was also the author of ' The Artifice,' played at Drury Lane for three nights in 1721. It has a cleverly-contrived plot, and the situations are ingenious and humorous. Her less important compositions are— ' Man's Bewitched,' a comedy, 1710 ; ' Bickerstaff's Burying,' a farce ; ' Gotham Election,' a farce, 1715 ; and a ' Wife Well Managed,' a farce, 1715.

Among the minor dramatists of the period must be mentioned AARON HILL. He was the eldest son of George

Hill, Esq., of Malmesbury Abbey, Wiltshire, and was born in Beaufort Buildings, London, on the 13th of February 1685. Sprung from an old and opulent family, he was the legal heir to an entailed estate worth about two thousand pounds per annum ; but the misconduct of his father, who, in daring defiance of the law, sold the property to defray his heavy liabilities, threw him and his brothers and sisters on the support of his mother and grandmother. The latter undertook the charge of Aaron Hill's education. At the age of nine he was sent to the Grammar School at Barnstaple, whence he was removed in due time to Westminster School. His talents and application soon gained him distinction ; and enabled him to add to the very scanty allowance of pocket money he received from his impoverished relatives, by the gratuities he received from his duller schoolfellows, for executing their tasks as well as his own.

He left Westminster in 1699, when only fourteen years old. A year later he was on his way to Constantinople, to seek the patronage of the English ambassador, Lord Paget, a close kinsman of his mother's. He was very cordially received by Lord Paget, who appreciated the lad's boldness of character and determination to make his way in the world. A tutor was provided for him, under whose care he was sent on an extended course of travel through Egypt, Palestine, and the greater part of the East—a system of education which rapidly developed his intellectual faculties, and gave him an early and a large experience of men and manners. When Lord Paget was recalled, Hill accompanied him on his visits to the principal courts of Europe, which the ex-ambassador included in his homeward route.

Hill continued to enjoy the friendship of his patron, who, it is said, would probably have made a generous provision for him at his death, but for the adverse influence of 'a certain female,' and the calumnies and misrepresentations to which she freely resorted. Hill was thus thrown upon the world to work out a career for himself. Good fortune attended him; his many estimable qualities recommended him to the notice of Sir William Wentworth, a wealthy Yorkshire baronet, and a very young man, who engaged Hill to accompany him in the capacity of governor or travelling tutor on an extensive Continental tour. The tutor was very little older than his pupil, but he was gifted with exceptional sobriety of temper and coolness of judgment, and discharged his important trust with entire satisfaction to his pupil and his pupil's friends.

In 1709 he began his career as an author, by the publication of his *History of the Ottoman Empire*, compiled from the materials he had collected during his Eastern travels and his residence at the Turkish Court. As the work of a young man, it is entitled to indulgent criticism; but of philosophical insight or critical research it exhibits not the slightest trace. It is singularly juvenile and deplorably heavy; and, to my thinking, nowhere sparkles with the 'fiery fancy' and 'imagination of the poet,' attributed to it by Hill's friendly biographer. With the 'imagination of the poet,' let it be understood, the gods most assuredly had not endowed our respectable friend, who ventured, however, to publish, in 1710, a poem—so he called it!—entitled, *Camillus*, in commemoration of Peterborough's Spanish campaign. It did not procure the suffrages of a much-enduring public,—compelled, during Queen Anne's reign, to read more bad poetry than has ever been published in any similar period of time,—but it pleased Lord Peterborough, who sought out the author, and appointed him his secretary; which post, however, Aaron quitted in the following year, on the occasion of his marriage.

The year which witnessed his appearance as an historian also witnessed his *début* as a dramatist. At the desire of Booth, the tragedian, he wrote his tragedy of 'Elfrid; or, The Fair Inconstant,' beginning and ending it, he says, in a week. Afterwards he entirely re-wrote it, and brought it out again at Drury Lane in 1731, under the title of 'Athelwold.' The ingenious reader will at once assume, and correctly, that it is founded on the romantic story of the marriage of Athelwold with the beautiful Elfrida, upon whose charms he had been commissioned by King Edgar to report. There are great possibilities of passion and pathos in the old legend, but Hill was incompetent to avail himself of them, and his drama sinks beneath an intolerable burden of commonplace. What can be expected from a dramatist who closes the tragic story of faithlessness and deceit and misguided love with such a 'moral' as the following?—

> 'Oh, Leolyn, be obstinately just ;
> Indulge no passion and deceive no trust :
> Let never man be bold enough to say,
> Thus, and no further, shall my passion stray :
> The first crime past compels us into more,
> And guilt grows *fate* that was but *choice* before.'

It is much to the credit of Mr Hill's audience that they would have none of his tragedy, either as 'Elfrid' or 'Athelwold ;' under the latter title, it was acted only three nights.

Hill was unquestionably a born speculator. He boldly took upon himself the management of the Queen's Theatre in the Haymarket, and commissioned Handel, who had just come over to England, to write an opera for him, of which he furnished the plot and situations. The Italian libretto was written by Giovanni Rossi. The story was adapted by Hill from that of Rinaldo and Armida in Tasso's 'Jerusalem Delivered.' 'Rinaldo,' which is esteemed one of its great composer's best operatic works, was produced on the 24th of February 1711, and enjoyed a run of fifteen nights. It was 'staged' with an exceptional degree of magnificence; and, among other novel scenic effects, the gardens of Armida were filled with living birds.

These innovations did not meet with general approval, and were good-humouredly ridiculed by Addison and Steele. In the fifth number of *The Spectator*, Addison tells us how he met a man in the streets carrying a cage of sparrows upon his shoulder, who, in answer to inquiries, said they were intended for the Opera,—how he was thereby induced to purchase the book of the opera, from which he learned that the sparrows were to act the part of singing-birds in a delightful grove; though, as a matter of fact, the music proceeded from 'a concert of flageolets and bird-calls' planted behind the scenes. 'At the same time,' he adds, 'that I made this discovery, I found, by the discourse of the actors, that there were great designs on foot for the improvement of the opera; that it had been proposed to break down a part of the wall, and to surprise the audience with a party of one hundred horse; and that there was actually a project of bringing the New River into the house, to be employed in jetteaus and waterworks. This project, as I have since heard, is postponed till the summer season. . . . In the meantime, the opera of "Rinaldo" is filled with thunder and lightning, illuminations and fireworks; which the audience may look upon without catching cold, and, indeed, without much danger of being burnt; for there are several engines filled with water, and ready to play at a minute's warning, in case any such accident should happen. However, as I have a very great friendship for the owner of this theatre, I hope that he has been wise enough to insure his house before he would let this opera be acted in it.' Addison concludes his paper by informing the reader that there is a treaty on foot with Loudon and Wise (the two principal landscape gardeners of the day), to furnish the opera with an orange-grove; and that the next time it is acted, the singing-birds will be personated by tom-tits—'the undertakers being resolved to spare neither pains nor money for the gratification of the audience.'

Steele followed suit in No. 14 of *The Spectator* in a sly contrast between the Opera and Powell's Puppet-Show, which was then on exhibition in the Little Piazza, Covent Garden. He says:—

The opera at the Haymarket, and that under the Little Piazza in Covent Garden, being at present the two leading diversions of the town, and Mr Powell professing in his advertisements to set up Whittington and his Cat against Rinaldo and Armida, my curiosity led me, the beginning of last week, to view both these performances, and make my observations upon them.

First, therefore, I cannot but observe that Mr Powell wisely forbearing to give his company a bill of fare beforehand, every scene is new and unexpected; whereas it is certain, that the undertakers of the Haymarket, having raised too great an expectation in their printed opera, very much disappoint their audience on the stage.

The King of Jerusalem is obliged to come from the city on foot, instead of being drawn in a triumphant chariot by white horses, as my opera-book had promised me; and thus while I expected Armida's dragons should rush forward towards Argantes, I found the hero was obliged to go to Armida, and hand her out of her coach. We had also but a very short allowance of thunder and lightning; though I cannot in this place omit doing justice to the boy who had the direction of the two painted dragons, and made them spit fire and smoke. He flashed out his resin in such just proportions, and in such due time, that I could not forbear conceiving hopes of his being one day a most excellent player. I saw, indeed, but two things wanting to render his whole action complete, I mean the keeping his head a little lower, and hiding his candle.

I observe that Mr Powell and the undertakers had both the same thought, and I think much about the same time, of introducing animals on their several stages—though, indeed, with very different success. The sparrows and chaffinches at the Haymarket fly as yet very irregularly over the stage; and instead of perching on the trees, and performing their parts, these young actors either get into the galleries, or put out the candles; whereas Mr Powell has so well disciplined his pig, that in the first scene he and Punch dance a minuet together. . . .

As to the mechanism and scenery, everything, indeed, was uniform, and of a piece, and the scenes were managed very dexterously; which calls on me to take notice that, at the Haymarket, the undertakers forgetting to change their side-scenes, we were presented with the prospect of the ocean in the midst of a delightful grove; and though the gentlemen on the stage had very much contributed to the beauty of the grove by walking up and down between the trees, I must own I was not a little astonished to see a well-dressed young fellow in a full-bottomed wig appear in the midst of the sea, and without any visible concern taking snuff.

I shall only observe one thing further. . . . . as the wit in both pieces is equal, I must prefer the performance of Mr Powell, because it is in our own language.

Hill continued, however, in the management of the Haymarket for some months longer, and was very successful in his endeavours to please the public. His knowledge of theatrical affairs was extensive, as may be seen in his poem—or rhymed essay—on *The Art of Acting*, and his periodical essays, entitled *The Prompter*, which contain some very sensible and judicious remarks. Towards the close of 1711 he married the only daughter of Edward Norris, Esq., of Stratford, in Essex, who brought him a considerable fortune, and thus enabled him to prosecute with vigour his numerous philanthropic and speculative enterprises. One of his earliest projects, for which, as inventor, he obtained a patent, was the manufacture of an oil, sweet as that of olives, from beech-nuts. The undertaking was too large for his unaided effort; and he launched a company, with a capital of £25,000 in shares and annuities, for the purchase of his patent rights, under the name of the Beech Oil Company. Disputes, however, arose between the shareholders and himself, which resulted, in 1716, in the failure of Hill's promising scheme, after three years of continuous labour, and a large pecuniary outlay.

He was next engaged with Sir Robert Montgomery in a design for planting, or colonising, a vast tract of land in the south of Carolina, which had been purchased from the lords proprietors of that province ; but here again he was baffled by the inadequacy of his means to the proper conduct of so large an enterprise ; and though the estate was afterwards largely cultivated, under the name of Georgia, it yielded no pecuniary profit to Mr Hill.

Though he was a restless speculator, and as bold a projector as any financing genius of the Victorian age, it is due to Hill to state that he was inspired rather by philanthropic zeal than by commercial greed. In 1727 he set on foot a scheme for turning to account the extensive woods in the north of Scotland for use in the national dockyards. The timber which they produced had always been deemed unfit for shipbuilding purposes. 'The falsity of this supposition, however, he clearly evinced, for one entire vessel was built of it, and on trial was found to be of as good timbers as that brought from any part of the world ; and, although, indeed, there were not many trees in these woods large enough for masts to ships of the largest burden, yet there were millions fit for those of all smaller vessels, and for every other branch of shipbuilding. In this undertaking, however, he met with various obstacles, not only from the ignorance of the natives of that country, but even from Nature herself ; yet Mr Hill's assiduity and perseverance surmounted them all. For when the trees were by his order chained together into floats, the inexperienced Highlanders refused to venture themselves on them down the river Spey ; nor would have been prevailed on, had he not first gone himself to convince them that there was no danger. And even the great number of rocks which choked up different parts of this river, and seemed to render it impassable, were another impediment to his expedition. But, by ordering great fires to be made upon them at the time of low tide, when they were most exposed, and throwing quantities of water upon them, they were, by the help of proper tools, broken to pieces and thrown down, and a free passage opened for the floats.'

Hill's project was carried on at first with a good deal of vigour, and, it would seem, with fair success; but after a while numerous obstacles were thrown in the way, and it gradually fell into disrepute. There is no evidence that its author ever made any pecuniary profit by his public-spiritedness, but it was recognised by the corporations of Inverness, Aberdeen, and other towns, who conferred upon him their freedom, and entertained him with true civic generosity. A great blow befell him in 1731 in the death of his wife, to whom he had been passionately attached, and he never again recovered his old elasticity of temper. In 1738 he withdrew from public life and retired to Plaistow, in Essex, where he devoted himself to study, to the enjoyment of domestic pleasures, and the cultivation of his garden. Not, wholly, however, to the neglect of the 'inventions and discoveries' in which he had always taken delight, for it is recorded that one of his latest, if not the latest, of his occupations was a new way of making potash equal to that exported from Russia.

In his rural seclusion at Plaistow he wrote and published several poetical pieces; including an heroic poem, called *The Fanciad;* another of the same kind, *The Impartial;* one upon Faith; and three books of an epic on the story of Gideon. The last work he lived to complete was an adaptation to the English stage of Voltaire's '*Merope*.' While engaged upon it he suffered from terrible attacks of pain, supposed to proceed from an inflammation of the kidneys. He sank rapidly, and died on the day before, by command of the Prince of Wales, 'Merope' was to have been performed for his benefit, in the very minute of the great earthquake shock of February 8, 1750.

Had he lived two days longer, he would have completed his sixty-fifth year. His friends buried him in the great cloister of Westminster Abbey, by the side of the wife whom he had loved so tenderly.

I pass on to enumerate the dramatic works of this very estimable man but dull writer, who expended all his imagination on his projects and speculations, and into his books put only a dreary residuum of sententious platitude and commonplace. I confess never to have read his farce of 'The Walking Statue; or, The Devil in the Wine Cellar,' which belongs to the year 1710. A comedy called 'Trick upon Trick; or, Squire Brainless,' was presented at Drury Lane Theatre, and immediately 'damned.' It was never printed. One can hardly imagine Hill, with his solemn style and entire lack of humorous invention, attempting farce or comedy. The common sense which he certainly possessed should have saved him from a blunder so egregious; but there is nothing in which a man is more easily deceived than in the limitations that cripple and confine his intellectual effort. At all events Hill wooed no more the Comic Muse. In 1716 he inflicted on the town another of those portentous five acts of stilted sentiment which he called a tragedy; and actually found audiences who tolerated for several nights, I think, 'The Fatal Vision; or, The Fall of Siam'—though *why* Siam, I am confident no one can conjecture. As far as local colouring goes—or does not go—it might just as well have been 'The Fall of Cambodia,' or 'The Fall of Annapolis.' The historical tragedy of King Henry V.; or, The Conquest of France by the English,' produced at Drury Lane in 1723, and acted for four nights, is a shameless perversion of the great Shakespearian chronicle-play. Imagine the monstrous egotism of the man who could ingraft a second plot upon it, and introduce a new female character,—Harriet, niece to Lord Scrope, whom Henry V. has seduced. She figures throughout in male costume, and is made the means of discovering to Henry the conspiracy against him. Hill presented the managers of the theatre, when his tragedy was brought forward, with new sets of scenes for this piece, which cost him £200.

The sole dramatic effort of Hill's which retains its place in our collections is his tragedy of 'Zara' (1736), founded upon the '*Zaire*' of Voltaire, but embodying a good deal of Hill's own. At its first representation, a young gentleman connected with Hill by the ties of relationship, attempted the character of Osman, but though he had been carefully instructed by the author himself, his failure was complete. Another, but infinitely more successful *début* on the same occasion, was that of the charming Mrs Cibber, the part of Zara being her first appearance in tragedy. A brief specimen of Hill's style will suffice the reader :—

    Osman. Shine out, appear, be found, my lovely Zara !
        Impatient eyes attend—the rites expect thee ;
        And my devoted heart no longer brooks
        This distance from its softener ! all the lamps
        Of nuptial love are lighted, and burn pure,
        As if they drew their brightness from thy blushes :
        The holy mosque is filled with fragrant fumes,
        Which emulate the sweetness of thy breathing :
        My prostrate people all confirm my choice,
        And send their souls to heaven in prayers for blessings.
        Thy envious rivals, conscious of thy right,
        Approve superior charms, and join to praise thee;
        The throne that waits thee seems to shine more richly,
        As all its gems, with animated lustre,
        Feared to look dim beneath the eyes of Zara !
        Come, my slow love, the ceremonies wait thee ;
        Come and begin from this dear hour my triumph.
    Zara. Oh, what a wretch am I ! Oh, grief ! oh, love !
    Osm. Come—come—

Zar. Where shall I hide my blushes?
Osm. Blushes—here, in my bosom, hide them.
Zar. My lord!
Osm. Nay, Zara—give me thy hand and come—
Zar. Mistrust me, Heaven!
    What should I say—alas! I cannot speak.
Osm. Away—this modest, sweet, reluctant trifling
    But doubles my desires, and thy own beauties.
Zar. Ah, me!
Osm. Nay—but thou shouldst not be too cruel.
Zar. I can no longer bear it. Oh, my lord—
Osm. Ha! what?—whence?—how?
Zar. My lord! my sovereign!
    Heaven knows this marriage would have been a bliss
    Above my humble hopes! yet, witness love!
    Not from the grandeur of your throne, that bliss,
    But from the pride of calling Osman mine.
    Would you had been no emperor! and I
    Possessed of power and charms deserving you!
    That, slighting Aria's throne, I might alone
    Have left a proffered world to follow you.
    Through deserts, uninhabited by man,
    And blessed with ample room for peace and love,
    But, as it is, those Christians—
Osm. Christians! what!
    How start two images into thy thoughts,
    So distant—as the Christians and my love!
Zar. That good old Christian, reverend Lusignan,
    Now dying, ends his life and woes together.
Osm. Well! let him die. What has thy heart to feel
    Thus pressing, and thus tender, from the death
    Of an old wretched Christian? Thank our prophet,
    Thou art no Christian! Educated here,
    Thy happy youth was taught our better faith:
    Sweet as thy pity shines, 'tis now mis-timed.
    What! though an aged sufferer dies unhappy,
    Why should his foreign fate disturb our joys?
Zar. Sir, if you love me, and would have me think
    That I am truly dear—
Osm. Heaven! if I love!
Zar. Permit me—

Osm. What?
Zar. To desire—
Osm. Speak out.
Zar. The nuptial rites
    May be deferred till—
Osm. What! Is that the voice
    Of Zara?
Zar. Oh, I cannot bear his frown!
Osm. Of Zara?
Zar. It is dreadful to my heart,
    To give you but a seeming cause for anger;
    Pardon my grief. Alas! I cannot bear it;
    There is a painful terror in your eye
    That pierces to my soul—hid from your sight,
    I go to make a moment's truce with tears,
    And gather force to speak of my despair.
                        [Exit disordered.
Osm. I stand immoveable, like senseless marble;
    Horror had frozen my suspended tongue;
    And an astonished silence robbed my will
    Of power to tell her that she shocked my soul!
    Spoke she to me? Sure I misunderstood her!
    Could it be me she left? What have I seen?

And so the dull stream flows on monotonously, undisturbed by any currents of thought, or feeling, or passion.

'Alzira; or, Spanish Insult Repented' (1736), is a close translation from Voltaire. So is 'Merope,' which Hill dedicated to Lord Bolingbroke, in verses rendered noteworthy by their simple pathos:—

> 'Covered in Fortune's shade, I rest reclined;
> My griefs all silent, and my joys resigned:
> With patient eye life's evening gleams survey;
> Nor shake the outhast'ning sands, nor bid them stay.
> Yet, while from life my setting prospects fly,
> Fain would my mind's weak offspring shun to die;
> Fain would their hope some light through time explore;
> The *name's* kind passport—when the *man's* no more.'

'Roman Revenge,' a tragedy (1753), founded on the

death of Julius Cæsar, is remarkable for a curious perversion of history, Brutus appearing as the great Dictator's natural son. 'The Insolvent ; or, Filial Piety' (1758), was produced at the Haymarket under the management of the younger Cibber. Hill adapted it from an old MS. play, 'The Guiltless Adulterer ; or, Judge in his own Cause,' which had long lain among the lumber of Drury, and, by a vague and ridiculous tradition, was attributed to Sir William Davenant. 'Merlin in Love ; or, Faith against Magic' (1759), is characterised as a pastoral opera. 'The Muses in Mourning' (1760) is a kind of burlesque on the growing partiality of the public for operas and pantomimes, the Tragic and the Comic Muses lamenting the neglect into which they have unhappily fallen. A similar theme runs through Hill's 'Snake in the Grass,' described as 'A Dramatic Entertainment of a new species, being neither Tragedy, Comedy, Pantomime, Farce, Ballad, nor Opera' (1760). This was never put upon the stage, but is printed among Hill's miscellaneous works. Of the tragedy of 'Saul' only one act was finished, and the pastoral opera of 'Daraxis' is also incomplete. The several publications enumerated in this paragraph were, of course, all posthumous.

Pope put Hill in 'The Dunciad,' and among very bad company—that of the Divers. There was no justification for the insult, and the general sympathy went with Hill when he retaliated on the spiteful little poet in his *Progress of Wit*, one of the best of his poetical compositions. Eventually Pope was forced to apologise. He withdrew the satirical reference in the enlarged edition of his poem, and contracted with Hill an apparent friendship.

Among his metrical compositions I must mention *The Northern Star*, in which he celebrated the achievements of Peter the Great, because it procured him from the Czar the gift of a gold medal, a distinction which now-a-days is chiefly dealt in by Exhibition Committees and Royal Humane Societies. You may read the poem thus honoured in Hill's collected works, and I fear your judgment of it will not be as favourable as the Czar's.

CHAPTER II.

THE STAGE IN QUEEN ANNE'S REIGN.

II. THE PERFORMERS.

Barton Booth—Thomas Doggett—Robert Wilks—George Powell—Richard Estcourt—Cave Underhill—Verbruggen—Betterton—Edward Kynaston—'Jubilee Dicky,' and others—William Penkethman—Mrs Verbruggen or Mountford—Mrs Bracegirdle—Mrs Betterton—Mrs Elizabeth Barry—Mrs Anne Oldfield—Mrs Porter.

TURNING over the time-stained pages of *The Daily Courant* for June 28th, 1712, you come upon this interesting theatrical notice:—' Not acted these 15 years. By Her Majesty's Company of Comedians. At the Theatre-Royal in Drury Lane, on Tuesday next, being the 1st of July, will be revived the second part of ' The Destruction of Jerusalem' [by Crowne]. . . The parts of Titus by Mr Booth; Phraastes, Mr Mills; Tiberius, Mr Keen; John, Mr Powell; Berenice, Mrs Rogers; Clarena, Mrs Bradshaw. *N.B.*—The Company will continue to Act on every Tuesday and Friday during the Summer Season. By Her Majesty's command no Persons are to be admitted behind the Scenes.' The interesting point in this announcement is 'the part of Titus by Mr Booth.' It was one of the best impersonations of that careful and intelligent actor; but inferior, I should suppose, to his Pyrrhus in 'The Distressed Mother.' Another of his great characters was that of Maximus in Lord Rochester's 'Valentinian,' the first in which he appeared on the

London stage in 1701. But he rose to his highest pitch of fame in Addison's 'Cato,' which owed not a little of its success to his stately impersonation of the Roman senator. I have already told how Bolingbroke called the hero of the piece on the first night of its performance into his box, and presented him with fifty guineas. A similar sum was presented by the managers. But a more important result followed; for Wilks and Cibber found themselves obliged, on Doggett's sulky retirement, to admit the great tragedian into partnership with themselves; and Lord Bolingbroke procured from Queen Anne a special licence which recognised this new triumvirate.

BARTON BOOTH came of an ancient and reputable family. By birth he was a distant relative of the Earls of Warrington, whose family name he bore. At the age of nine he was sent to Westminster School, at first under the care of Dr Busby, of flagellating fame; and afterwards under that of Dr Knipe. Baker, in one of his long-winded sentences, which you can hardly read without half-a-dozen pauses, says:—' Here he showed a strong passion for learning in general, and more particularly for an acquaintance with the Latin poets, the finest passages in whose works he used with great pains to imprint in his memory; and had, besides, such a peculiar propriety and judicious emphasis in the repetition of them, assisted by so fine a tone of voice, and adorned with such a natural gracefulness of action, as drew on him the admiration of the whole school; and, added to the sprightliness of his parts in general, strongly recommended him to the notice of his master, Dr Busby, who having himself when young obtained great applause in the performance of a part in "The Royal Slave" (by Cartwright), had ever after held theatrical accomplishments in the highest estimation.'

On one of the annual speech-days Terence's 'Andria' was chosen for performance, and to young Booth was assigned the part of Pamphilus. He represented it with so much intelligence, with such graceful action, and with so silvery a voice, that he carried off the plaudits of the spectators. Fired by their cheers, he became one of the glorious army of stage-struck youths, and while his father intended him for the Church, was seeking a speedy means of entrance into the Theatre. He was only seventeen when he stole away from home, joined a strolling company, and afterwards played in 'a droll' at Bartholomew Fair. Next he contrived to obtain an engagement in Dublin, where, in June 1678, he opened as Oroonoko, in Southern's tragedy, under decidedly adverse conditions. For, in the stress of his passion, he wiped the sweat from his blackened face, and in the last act appeared like a sweep half washed; while, on the second night, in his excitement he tore away some crape with which a lady had covered his features, and stood before the laughing audience with a countenance half black half white. 'When I came off,' he says, 'they so lampblacked me for the rest of the night, that I was flayed before it could be got off again.' Nevertheless he made a success. Nor was this surprising: he had a good figure, an expressive countenance, and a fine voice; to which physical advantages he added quickness of perception, soundness of judgment, and considerable measure of that sympathetic faculty without which no man can be a great actor. After two prosperous seasons in Dublin, he resolved to seek the suffrages of a London audience; and returning to England in 1701, he obtained from Lord Fitzhardinge an introduction to Betterton. The veteran gave him some instruction; after which he made his *début* at Lincoln's Inn Fields in Rochester's 'Valentinian,' together with Betterton and the irresistible Mrs Barry. He was received with much cordiality; and thenceforward his advancement was swift and sure.

It was greatly in his favour that he led a life of moderation and sobriety. He told Cibber that he had for some time been 'too frank a lover of the bottle,' but having observed the contempt and distress in which Powell had involved himself by the same vice, he was so deeply impressed that he made a resolution thenceforward to abstain from it, and kept that resolution to the end of his days.

I have alluded to one or two of his great parts. He excelled also in the Ghost in 'Hamlet,' in which it would appear that no actor has ever approached him. 'His slow, solemn, and under tone of voice,' says Davies; 'his noiseless tread, as if he had been composed of air, and his whole deportment, inspired the audience with that feeling which is excited by awful astonishment! The impression of his appearance in this part was so powerful upon a constant frequenter of the theatres for nearly sixty years that he assured me, when, long after Booth's death he was present at the tragedy of "Hamlet," as soon as the name of the Ghost was announced on the stage he felt a kind of awe and terror, " of which," said he, " I was soon cured by his appearance."'

Of his assumption of the part of Cato an interesting story is told. The then managers, Wilks, Cibber, and Doggett, did not clearly apprehend all that could be made of it, and Wilks was doubtful whether young Booth would accept so venerable a character. He therefore took the manuscript himself to Booth's lodgings for the purpose of overruling his objections, and cajoling him into a consent. A rapid glance at the poet's pages convinced the actor that a great opportunity lay before him; but he professed a polite indifference, and allowed the managers to understand that he yielded only out of complaisance. What the young tragedian made of it I have already stated. For thirty-five nights Drury Lane was filled from floor to ceiling by an applauding crowd. At Oxford an equally enthusiastic reception awaited him. That year the Drury Lane triumvirs made a profit of £1500 each, and as for Booth, he was hailed as the only successor of Betterton, and before long admitted to a share of the management.

In Shakespeare's 'Henry VIII.' he embodied the idea of royal dignity. 'Hans Holbein,' says Victor, 'never gave a higher picture of King Henry. . . . When angry, his eye spoke majestic terror; the noblest and bravest of his courtiers were awe-struck. He gave you the fullest idea of that arbitrary prince, who thought himself born to be obeyed; the boldest dare not dispute his commands: he appeared to claim a right divine to exert the power he imperiously assumed.' The same writer adds that 'his voice was completely harmonious, from the softness of the flute to the extent of the trumpet.' Pope, by the way, speaks of 'well-mouthed Booth.' Aaron Hill sums up his general qualifications as an actor in these words:—'He had learning to understand whatever it was his part to speak, and judgment to know how far it agreed or disagreed with his character. It was this actor's peculiar felicity to be heard and seen the same, whether as the pleased, the grieved, the pitying, the reproachful, or the angry. One would be almost tempted to borrow the aid of a very bold figure, and to express his excellency more significantly, by permission to affirm that the blind might have seen him in his voice, and the deaf have heard him in his visage.'

In 1704 Mr Booth married a daughter of a Norfolk baronet, who died in 1710, without issue. He afterwards formed a *liaison* with Mrs Mountford, who placed in his hands her whole fortune, estimated at eight thousand pounds, which he promptly returned on discovering that that fair, but, unfortunately, frail lady had contracted another attachment. In 1709 he took to wife the beautiful and popular dancer, Miss Hester Santlow, whose charms had brought to her feet some of the most eminent men of the time, including 'the hero of Blenheim.' She was a very amiable and fascinating woman, and brought with her an ample dowry. After her marriage she abandoned the ballet, and made her appearance as Dorcas Zeal in Shadwell's 'Fair Quaker of Deal,' with very genuine success. 'The gentle softness of her voice,' says Cibber, 'the composed innocence of her aspect, the modesty of her dress, the reserved decency of her gesture, and the simplicity of the sentiments that naturally fell from her, made her seem the amiable maid she represented.'

This second marriage made the happiness of Booth's later life, until, in 1727, he was attacked by a violent fever. Though he shook off its worst effects, the physical debility which it induced compelled him to quit the stage. He reappeared only for eight nights, in 1729, in the play of 'The Double Falsehood.' His health continued to decline, and on the 10th of May 1733, in the fifty-third year of his age, he passed away. He was buried in Cowley Churchyard (near Uxbridge), and forty years later (January 1773), his widow was laid by his side. Booth had property in Cowley, which was afterwards held by John Rich, the original harlequin. He also built Booth Street, Westminster. Notwithstanding his large earnings, he would have died in comparative poverty, but for the fortune brought him by his second wife, to whom he honourably bequeathed all that he had to leave.

To one utterance of Booth's, which shows that he had no mean conception of his art, I ask the reader's attention:—'The longest life is too short for the almost endless study of the actor.' These are golden words; but the idea which they embody is, I apprehend, foreign to the minds of a great many stage-struck aspirants of the present day.

Booth was the author of a masque, 'The Death of Dido,' received with favour in 1716.

'His character as a man,' says one of his biographers, 'was adorned with many amiable qualities, among which a perfect goodness of heart, the basis of every virtue, was remarkably conspicuous. He was a gay, lively, cheerful companion, yet humble and diffident of his own abilities, by which means he acquired the love and esteem of every one; and so particularly was he distinguished and caressed, and his company sought by the great, that, as Chetwood relates of him, although he kept no equipage of his own, not one nobleman in the kingdom had so many sets of horses at his command as he had. For at the time that the patentees, jealous of his merit, and apprehensive of his influence with the ministry, in order to prevent his application to his friends at court, which was then kept at Windsor, took care to give him constant employment in London, by giving out every night such plays as he had principal parts in; yet even this policy could not avail them, as there was punctually every night the chariot and six of some nobleman or other waiting for him at the conclusion of the play, which carried him the twenty miles in three hours at furthest, and brought him back again next night, time enough for the business of the theatre.'

But it was no doubt this social popularity which brought about the great actor's premature end.

THOMAS DOGGET or DOGGETT, was born in Castle Street, Dublin, and on the Dublin stage made his first appearance as an actor. His unctuous style of acting does not seem to have been appreciated by the audience there, and he came over to England to seek fame and—what he valued far more—fortune. After some short experience as a strolling player,* he was invited to London, where he soon became a favourite, and at Drury Lane and Lincoln's Inn Fields was established as a leading member of the stock company. Congreve keenly enjoyed his rich original humour, and to some extent 'measured' him for the characters of Fondlewife in 'The Old Bachelor,' and Ben in 'Love for Love,' which he rendered in the most masterly manner.

Eventually he attached himself exclusively to Drury Lane, where he became joint manager with Wilks and Cibber, the latter of whom has described his qualifications as an actor with his usual felicity of criticism. 'He was the most original and the strictest observer of nature,' says Cibber, 'of all his contemporaries. He borrowed from none of them; his manner was his own; he was a pattern to others, whose greatest merit was that they had sometimes tolerably imitated him. In dressing a character to the greatest exactness, he was remarkably skilful; the least article of whatever habit he wore, seemed in some degree to speak and mark the different humour he presented: a necessary care in a comedian, in which many have been too remiss or ignorant. He could be extremely ridiculous, without stepping into the least impropriety to make him so. His greatest success was in characters of lower life, which he improved from the delight he took in his observations of that kind in the real world. Congreve was a great admirer of him. . . . . He was very acceptable to several persons of high rank and

---

* Aston gives a curious account of the life of a strolling player in Queen Anne's time. He travelled with Doggett, who was manager, and each player he says, wore a brocaded waistcoat, kept his own horse, and was welcomed everywhere as a gentleman.

taste, though he seldom cared to be the comedian but among his more intimate acquaintance.'

In like manner Downes, in the *Roscius Anglicanus*, speaks of him as 'the only comic original now extant.' He wore farce in his face; and his thoughts deliberately framed 'his utterance congruous to his looks.' Tony Aston furnishes a few particulars which enable us to see the man in his habit as he lived: he was a little, lively, 'spract man,' who dressed neat and something fine, in a plain cloth coat, and a brocaded waistcoat. He danced the 'Cheshire Rounds' full as well as the famous Captain George, but 'with more nature and nimbleness.' He was a man of very good sense, but, it seems, illiterate; 'for he wrote one word,' says Aston, 'thus—Sir, I will give you a hole [instead of "whole"] share.' This orthographical lapse, however, may have been an accident; and, besides, orthography was not a fashionable study in the reign of Anne. That a man who attained Doggett's position as an artist—who kept the company of men of parts—who was the author of a once-popular comedy—could fairly be described as 'illiterate,' I am not at all inclined to believe.*

When Booth was introduced into the management of Drury Lane, under circumstances very graphically narrated by Colley Cibber, but of no earthly interest to any of my readers, Doggett, who appears to have been a man of avaricious disposition and cross-grained temper, surlily withdrew. He had, by his frugality and industry, acquired a considerable fortune, which he contrived to increase, it is said, by keeping a booth at Bartholomew Fair. He took up his residence at Eltham, where he employed his

---

* To these notices I may add that he 'made up' his face with great skill to imitate any age from manhood to extreme senility; wherefore Sir Godfrey Kneller said that Doggett excelled him in his own art; for he could only copy nature from the originals before him, whilst the actor could vary them at pleasure, and yet always preserve a true resemblance.

leisure in rural pursuits, and where he died, on the 22d of September 1721. He lies buried in the churchyard.

Doggett was a politician of strong Whig principles—a firm believer in, and upholder of the Protestant succession—a devoted partisan of the House of Hanover. In honour of the accession of George I. to the throne, he gave a waterman's coat and badge to be rowed for on the first anniversary of that happy event; and at his death, he bequeathed a sum of money, the interest of which was to be appropriated annually, in perpetuity, to the purchase of a similiar coat and badge; and with that close regard for appropriate details of dress which had marked him as an actor, he directed that the coat should be of an orange colour, and that the badge should represent the white horse of Hanover. The race for the prize takes place on the 1st of August, and the course extends from the Old Swan at London Bridge to the White Swan at Chelsea, when the tide is running out.

The theatrical annals of Queen Anne's time, present few more eminent names than that of ROBERT WILKS. He was descended from a reputable Worcestershire family, that had for some time been settled at Bromsgrove. His grandfather, a lawyer of eminence, raised a troop of horse for Charles I., and, like many another good cavalier, sank into penury. His son went over to Ireland, and found employment in Dublin, where *his* son was born in 1665. Robert Wilks cannot have received more than a scanty education, but he had a ready talent, and picked up a good deal of information as he went through the world. His father found a vocation for him as a clerk in the secretary's office: he fell, however, into the society of actors; strutted in sock and buskin on the amateur stage; played Othello with so much vigour, that everybody predicted for him fame and fortune 'in the profession;' made his way to London, and obtained, through Betterton, an introduction to Manager Rich, who was so much impressed by his ease and gaiety of manner, and his handsome person, that he engaged the promising young amateur at a salary of fifteen shillings a week, less two shillings and sixpence for instruction in dancing. Buoyed up by sanguine hopes of speedy success, Wilks, who was already in love, did not fear to marry even upon this small pittance. He was at that time (1690) twenty-five years of age. It was soon apparent that in the young Irishman the stage had gained a valuable recruit; but he had old-established rivals, who, as a matter of course, took the best parts, and his progress was so slow that, being refused an increase of salary, he determined to return to Ireland. 'I fancy,' said Betterton, 'that that gentleman (the autocratic manager), if he has not too much obstinacy to own it, will be the first that repents your parting, for, if I foresee aright, you will be greatly wanted here.' And he recommended him to Ashbury, the Dublin manager, who offered him sixty pounds a year and a clear benefit.

In the Irish capital he rapidly gained a good position; and such favourable reports of his progress reached London that, on the death of William Mountford, in 1696, Rich invited him back to Drury Lane, with a salary of four pounds a week. Then, indeed, his expectations of fame and fortune seemed in a direct way of being fulfilled. Ashbury was so reluctant to lose him, that he persuaded the Lord-Lieutenant to issue an order prohibiting him from leaving the country; but apprised of this intrigue, Wilks stole away immediately, crossed the Channel in safety, and made his re-appearance on the stage of Drury Lane Theatre as Palamede in Dryden's '*Marriage à la Mode.*' In this character he was inferior to Powell, its former representative, and Cibber says that he still showed a good deal of rawness. But he was 'young, erect, and of pleasing aspect,' and, on the whole, an actor of considerable promise. This promise he speedily fulfilled, for he was thoroughly in earnest in his work, and by careful study soon amended his defects. He was wise enough to learn by experience, and to profit by the advice of competent critics.

His success awakened the jealousy of Powell, who, since the death of Mountford, had held the stage without a rival, and a desperate feud broke out between the two comedians. In short, a challenge, says Cibber, came from Powell in one of his hot-headed fits; but the next morning he was cool enough to let it end in Wilks's favour. Discovering that intimidation availed him nothing, and that Wilks, when really provoked, was ready to give battle, he grew so out of humour that he cocked his hat, and in high dudgeon transferred his services to the company at Lincoln's Inn Fields. But there he found more competitors than in his old scene of action, and made a still worse figure; so that, after staying but one winter with them, he returned to Drury Lane, and having made these 'unsuccessful pushes of his ambition,' sank into a negligent and apathetic mood, submitting quietly to the superiority which Wilks had acquired during his ill-judged desertion.

By nature Powell had been more richly endowed than Wilks, and his memory was not less tenacious than his rival's; but he lacked his patience, perseverance, and resolution. He often appeared before the public unprepared: Wilks never. Cibber doubts whether the latter, in a career of forty years, ever changed or misplaced an article five times in any one of his parts; and relates a remarkable example of his extraordinary diligence:—'In some new comedy he happened to complain of a crabbed speech in his part, which, he said, gave him more trouble to study than all the rest of it had done; upon which he applied to the author either to soften or shorten it. The author, that he might make the matter quite easy to him, fairly cut it all out. But when he got home from the rehearsal, Wilks thought it such an indignity to his memory that anything should be thought too hard for it, that he actually made himself perfect in that speech, though he knew it was never to be made use of.' This may have been, as Cibber styles it, ' an act of supererogation,' but a man capable of such an act—so resolute in applying and perfecting his natural powers—could not but achieve success. For him there was no such word as 'fail.'

No wonder, then, that Wilks grew daily into greater favour with the public, and attained to so eminent a position that even Rich, his tyrannical manager, was compelled to accede to his demands. He became his first minister, or, as Cibber puts it, ' bustle-master-general of the company,' a kind of acting-manager, in which capacity his critic admits that he did good service, by insisting that every play should be put upon the stage with proper care. The rigid discipline he maintained did not secure him the goodwill of the company, though their success was in no small measure due to it ; and evidently his recollection of its stringency colours Cibber's estimate of Wilks's character. He denounces him as of an imperious temper, fond of authority, and jealous of competitors ; but, he adds, with a half-regretful sigh, ' had I had half his application, I still think I might have shown myself twice the actor that in my highest state of fervour I appeared to be.'

Downes speaks of this fine artist as 'proper and comely in person, of graceful port, mein, and air,—void of affectation ; his elevations and cadences just, congruent to elocution.' Steele, in *The Tatler*, No. 182, does him homage,—'To beseech gracefully, to approach respectfully, to pity, to mourn, to love, are the places wherein Wilks may be said to shine with the utmost beauty.' We are told by Chetwood that he was unequalled in the just expression of manly sorrow. The deeper passions lay beyond his province, though his Hamlet was admirable, and in Macduff he could always move his audience to tears. But it was in the light and lively comedies of Farquhar and Cibber—as Mirabel, and Plume, and Archer; as Don Felix in 'The Wonder,' and Sir Harry Wildair in 'The Constant Couple'[1]—that he distanced all competitors. In the last-named part he became the idol of the town, and crowds flocked night after night to see him, as they now flock to see Mr Irving. He had all that ease, and vivacity, and spontaneous grace which endeared the late Charles Mathews to the elder playgoers of the Victorian age, with a capacity for expressing emotion in which Mathews was unhappily deficient. I can never read Cibber's vivid account of his artistic acting, without wishing that it were possible to resuscitate him for the benefit of our modern comedians! 'Whatever he did upon the stage, let it be ever so trifling, whether it consisted in putting on his gloves, or taking out his watch, lolling on his cane, or taking snuff, every movement was marked by such an ease of breeding and manner, everything told so strongly the involuntary motion of a gentleman, that it was impossible to consider the character he represented in any other light than that of reality.'

Wilks died in 1732, at the age of seventy-six, and was buried in St Paul's, Covent Garden. He left directions that his funeral should take place at midnight, without any pomp or circumstance; but the King's Chapel choir voluntarily attended, and sang an anthem.

To what I have already said of GEORGE POWELL, the comedian, I shall add but little. He might have held his ground as the successor of Mountford, and

---

[1] Steele speaks of 'the inimitable strain and run of great humour' which he kept up in this character.

have more than rivalled Wilks, for he was better gifted by nature, but for his idleness and intemperance. Cibber draws of him a darkly-coloured portrait, in which some of the touches may be due to ill-feeling, but the substantial accuracy of which is proved by much contemporary evidence. For instance, Gildon describes him as an idle fellow that neither minded his business nor lived quietly in any community. Love of drink and the dice was his ruin. Sometimes he appeared upon the stage in a drunken condition; and he was so constantly pursued by sheriffs' officers, that he used to promenade the streets with sword drawn to keep them at bay. On one occasion he compelled a terrified bailiff to retreat to the other side of the road, with the deprecatory exclamation of ' We don't want you *now*, Mr Powell!' In several respects he reminds us of George Frederick Cooke. Like him, he might have stood foremost among the actors of his time, had he been sober and industrious. But he was careless in his study, and dissipation weakened his memory and deteriorated his powers. Among his latest impersonations were Orestes in 'The Distressed Mother,' and Portius in Addison's 'Cato.' He died on the 14th of December 1714, and lies buried in St Clement Danes.

According to Chetwood, in his *History of the Stage*, RICHARD ESTCOURT was born at Tewkesbury, in 1668, and educated at the Grammar School of that ancient town. Like many other high-spirited lads, he was seized at the age of fifteen with a strong desire to appear upon the stage, and joined a travelling company of comedians, then at Worcester. That no friend or acquaintance might recognise him, he made his *début*, in female attire, as Roxana in Lee's ' Alexander the Great.' His father, however, had obtained notice of it, and sent to secure the runaway, who hastily effected his escape in a suit of woman's clothes, lent him by one of the ladies of the company, and tramped away to Chipping Norton, a distance of five-and-twenty miles. At the inn there he found the beds all engaged, and was invited to partake of the daughter's, behind the bar. The young woman, on retiring, found the wearied and foot-sore traveller in a profound sleep ; but, observing a shirt instead of the corresponding article of female attire, she grew suspicious, and among the clothes that lay on the floor were a pair of men's shoes, which confirmed her mistrust. She roused the people of the house, and her father, on learning the reason, prepared to fling Master Dick Estcourt into the horse-pond ; but his frank and full confession of his adventure, and the arrival on the scene of a person from Tewkesbury who knew the truant, led to a peaceful settlement of the affair.

To prevent a repetition of this escapade, his father conveyed him to London, and bound him apprentice to an apothecary in Hatton Garden. Estcourt wearied quickly of mortar and pestle, pills and potions, and deserting his new master at the first favourable opportunity, wandered about England for two years. He spent some time afterwards in Dublin, slowly developing into an accomplished actor ; and, with a tolerable reputation, returning to England, was engaged at Drury Lane Theatre. There his first appearance was in the character of Dominic in Dryden's tragedy of ' The Spanish Friar ; ' and he achieved a considerable degree of success by his close imitation of Leigh, its original impersonator. According to Downes, he was ' *histrio naturæ*—a true actor—he has the honour (Nature endowing him with an easy, free, unaffected mode of elocution) in comedy always to *lætificate* his audience, especially quality.' But Cibber does not stand alone in representing him as a comparatively indifferent performer, who owed such measure of popularity as he enjoyed to his singularly faithful imitation of his predecessors. So, too, Baker affirms that in all his parts he was mostly indebted for the applause he received to his extraordinary powers of mimicry, which enabled him to copy 'very exactly' several performers of capital merit, whose manner he remembered and assumed. It is also charged against him that he indulged in the evil practice of 'gagging' —'throwing in additions of his own, which the author not only had never intended, but perhaps would have considered as most opposite to his main intention.' Steele, however, valiantly takes up the cudgels on his behalf. 'It has as much surprised me as anything in nature to have it frequently said that he was not a good player;' and he ascribed this unfavourable judgment to 'a partiality for former actors in the parts in which he succeeded them, and judging by comparison of what was liked before rather than by the nature of the thing.' And he exclaims, with a fine air of assured conviction,—'When a man of his wit and smartness could put on an utter absence of common sense in his face, as he did in the character of Bullfinch in "The Northern Lass" [by Richard Brome], and an air of insipid cunning and vivacity in the character of Pounce in "The Tender Husband" [by Steele himself], it is folly to dispute his capacity and success, as he was an actor.'

Whatever he was on the stage, it is certain that in society he was a very lovable and agreeable companion; and even a better man might have been proud to draw forth by his amiable qualities so gracious an 'In Memoriam' as Steele has dedicated to him in *The Spectator*.[1] It was worth living to be remembered after death with so sincere an affection and with such exquisite praise. For instance, Steele speaks of his 'quick wit in conversation,' his 'nice judgment upon any emergency that could arise,' and his 'blameless, inoffensive behaviour.' He con-

---

[1] No. 468, August 27, 1712.

demns very strongly the artificial social distinctions which could not raise such a man 'above being received only upon the foot of contributing to mirth and diversion.' And he adds, with a sigh :—' Poor Estcourt ! let the vain and proud be at rest, thou wilt no more disturb their admiration of their dear selves ; and thou art no longer to drudge in raising the mirth of stupids, who know nothing of thy merit, for thy maintenance.' And, in conclusion, he says, 'I speak of him as a companion, and a man qualified for conversation. His fortune exposed him to an obsequiousness towards the worst sort of company, but his excellent qualities rendered him capable of making the best figure in the most refined. I have been present with him among men of the most delicate taste a whole night, and have known him (for he saw it was desired) keep the discourse to himself the most part of it, and maintain his good-humour with a countenance, in a language so delightful, without offence to any person or thing upon earth, still preserving the distance his circumstances obliged him to ; I say, I have seen him do all this in such a charming manner, that I am sure none of those I hint at will read this without giving him some sorrow for their abundant mirth, and one gush of tears for so many bursts of laughter. I wish it were any honour to the pleasant creature's memory, that my eyes are too much suffused to let me go on.'

Of Estcourt's powers of mimicry there can be no doubt. ' In the accounts he gave of persons and sentiments,' says Steele, ' he did not only hit the figure of their faces, and manner of their gestures, but he would in his narrations fall into their very way of thinking, and this when he recounted passages wherein men of the best wit were concerned, as well as such wherein were represented men of the lowest rank of understanding.' And Cibber is not less emphatic :—' This man was so amazing and extraordinary a mimic, that no man or woman, from the coquette to the privy councillor, ever moved or spoke before him, but he would carry their voice, look, mien, and motion instantly into another company: I have heard him make long harangues, and form various arguments, even in the manner of thinking, of an eminent pleader at the bar, with every the least article and singularity of his utterance so perfectly imitated, that he was the very *alter ipse*, scarce to be distinguished from his original.' One day Mr Secretary Craggs with some friends, carried the great mimic to Sir Godfrey Kneller's, where he gave many of his most amusing imitations. Among others, that of Lord Somers, which hugely delighted the artist. Then, at a signal from Craggs, Estcourt mimicked Sir Godfrey himself, who exclaimed,—'Nay, there you are out, man; by G—! that is not me.'

Estcourt was a great favourite with the Duke of Marlborough, and with many other illustrious personages. At the time that the Beefsteak Club was established, he was unanimously elected to the post of *Providore;* and as a badge of office wore a small golden gridiron suspended from his neck by a green silk ribbon. He retired from the stage in 1711, and became landlord of 'The Bumper' tavern, in St James Street, which he opened on the 1st of January 1712. In No. 264 of *The Spectator*, Steele good-naturedly advertises the actor-Boniface, in a letter purporting to be written by Sir Roger de Coverley.

Estcourt was the author of a comedy, 'The Fair Example,' and of an interlude. 'Prunelia,' burlesquing the Italian operas which were then slowly struggling into popularity.

He died in 1713, and was buried in the churchyard of St Paul's, Covent Garden—the Necropolis of actors.

CAVE UNDERHILL'S portrait is hung up in Cibber's

gallery. 'His particular excellence was in characters that may be called still life—I mean the stiff, the heavy, and the stupid. To those he gave the exactest and most expressive colours, and in some of them looked as if it were not in the power of human passions to alter a feature of him. In the solemn formality of Obadiah in "The Committee," and in the boobily heaviness of Lolprop in "The Squire of Alsatia," he seemed the immovable log he cared for: a countenance of wood could not be more frigid than his when the blockhead of a character required it. His face was full and long: from his crown to the end of his nose was the shorter half of it; so that the disproportion of his lower features, when soberly compressed, with an unwondering eye hanging over them, threw him into the most lumpish, moping mortal that ever made beholders merry; not but, at other times, he could be wakened into spirit equally ridiculous. In the coarse rustic humour of Justice Clodfeet, in "Epsom Wells," he was a delightful brute; and in the blunt vivacity of Sir Sampson, in "Love for Love," he showed all that true perverse spirit that is commonly seen in much wit and ill-nature.'

One of Underhill's best characters was the First Gravedigger in 'Hamlet.' He continued on the stage until years had brought him to the winter of discontent,[1] and in 1709 Steele made an earnest appeal on his behalf to the generosity of the playgoing public:—'He has been a comic for three generations: my father admired him extremely when he was a boy.' An allowance was afterwards made to him in his old age by the patentees of Drury Lane, and he had a benefit given him on the 3d of June 1709, when he played his favourite part of the First Gravedigger; 'but, alas!' says Cibber, 'so worn and disabled as if he himself was to have lain in the grave he was digging.'

[1] He was on the stage from 1661 to 1710.

Of VERBRUGGEN, the second husband of our charming Mrs Mountford, I have little to tell. He was a respectable tragedian—the original *Oroonoko*. 'Nature without extravagance,' says Downes, 'freedom without licentiousness, and vociferous without bellowing.' Gildon affirms that he had 'a cracked voice,' and Downes adds, that though tall and well built, he was 'a little inkneed.' On the whole, it is matter for wonder that he gained the hand—and, I suppose, the heart—of beautiful Mrs Mountford. Tony Aston describes him as of a fiery temper—his sword drawn on the least occasion. Altogether his character does not commend itself to notice as particularly genial or attractive.

BETTERTON, the greatest actor of the Restoration Drama, lived into the reign of Anne, and was buried in Westminster Abbey on the 2d of May 1710.[1] His last years were years of poverty and decay, and he was very thankful for the benefit given to him in the season of 1708-9. He played Valentine in 'Love for Love,' and cleared five hundred and twenty pounds. In the year following it was repeated, and Betterton, who was suffering severely from gout, played Melantius in 'The Maid's Tragedy' (April 20th). The effort proved too much for the aged actor, and he died on the 28th.

EDWARD KYNASTON, at one time so famous for his performance of female parts, made his first appearance on the stage in 1659, and remained on it until 1699. At the

[1] 'Having received notice,' says Steele, 'that the famous actor, Mr Betterton, was to be interred in the cloisters near Westminster Abbey, I was resolved to walk thither, and see the last offices done to a man whom I always very much admired, and from whose action I had received more strong impressions of what is great and noble in human nature, than from the arguments of the most solid philosophers, or the descriptions of the most charming poets I have ever read.'

time of his death, in 1712, he was probably about sixty-seven years old.

With a passing allusion to HILDEBRAND HORDEN, a rising young actor, who was killed in a brawl at the Rose Tavern; to LEIGH, the post-Restoration comedian, who died in the reign of Anne; to BENJAMIN JOHNSON, a solid and serious actor, born in 1665 died 1740; to BOWMAN, best known as the husband of the attractive Mrs Bowman, Betterton's adopted daughter and pupil; and NORRIS, a man with a great deal of dry and original humour, who was called 'Jubilee Dicky,' from the part which he had created in Farquhar's 'Constant Couple,' I proceed to notice briefly the celebrated WILLIAM PENKETHMAN.

In *The Spectator*, No. 370, Steele has commemorated this popular actor. 'The petulancy of a peevish old fellow,' he says, 'who loves and hates he knows not why, is very excellently performed by the ingenious Mr William Penkethman in "The Fop's Fortune" [by Colley Cibber], where, in the character of Don Choleric Snap Shorto de Testy, he answers no questions but to those whom he likes, and wants no account of anything from those he approves. Mr Penkethman is also master of as many faces in the dumb scene as can be expected from a man in the circumstances of being ready to perish out of fear and hunger. He wonders throughout the whole scene very masterly, without neglecting his victuals. If it be, as I have sometimes heard it mentioned, a great qualification for the world to follow business and pleasure too, what is it in the ingenious Mr Penkethman to represent a sense of pleasure and pain at the same time?'

Penkethman was what is now called a low comedian. He first appeared on the stage in 1692. and gradually rose into favour with the public. As a speaking harlequin and pantomime actor, he acquired both popularity and wealth.

'He's the darling of Fortunatus,' says Downes, 'and has gained more in theatres and fairs in twelve years than those that have tugged at the oar of acting those thirty.' To please the groundlings, he would condescend to any artifice. On one occasion he spoke an epilogue, straddling on an ass. Steele refers to his somewhat vulgar fooling in *The Tatler*, No. 188, joining him with Bullock, another low comedian, whose style was very similar. 'Mr William Bullock and Mr William Penkethman are of the same age, profession, and sex. They both distinguish themselves in a very particular manner under the discipline of the crab-tree, with this only difference, that Mr Bullock has the more agreeable squall, and Mr Penkethman the more graceful shrug. Penkethman devours a cold chick with great applause; Bullock's talent lies chiefly in asparagus. Penkethman is very dexterous at conveying himself under a table; Bullock is no less active in jumping over a stick. Penkethman has a great deal of money; but Mr Bullock is the taller man.'

Both Penkethman and Bullock had a booth at Bartholomew Fair. The character of the entertainments they gave may be inferred from the following advertisement:[1] —

At Pinkeman's, Mills', and Bullock's Booth. In the Old Place over against the Hospital Gate, During the time of Bartholomew Fair, will be presented, a New Droll called The Siege of Barcelona, or The Soldier's Fortune, with the Taking of Fort Mountjouy. Containing the pleasant and comical exploits of that renouned hero Captain Blunderbuss and his man Squib; his Adventures with the Conjuror; and a Surprising Scene of the Flying Machine, where he and his man Squib are enchanted. Also the Diverting Humour of Corporal Scare Devil.

The Principal Parts acted by the Comedians of the Theatre Royal, viz., Colonel Loverwell, Mr Mills; Captain Blunderbuss, Mr Bullock; Squib, his man, Mr Norris, *alias* Jubilee Dicky; Corporal

[1] Quoted by Ashton, i. 255.

Scare Devil, Mr Bickerstaff; Maria, the Governor's daughter, Mrs Baxter; and The Dame of Honour, Mrs Willis.

To which will be added the Wonderful Performance of the most celebrated Master, Mr Simpson the famous Vaulter; who has had the honour to teach most of the Nobility in England; and at whose request he now performs with Mr Pinkeman to let the world see what Vaulting is. Being lately arrived from Italy.

The Musick, Songs, and Dances are all by the best Performers of their kind, whom Mr Pinkeman has entertained at extraordinary charge, purely to give a full satisfaction to the town. *Vivat Regina!*

Penkethman did not disdain to visit any public place where the multitude congregated, and carried his itinerant company to Greenwich or to May Fair. At the last named (abolished in 1709), he apparently provided an entertainment of a lower class than he put before his patrons in Smithfield. Here is his programme in 1704, as quoted by Mr Ashton:—

In Brookfield Marketplace at the East corner of Hide Park, is a Fair to be kept for the space of sixteen days, beginning the First of May; The first three days for live cattle and leather, with the same entertainment as at Bartholomew Fair, where there are shops to be let, ready built, for all manner of tradesmen that usually keep Fairs; and so to continue yearly at the same time and place; being a free Fair: and no person to be arrested or molested during the time of this Fair by virtue of Pye Powder [Pie Powdre] Court. And at Mr Pinkeman's Droll Booth will be performed several entertainments which will be expressed at large upon the bills, especially one very surprising that the whole world never yet produced the like, viz.,—He speaks an epilogue upon an elephant between nine and ten feet high, arrived from Guinea, led upon the stage by six Blacks. The Booth is easily known by the picture of the Elephant and Mr Pinkethman sitting in state on his back, on the outside of his Booth.

Again, in 1707:—

At Pinkeman's Booth in May Fair, to entertain the Quality, Gentry, and others, he has got eight dancing dogs, brought from Holland, which are admired by all that see them; and they will dance upon Mr Pinkeman's stage in each show. This extraordinary charge he's at (in procuring these dogs), is purely to divert the town.

They are the Wonder of the World. The last show beginning between eight and nine o'clock for the entertainment of the Quality, as the Park breaks up.

Pinkethman, or Pinkeman, retired from the stage in May 1724, and died in 1740.

Among the actresses of the time, I scruple to introduce Mrs VERBRUGGEN—better known by her earlier married name of Mrs Mountford—because her career belongs rather to the reign of William III. than that of Anne, terminating soon after the accession of the latter. She made her *début* on the stage as Miss Percival, and won the suffrages of the playgoing public by her impersonation of Nell in 'The Devil to Pay.' While still in the bloom of womanhood, she married the brilliant comedian, William Mountford, who was killed by Captain Hill in 1692. According to Betterton, her father was involved in the assassination plot against King William; 'for this he lay under sentence of death, which he received on the same night that Lord Mohun[1] killed her husband, Mr Mountford.' He adds that, while suffering under this double affliction, she was introduced to Queen Mary, 'who being, as she was pleased to say, struck to the heart upon receiving Mrs Mountford's petition, immediately granted all that was in her power, a remission of her father's [sentence of] execution for that of transportation. But Fate had so ordered it, that poor Mrs Mountford was to lose both father and husband. For as Mr Percival was going abroad, he was so weakened by his imprisonment, that he was taken sick on the road, and died at Portsmouth.'

Mrs Mountford did not long wear her widow's weeds. Verbruggen, the tragedian — that tall, well-limbed and choleric fellow,—prevailed upon her to relinquish them in his favour; but whether her second marriage was al-

---

[1] Lord Mohun was an accessory; Hill was the real murderer.

together a happy one, seems open to doubt. Tony Aston is not, perhaps, an unimpeachable authority, and the reader must take his statement for what it is worth. 'She was the best conversation possible,' he says, which we can well believe : ' never captious or displeased at anything but what was gross or indecent: for she was cautious lest fiery Jack should so resent it as to breed a quarrel ; for he would often say, " Dammee! though I don't much value my wife, yet nobody shall affront her, by G—!" and his sword was drawn on the least occasion, which was much the fashion in the latter end of King William's reign.'

A woman of rare talent and great personal charm—with a fine and well-proportioned figure, not too thin, and a smooth oval countenance, expressive eyes, and a fine complexion—she was the very genius of comedy. How one would have delighted to see her play Melantha to the Palamede of Wilks in Dryden's '*Marriage à la Mode!*' There is an admirable portrait of her, drawn in vivid colours, in that gallery of characters which Colley Cibber has bequeathed to us. I shall make bold to copy it :—

'She was mistress of more variety of humour,' he says, 'than I ever knew in any one woman actress. This variety too, was attended with an equal vivacity, which made her excellent in characters extremely different. As she was naturally a pleasant mimic, she had the skill to make that talent useful on the stage ; a talent which may be surprising in a conversation, and yet be lost when brought to the theatre. . . . When the elocution is round, distinct, voluble, and various, as Mrs Mountford's was, the mimic then is a great assistant to the actor. Nothing, though ever so barren, if within the bounds of nature, would be flat in her hands. She gave many heightening touches to characters but coldly written, and often made an author vain of his work, that in itself had but little merit. She was so fond of humour, in what her part soever to be found, that she would make no scruple of defacing her fair form to come heartily into it : for when she was eminent in several desirable characters of wit and humour in higher life, she would be in as much fancy, when descending into the antiquated Abigail of Fletcher, as when triumphing in all the airs and vain graces of a fine lady; a merit that few actresses care for. In a play of D'Urfey's, now forgotten, called 'The Western Lass,' which part she acted, she transformed her whole being, body, shape, voice, language, look, and features into almost another animal; with a strong Devonshire dialect, a broad, laughing voice, a poking head, round shoulders, an unconceiving eye, and the most bedizening, dowdy dress that ever covered the untrained limbs of a Joan Trot. To have seen her here, you would have thought it impossible the same creature could ever have been covered to what was as easy to her—the gay, the lively, and the desirable. Nor was her humour limited to her sex; for while her shape permitted, she was a more adroit pretty fellow than is usually seen upon the stage; her easy air, action, mien, and gesture, quite changed from the coif to the cocked-hat and cavalier in fashion. People were so fond of seeing her a man, that when the part of Bayes, in 'The Rehearsal,' had for some time lain dormant, she was desired to take it up, which I have seen her act with all the true coxcombly spirit and humour that the sufficiency of the character required.

But what found most employment for her whole various excellence at once, was the part of Melantha in '*Marriage à la Mode.*' Melantha is as finished an impertinent as ever fluttered in a drawing-room, and seems to contain the most complete system of female foppery that could possibly be crowded into the tortured form of a fine lady. Her language, dress, motion, manners, soul, and body, are in a continual hurry to be something more than is necessary or commendable. And though I doubt it will be a vain labour to offer you a just likeness of Mrs Mountford's action, yet the fantastic impression is still so strong in my memory that I cannot help saying something, though fantastically, about it. The first ridiculous airs that break from her are upon a gallant never seen before, who delivers her a letter from her father, recommending him to her good graces as an honourable lover. Here now one would think she might naturally show a little of the sex's decent reserve, though never so slightly covered. No, sir, not a tittle of it; modesty is the virtue of a poor-souled country gentlewoman; she is too much a court lady to be under so vulgar a confusion; she reads the letter, therefore, with a careless, dropping lip, and erected brow, humming it hastily over, as if she were impatient to outgo her father's commands by making a complete conquest of him at once; and that the letter might not embarrass her attack, crack! she crumbles it at once into her palm, and pours upon him her whole artillery of airs, eyes, and motion; down goes her dainty diving body to the ground, as if she were sinking under the conscious load of her own attractions; then launches into a flood of fine language and compliment, still playing her chest forward in fifty falls and risings, like a swan upon waving water; and to complete her impertinence, she is so rapidly fond of her own wit that she will not give her lover leave to praise it; silent assenting bows, and vain endeavours to speak, are all the show of the conversation he is admitted to, which at last he is relieved from by her engagement to half a score visits, which she swims from him to make, with a promise to return in a twinkling.

Mrs Verbruggen died in 1703; her husband in 1708.

With the death of William Mountford, the actor, Mrs BRACEGIRDLE was indirectly concerned. Like Mrs Mountford, she made her *début* in Charles the Second's reign, but her fame was won in later years. She was the ornament of the stage and the delight of the public, who respected as well as admired her, from 1680 to 1707, when her lustre paled before the rising glory of Mrs Oldfield. 'Never,' says Cibber, ' was any woman in such general favour of the spectators. . . . She was the darling of the theatre; for it will be no extravagant thing to say, scarce an audience saw her that were less than half of them lovers, without a suspected favourite among them; and though she may be said to have been the universal passion, and under the highest temptations, her constancy in resisting them served but to increase her admirers. It was even the fashion among the gay and young to have a taste or *tendre* for Mrs Bracegirdle.' The old, too, were not out of the fashion. One day the Earl of Burlington sent her a present of some fine old china. She told the servant he had made a mistake; that it was true the letter was for her, but the china was for his lady, to whom she bade him carry it. 'Lord!' exclaims Walpole, 'the Countess was so full of gratitude when her husband came home to dinner.' Lord Lovelace was another of her suitors; but so reserved and prudent was her conduct, that never a breath of scandal sullied it. To the number and variety of love-tokens and love-gifts which poured in upon her Dryden makes her allude in one of his epilogues:—

'I have had to-day a dozen *billets-doux*
From fops, and wits, and cits, and Bow Street beaux:
Some from Whitehall, but from the Temple more:
A Covent Garden porter brought me four.'

Congreve also entered the lists, and it is supposed that his addresses were not unwelcome to her; but she did not permit herself to be beguiled from the path of virtue. This he admits in some saucy verses, which, however, no man sincerely in love could ever have written.

The Diana of the stage—a title given to her by Aston, and one she well deserved—was the daughter of a Mr Justinian Bracegirdle, of Northamptonshire. She was born about 1674, and in some unexplained way passed into the charge of the actor Betterton and his wife, who brought her up to the stage. She acted as a page in 'The Orphan' when she was only six years old. Her advance was very rapid, and in 1690 she was already esteemed one of the finest actresses of her time. There was an indescribable charm in her manner, a rare refinement and expressiveness in her acting; and then, again, her personal advantages were of a very rare order. 'She was of a lovely height, with dark brown hair and eyebrows, black, sparkling eyes, and a fresh, blushy complexion; and whenever she exerted herself, had an involuntary flushing in her breast, neck, and face, having continually a cheerful aspect, and a fine set of even white teeth; never making an exit but that she left the audience in an imitation of her pleasant countenance. Genteel comedy was her chief essay, and that, too, when in men's clothes, in which she far surmounted all the actresses of that age.'

One Captain Richard Hill, a dissolute man about town, fell so violently in love with her person—her qualities of mind and heart he was unable to appreciate—that he resolved to carry her off by force, and persuaded Lord Mohun, who was as wild and wicked as himself, to assist. Having ascertained that she was to sup one evening with her mother and brother, at the house of a friend, Mr Page, in Prince's Street, Drury Lane, they hired six soldiers for the deed of violence, and posted them in convenient proximity. It was the 9th of November 1692, and about ten at night, as she left Mr Page's, the ruffians pounced upon her; but she screamed so loudly, and her brother and friend made so gallant a resistance, that the attempt failed. An excited crowd assembled; and Lord Mohun and Hill thought it prudent to undertake her escort to her residence in Howard Street, Strand. Close at hand lived Will Mountford, the comedian; and Mrs Bracegirdle, overhearing Captain Hill, who chose to think that Mountford was a favoured lover, indulging in violent threats against him, sent to Mrs Mountford instructions to warn her husband, who had gone home, to be on his guard. The gay young actor, apprehending no danger, came round into Howard Street, and saluted Lord Mohun. At the same moment Hill stepped up behind, struck him on the head, and before he could draw in his defence, ran his sword through the unfortunate man's body. The murderer fled to the Continent; but Lord Mohun was tried as an accomplice, and acquitted by threescore peers to fourteen. He afterwards fell, as everybody knows, in the fatal duel with the Duke of Hamilton.

Lord Macaulay is pleased to sneer at this brilliant lady's chastity. 'She seems to have been,' he says, 'a cold, vain, and interested coquette, who perfectly understood how much the influence of her charms was increased by the fame of a society which cost her nothing; and who could venture to flirt with a succession of admirers, in the just confidence that no flame which she might kindle in them would thaw her own ice.' The great Whig historian had his prejudices; and, for some reason or other, cherished one against Mrs Bracegirdle, which is certainly not justified by anything to be found in contemporary authorities of good repute.

She retired from the stage in 1707; but lived in the enjoyment of adequate means, and flattered by the attention of men of parts and women of virtue, until 1748.

Had Mrs BETTERTON figured in any great scandal, we should have known more of her history than now we do; the chronicles of the theatre being ever more devoted to tales of vice than records of virtue. For thirty years she did good service on the stage, representing, with skill and intelligence, a wide extent of characters. She was a Mistress Mary Saunderson, when, in 1662, she married Betterton, and was then about twenty-five years of age. It is remembered that, during the period of their courtship, she played Ophelia to his Hamlet; and on their dramatic love passages the audience dwelt with admiring interest, knowing what tender relations off the stage existed between them.

'She was so great a mistress of Nature,' says Colley Cibber, 'that even Mrs Barry, who acted Lady Macbeth after her, could not in that part, with all her superior strength and melody of voice, throw out those quick and careless strokes of terror, from the disorder of a guilty mind, which the other gave us, with a facility in her manner that rendered them at once tremendous and delightful.' Her powers as an artist she retained to the last. 'Time could not impair her skill, though he had brought her person to decay.'

Pepys always refers to this great actress as Ianthe, from the part she played in Davenant's 'Siege of Rhodes;' but it was in Shakespeare's plays she chiefly excelled, and in these she was 'without a rival.' It was due to her singular artistic merit, as well as her unblemished character, that she was chosen, in 1674, to instruct the Princesses Mary and Anne in elocution. Afterwards she was engaged to teach the Princess Anne to play the part of Semandra in Lee's noisy play of 'Mithridates,' which was acted before Charles II. and his court.

Far into the reign of Anne she retained the respect and regard of the public. It so befell that her declining years were darkened with the clouds of misfortune; but the heaviest affliction under which she succumbed was the death of her beloved husband in May 1710. The burden proved to be more than she could bear; she lost her reason, and survived him only eighteen months. In her distress and penury she was first befriended by Lady Elizabeth Hastings; but afterwards Queen Anne interposed, and granted her a pension—which she enjoyed only half a year. To those pathetic circumstances Steele, with characteristic sensibility, alludes (in *The Tatler*, No. 167):—'His wife,' he says, 'after a cohabitation of forty years in the strictest amity, has long pined away with a sense of his decay, as well in his person as in his little fortune; and, in proportion to that, she has herself decayed both in her health and reason. Her husband's death, added to her age and infirmities, would certainly have determined her life, but that the greatness of her distress has been her relief, by a present deprivation of her senses. This absence of reason is her best defence against age, sorrow, poverty, and sickness. I dwell upon this account so distinctly, in obedience to a certain great spirit [Lady Elizabeth Hastings], who hides her name, and has by letter applied to me to recommend to her some object of compassion, from whom she may be concealed.'

A name not less famous, though less pure, is that of ELIZABETH BARRY, the original Belvidera of Otway's 'Venice Preserved,' and the Zara of Congreve's 'Mourning Bride.'

This fair, frail, and fascinating lady was the daughter of Robert Barry, a barrister and a Royalist, who, in the Civil War, raised and equipped an army for the King, and was rewarded with the rank of Colonel. He fell into great poverty during the Protectorate, and bequeathed to his daughter, who was born in 1658, nothing but the memory of his unrewarded loyalty. As she grew in years and in maiden charms, Elizabeth found a friend in Sir William Davenant, who, much impressed by her beauty and vivacity, endeavoured to train her for the stage, which then offered to a handsome woman a successful, if too seldom an honourable, career. The natural talent was there, like the statue in the block of marble; but he did not succeed in bringing it forth, and she was thrice, it is said, rejected by the managers, as possessing none of the qualifications of an actress. This was not the judgment at which Rochester arrived,[1] and, according to Curll, he made a wager that in six months she should be the finest actress on the stage. Taking her under his protection, he lodged her in his house in Lincoln's Inn Fields, and educated her with equal skill and patience. He made her repeat every sentence of her author until she fully understood its meaning, and could render it with appropriate expression. The management of the voice, the employment of eloquent and becoming gesture, nothing was neglected which could assure her proficiency in her art;

---

[1] Aston asserts that 'she was woman to Lady Shelton of Norfolk (my good mother) when Lord Rochester took her on the stage.'

and, finally, to accustom her to the business of the stage, he took her through thirty rehearsals, twelve of which were 'dress rehearsals' of each of the characters she was to impersonate.

At length she made her *début*. She was received with coldness, and it was not until she played Isabella, the Hungarian Queen, in Lord Brooke's tragedy of 'Mustapha,' that she made a decided 'hit.' With her combined grace and dignity in this part, the Duchess of York—Mary of Modena—was so enraptured, that she engaged her as her instructess in elocution, and when she became Queen, presented her with her marriage dress and coronation robes. In 1680 she gained a foremost place amongst living actresses by her representation—very touching and tender it appears to have been—of Monimia in Otway's tragedy of 'The Orphan.' This was the nineteenth of her original characters, but the first which she indissolubly associated with her name. In 1682 all London flocked to see her Belvidera, and to be moved to tears by the sincerity of her pathos and the intensity of her conjugal devotedness. So true and so full of resource was her genius, that she would take the lay figure of the dramatist—as in the Cassandra of Dryden's 'Cleomenes' (1692)—and clothe it with flesh and blood, and infuse into it life and motion. 'Mrs Barry,' says the poet, in the preface to his play, 'always excellent, has in this tragedy excelled herself, and gained a reputation beyond any woman I have ever seen in the theatre.' 'In characters of greatness,' says Colley Cibber, 'Mrs Barry had a presence of elevated dignity; her mien and motion superb, and gracefully majestic; her voice full, clear, and strong, so that no violence of passion could be too much for her; and when distress or tenderness possessed her, she subsided into the most affecting melody and softness. In the art of exciting pity she had a power beyond all the actresses I have yet seen, or what your imagination can conceive. In scenes of anger, defiance, or resentment, while she was impetuous and terrible, she poured out the sentiment with an enchanting harmony; and it was this particular excellence for which Dryden made her the above-recited compliment upon her acting Cassandra in his 'Cleomenco.' She was the first person whose merit was distinguished by the indulgence of having an annual benefit play, which was granted to her alone in King James's time, and which did not become common to others till the division of this [the old Drury Lane] company, after the death of King William and Queen Mary.'

There is no art so fugitive as that of acting. The genius of a great actor lives only in the memory of those who have seen him,—who have watched his lightning play of countenance, the mobility of his gestures and attitudes, his living embodiment of character, his eloquent expression of feeling, sentiment, or passion. We can convey no accurate idea of all this to others; and the most felicitous and successful criticisms can do no more than impress upon us a vague idea of something beyond ordinary excellence. Admirable as is Charles Lamb's account of Elliston, or Cibber's of Mrs Bracegirdle, we cannot actually realise a definite conception of either. We know that Garrick must have been an artist of singular capacity and capability, because it is evident that he produced an immense effect upon his audiences; but we cannot compare him with any of his successors or predecessors, because no permanent standard of criticism exists or is possible. To the admirers of Edmund Kean he might have been as unacceptable as Edmund Kean might prove to the admirers of Mr Irving. We have nothing to guide us to a decision—we have nothing before us. To compare or contrast Turner with Claude, or Rembrandt with Titian, is easy enough for the skilled critic, because he has their works—their glowing canvases—to assist him to a judgment, and because art-criticism, as applied to painting or music, has its fixed rules and canons. The artist and the musician leave behind them imperishable monuments, but such is not the case with the great actors: they bequeath to posterity only a memory and a name.

We must take Mrs Barry, therefore, for what she was in the opinion of her contemporaries. One of her finest parts seems to have been that of Isabella in Southern's tragedy of 'The Fatal Marriage' (1694). In 1697 she enabled the public to appreciate her versatility by performing the two very opposite characters of Lady Brute in Vanbrugh's 'Provoked Wife,' and Zara in Congreve's 'Mourning Bride.' In 1703 she appeared as Calista in Rowe's tragedy of 'The Fair Penitent' (founded upon Massinger's 'Fatal Dowry'); and in 1705, Clarissa in Sir John Vanbrugh's comedy of 'The Confederacy.' About three years later, ill health compelled her to retire from the stage, her last new character of importance being that of Phædra, in Edmund Smith's tragedy (1708). She re-appeared for one night in the following year, to play with Mrs Bracegirdle; and she enacted Mrs Frail, in Congreve's 'Love for Love,' on the occasion of Betterton's benefit. Her last years were spent at Acton, in the enjoyment of the wealth she had acquired by her theatrical successes and the gifts of her lovers, and preserved by her excessive parsimony; and she died of fever, on the 7th of November 1713.'[1] She lies buried in Acton churchyard.

Davis says that the stage perhaps never produced four such handsome women at once as Mrs Barry, Mrs Bracegirdle, Mrs Mountford, and Mrs Bowman. When they stood together in the last scene of 'The Old Bachelor,' the

---

[1] Cibber says that in the delirium of her last hours she broke out into blank verse, alluding, apparently, to Queen Anne's creation of twelve peers at once. . . . 'Ha, ha! and so they make us lords by dozens!'

audience was struck with so fine a group of beauty, and broke into loud applause. Mrs Barry's great charm was expression. Her eyes and forehead were fine, but it was 'the mind, the music breathing o'er the face' that fixed the gaze of the beholder. The rich dark hair, drawn back from her brow, revealed its gracious curve. The mouth was infinitely sympathetic, though, according to Tony Aston, it was drawn a little too much on the right side. She was not below the average height, and her figure, though plump, was harmonious in proportion and exquisitely graceful in carriage.

Her powers were displayed to most advantage in tragedy. Two of her speeches, which by their forcible delivery always electrified her audiences, were:—' Oh, poor Castalio!' in Otway's 'Orphan,' and 'What mean my grieving subjects?' in Banks's 'Unhappy Favourite.' 'In comedy,' according to Aston, 'she was alert, easy, and genteel, pleasant in her face and action, filling the stage with variety of gesture.' She surrendered herself so entirely to the emotions of the characters she depicted, that 'in stage dialogues' she often turned pale or flushed red, as varying passions prompted.

In Nat Lee's 'Rival Queens; or, The Death of Alexander the Great,' she, on one occasion, played Roxana to Mrs Boutell's 'Statira.' A dispute had arisen between the two ladies as to the wearing of a certain veil, which the latter affirmed to belong to her part, and the stage manager decided in her favour. Both actresses went upon the stage with tempers fairly roused; and probably the anger and jealousy with which the dramatist endows the rival queens were never more faithfully represented. When, in the gardens of Semiramis, Roxana seizes her hated enemy, and a final struggle takes place, Mrs Barry exclaiming, ' Die, sorceress, die! and all my wrongs die with thee!' drove her keen dagger right through Statira's steel-bound stays. A slight wound was the result; and a considerable commotion. When the matter came to be investigated, Mrs Barry protested that she had been carried away by the excitement of the scene; but there were not wanting censorious tongues to declare that she enjoyed the punishment she had inflicted on a rival.

To dwell on the record of Mrs Barry's frailties would be humiliating and unprofitable. Like too many of the actresses of her time, she lived a life of sensual indulgence, which the contemporary gossip of the coffee-houses has probably represented in the darkest possible colours. She had a daughter by the Earl of Rochester, who died, however, before her mother. Tom Brown censures her avarice; others speak of her as cold and heartless; but the woman to whom poor Otway addressed the six pathetic letters preserved in his published works, could not have been without some singular attraction.

The unquestionable successor to Mrs Bracegirdle was the beautiful and notorious ANNE OLDFIELD, the daughter of an officer of the Guards, who [1] at an early age had been left an orphan, and had passed into the charge of her aunt, the hostess of the Mitre Tavern in St James's Market. It was there that Farquhar, one day, overheard her reading Beaumont and Fletcher's 'Scornful Lady,' with an animation, an intelligence, and a judiciousness of emphasis, which completely delighted him, and led him to speak of her talents to Sir John Vanbrugh. Thus she came to be introduced to Rich, the manager, who engaged her at a salary of fifteen shillings a week. This was in 1699, when she played Candiope in Dryden's 'Secret Love; or, The Maiden Queen.'[2] Her elocution was bad, however;

[1] She was born in Pall Mall in 1683.
[2] Revived by the Dramatic Students' Club, and played at the Court Theatre, London, January 19, 1886.

her delivery forced and artificial; so that for a twelve-month she remained almost a mute and unheeded, till Sir John Vanbrugh gave her the part of Alinda in 'The Pilgrim.' Gradually her powers developed under the combined influences of study and experience; and she needed only an opportunity to show the theatrical world of what she was capable. Such an opportunity was afforded by the death of Mrs Verbruggen, when her character of Leonora in Craven's 'Sir Courtly Nice' fell to Mrs Oldfield. Cibber, who played the hero, tells us that 'he had so cold an expectation from her abilities' that he was unwilling to rehearse with her the scenes in which he figured as Sir Courtly. 'We ran them over, he says, 'with a mutual inadvertency of one another. I seemed careless, as concluding that any assistance I could give her would be to little or no purpose; and she muttered out her words in a sort of misty manner at my low opinion of her. But when the play came to be acted, she had a just occasion to triumph over the error of my judgment, by the (almost) amazement that her unexpected performance awaked me to; so forward and sudden a step into nature I had never seen; and what made her performance more valuable was that I knew it all proceeded from her own understanding, untaught and unassisted by any one more experienced actor.'

So great was her triumph—such a potency of comic spirit did she manifest—that Cibber immediately set to work to finish his play of 'The Careless Husband,' which he had previously thrown aside in despair of finding any actress able to do justice to the character of Lady Betty Modish. It was produced in 1709; and the public enthusiastically declared, with charming unanimity, that she was the most perfect lady of fashion the stage had ever seen. To her brilliant acting its success was largely due. 'There are many sentiments in the character,' says Cibber, 'that I may almost say were originally her own, or only dressed with a little more care than when they negligently fell from her lively humour. Had her birth placed her in a higher rank of life, she had certainly appeared in reality, what in this play she only excellently acted, an agreeable gay woman of quality, a little too conscious of her natural attractions. . . . After her success in this character, all that nature had given her of the actress seemed to have risen to its full perfection; but the variety of her power could not be known until she was seen in as great variety of characters, which, as fast as they fell to her, she equally excelled in. Authors had much more from her performance than they had reason to hope for from what they had written for her; and none had less than another, but as their genius in the parts they allotted her was more or less elevated. In the wearing of her person,' he adds, 'she was particularly fortunate; her figure was always improving to her thirty-sixth year; but her excellence in acting was never at a stand, and the last new character she shone in, Lady Townly, was a proof that she was still able to do more, if more could have been done for it.'

Her rare gifts of mind and person were accompanied by a charming modesty. She never undertook any part in which she wished to excel, without being 'importunately desirous' of all the help that others could give her. She was entirely free from the airs and affectations in which so many leading actresses have been prone to indulge; less presuming, says Cibber, than several who had not half her pretensions to be troublesome. It was some time before she could be persuaded that she had any talent for tragedy, and she would say, with that musical, infectious laugh of hers,—'Oh, give those parts to Porter, she can put on a tragedy face better than I can.' Yet in the parts of Jane Shore and Calista she moved the audience to tears by the truth and force and simple pathos of her acting. 'The excellent clear voice of passion,' writes Chetwood. 'her piercing, flaming eye, with manner and action suitable, used to make me shrink with awe.' The last part she created was Sophonisba, in Thomson's tragedy of that name ; and the poet afterwards owned that ' she excelled what even in the fondness of an author I could wish or imagine.'

But it was in comedy that she was most herself. It was in comedy—and especially in such parts as Lady Townly in ' The Provoked Husband '—that all her powers found a fit field of exercise ; that she could employ all her natural and acquired graces ;—could be gay and *riante*, saucy without impertinence, easy without carelessness—a fine lady, and yet with something womanly at bottom—in a word, Anne Oldfield.

I cannot pretend that her private life was without moral flaws, though she never offended like a Barry or a Woffington. At one time she lived under the protection of a Mr Maynwaring, and after his death under that of General Churchill, to whom she appears to have been loyally attached. ' I hear you and the General are married,' said Queen Caroline to her one day. ' Madam, the General keeps his own secrets.' Her dubious position did not affect the estimation in which she was held by the best circles, where you may be sure she was fully able to hold her own. ' I have often seen her,' says Cibber, ' in private societies, where women of the best rank might have borrowed some part of her behaviour without the least diminution of their sense or dignity.'

Mrs Oldfield had a great taste in, and a strong liking for, dress,—not, indeed, for itself, but because it helped to bring out her gifts of person. ' Flavia,' says Steele, ' is ever well dressed, and always the genteelest woman you meet ; but the make of her mind very much contributes to the ornament of her body. She has the greatest simplicity of manners of any of her sex. This makes everything look native about her, and her clothes are so exactly fitted, that they appear, as it were, part of her person.' Pope, in a well-known passage, takes her as one of his examples of the ruling passion strong in death, and represents her, when dying, as giving particular directions for the special adornment of her dead body:—

> '" Odious! in woollen! 'twould a saint provoke,"
> Were the last words that poor Narcissa spoke;
> " No, let a charming chintz and Brussels lace
> Wrap my cold limbs and shade my lifeless face;
> One would not, sure, be frightful when one's dead—
> And, Betty, give this cheek a little red." '

But one of her biographers notes that this ghastly death toilette was appointed by the order of the said 'Betty,' her old and faithful servant—an actress named Mrs Saunders, who played old maids' and widows' parts:—'As the nicety of dress was her delight when living, she was as nicely dressed after her decease, being, by Mrs Saunders' direction, thus laid in her coffin:—she had on a very fine Brussels lace head; a Holland shift, with tucker and double ruffles of the same lace; a pair of new kid gloves, and her body wrapped up in a winding-sheet.'

Her last appearance on the stage was on the 28th of April 1780; she died on the 23d of the following October, and after lying in state in the Jerusalem Chamber, was buried in Westminster Abbey, her pall being supported by peers. She left several children, who married into noble houses.

The last great actress of Queen Anne's reign who claims notice in these pages, is Mrs PORTER. Betterton saw her act, when a child, the Genius of Britain, in a Lord Mayor's pageant, and was so pleased by her quick intelligence, that he undertook to train her for the stage. She was so small at this time that he used to threaten, if she did not perform her tasks, to put her in the basket of one of the orange-women, and cover her with a vine-leaf. Her career on the stage was eminently respectable. During Mrs Betterton's life, she played only secondary characters; but after her death she acceded to the principal *rôles* in the tragic drama. Though not handsome, she was tall, with a good figure, and a dignified presence; her voice was naturally harsh, but by diligent practice she had contrived to soften and vary its intonation; her grasp of character was complete, and she sounded the depths of passion with unfailing power. An artist to her very finger-ends, she knew how to conceal her art; and realised her conceptions with a truth and force that could hardly be surpassed. Her career was a long one; she made her *début* on the stage in 1699, and her last appearance in 1742. So that she who in her youth had played to Steele and Addison, lived to play in her later womanhood to Burke, and Walpole, and Dr Johnson. The illustrious author of *The Rambler* informed Mrs Siddons, who may be considered her successor, that in the vehemency of tragic rage he had never seen her equalled. She was specially happy in the grace and dignity with which she assumed the regal character; and playgoers long loved to talk of her Queen Katherine in ' Henry VIII.,' and her Queen Elizabeth in 'The Unhappy Favourite.' On one occasion, when she was performing in the latter part, Queen Anne, who was present in the stage box, accidentally dropped her fan; and it is said that, in her full possession of the character she was representing, Mrs Porter turned with a stately air to an attendant, and said, ' Take up our sister's fan.' It is added that it was only the applause of the audience which recalled her to the real nature of the situation. But a very similar anecdote has been invented in reference to Shakespeare and Queen Elizabeth.

In addition to the parts we have mentioned, Mrs Porter was excellent as Hermione in Phillips's 'Distressed Mother,' and Olivia in 'Jane Shore.'

She died in 1762, when she must have been nearly eighty years of age.

CHAPTER III.

MUSIC AND MUSICIANS IN QUEEN ANNE'S REIGN.

Introduction of Operatic Representations—'Rosamond'—Italian Opera—'Hydaspes'—Nicolini and the Lion—'Rinaldo'—Various Operas—Operatic Airs—Handel's Operas—The Singers—John Abell—Richard Leveridge — Lawrence — Lewis Ramondon — Margarita de l'Epine — Mrs Tofts—The Cavaliere Nicolini—The Musical Composers — Congreve's Masque— The Competitors—John Weldon — John Eccles—Daniel Purcell—Godfrey Finger—Dr Blow—Dean Aldrich — Dr Croft — Jeremiah Clark — Maurice Greene — Charles King — Richard King—Nicolo Haym—Harry Carey—Thomas Britton—'The Musical Small-Coal Man'— Dr Pepusch—Galliard— Dr Tudway— Marshall—Dr Turner—Some celebrated Organists.

FOR the musical student, the reign of Queen Anne has a special and peculiar interest, because it witnessed the establishment of Opera in England, and a consequent development on a large scale of musical taste and musical ability. As early as 1704 we read of a new musical entertainment, written by Motteux, and entitled 'Britain's Happiness,' which partook of the operatic character. It was produced almost simultaneously at Drury Lane and Lincoln's Inn Fields; and its reception seems to have been so favourable as to encourage the introduction in the following season of a full-blown opera, on a foreign model. On the 13th of January 1705, the public were invited to Drury Lane to pronounce judgment upon 'Arsinoe, Queen of Cyprus,'—an English version, by Motteux, of an Italian opera (first performed at Venice in

1677), set to music by Thomas Clayton. This Clayton was a member of the royal band, who in Italy had acquired 'a little taste and much vanity,' and bringing home a number of Italian airs, he altered and adapted them, worked them up into 'Arsinoe,' and claimed them as his own. The singers in 'Arsinoe' were all English; and the whole of the narrative was given in recitative. Its success was complete: and in December 1707, another opera, that of 'Camilla'—translated by Owen M'Swiney, and the music (chiefly from Buononcini) arranged by Nicolo Haym—was also well received. The principal parts were thus distributed:—*Latinus*, Mr Turner; *Preneste*, Signora Margarita de l'Epine; *Turnus*, Signor Valentini;[1] *Metius*, Mr Ramondon; *Linico*, Mr Leveridge; *Camilla*, Mrs Tofts; *Lavinia*, The Baroness; and *Tullia*, Mrs Lindsey. The English vocalists sang in English; the Italians also in their own language—a confusion of tongues which must have had a singular and distressing effect.

Meanwhile, a new and stately theatre had been erected in the Haymarket by Sir John Vanbrugh, who, to defray the expense, had raised a subscription from thirty persons of quality of one hundred pounds each. The management, at first was in the hands of Vanbrugh and Congreve; and, to take advantage of the new direction of the public taste, they opened, on the 9th of April 1705, with a 'pastoral opera,' 'The Temple of Love,' translated from the Italian by Motteux, the music by Signor Saggioni. This had been preceded, according to Hawkins, by an entertainment called 'The Loves of Ergasto,' with music by Greber. The entertainment had proved a failure, and the pastoral opera met with no greater success. A similar ill-fortune befell D'Urfey's whimsical extravaganza, 'Wonders in the Sun; or, The Kingdom of the

[1] Valentini Urbani, a male soprano (an *evirato*).

Birds,' which did not pay half the cost of its getting up. It was illustrated, we are told, ' with a great variety of songs in all kinds by several of the most eminent wits of the age,' and these were set to music by English composers. But the public would have none of it: they wanted opera undiluted ; and they flocked to Drury Lane to hear ' Camilla ; ' though it cannot be said that its libretto possessed any potency of poetical attraction. Here are two brief samples of its nakedness :—

> ' Since you from death thus save me,
>   I'll live for you alone ;
>   The life you freely gave me,
>   That life is not my own.

> Charming fair,
>   For thee I languish,
>   But bless the hand that gave the blow ;
>   With equal anguish,
> Each swain despairs,
> And when she appears
>   Streams forget to flow.'

The popularity of these operatic representations grew so formidable to the old theatrical companies, that in 1707 a subscription was actually opened ' for the better support of the comedians acting in the Haymarket, and to enable them to keep up the diversion of plays under a separate interest from operas.' The new idol of the public is described in caustic terms by Colley Cibber, who says that ' the Italian Opera was a long time stealing into England ; but in so rude a disguise, and unlike itself as possible, in a lame, hobbling translation into our language, with false quantities, or metre out of measure, to its own original notes, sung by our own unskilful voices, with graces misapplied to almost every sentiment, and with action lifeless and unmeaning through every character.' In his *Essay on the Operas after the Italian Manner*, John Dennis attacks it with characteristic surliness:—'If that is truly the most Gothic which is most opposed to Antique, nothing can be more Gothic than an opera, since nothing can be more opposed to the ancient tragedy than the modern tragedy in music, because the one is reasonable, the other ridiculous; the one is artful, the other absurd! the one beneficial, the other pernicious; in short, the one natural, and the other monstrous. And the modern tragedy in music is as much opposed to the chorus, which is the musical part of the ancient tragedy, as it is in the episodic: because, in the chorus, the music is always great and solemn, in the opera 'tis often most trifling and most effeminate; in the chorus the music is only for the sake of the sense; in the opera the sense is most apparently for the sake of the music.' He thus began the unprofitable controversy which, even in our own days, shows occasional symptoms of revival.

The inclination of the public, however, is stronger than the wrath of critics; and the ingenious Mr Addison, with all the honours of his poem of *The Campaign* upon him, did not scruple to yield to it. In 1707 his opera of 'Rosamond' was put upon the Drury Lane stage, with a great flourish of trumpets. The cast comprised the best English singers of the day:—*Queen Eleanor*, Mrs Tofts; *Page*, Mr Holcombe; *Sir Trusty*, Mr Leveridge; *Grideline*, Mrs Lindsey; *Rosamond*, Signora Maria Gallia;[1] *King Henry II.*, Mr Hughes; *War*, Mr Lawrence; and *Peace*, Miss Reading. The versification is easy and agreeable; but there is no dramatic force in the piece—the characters are without form and substance—the comic personages do not happen to be comic—and situations in themselves effective, are marred by their unskilful treatment. Partly for these reasons, and partly on account of

[1] Sister of Margarita de l'Epine.

the triviality of Clayton's music, 'Rosamond' ran only three nights. I insert a specimen of Clayton's composition :—

We may note that 'Rosamond' was more successful in 1733, when it was produced with new and charming music by Dr Arne. The airs, 'No, no, 'tis Decreed,' 'Was Ever

Nymph like Rosamond?' and 'Rise, Glory, Rise,' were for a long time popular favourites.

To 'Rosamond' succeeded the opera of 'Thomyris, Queen of Scythia,' written by Motteux. The songs in it were adapted to music by Buononcini, Scarlatti, Steffani, Gasparini, and Albinoni, selected by John James Heidegger, who had undertaken the conduct of the opera in the Haymarket, and had had the address to secure a large subscription from the nobility and gentry to enable him to put 'Thomyris' on the stage. It could not compete, however, with 'Camilla,' and its combination of first-rate vocalists. Its performance was suspended; and, in the following year, it was transferred to Drury Lane, where, during six weeks, it was presented alternately with 'Camilla.' At this time the Drury Lane operatic company was very strong; including Valentini Urbani, Hughes, Lawrence, Leveridge, with Margarita de l'Epine, Mrs Tofts, and Mrs Lindsey.

Next came a pastoral called 'The Triumph of Love.' produced at the Haymarket by Valentini. Motteux translated it from the Italian of Cardinal Ottoboni; the music was by Francesco Gasparini and Carlo Cesarini Giovanni. A number of choruses were introduced, with dances (*analogues*), after the French manner: but the experiment failed, and Valentini abandoned the cares of management to resume his profession of a singer. In the following winter appeared the last of these hybrid Anglo-Italian mixtures, 'Pyrrhus and Demetrius,' written by Owen Swiney (or M'Swiney), with music by Scarlatti, arranged by Nicolo Haym, who composed a new overture and several additional songs of considerable merit. In this opera the celebrated singer Nicolini made his *début* on the English stage. At this time the orchestra included Charles Dieupart, Pepusch. and Leoillet, on the harpsichord; John Baniste, William Corbet, and Signor Claudio, violinists; Haym, violoncello; and Saggioni, double bass.

'Pyrrhus and Demetrius' incurred the ridicule of Steele in *The Tatler*. 'Letters from the Haymarket inform us,' he says, 'that the opera was performed with great applause. This intelligence is not very acceptable to us friends of the theatre; for the stage being an entertainment of the reason and all our faculties, this way of being pleased with the suspense of them for three hours together, and being given up to the shallow satisfaction of the eyes and ears only, seems to arise rather from the degeneracy of our understanding than an improvement of our diversions. That the understanding has no part in the pleasure is evident, from what these letters very positively assert, to wit, that a great part of the performance was done in Italian; and a great critic (John Dennis) fell into fits in the gallery, at seeing, not only time and place, but languages and nations, confused in the most incorrigible manner. His spleen is so extremely moved on this occasion, that he is going to publish another treatise against operas, which, he thinks, have already inclined us to thoughts of peace, and, if tolerated, must infallibly dispirit us from carrying the war on.'

In March 1709, an opera called 'Clotilda,' with music selected by Heidegger, from Buononcini, Scarlatti, and Conti, was unsuccessful. In the following November, a difference having arisen between Rich, the patentee of Drury Lane, and his principal performers, the latter, including Wilks, Cibber, Doggett, and Mrs Oldfield, were engaged at the Haymarket, where, for some months, operatic and dramatic representations were given alternately. On January 10th, 1710, the operatic company appeared in 'Almahide,' in which songs, both in Italian and English, were adapted to Italian airs; the former being sung by Nicolini, Valentini, Cassani, Isabella

Girardeau, and la Margharita,—the latter by Doggett, the comedian. 'The songs given to Nicolini and Margharita are more rapid and difficult than any in the preceding dramas; and if their style does not evince much advance in the great secret of expressing the passions, it at least demonstrates the improved power of vocal execution.'

In March, the public were amused with the opera of 'Hydaspes'; or, '*L'Idaspe Fideli*,' set to music by Francesco Mancini, a Roman composer. Its scenic effects furnished Addison with a theme for one of his liveliest papers in *The Spectator* (No. 13), which, it is said, so diverted the Pope that, on reading it, he laughed till his sides shook. 'There is nothing,' he says, 'that of late years has afforded matter of greater amusement to the town than Signor Nicolini's combat with a lion in the Haymarket, which has been very often exhibited to the general satisfaction of most of the nobility and gentry in the kingdom of Great Britain.' He proceeds to describe the various individuals who have successively represented the king of beasts. The first, he says, was a candle-snuffer, a fellow of a testy, choleric temper, who overdid his part, and would not suffer himself to be killed so easily as he ought to have done. He declared that he would wrestle with Mr Nicolini for what he pleased, out of his lion's skin; and grew so surly, that it was thought advisable to dismiss him, lest he should do mischief. Besides, it was objected against him, that he reared himself so high upon his hinder paws, and walked in so erect a posture, that he looked more like an old man than a lion.

Addison continues:—'The second lion was a tailor—a mild and peaceable man in his profession—who proved to be "too sheepish" for his part; so much so, that, after a short and modest walk upon the stage, he would fall at the first touch of Hydaspes,—not venturing to grapple with him, and giving him no opportunity of exhibiting "his variety of Italian trips." At present,' adds the essayist, 'the acting lion is a country gentleman, who does it for his diversion, but desires his name may be concealed. He says very handsomely, in his own excuse, that he does not act for gain; that he indulges an innocent pleasure in it; and that it is better to pass away an evening in this manner than in gaming and drinking; but at the same time says, with a very agreeable raillery upon himself, that if his name should be known, the ill-natured world might call him "the ass in the lion's skin." This gentleman's temper is made out of such a happy mixture of the mild and the choleric, that he outdoes both his predecessors, and has drawn together greater audiences than have been known in the memory of man. . . .

'I would not be thought,' adds the essayist, 'in any part of this relation, to reflect upon Signor Nicolini, who, in acting this part, only complies with the wretched taste of his audience; he knows very well that the lion has many more admirers than himself; as they say of the famous equestrian statue on the Pont Neuf at Paris, that more people go to see the horse than the king who sits upon it. On the contrary, it gives me a just indignation to see a person whose action gives new majesty to kings, resolution to heroes, and softness to lovers, thus sinking from the greatness of his behaviour, and degraded into the character of the London Prentice. I have often wished that our tragedians would copy after this great master in action. Could they make the same use of their arms and legs, and inform their faces with as significant looks and passions, how glorious would our English tragedy appear with that action which is capable of giving a dignity to the forced thoughts, cold conceits, and unnatural expressions of an Italian opera. In the meantime, I have related this combat of the lion, to show what are at present the reigning entertainments of the politer part of Great Britain.'

We have already referred to Aaron Hill's management of the Haymarket Theatre. Its noteworthy feature was the engagement of Handel to set to music his opera of 'Rinaldo.' The great composer accomplished his task in a fortnight; and 'Rinaldo' was produced on the 24th of February 1711. This was, unquestionably, the finest opera the stage in any country had as yet seen; and its success was as enduring as it was brilliant. On its first production, it was played fifteen nights consecutively. In the following year, it had a second run of nine nights; a third in 1715; a fourth in 1717; while abroad it commanded an enthusiastic reception at Hamburg and Naples. To ears hitherto accustomed only to the bald and *jejune* musical commonplaces of illiterate composers, Handel's beautiful arias came like revelations of a new world of light and melody. Like everything possessed of true beauty, such airs as 'Lascia ch'io pianga,' 'Cara sposa,' 'Vieni o cara,' 'Figlia mia,' 'Il tricerbero umiliato,' and the splendid march, afterwards introduced by Dr Pepusch into 'The Beggar's Opera' ('Hark! I hear the sound of coaches!') will never be forgotten.

In this year, on the 10th of November, the opera theatre opened with a repetition of 'Almahide,' in which Mrs Barbier, a new English singer,[1] assumed the character of Almanzar, originally sustained by Valentini. The sensitive diffidence displayed by this lady on her first appearance gave occasion to some sympathetic remarks

---

[1] Mistress or Miss Barbier afterwards performed Daphne in Hughes's masque, set to music by Pepusch, and performed in 1716. Her last appearance on the stage was in the pantomime of 'Perseus and Andromeda' in 1729. She is described as a very capricious and indiscreet, but charming woman :—

'Brown skin, her eyes of sable hue;
Angel when pleased, when vexed a shrew.'

by Addison (*The Spectator*, No. 231). Commenting upon 'the awe' that public assemblies often strike on such as are obliged to exert any talent before them, he says:— 'As this sudden desertion of one's self shows a diffidence which is not displeasing, it implies at the same time the greatest respect to an audience that can be. It is a sort of mute eloquence, which pleads for their favour much better than words could do; and we find their generosity naturally moved to support those who are in so much perplexity to entertain them. I was greatly pleased with a late instance of this kind at the opera of "Almahide," in the encouragement given to a young singer, whose more than ordinary concern on her first appearance recommended her no less than her agreeable voice and just performance.'

In the following December an opera, called 'Antiochus,' originally composed for the theatre at Venice by Francesco Gasparini, was produced; but it did not command the approval of the public, and 'Rinaldo' was revived. On February 1712, another opera, composed by Gasparini for the Venetian theatre, entitled '*Ambleto*' (Hamlet), was put on the stage. But Gasparini's music seems to have been mutilated and modified, and a variety of airs introduced from other sources, a barbarous proceeding which explains and justifies the failure of the opera. In May appeared an English opera, 'Calypso and Telemachus,' written by John Hughes (author of 'The Siege of Damascus') on the Homeric story as adapted by Fénélon, and set to music by Galliard, a German musician well acquainted with the English taste. The dialogue and songs are much above the average, and Galliard's setting is judicious and animated, but the opera ran only five nights.

A new season began at the Queen's Theatre (as the Opera House was then called) in the ensuing November with Gasparini's '*Il Trionfo d'Amore*' ('Love's Triumph'), which, after two performances, was succeeded by '*Il Pastor Fido*' ('The Faithful Shepherd'), written by Rossi, and composed by Handel.

Here we may pause to note the arbitrary conditions under which the composer of an opera wrought in those early years of the eighteenth century. Even as regarded the distribution of the voices he employed, existing conventionalities limited him. His *dramatis personæ* were six in number—three men and three women; sometimes a fourth male was added. The *prima donna*, or first woman, was always a high soprano, and the second or third a contralto. Occasionally a woman was permitted to sing a man's part, especially if her voice, like that of Mrs Barbier or Mrs Anastasia Robinson, chanced to be a low one; but it was an unchanged and unchangeable law that the *primo uomo*, or first man, should be an artificial soprano (*evirato*), though the part he had to play was that of Theseus or Hercules. The second man was either a soprano, like the first, or an artificial contralto, and the third was a tenor. When a fourth male character was made use of, the part assigned to him was generally that of a bass; but operas were frequently so constructed that, as in Handel's 'Teseo,' all the male singers were artificial sopranos and contraltos, who monopolised the principal airs, and upon whose popularity the success of the piece depended.

The airs entrusted to these several performers were arranged in five unvarying classes, each distinguished (says Mr Rockstro) by some well-defined peculiarity of style, though not of general design: the same mechanical form, consisting of a first and second part, followed by the indispensable *da capo*, governing them all.

1st. The *Aria cantabile*, a quiet and pathetic slow movement, with its accompaniment generally confined to a plain thorough-bass, the chords of which were filled in upon the harpsichord.

2d. The *Aria di portamento*, also a slow movement, with a strongly-marked rhythm, and a symmetrical melody, freely interspersed with sustained and swelling notes. The accompaniment rarely extended beyond a well-phrased thorough-bass, with one or two violins, used generally in the symphonies.

3d. The *Aria di mezzo carattere* was capable of much variety of treatment, but, as a rule, showed less pathos than the *Aria cantabile*, and less dignity than the *Aria di portamento*, while expressing greater depths of passion than either. The accompaniment introduced all the strings, and sometimes the oboes and other wind instruments. As a fine example of this class, Mr Rockstro indicates the 'Vieni torna, idolo mio' in Handel's 'Teseo,' sung by Margarita de l'Epine in 1713.

4th. The *Aria parlante*, was of a freer, fuller, and more declamatory character than either of the preceding, and its accompaniment was usually very elaborate.

And 5th. The *Aria di bravura*, or *d'agilità*, explains itself. It was a dashing allegro, filled with passages of rapid position, adapted to exhibit the executive powers of the performer. 'Some of the passages written for Elizabeth Pilotti Schiavonetti, Cuzzoni, Faustina, Nicolini, Farinelli, and other great singers of the period, were so amazingly difficult, that few artists of the present day would care to attack them without a considerable amount of preparatory study, though it is certain that the vocalists for whom they were originally composed overcame them with ease.'

The opera, or '*drama tragica*,' of 'Teseo,' one of the best of Handel's operatic compositions, was performed on the 21st of January 1713, 'with all the scenes, decorations, flights, and machines.' It ran for twelve nights, the last performance (May 16th) being for the composer's benefit.

In January 1714 was produced 'Dorinda'; but it did not awaken any public enthusiasm. It was followed by 'Creso,' a *pasticcio*—a thing of shreds and patches, without coherence; and by 'Arminio,' the name of whose composer is unknown. In May 1715, Handel brought forward his 'Amadigi,' or 'Amadis of Gaul,' which was received with considerable favour. In this opera was introduced 'the effective and happy practice,' as it has been characterised, ' of arranging the violin parts in octaves.'

The season of 1716 bore fruit in 'Lucio Vero,' which contrasted strongly with 'Pyrrhus and Demetrius,' revived. In the course of it, 'Cleartis,' a new opera, by an anonymous composer, was thirteen times performed; and at its close was repeated 'Amadis,' between the acts of which a new 'symphony' was executed by Signor Attilio Ariosti (the operatic composer), on the viola d'amour, an instrument which had never before been heard in England. In the following January 'Rinaldo' was revived, and repeated ten times. Then 'Amadis' was repeated 'by command;' and in March a new opera called 'Venceslao,' written by Apostolo Zeno, the music by an anonymous composer, struggled through three representations.

From this date operatic performances ceased until 1720, when a movement was made for placing them on a broader and securer basis. A fund of fifty thousand pounds was raised by subscription, and the Royal Academy of Music founded, under the direction of a governor, deputy-governor, and twenty directors. But our historical survey is carrying us too far beyond our limits, and with this brief note of the establishment of an institution which has largely contributed to the progress of the musical art in England, I proceed to another branch of my subject.

THE SINGERS.

Among the most popular in the reign of 'Good Queen Anne' was JOHN ABEL or ABELL, who attained distinction both on the concert-platform and the stage. He was probably educated in the choir of the Chapel Royal, to which establishment he was appointed as 'gentleman extraordinary' in 1679. His fine counter-tenor, and his skill as a lutanist, obtained the frequent and liberal recognition of Royalty; and it is affirmed that between 1679 and 1688 he received in gifts no less a sum than seven hundred and forty pounds (probably equal to two thousand pounds at the present value of money). Through the munificence of Charles II., who was a liberal patron of music and musicians, he was sent to Italy to complete his studies. On his return to England, Evelyn had the pleasure of hearing him (January 24, 1683). 'After supper,' he writes, 'came in the famous treble, Mr Abel. . . . I never heard a more excellent voice, and would have sworn it had been a woman's, it was so high, and so well and skilfully managed.' Abell continued in the service of the Chapel until the Revolution of 1688, when his attachment to Romanism led to his removal. Afterwards he travelled on the Continent, and visited France, Holland, Germany, and even Poland—an itinerant musician, supporting himself by his lute and voice. He underwent a curious experience during his sojourn at Warsaw. The king sent for him to his Court. Abell excused himself from going, but on being cautioned that he would have everything to dread from the royal resentment, he made an apology, and offered to attend the king on the day following. 'Upon his arrival at the palace, he was seated in a chair in the middle of the spacious hall, and immediately drawn up to a great height. Presently the king with his attendants appeared in a gallery opposite to him, and at the same instant a number of wild bears were turned in. The king bade him then choose whether he would sing or be let down among the bears. Abell chose the former, and declared afterwards that he never sang so well in his life.'[1]

Abell came back to England in the last years of Dutch William's reign, and throughout that of Anne continued to hold a high position in his art. To his eccentricity of character, as well as to his rare musical gifts, Congreve bears witness (December 10, 1700): 'Abell,' he writes, 'is here: has a cold at present, and is always whimsical, so that when he will sing or not upon the stage is very disputable, but he certainly sings beyond all creatures upon earth, and I have heard him very often, both abroad and since he came over.'

Abell had some ability as a composer. There is an announcement of *The Queen's Coronation Song*, as 'composed and sung by Mr Abell.' He had just before published, in 1700, *A Collection of Songs in Several Languages*, which he dedicated to William III.; and *A Collection of Songs in English*. The latter contains a remarkable poem of his own inditing, in which he describes, with a good deal of egotism, some of his experiences of Continental travel.

The date of his death is not recorded; but as late as 1716 he gave a concert at Stationers' Hall, where, in Queen Anne's time, musical entertainments seem frequently to have been given.

RICHARD LEVERIDGE, a bass singer, long famous for his deep, resonant voice, was born in 1670; and probably, like most of his musical contemporaries, received his education in connection with the Chapel Royal. One of the earliest notices of him extant refers to his fine singing in Dr Blow's

---

[1] This incident appears very apocryphal.

'Te Deum' and 'Jubilate,' composed for the St Cecilia's Day Festival in 1685. He was engaged as principal bass at Drury Lane Theatre from 1705 to 1707, and took part in the succession of Anglo-Italian operas on which I have commented,—'Arsinoe,' 'Camilla,' 'Rosamond,' and 'Thomyris.' He migrated to the Queen's Theatre in 1708, and sang in various operatic works. In Handel's 'Pastor Fido' he 'created'—to use the slang of the day— the principal character (1712). Afterwards he was engaged by Rich, and for nearly thirty years sang in masque and pantomime at Covent Garden and Lincoln's Inn Fields with few signs of diminishing vigour. In 1730, at the age of sixty, he had issued a challenge to sing against any bass singer in England, for a sum of one hundred guineas. He was upwards of eighty years old before he retired from the stage, and to the very last his audiences appear to have listened to him with pleasure.

Leveridge had a considerable knowledge of his art, and composed several very good Bacchanalian songs. In 1699, along with Clarke and Dan Purcell, he wrote the music for Motteux's 'Island Princess; or, The Generous Portuguese,' an adaptation from Beaumont and Fletcher. In 1716 he compiled and set to music a comic masque of 'Pyramus and Thisbe,' which was, of course, taken from 'The Midsummer Night's Dream.' It was performed with some success at the Lincoln's Inn Fields Theatre.

It was in or about 1726, that, to increase his income, he opened a coffee-house in Tavistock Street; but the speculation did not turn into his coffers a Pactolian flood; and during the last years of his life, he fell into such poverty that he was indebted for a sustenance to the annual subscriptions of a few friends. He died on the 22d of March 1788 at an advanced age.

LAWRENCE was a tenor singer, whose knowledge of

Italian enabled him to take part in Italian Opera; but he fades away into oblivion after 1717. HUGHES, a counter-tenor, played the leading *rôle* until he was superseded by Valentini. The Italian singers, even when their natural gifts were inferior, triumphed over their rivals by their superiority of method.

LEWIS RAMONDON made his first appearance on the stage in the opera of 'Arsinoe.' He was the composer of several attractive airs, one of which ('All you that must take a leap in the dark') Pepusch adapted to a song in 'The Beggar's Opera.' Ramondon's career on the stage extended from 1704 to 1711.

Among female singers, the largest share of popularity at this time was enjoyed by FRANCESCA MARGARITA DE L'EPINE. She was a native of Tuscany, and came from Italy into England in charge of a German musician named Greber—whence she was familiarly known as Greber's Peg. An advertisement in *The London Gazette* (No. 2834) intimated 'that the Italian Lady (that is lately come over, that is so famous for her singing), though it has been reported that she will sing no more in the consert in York Buildings; Yet this is to give notice that next Tuesday, January 10th, she will sing there, and so continue during the season.' A fortnight later it was announced that she would sing not only at York Buildings every Tuesday, but on Thursday, in Freeman's Yard, Cornhill. On the first of June 1703, the programme of the Lincoln's Inn Theatre advertised that 'Signora Francesca Margarita de l'Epine would sing, being positively the last time of her singing on the stage during her stay in England.' She continued to sing, however, throughout the season; and her stay in England lasted until her death.

On the 29th of January, 1704, Margarita made her first

appearance at Drury Lane, and was cordially received. On her next appearance, a cabal was formed against her, in which a servant of the English *prima donna*, Mrs Tofts, was actively concerned ; it was not unnaturally conjectured, therefore, that Mrs Tofts had been at the bottom of it. The supporters of Margarita raised a clamour against the English *prima donna*, which was scarcely allayed by her public denial of complicity. Hughes, in a song called ' Tofts and Margaretta,' has commemorated this theatrical feud :—

> Music has learned the discords of the State,
> And concerts jar with Whig and Tory hate,
> Here Somerset and Devonshire attend
> The British Tofts, and every note commend ;
> To native merit just, and pleased to see
> We've Roman arts, from Roman bondage free ;
> Then famed l'Epine does equal skill employ,
> Whilst list'ning peers crowd to th' ecstatic joy.
> Bedford, to hear her sing, his dice forsakes,
> And Nottingham is raptured when she shakes ;
> Lulled, statesmen melt away their drowsy cares
> Of England's safety, in Italian airs.
> Who would not send each year blank passes o'er
> Rather than keep such strangers from our shore ?

The 'Margarita' sang in Clayton's 'Arsinoe' in 1705 ; in Greber's 'Temple of Love' in 1706 ; in Scarlatti and Buononcini's 'Thomyris,' in 1707 ; and in Haym's 'Camilla,' performing her part in Italian, while the English vocalists sang in English, in 1708. In the following year she 'created' the part of Marius in 'Pyrrhus and Demetrius.' She also appeared as *prima donna* in 'Almahide,' 'Hydaspes,' 'Antiochus,' and 'Ambleto.' In 1711, we meet with an allusion to her in *Swift's Journal* (August 6). 'We have a music meeting,' he writes, 'in our town to-night. I went to a rehearsal of it, and there was Margarita, and her sister, with another drab, and a parcel of fiddlers. I was weary, and would not go to the meeting, which I am sorry for, because I heard it was a great assembly.'

Margarita was, unquestionably, a vocalist of no ordinary powers ; and in Handel's 'Rinaldo' and 'Il Pastor Fido,' she rendered the difficult soprano music with much brilliancy of execution. She was also a skilful performer on the harpsichord. She continued on the stage until 1718, when she married Dr Pepusch, having amassed by her industrious exertions a fortune of ten thousand pounds. Dr Burney speaks of her as unprepossessing in person, with an ill-favoured countenance and a swarthy complexion. 'The tawny Tuscan,' an epigrammatist of the time calls her—so that her husband jocosely nicknamed her *Hecate*, 'a name to which she answered with as much good-humour as if he called her Helen.' She died in 1740.

Mrs TOFTS owed to nature the gift of a very fine voice which art had done but little to cultivate. She had also a handsome person ; and her action on the stage was graceful and impressive. Until the appearance of Margarita she reigned on the operatic stage supreme ; and for some time afterwards she divided the suffrages of the public with her rival. But in 1709 a sudden failure of her mental powers compelled her to retire into private life. In No. 20 of *The Tatler*, Steele, commenting upon the vicissitudes of theatrical life, refers to 'the distress of the unfortunate Camilla, who has had the ill-luck to break before her voice, and to disappear at a time when her beauty was in the height of its bloom. This lady entered so thoroughly into the great characters she acted, that when she had finished her part, she could not think of retrenching her equipage, but would appear in her own lodgings with the same magnificence that she did upon the stage. This greatness of soul has reduced that unhappy princess to an involuntary retirement, where she now passes her time among the woods and forests, thinking on the crowns and sceptres she has lost, and often humming over in her solitude :—

> "I was born of royal race,
> Yet must wander in disgrace," etc.

But, for fear of being overheard, and her quality known, she usually sings it in Italian.

> " Nacqui al regno,
> E par sono qui
> Sventurata."' [1]

After an interval of seclusion, Mrs Tofts recovered her intellect—at least for a time—and in the flush of her beauty married a wealthy art patron and connoisseur, Mr Joseph Smith, accompanying him to Venice on his appointment there as English consul. But her mental disorder returned, and she lived sequestered from the world in a remote part of her house, frequently wandering in the garden, and singing snatches of her favourite songs. She was living in 1735.

Colley Cibber bears testimony to her charms :—'Mrs Tofts, who took her first grounds of music here in her own country, before the Italian taste had so highly prevailed, was then but an adept in it : yet, whatever defect the fashionably skilful might find in her manner, she had, in the general sense of her spectators, charms that few of the most learned singers ever arrive at. The beauty of her fine-proportioned figure, and the exquisitely sweet silver tone of her voice, with that peculiar rapid swiftness of her throat, were perfections not to be imitated by art or labour.'

A once-popular epigram, sometimes attributed to Pope, reminds us that this brilliant picture was not without its shadows :—

[1] Her song in 'Camilla'; the first in the opera.

'So bright is thy beauty, so charming thy song,
  As had drawn both the beasts and their Orpheus along;
  But such is thy avarice and such is thy pride,
  That the beasts must have starved and the poet have died.'

No singer of the day attained or deserved a greater reputation than the Cavaliere NICOLINI GRIMALDI, also known as NICOLINI DI NAPOLI. He was born at Naples about 1673, and received an excellent education. Nature had endowed him with rare personal gifts, and with the dramatic faculty: the libretti which he invented and wrote are of much more than ordinary merit. It was soon discovered that he had a splendid voice, and after a preliminary training such as few singers now-a-days think it necessary to undergo, he went on the stage. We find him singing at Rome in 1694. During 1697 and 1698 he played the leading parts in the opera at Naples. In 1699 and 1700 he was again at Rome, after which he sang in the principal Italian cities with great acceptance. For his personal merits as much as for his singing, he was made a Cavaliere di San Marco.

He came over to England in 1708, without any particular invitation or engagement, but attracted by the report of our strong partiality for foreign music. He made his first appearance in the opera of 'Camilla,' or, according to some authorities, in that of 'Pyrrhus and Demetrius.' Steele, in *The Tatler*, declares himself 'fully satisfied with the sight of an actor who, by the grace and propriety of his action and gesture, does honour to an human figure, and sets off the character he bears in an opera by his action, as much as he does the words of it by his voice; every limb and finger contributes to the part he acts, in so much that a deaf man might go along with him in the sense of it. There is scarce a beautiful posture in an old statue which he does not plant himself in, as the different circumstances of the story give occasion for it. He performs the most ordinary action in a manner suitable to the greatness of his character, and shows the prince even in the giving of a letter or the despatching of a message.'

Dr Burney speaks of him as 'the first truly great singer who had ever sung in our theatre.' Colley Cibber, who was certainly a competent judge, says :—' Whatever praises may have been given to the most famous voices that have been heard since Nicolini, upon the whole I cannot but come into the opinion that still prevails among several persons of condition, who are able to give a reason for their liking, that no singer since his time has so justly and gracefully acquitted himself, in whatever character he appeared, as Nicolini. At most, the difference between him and the greatest favourite of the ladies, Farinelli, amounted but to this, that he might sometimes most exquisitely surprise us; but Nicolini (by pleasing the eye as well as the ear) filled us with a more various and rational delight.' It has been doubted whether a very great singer can also be a very fine actor, but Galliard expressly affirms that 'Nicolini had both qualities, more than any that have come hither since. He acted to perfection, and did not sing much inferior. His variations in the airs were excellent; but in his cadences he had a few antiquated tricks.'

Addison, in *The Spectator*, No. 405, expresses his regret that 'we are likely to lose the greatest performer in dramatic music that is now living, or that perhaps ever appeared upon the stage. I need not acquaint my reader,' he says, 'that I am speaking of Signor Nicolini. The town is highly obliged to that eminent artist for having shown us the Italian music in its perfection, as well as,' he continues, 'for that generous approbation he lately gave to an opera of our own country, in which the composer endeavoured to do justice to the beauty of the words, by following that noble example which has been set him by the greatest foreign masters in that art.' This was the opera of 'Calypso and Telemachus,' written by Hughes, and set by Galliard. Nicolini was on friendly terms both with Steele and Addison. He was partial to the men and to their writings; and was disposed to study the English language, in order to have the pleasure of reading *The Tatler*. When he left England after his visit, it was supposed, as Addison hints, that he would not return; whereupon some verses appeared in *Steele's Miscellany*, which curiously blended admiration with satirical criticism:—

'Begone, our nature's pleasure and reproach!
Britain no more with idle trills debauch.

Back to thy own unmanly Venice sail,
Where luxury and loose desires prevail;
There thy emasculating voice employ,
And raise the triumph of the wanton boy.
Long, ah! too long, the soft enchantment reigned,
Seduced the wise and ev'n the brave enchained:
Hence with thy curst deluding song! away!
Shall British freedom thus become thy prey?
Freedom which we so dearly used to prize,
We scorned to yield it—but to British eyes.
Assist, ye gales, with expeditious care,
Waft this prepost'rous idol of the fair;
Consurb, ye fair, and let the trifler go,
Nor bribe with wishes adverse winds to blow;
Nonsense grew pleasing by his syren arts,
And stole from Shakespeare's self our very hearts.'

Nicolini's salary, while in England, was eight hundred guineas a year, which, even after allowing for the change in the value of money, would be laughed at contemptuously by an operatic 'star' of the present day. 'Starring,' however, had not yet come into vogue; and Cibber remarks that none but the best performers that could be found were engaged even for the inferior parts. To meet the increased expenditure, the prices were raised; and though the cast included not only Nicolini, but Mrs Tofts and Valentini, the audiences were so large that Swiney, the director, cleared in the first season 'a moderate younger brother's fortune.' It must, however, be added that this prosperity was exceptional; and in the following season the diminished receipts led Nicolini to suggest an alteration in the terms of subscription, and that an application should be made to the Queen for assistance to the amount of one thousand guineas.

In June 1710 a quarrel broke out between Swiney and his great singer, and the latter endeavoured to get released from his *impresario*, describing his engagement as 'un esclavage inquiet et houteux qu'on ne scauroit une plus immaginer ailleurs hors de l'Angleterre.' The original cause of this anger was the irregularity of payment affected by Swiney. The Vice-Chancellor took up the quarrel, and succeeded in effecting a reconciliation, thus preserving to the opera its most brilliant ornament. Nicolini sang in 'Almahide' and 'Hydaspes'—of the latter the libretto was his own. In 'Rinaldo' his success was legitimate and complete, Handel's noble music enabling him to display the full scope of his powers. He next sang in 'Antioco' (December 1711), and in 1712 in 'Ambleto,' in which he again appeared as author. He then proceeded to the Continent, and did not return until 1714, when his stay was very brief. He came back in the following winter, and sang in 'Rinaldo' and 'Amadigi.' In 1716 he sang *à merveille* in 'Lucio Vero,' 'Amadigi,' and 'Clearti'; and in 1717 he again appeared in 'Rinaldo' and 'Amadigi.' We hear of him afterwards as at Venice in 1718, 1723, and 1726, when time had begun to impair his vocal powers. The date of his death is unknown.[1]

---

[1] Among the foreign singers of the time I must refer to the celebrated basso, Guiseppe Boschi, a native of Viterbo, who came to London about 1710-1711, and sang the part of Argante in Handel's 'Rinaldo.' He long held a foremost place on the English operatic stage.

Let us now glance at the MUSICAL COMPOSERS of the age of Anne. The opening of the eighteenth century was synchronous with a marked development of the art in England, leading, as we have seen, to the establishment of opera, which was followed, through the sublime inventiveness of Handel, by that of oratorio, the grandest artistic creation inspired by music. A love of music, and a taste and feeling for its higher manifestations, began to awake among the people; and sacred compositions in the sanctuary, and secular in the concert-room and on the stage, found ready and appreciative audience. England, in the reign of Charles II., had produced a great musical composer of her own in Henry Purcell, a man whose genius was capable of noble effort and splendid achievement, who, but for his premature death, might have taken rank among the greatest masters of the art. He had no successors equal to himself, yet the English school was not without some respectable names, and the public was not left to depend wholly upon foreign supplies.

In 1710 an advertisement appeared in *The London Gazette* acquainting English composers with the fact that 'several persons of quality' had subscribed a sum of two hundred guineas, to be distributed in four prizes of fifty guineas each, for the best settings of Congreve's masque, 'The Judgment of Paris.' From the compositions sent in the judges selected that of John Weldon for the first prize, of John Eccles for the second, of Daniel Purcell for the third, and of Godfrey Finger for the fourth. The public performance of these pieces at the Theatre in Covent Garden is described by Congreve himself in his *Literary Relics*. 'I don't think any one place in the world,' he says, 'can show such an assembly. The number of performers, besides the verse-singers, was eighty-five. The front of the stage was all built into a concave with deal boards, all which are faced with tin, to increase and throw forwards the sound. It was all hung with sconces of wax candles, besides the common branches of lights usual in the playhouses. The boxes and pit were all thrown into one, so that all sat in common; and the whole was crammed with beauties and beaux, *not one scrub being admitted.* The place where formerly the music used to play, between the pit and stage, was turned into Chiti's chocolate-house, the whole family being transplanted thither with chocolate, cooled drinks, ratifia, postico, etc., which everybody that would called for, the whole expense of everything being defrayed by the subscribers. I think, truly, the whole thing better worth coming to see than the jubilee.'

JOHN WELDON, who on this occasion won the first prize, was born at Chicester about 1679. He received his musical education under John Walter, the organist of Eton College and afterwards under Henry Purcell. His admirable qualifications successively preferred him to the posts of organist of New College, Oxford; Gentleman Extraordinary of the Chapel Royal, in 1701; organist of the same in 1708, succeeding Dr Blow; and Second Composer in Ordinary to George I. in 1715. He died in 1736, and lies buried in the churchyard of St Paul's, Covent Garden. Weldon's services and anthems—especially his anthems. 'In Thee, O Lord,' and 'Hear my Crying'—are characterised by much suavity and refinement, and by considerable variety and skill in harmony and counterpoint, but they miss that breadth of style which is peculiar to our best church music. Some of his fugitive songs are very pleasing: as, for instance, his 'From Grave Lessons and Restraint.'[1]

The second prize-winner, JOHN ECCLES, was born in London about 1660. His musical teaching came from

[1] Printed by Hawkins, ii. 785.

his father (Solomon Eccles), and rapidly bore good fruit; as a young man he was engaged in composing for the theatres, and he continued to practise in this branch of his art for a quarter of a century. The plays which he illustrated and brightened by songs and intermezzi, includes Motteux's 'Europe's Rivals for the Peace [of Ryswick],' 1697; 'The Sham Doctor,' 1697; Dennis's 'Rinaldo and Armida,' 1699; and Congreve's 'Semele,' 1707. He collaborated with the illustrious Purcell in D'Urfey's 'Don Quixote' (1694)—in itself a stamp and seal of his ability as a composer. In 1698, on the death of Dr Staggins, he was made Master of the King's Band of Music, a post which entailed upon him the production of numerous Birthday and New Year's Day odes. In 1701 he set to music Congreve's Ode for St Cecilia's Day—by no means an inspiring theme. Throughout the reign of Anne, and her successor, he continued to pour out his musical ideas with an astonishing fertility, and a uniformity of excellence which is not less astonishing. I believe that some of the melodies contained in the collection of songs which he published *in tempore Annæ*, would even now be heard with pleasure. To enumerate all his compositions would be impossible; it is enough to note that he provided airs and graces for no fewer than forty-six dramas. In his old age he retired to Kingston-upon-Thames, and amused his leisure with rod and line—Izaak Walton having few stauncher disciples than John Eccles. He died in January 1735. His two brothers, Henry and Thomas, were also celebrated for their ability as musicians.

DANIEL PURCELL, the brother of the greatest of our early English musicians, does not seem to have been educated in any choir, and probably received his instruction from his brother. He was for some time organist of Magdalen

College, Oxford, and afterwards of St Andrew's, Holborn. He composed the music to an opera entitled 'Brutus of Alba; or, Augusta's Triumph,' written by George Powell, the comedian, and performed at the Dorset Garden Theatre in 1697. Many of his songs, but without the basses, are preserved in Thomas D'Urfey's *Pills to Purge Melancholy*. They exhibit no interesting or meritorious points; and for years Dan Purcell was best known by the puns which he poured out in profusion.

The fourth prize-winner was GODFREY FINGER, a Moravian by birth, but for many years a resident in England. He came over in 1685; was appointed chapel-master to James II.; published in 1688 twelve sonatas for divers instruments, and in 1690 six sonatas or solos, three for violin and three for flute; joined John Barrister in 1691 in 'Ayres, Chasones, Divisions and Sonatas for Violins and Flutes'; and laboured on at the work of composition with laudable tenacity of purpose. The instrumental music in the following plays flowed from his prolific fancy:—Southern's comedy, 'The Wives' Excuse,' 1692; Congreve's 'Love for Love,' 1695; Otway's 'Mourning Bride,' 1697; Catherine Trotter's 'Love at a Loss,' 1701; Colley Cibber's 'Love makes a Man,' 1701; and Farquhar's 'Sir Harry Wildair,' 1701. In conjunction with Eccles he composed the music for Motteux's masque, 'The Loves of Mars and Venus,' in 1696, and for Ravenscroft's comedy of 'The Anatomist; or, The Sham Doctor.' In 1701 he set to music Elkanah Settle's opera, 'The Virgin Prophetess,' performed at the Theatre Royal. In the same year, as we have seen, the fourth prize was awarded to his setting of Congreve's 'Judgment of Paris.' His vanity was wounded at this public discrediting of his composition, and in the following year he abandoned ungrateful Albion and returned to Germany.

Dr JOHN BLOW, an honoured name in the records of English church music, was born at North Collingham, in Nottinghamshire, in 1648, so that at the accession of Anne he was fifty-four years old. He died in 1708, just half-way into the Queen's reign. He was educated in the choir of the Chapel Royal under Harry Cooke; and at the age of fifteen began his career as a composer. Three anthems by 'John Blow, one of the Children of His Majesty's Chapel,' are included in Clifford's *Divine Hymns and Anthems* (1663); and, in collaboration with Pelham Humfrey and William Turner, he produced an anthem with orchestral accompaniments, which is still extant. On leaving the choir, Blow became a pupil, first of Hingiston, and next of Dr Christopher Gibbons. His sound scholarship and natural capacity soon obtained recognition; and in 1669, at the early age of twenty-one, he was appointed organist of Westminster Abbey. In 1680 he was removed to make way for Purcell, but on the latter's death in 1695, was re-appointed. He had previously received the post of Composer to the King, and in 1699 was made Composer to the Chapel Royal. But an enumeration of the various offices he held will scarcely be of interest to the reader, except so far as they show the value set upon his acquirements as a musician. His degree of Doctor of Music he received from Sancroft, Archbishop of Canterbury.

Dr Blow died on the 1st of October 1708, and was buried under the organ in Westminster Abbey, which for so many years had pealed forth harmonious strains at his bidding. As a composer his eminent qualities were soundness of knowledge, great structural skill, contrapuntal exactness, and considerable breadth of style. The reader will find these displayed in the anthems (more than a hundred) and services which have come down to us: though many are not in print, they are all extant. A collection of his songs, under the title of *Amphion Anglicus*, was issued in 1702; others will be found in Playford's *Harmonia Sacra*. But perhaps his most enduring title to remembrance is, that he was the teacher [1] of the illustrious Purcell.

DEAN ALDRICH, born at Westminster in 1647, lived into the reign of Anne, and died two years after his contemporary Dr Blow—that is, on the 14th of December 1710—at the age of sixty-four. Everybody knows the famous and beautiful round, 'Hark! the bonny Christchurch Bells,' composed by the worthy Dean; but less known, though not less admirable, are his 'Morning and Evening Services,' in G and A, and his fine anthem, 'O Praise the Lord,' which is distinguished by true musicianly skill and fervour. He wrote also a number of very good motets, catches, rounds, madrigals, masses, services, and anthems; in each composition exhibiting ingenuity, taste, and thorough knowledge of his art.

Henry Aldrich was educated at Westminster School, under the celebrated Dr Busby, and thence removed to Christ Church, Oxford, where he received the degree of M.A. in 1669. He took holy orders, and was appointed to the living of Wem, in Shropshire, but continued to reside in his college, and as a tutor drew round him a large number of pupils. He took his degrees as B.D. and D.D. in 1681; and eight years later was installed as Dean of Christ Church—a post which he filled with eminent success, gaining all hearts by his genial and sympathetic manners, and zealously promoting the interests of his college by his energy and zeal. 'As dean of a college and a cathedral,' says Hawkins, 'he regarded it as a duty, as it undoubtedly was in his case a pleasure, to advance the study and progress of church music. His choir was

---

[1] In conjunction with Pelham Humfrey.

well appointed, and every vicar, clerical as well as lay, gave his daily and efficient aid in it. He contributed also largely to its stock of sacred music; and some of his services and anthems, being preserved in the collections of Bryce and Arnold, are known and sung in every cathedral in the kingdom.'

Dean Aldrich was an 'all-round' man—a fine scholar, musician, architect, and humorist. His compendium of Logic[1] was long held in high repute, was, in fact, an Oxford class-book; he was one of the editors of Clarendon's *History of the Rebellion*, and he wrote numerous classical and theological tracts. As an architect he designed the chapel of Trinity College, All Saints' Church, and the Peckwater quadrangle at Christ Church. Of his musical abilities I have already furnished proofs; and I may add here that he collected and bequeathed to his college a musical library of very great value. The man who composed the catch, 'Hark! the bonny Christ Church Bells,' and that one in praise of smoking[2]—he was an ardent devotee of the pipe—in which a rest is afforded to each singer to enable him to enjoy a puff—could not be other than a humorist. All honour to the memory of Dean Aldrich! Smokers and musicians should unite to keep it green.

I subjoin the notation of the Dean's famous catch:—

[1] *Artis Logicæ Rudimenta.*
[2] Both were printed in *The Pleasant Musical Companion*, 1726.

Queen Anne's reign can boast of a sound Church Musician in Dr CROFT—perhaps, among earlier English composers, second only to Purcell. Who has not felt the solemn dignity and pathos of his grand Burial Service, when its sublime strains peal out in Westminster Abbey over the dust of some English worthy whom his country has chosen to honour with a resting place in that reverend pile? Or the full harmonious swell of his fine anthems, such as 'Put me not to rebuke,' 'God is gone up,' and 'O Lord, Thou hast searched me out?' Or, again, the impressive sublimity of his Psalm tunes, especially those evergreen favourites, 'St Ann's' and 'St Matthew's?' In secular music Dr Croft's workmanship was always deft and sound, as in the songs and accompaniments which he wrote for David Craufurd's 'Courtship à la Mode' (1700); Steele's 'Funeral' (1702); Farquhar's 'Twin Rivals' (1703); and Steele's 'Lying Lover' (1704). He also published numerous songs and sonatas for both violin and flute.

William Croft was born in 1677 at Nether Eatington, in Warwickshire, and educated among the children of the Chapel Royal by Dr Blow. On the erection of an organ in St Anne's Church, Soho, he was appointed organist (1699); and in May 1704, joint organist with Jeremiah Clark, of the Chapel Royal. In 1707, on Clark's death, he became sole organist; and in the following year succeeded Dr Blow as organist of Westminster Abbey, and master of the children and composer to the Chapel Royal. His noble anthems, so deservedly cherished in the Anglican Church, were produced by him in discharge of his official duties, on occasions of public thanksgiving and the like. On the 9th of July 1713 he took the degree of Doctor of Music in the University of Oxford, his exercise being two odes, published under the title of *Musicus Apparatus Academicus*, one in English and the other in Latin, in celebration of the Peace of Utrecht. Under the title of *Musica Sacra* he published, in 1724, thirty anthems[1] and a Burial Service of his own composition.

He died on the 14th of August 1727, and, like his teacher, Dr Blow, was buried in Westminster Abbey, where both composers are commemorated by monuments.

The inscription on Dr Croft's runs as follows:—

> NEAR TO THIS PLACE LIES INTERRED
> WILLIAM CROFT,
> DOCTOR IN MUSIC,
> ORGANIST OF THE ROYAL CHAPEL AND
> OF THIS COLLEGIATE CHURCH.
> HIS HARMONY HE DERIVED FROM THAT EXCELLENT ARTIST[2]
> IN MODULATION WHO LIES ON THE OTHER SIDE OF HIM.
> IN HIS CELEBRATED WORKS, WHICH FOR THE MOST PART HE
> CONSECRATED TO GOD, HE MADE A DILIGENT PROGRESS;
> NOR WAS IT BY THE SOLEMNITY OF THE NUMBERS ALONE,
> BUT BY THE FORCE OF HIS INGENUITY AND THE
> SWEETNESS OF HIS MANNERS, AND EVEN HIS COUNTENANCE,
> THAT HE EXCELLENTLY RECOMMENDED THEM.
> HAVING RESIDED AMONG MORTALS FOR FIFTY YEARS,
> BEHAVING WITH THE UTMOST CANDOUR
> (NOT MORE CONSPICUOUS FOR ANY OTHER OFFICE OF HUMANITY
> THAN A FRIENDSHIP AND LOVE
> TRULY PATERNAL TO ALL WHOM HE HAD INSTRUCTED),
> HE DEPARTED TO THE HEAVENLY CHOIR ON THE
> FOURTEENTH DAY OF AUGUST, 1727,
> THAT, BEING NEAR,
> HE MIGHT ADD HIS OWN HALLELUJAH TO THE CONCERT
> OF ANGELS.
> AWAKE UP, MY GLORY, AWAKE LUTE AND HARP,
> I MYSELF WILL AWAKE RIGHT EARLY.

JEREMIAH CLARK, to whom I have above alluded, was, like Croft, a chorister in the Chapel Royal, under Dr Blow,

---

[1] These include 'Praise the Lord, O my Soul,' 'God is gone up,' O Lord, rebuke me not,' and 'O Lord, Thou hast searched me out.'

[2] Dr Blow.

whom he succeeded in 1693, as almoner and master of the children of St Paul's Cathedral. Two years later, he was promoted to be organist and one of the vicars-choral of St Paul's; and in May 1704 he and Croft became joint-organists of the Chapel Royal. Clark having fallen in love with a lady whose position in life rendered it impossible for him to aspire to her hand, sank into a despondent condition, and committed suicide by shooting himself, sometime in October 1707. A few weeks before, when riding to town, accompanied by a servant, he had been seized with an attack of suicidal mania, and dismounting by a field in which lay a pond surrounded with trees, he tossed up whether he should hang or drown himself. The coin fell on its edge, sticking in the soil, and this accident induced him temporarily to forego his design. Clark is the author of several beautiful anthems, dignified and pathetic in their style, such as 'Please the Lord, O Jerusalem,' and 'Bow down Thine ear;' of a cantata, and of numerous songs. His setting of Dryden's 'Alexander's Feast' (in 1697) has unfortunately not been preserved. Conjointly with the younger Purcell, he composed Elkanah Settle's opera, 'The World in the Moon;' and, with Purcell and Leveridge, Motteux's 'Island Princess.' He also furnished the music for D'Urfey's 'Fond Husband,' 1676 —in which occurs the simple sweet air, 'The bonny grey-eyed Man,' which Dr Pepusch, in Gay's 'Beggar's Opera,' adapted to the words, 'Tis woman that seduces all mankind'—Sedley's 'Antony and Cleopatra,' 1677; 'Titus Andronicus,' 1687; and 'A Wife for Any Man,' 1690.

Both as a composer and a practical musician, MAURICE GREENE—whose anthem, 'O clap your hands,' is still popular—ranks considerably above Clark. He was the son of the Rev. Dr Greene, a London clergyman, and born in London about 1695. He received his early training under Charles King as a chorister of St Paul's Cathedral, and when his voice broke, was placed under Richard Brind, then organist of the Cathedral. On the organ he acquired a remarkable proficiency—he is always spoken of as one of the first organists of his time—and at the age of twenty officiated with much success at St Dunstan's, Fleet Street, (1715), and St Andrew's, Holborn (1717). In 1718 he succeeded his master, Brind, at St Paul's, and in 1727, Dr Croft, at the Chapel Royal. He was a hearty admirer of the genius of Handel; and by admitting the great German to perform on the organ at St Paul's, grew into cordial intimacy with him ; but Handel broke it off, on discovering that Greene extended a similar courtesy to his rival Buononcini.

In 1728 the latter contrived to make Greene the instrument of introducing to the Academy of Ancient Music [1] one of Lotti's madrigals ('In una siepe ombrosa') as his own. The deception was discovered, three or four years later, and was punished by Buononcini's expulsion from the Academy. For some unexplained reason, Greene believed that his friend had been ill-treated, and withdrew from the Academy, taking with him the St Paul's choristers ; and, in conjunction with Michael Festing, the violinist, established a rival series of concerts in the famous Apollo Room at the Devil Tavern near Temple Bar, whence Handel was able to make his little joke that ' Toctor Greene had gone to the Devil.'

In 1730, on the death of Dr Tudway, Greene was elected Professor of Music in the University of Cambridge, with the degree of Doctor of Music. As his exercise on this occasion he produced a setting of Pope's 'Ode on St Cecilia's Day,' shortened in some respects, but with a new stanza composed for the occasion by the poet himself

[1] Founded in 1710 by professional and amateur musicians, for the study and practice of vocal and instrumental works.

(July 6, 1730). Five years later, on the death of Eccles, he was appointed Master of the King's band of music, in which capacity he set several odes for the King's Birthday and New Year's Day. In 1743 he published his *Forty Select Anthems*, which 'place him at the head of the list of English ecclesiastical composers, for they combine the science and vigour of our earlier writers with the melody of the best German and Italian masters who flourished in the first half of the eighteenth century.'

Greene died on the 1st of December 1755. His compositions include—the oratorios of 'Jephtha' and 'The Force of Truth'; a *Te Deum* in D major; Addison's ode, 'The Spacious Firmament'; the dramatic pastoral of 'Florimel: or Love's Revenge'; 'The Judgment of Hercules,' a masque; the pastoral opera of 'Phœbe,' written by Dr Hoadley; two books, each containing 'A Cantata, and four English Songs'; 'The Chaplet: a Collection of Twelve English Songs;' and 'Spenser's Amoretti,' a collection of twenty-five Sonnets.

Greene joined Festing (in 1738) in establishing that excellent benevolent institution, 'The Royal Society of Musicians,' for the support and maintenance of decayed musicians and their families.

It was a quip of Dr Greene that CHARLES KING, the musician, was a very *serviceable* man—the quip being an allusion to the 'services' he had composed, and particularly to those in C and F, which are still occasionally performed. He was born at Bury St Edmunds in 1687; graduated as Mus. Bac. Oxon., in 1707; was afterwards organist of St Benet Fink; in 1730 was admitted a vicar choral of St Paul's; and died in 1748.

There was another King among the musicians of Queen Anne's reign—RICHARD KING, who graduated as Mus. Bac.

in 1696. His compositions include the songs in Crowne's comedy of 'Sir Courtly Nice'; and a setting of Shadwell's ode for St Cecilia's Day, 'O Sacred Harmony.' The date of his death is not known; but he was living in 1711.

JAMES HART, a sound Church musician, was born in 1700; TRAVERS in 1708; WILLIAM BRYCE in 1710; and Dr ARNE in 1710. Their works lie beyond the scope of the present review.

I pass on to NICOLO FRANCESCO HAYM. He was an Italian by birth, but spent several years of his life in England, and took no unimportant part in the establishment of Italian opera among us. He came to this country in 1704; and soon afterwards joined Clayton and Dieupart[1] in the formation of an Italian opera company. He played the principal 'cello in Clayton's 'Arsinoe'; and in April 1706, produced an opera of his own, the 'Camilla,' to which reference has already been made. Afterwards he adapted Buononcini's 'Thomyris' and Scarlatti's 'Pyrrhus and Demetrius' for the English stage. For his work on the latter Rich paid him the handsome sum of three hundred pounds. In 1711 appeared his 'Etrarco.' The arrival of Handel, and the success of 'Rinaldo,' aroused Haym's jealousy; and, with Clayton and Dieupart, he publicly protested, in *The Spectator*, against the new style of opera, at the same time soliciting patronage for their concerts at Clayton's house in York Buildings. I suspect that Haym's secret cause of complaint was not the supreme genius of Handel, but the pecuniary loss he had reason to apprehend. I think he was an avaricious man,

---

[1] Charles Dieupart, a Frenchman, arrived in England about 1690-5. He was an admirable performer on the violin and harpsichord; but fell into low habits and vicious company, frequented alehouses, and died in indigence about 1740.

and that he was always ready to take any side which
paid him well. He soon went over to Handel; no doubt,
for 'a consideration'; and we find him writing libretti
for some of the Handelian operas—'Teseo,' 'Rada-
misto,' 'Othone,' 'Flavio,' 'Guilio Cesare,' 'Tamerlano,'
'Rodolinda,' 'Siroc,'[1] 'Tolomeo.' He also wrote libretti
for Ariosti and Buononcini.

Haym was a good musician, and it is to be regretted
he could not carry out his proposed *History of Music*, as
it would unquestionably have contained much sound criticism. He was a man of refined taste ; published a good
edition of Tasso's *Gierusalemme Liberata;* and wrote a
couple of tragedies, 'Merope' and 'Demodice.' He drew
with spirit and accuracy; witness his portraits of Tallis
and Byrd, engraved by Vander Gucht, than which none
other are known to be in existence. He was a connoisseur
in medals, and a collector of pictures; and it must be owned
that if in the acquisition of money he showed a keen desire, in its disposal he showed a judicious discrimination.
The date of his death is unknown, but it must have been
in 1730 or 1731.

HARRY CAREY, to whom England is indebted for that
most exquisite and homeliest of ballads, 'Sally in our
Alley,' and also (it is said) for the immortal anthem, 'God
Save the Queen,' which has in no small degree contributed
to fan the flame of English loyalty. lived through the reign
of Anne, but as composer and dramatist really belongs
to the next two reigns. He is reputed to have been an
illegitimate son of the Marquis of Halifax. His instruc-
tors in music were Linnert, and (subsequently) Roscin-
grave and Geminiani, but he never acquired a thorough
knowledge of his art, and his compositions, while marked

[1] Though Haym claimed the authorship of 'Siroc,' the book was really
written by Metastasio.

by fertile invention, and a strong vein of spontaneous melody, suffer from this important limitation. His dependence for a livelihood, therefore, was upon teaching in schools and in private families, and upon his writings for the stage, which were almost uniformly successful. Hawkins, I think, defines his literary and musical position pretty accurately when he says:—'As a musician, Carey seems to have been one of the first of the lowest rank; and as a poet, the last of that class of which D'Urfey was the first, with this difference, that in all the songs and poems written by him on wine, love, and such kind of subjects, he seems to have manifested an inviolable regard for decency and good manners.' But I shall claim for Carey a depth of feeling and a purity of sentiment to which D'Urfey was wholly a stranger.

The origin of his sweet and striking ballad, 'Sally in our Alley,' is thus described by Carey himself:—' A shoemaker's prentice, making holiday with his sweetheart, treated her with a sight of Bedlam, the puppet-shows, the flying chairs, and all the elegancies of Moorfields, from whence, proceeding to the Farthing Pie House, he gave her a collation of buns, cheese-cakes, gammon of bacon, stuffed beef, and bottled ale, through all which scenes the author dodged them. Charmed with the simplicity of their courtship, he drew from what he had witnessed this little sketch of nature.'

Good nature, a ready humour, geniality of temper, and musical ability are dangerous gifts when not united with firmness of will and tenacity of purpose. Carey's society was always welcome, and he yielded to the pleasures of gay companionship to such an extent as to reduce his family and himself to poverty, and overcloud his later years with pecuniary embarrassments. It is said that he terminated his life by his own hand at the age of eighty; but a newspaper notice at the time simply speaks of his death as sudden. It took place on the 4th of October 1743. There is no evidence in confirmation of the patriarchal longevity attributed to him.

Carey's songs and cantatas were very numerous; and in 1739-40 he published *The Musical Century*, or One Hundred English Ballads on various subjects and occasions, adapted to several characters and incidents in Human Life, and calculated for innocent conversation, mirth, and instruction.'

A few words must be given to his dramatic efforts:—

In 1715 he wrote and composed the music for the entertaining farce of 'The Contrivances; or, More Ways than One,' which was brought out with great success at Drury Lane. The character of Arethusa 'used to be the probationary part for female singers, before they were bold enough to venture upon characters of more consequence.'

In March 1722, at Lincoln's Inn Fields, was performed his farce of 'Hanging and Marriage; or, The Dead Man's Wedding.' It was acted for the benefit of the comedian Quin.

In 1732 he wrote the operas of 'Amelia' (music by Lampe), and 'Teraminta' (music by John Christopher Smith). In December of the same year he brought out at Drury Lane his ballad opera of 'Betty; or, The Country Bumpkins."

In 1733 his indefatigable invention produced a musical entertainment called 'Cephalus and Procris,' with a pantomime interlude called 'Harlequin Grand Volgi.'

Next came (in February 1734) his amusing burlesque extravaganza—'The most Tragical Tragedy that ever was Tragedized by any company of Tragedians. called *Chrononotonthologos.*' Some of the parodies and bits of extravagance are very diverting; and there is real humour in the idea of a warrior piling himself up on the bodies of his victims until he reaches the gods, who, in admiration of his heroism, invite him to remain with them—an invitation he declines, because summoned to earth by the eyes of his mistress :—

> 'Oh ! had you seen him, how he dealt out death,
> And at one stroke robbed thousands of their breath ;
> While on the slaughtered heaps himself did rise,
> In pyramids of conquest, to the skies.
> The gods all hailed, and fain would have him stay ;
> But your bright charms have called him thence away.'

The pompous and stilted style of the contemporary drama is thus ridiculed :—

> 'But lo, the king, his footsteps this way bending,
> His cogitative faculties immured
> In cogitundity of cogitation :
> Let silence close our folding-doors of speech,
> Till apt attention tell our heart the purport
> Of this profound profundity of thought.'

The following passage is not wholly forgotten :—

> 'Go, call a coach, and let a coach be called ;
> And let the man that calls it be the caller ;
> And in his calling let him nothing call,
> But "Coach—coach—coach !" Oh, for a coach, ye gods !'

The ballad-opera of 'A Wonder ; or, The Honest Yorkshireman,' produced in 1735, was long a stock piece in our theatres. From one of the songs we quote a stanza which embodies a sound sentiment, though deficient in the graces of poetic expression :—

> 'A noble mind
> Is ne'er confined
> To any shire, or nation ;
> He gains most praise
> Who best displays
> A generous education.
> While rancour rolls
> In narrow souls,

> By narrow views discerning,
> The truly wise
> Will only prize
> Good manners, sense, and learning.'

An even greater success was won by Carey with his burlesque opera (the music by Lampe) of 'The Dragon of Wantley,' a sharp and amusing satire on the Italian opera of the day, which was acted sixty-seven times in the first season. 'The plot, taken from the old ballad of *Moore of Moorehall*, is worked up into all the incidents of love, heroism, rivalry, and fury, which most of the Italian operas indiscriminately were stuffed with. To help this forward, the characters were dressed in the utmost extravagance of theatric parade: the machinery truly burlesque, and the songs, though ludicrous in the highest degree, were set perfectly in the Italian taste.'

The success of this venture induced Carey, in the following year, to bring forward another burlesque, in the form of a sequel or second part, entitled 'Margery; or, A Worse Plague than the Dragon.' This was received with a good deal of applause, but cannot escape the critical censure which almost invariably falls upon sequels or continuations.

'Betty; or, The Country Bumpkin' (1739), did not hit the taste of 'the town;' but better fortune attended Carey's last dramatic production, the musical interlude of 'Nancy; or, The Parting Lovers' (also known as 'The Pressgang'). It is said to have been suggested by an incident which came under the author's observation. 'At the beginning of the late impress, the author saw a young fellow hurried away by a pressgang, and followed by his sweetheart, a very pretty wench, and perfectly neat, though plain in her dress: her tears, her distress, and moving softness drew attention and compassion from all who beheld her.'

One of the 'characters' of Queen Anne's reign, and an enthusiast who, though homely born and bred, contributed largely to the cultivation of a refined musical taste in England, was THOMAS BRITTON, popularly known as 'the Musical Small-Coal Man.' Hearne furnishes the following biographical sketch of this celebrity:—

He was born [about 1651] at or near Higham Towers, in Northamptonshire. From thence he went to London, where he bound himself apprentice to a small-coal man in St John Baptist's Street. After he had served his full term of seven years, his master gave him a sum of money not to set up. Upon this Tom went into Northamptonshire again, and, after he had spent his money, he returned again to London, set up the small-coal trade (notwithstanding his master was still living), and, withal, he took a stable and turned it into a house, which stood the next door to the little gate of St John's of Jerusalem, next Clerkenwell Green. Some time after he had settled here, he became acquainted with Dr Garenciers, his near neighbour, by which means he became an excellent chemist, and perhaps he performed such things in that profession as had never been done before, with little cost and charge, by the help of a moving laboratory, that was contrived and built by himself, which was much admired by all of that faculty that happened to see it, insomuch that a certain gentleman of Wales was so much taken with it, that he was at the expense of carrying him down into that country on purpose to build him such another, which Tom performed to the gentleman's very great satisfaction, and for the same he received of him a very handsome and generous gratuity. Besides his great skill in chemistry, he was as famous for his knowledge in the theory of music; in the practical part of which faculty he was likewise very considerable. He was so much addicted to it that he pricked with his own hand (very neatly and accurately), and left behind him a valuable collection of music, mostly pricked by himself, which was sold upon his death for near an hundred pounds. Not to mention the excellent collection of printed books that he also left behind him, both of chemistry and music.

Besides these books that he left behind him, he had some years before his death sold by auction a noble collection of books, most of them in the Rosicrucian faculty (of which he was a great admirer), whereof there is a printed catalogue extant (as there is of those that were sold after his death), which I have often looked over with no small surprise and wonder, and particularly for the great number of manuscripts in the before-mentioned faculties that are specified in it. He had, moreover, a considerable collection of musical instruments, which were sold for fourscore pounds upon his death, which happened in September 1714, being upwards of threescore years of age, and lies buried in the churchyard of Clerkenwell, without monument or inscription, being attended to his grave in a very solemn and decent manner by a great concourse of people, especially of such as frequented the Musical Club, that was kept up for many years at his own charges (he being a man of a very generous and liberal spirit), at his own little cell. He appears by the print of him, done since his death, to have been a man of an ingenious countenance, and of a sprightly temper. It also represents him as a comely person, as indeed he was, and withal there is a modesty expressed in it every way agreeable to him. Under it are these verses, which may serve instead of an epitaph :—

> 'Though mean thy rank, yet in thy humble cell
> Did gentle peace and arts unpurchased dwell ;
> Well pleased, Apollo thither led his train,
> And Music warbled in her sweetest strain.
> Cyllenius so, as fables tell, and Jove
> Came willing guests to poor Philemon's grove ;
> Let useless pomp behold, and blush to find
> So low a station, such a liberal mind.'[1]

In short, he was an extraordinary and very valuable man, much admired by the gentry, even those of the best quality, and by all others of the more inferior rank that had any manner of regard for probity, sagacity, diligence, and humility. I say humility, because, though he was so much famed for his knowledge, and might therefore have lived very reputably without his trade, yet he continued it to his death, not thinking it to be at all beneath him.

Some further particulars are furnished by Ned Ward, the author of *The London Spy*, who at that time kept a public-house in Clerkenwell, and afterwards in Moorfields,

---

[1] Written by John Hughes (author of 'The Siege of Damascus'), who frequently played the violin at Britton's concerts.

where he sold ale of his own brewing. In his *Satirical Reflections on Clubs* he speaks of Britton's musical meetings as 'just begun, or at least confirmed, by Sir Roger L'Estrange, a very musical gentleman, and who had a tolerable perfection on the bass viol.' He adds that 'the attachment of Sir Roger and other ingenious gentlemen, lovers of the Muses, to Britton, arose from the profound regard that he had in general to all manner of literature; that the prudence of his deportment to his betters procured him great respect; and that men of the best wit, as well as some of the best quality, honoured his musical society with their company; that Britton was so much distinguished, that when passing the streets in his blue linen frock, and with his sack of small coal on his back, he was frequently accosted with such expressions as these, 'There goes the famous small-coal man, who is a lover of learning, a performer in music, and a companion for gentlemen.'

It is said that his cry, as he perambulated the streets with his wares, was 'the most perfect of all musical intervals, the diapason,' as thus:—

Britton's house, where he held his weekly concerts,[1] was on the south side of Aylesbury Street, at the corner of the passage which leads by the old Jerusalem Tavern into St John's Square. On the ground floor was his store of small-coal, and above it the concert-room, which was curiously long and narrow, with so low a ceiling, that a tall man could scarcely stand upright. Access to this room was obtained

---

[1] At first, these concerts were free to all comers; afterwards the visitors paid 10s each. Coffee was provided at a penny a dish.

by an outside flight of stairs,[1] which ladies ascended with difficulty. In this dingy den, however, the lovers of music gathered with eagerness to listen to fine performances of the best compositions—men of letters and science, peers and commoners, ladies of high rank, and foreigners of distinction. Among the performers were Dr Pepusch, and even Handel himself, on the harpsichord; Banister and Henry Needler, as first violins; and as second violins, John Hughes, the artist Woolaston, Philip Hart, Henry Symonds, Abriel Whichells, and Obadiah Shuttleworth.

'That fine performer Mr Matthew Dubourg, was then but a child, but the first solo that ever he played in public, and which probably was one of Corelli's, he played at Britton's concert, standing upon a joint-stool; but so terribly was the poor child awed at the sight of so splendid an assembly, that he was near falling to the ground.'

Britton's death took place under remarkable circumstances. A Mr Justice Robe, who frequently played at his concerts, introduced to him a notorious ventriloquist named Honeyman, who, without moving his lips or seeming to speak, announced, as from some mysterious and remote source, that his death would take place within a few hours, unless he immediately fell on his knees, and repeated the Lord's Prayer. Britton complied; but his nerves were so shaken by the rude practical joke, that on returning home, he took to his bed, from which he never

---

[1] So we read in Ned Ward's verses:—

1	2
Upon Thursdays repair	And without e'er a souse
To my palace, and there	Paid to me or my spouse,
Hobble up, stair by stair,	Sit as still as a mouse
But I pray ye take care	At the top of the house,
That you break not your shins by a stumble.	And there you shall hear how we fumble.

rose again alive. This sad event took place on the 27th of September 1714.[1]

After Britton's death, his weekly concerts were continued by Woolaston, the painter, at his house in Warwick Court, Warwick Lane, Newgate—not exactly the locality where one would now-a-days cultivate the Muse! Vocal and instrumental concerts were also given regularly at the Angel and Crown Tavern in Whitechapel. But these yielded in popularity, as they were inferior in excellence, to those established by Caslon, the type-founder, at his house in Chigwell Street. They took place once a month; and for the convenience of those of his friends who had to walk home, on that Thursday in the month which was nearest full moon—whence his guests were wont 'humorously' to call themselves Lunatics. The performers were Mr Woolaston, and oftentimes Mr Charles French, organist of Cripplegate Church; Mr William De Sautherns, organist of Spittalfields; Mr Samuel Peacock, and many others. The performance consisted mostly of Corelli's music, intermingled with the overtures of the old English and Italian operas, namely 'Clotilda,' 'Hydaspes,' 'Camilla,' and others, and the more modern ones of Mr Handel. In the intervals of the performance, the guests refreshed themselves at a sideboard, which was amply furnished; and, when it was over, sitting down to a bottle of wine, and a decanter of excellent ale, of Mr Caslon's own brewing, they concluded the evening's entertainment with a song or two of Purcell's, sung to the harpsichord, or a few catches, and about twelve retired.'

A respectable name among the Queen Anne musicians is that of JOHN CHRISTOPHER PEPUSCH. The son of a Protestant clergyman, he was born at Berlin in 1667. Displaying a talent for music at an early age, his father placed

---

[1] Britton was a widely read man. He collected the Somers Tracts, and took part in the formation of the celebrated Harleian Library.

him to study the practice under Klingenberg, organist at Stettin, and the theory under Grosse, a Saxon. This course of instruction he enjoyed only for a twelvemonth, owing to the narrow circumstances of his family; but he made such good use of his time that at the age of fourteen he was engaged to teach the harpsichord to the Crown Prince of Prussia. He continued to prosecute his studies with unremitting diligence; and having acquired a knowledge of the classic languages, investigated the early principles of his art as laid down in the ancient Greek writers. He became, in fact, a profoundly skilled musician, and as a theorist had scarcely his equal among his contemporaries. He remained in the service of the Prussian Court until he was about thirty years old, when an act of irresponsible power on the part of the king—the decapitation without trial of an officer who had given some slight offence—so disgusted him, that he resolved on quitting his native land, and seeking some country where individual freedom was secured by the law. In Holland he resided for about a year, and then, in 1700, passed over into England, and, settling in London, was engaged in the orchestra at Drury Lane. It is probable, as Hawkins says, that he assisted in putting the operas on the stage that were performed there, for in that of 'Thomyris' is introduced a song of his composition, 'How blest is a Soldier.'

Soon afterwards he set to music, in the Italian style—that is, airs intermixed with recitative—six cantatas for voice and instruments, written by John Hughes; and as those were very favourably received, he published a second collection. In 1710 he took an active part in the establishment of the Academy of Ancient Music; and in 1712 was engaged by the Duke of Chandos as organist and composer to his chapel at Canons, for which he prepared several services and anthems. As a composer, however, it is not probable that, even if Handel had not been living, he would have won an extensive or permanent popularity. His music is that of a man thoroughly sound in all the secrets of his art, but without any natural gift of smooth and flowing melody. It was as a teacher of the principles of harmony and of the science of composition that he did good and faithful service in his generation.

In July 1713, at the same time with Croft, he took the degree of Doctor of Music at Oxford, his exercise being a a dramatic ode in celebration of the Peace of Utrecht— which seems to have been more popular with poets and musicians than it was with the great body of the people. About the same time, we are told, he revived the practice of 'solmisation by hexachords,'[1] which for almost a century had been disused. The non-musical reader is solemnly assured that there is nothing terrible in the said practice, notwithstanding the gruesome terms by which it is known. In 1714 he became director of the music at Lincoln's Inn Fields Theatre, for which he composed and arranged the masques of 'Venus and Adonis,' 1715; 'Apollo and Daphne,' and 'The Death of Dido,' 1716; and 'The Union of the Three Sister Arts,' St Cecilia's Day, 1723. His laborious and useful career he continued in this direction until 1724, when he was persuaded to co-operate in Berkeley's fantastic scheme for propagating religion and learning in America by the erection of a college in the Bermuda Islands. He and his associates had actually embarked, but the ship being wrecked, the enterprise was abandoned, and Dr Pepusch returned to England.

He did a much better thing for himself by his marriage with Signora Margarita de l'Epine; she brought him a fortune of £10,000, and settling down in Boswell Court, Carey Street,[2] he was able to organise his house-

[1] That is, the art of constructing the Musical Scale on the six sounds of the hexachord,—*Do, Re, Mi, Fa, Sol, La.*

[2] He afterwards removed to Fetter Lane, 'the next door but one to the south corner of the passage leading from thence into Bartlett's Building.'

hold on a liberal scale. In 1727 he largely increased his popularity by the admirable taste and skill with which he arranged the airs for Guy's 'Beggar's Opera.' Its successful reception was in no small measure due to Pepusch's labours. In 1730-31 appeared his well-known *Treatise on Harmony*. Six years later he was appointed organist of the Charter House, where he spent the remainder of his long and honourable life, still prosecuting his well-loved studies, and watching over the interests of his favourite institution, The Academy of Ancient Music. He lost his wife about 1746. In the same year he gave a proof of intellectual vigour by contributing a paper on the Ancient Genera to 'The Transactions of the Royal Society,' of which body he was elected a Fellow. He died on the 20th of July 1752, and was interred in the chapel of the Charter House. He produced a large number of compositions besides those I have mentioned; but the dust of oblivion rests upon them. Pepusch's great merit was the perseverance with which he taught and vindicated the scientific principles of the art, and helped to cultivate the public taste in a right direction.

He bequeathed a valuable collection of music to the Academy of Ancient Music.

JOHN ERNEST GALLIARD, the son of a perruquier of Zell, in Hanover, was born in or about 1687, and was taught music by Farinelli (not the great singer, but his uncle) and Steffani. After he had completed this course of instruction, he applied himself to the practice of the flute and the oboe; and was taken into the household of Prince George of Denmark as one of his chamber musicians. With that fortunate prince he came over to England, and succeeded Draghi in the then sinecure appointment of organist at Somerset House. Unlike a good many foreign artists who have profited by English patronage, he paid his adopted country the compliment of learning its language; and composed a Te Deum and Jubilate, and three anthems ('I will magnify Thee, O Lord,' 'O Lord God of Hosts,' and 'I am well Pleased'), which were performed at St Paul's and the Chapel Royal on occasions of public thanksgiving.

In 1712 Galliard set to music Hughes's opera of 'Calypso and Telemachus,' which was performed at the Haymarket, the cast including Signora Margarita, Signora Manina, Mrs Barbier, Mrs Pearson, and Mr Leveridge. Notwithstanding the exertions of these great artists, and the superior merit of both the words and music, the opera was not very successful, the 'Italian Opera' faction using their utmost exertions to secure its condemnation. In 1717 he composed the opera of 'Pan and Syrinx,' the libretto of which was furnished by Lewis Theobald (Pope's 'piddling Tibbald'); and for some years afterwards was engaged by Rich to adapt, arrange, and compose the music for the 'strange conjunction of opera and pantomime' which that energetic manager—an eighteenth-century Hollingshead—loved to put before his patrons at Lincoln's Inn and afterwards at Covent Garden. Even in these trifles Galliard showed the rare qualifications of a sound musician; and modern composers might find much to approve in his 'Jupiter and Europa,' 1723; his 'Necromancer; or, Harlequin Dr Faustus,' 1723; 'The Loves of Plato and Proserpine, with the Birth of Harlequin, 1725; and 'Apollo and Daphne; or, The Burgomaster Tricked,' 1726. One of the last of his works of this kind was 'The Royal Chase; or, Merlin's Cave,' 1736, in which for a hundred nights the popular singer, Mr Beard, delighted the audience by his rendering of the celebrated song, 'With early Horn.' He also composed the music for Lee's tragedy of 'Œdipus': it was never printed, but was preserved in the library of the Academy of Ancient Music. He contributed a considerable number of songs to *The Musical Miscellany*; and about 1740 published on his own account a volume of twelve songs composed by him at sundry times.

One of his finest compositions, which, if republished, might even now be acceptable, is his setting as a duet of Adam and Eve's Morning Hymn, from *Paradise Lost*. It was enlarged by Dr Cooke into a cantata, with orchestral accompaniment, and some of the airs arranged as choruses. In 1742 this scholarly and accomplished musician published a translation of Tosi's *Opinioni di Cantori Antichi e Moderuis, o Sieno Ossavazioni Sopra il Canto Figurato*, under the title of *Observations on the Florid Song; or, Sentiments of Ancient and Modern Singers*. In 1745 he held a benefit concert at Lincoln's Inn Fields Theatre, at which were performed his settings of the choruses to Sheffield, Duke of Buckingham's tragedies of 'Brutus' and 'Julius Cæsar.' Galliard died early in 1749.

Among the Church musicians of the period, honourable mention must be made of Dr THOMAS TUDWAY, one of Dr Blow's pupils in the Chapel Royal, and contemporary there with Purcell, Turner, and Estwick. His acquirements were so considerable that in 1671 he obtained the post of organist at King's College Chapel, Cambridge, and in 1681 was admitted to the degree of Mus. Bac. When Queen Anne paid her celebrated visit to the University in 1705, he composed a special anthem for the occasion. 'Thou, O God, hast heard my Vows,' which he performed as an exercise for the degree of Doctor of Music. He then received the honorary appointment of Professor of Music.

A few songs and catches are all of Dr Tudway's compositions that are in print, but he seems to have been a very industrious writer of anthems. Perhaps nothing from his pen is more interesting than his letter on Music and Musicians, from which Hawkins quotes. 'Many very curious particulars are related in it, and some facts which, but for him, must have been buried in oblivion; among which are the contest between Father Smith and Harris about the making of the Temple organ, and the decision of it by Jefferies, afterwards Lord Chancellor'—a contest of which, I fancy, few of my readers have ever heard, though it was not wholly without interest. In this letter Tudway alludes to Purcell in eulogistic terms :—' He had a most commendable ambition of exceeding every one of his time, and he succeeded in it without contradiction, there being none in England, nor anywhere else that I know of, that could come in competition with him for compositions of all kinds.'

Whether it was to the credit of Dr Tudway that he was an incorrigible punster, I leave it to my readers to determine.

The following notice I borrow verbatim from Sir John Hawkins :—

Samuel Marshall, a young man of a promising genius and amiable character, merits a place among the Church musicians of the time. He was a scholar of Bowl, and organist of St Catherine Cree Church, London. An anthem, 'Behold how good and joyful,' in the key of C with the greater third, extant only in manuscript, and a few songs, printed with his name, are all of his compositions that at this day are known; among them is one for two voices : 'Earth's Treasure,' which, being sung at a concert at Stationers' Hall, was received with great applause. It was reprinted about twenty years ago, but without a name, in a collection entitled *The Essex Harmony*. He died in 1714, at the age of twenty-seven, and lies buried under the organ of his church. Over the place of his interment is a marble tablet, erected by the Rev. Mr Prat.

An anthem in occasional use, 'I will arise and go to my Father,' was composed by Dr ROBERT CREIGHTON, son of the Bishop of Bath and Wells of that name, who attended Charles II. in his exile, but did not succeed in correcting his morals. Dr Creighton was in holy orders, and in 1674 was appointed canon residentiary of Wells; and in this position devoted his leisure to the study and practice of his beloved art. Music is a jealous mistress and reserves her chiefest favours for those who give her their exclusive devotion. Creighton died at Wells, in 1736, at the ripe old age of ninety-seven.

Dr WILLIAM TURNER, another of Blow's pupils, attained to the age of eighty-eight. He died on the 13th of January 1746; and was buried in the same grave and at the same time with his wife Elizabeth, whose death happened but four days before his own. They had been married nearly seventy years. Those facts are singular enough to be worth recording. Turner took his degree of Mus. Doc. in 1696. Along with Blow, Humphrey, and Turner, and as a memorial of their close and enduring friendship, he composed the 'Club Anthem,'—'I will alway give thanks.'

JOHN GOLDWIN, who died in 1719, composed several anthems of an original character. He was organist and master of the choristers at St George's Chapel, Windsor, being appointed to these posts in 1703.

JOHN ISHAM, or ISUM, a good organist and sound musician, made sundry valuable compositions for the use of the Church.

As leader of the first opera orchestra in England, and a celebrated violinist, WILLIAM CORBETT deserves mention here. He was a good musician, and published several concertos for all instruments, and two or three sonatas for violins and flutes. He died in 1748.

Among popular organists and composers we may record THOMAS ROSEINGRAVE, organist of St George's, Hanover Square—so enthusiastic an admirer of Palestrina, that his bedchamber was covered with scraps of paper containing select passages from the Italian master's compositions; PHILIP HART, died 1750, organist of St Dionis Backchurch; GEORGE MONRO, organist of St Peter's, Cornhill, an agreeable song-writer; GEORGE HAYDEN, organist of St Mary Magdalen's, Bermondsey, whose two-part song, 'As I saw fair Chlora walk alone,' has an elegant and attractive melody; and WILLIAM BABELL, organist of Allhallows, Praed Street, who deserves notice as, perhaps, the first composer of fantasias or sonatas upon airs selected from popular operas. He died in 1723. There were also OBADIAH SHUTTLEWORTH, organist of the Temple; HENRY SYMONDS, of St Martin's, Ludgate; ABELL WHICHELLS, of St Edmund the King's, who published a collection of lessons for the harpsichord or spinnet; and JOHN ROBINSON, organist of Westminster, who was also a proficient on the harpsichord.

Of the Music and Musicians of Queen Anne's time, the preceding pages have, I hope, furnished the reader with a comprehensive survey.

CHAPTER IV.

ART AND ARCHITECTURE.

Characteristics of the 'Queen Anne' Architecture—Wood Carving and Grinling Gibbons—Francis Buol-Boit, the Painter in Enamel—Jervas—Howard—Cradock—Crowe—Jonathan Richardson—Wollaston—Dahl—Ricci—Pellegrini—John Closterman—Sir Godfrey Kneller—Anecdotes—Sir James Thornhill—Sir Christopher Wren—Sir John Vanbrugh—James Gibbs — Landscape Gardening — William Kent — Orlando Bridgman.

THE Age of Queen Anne not only failed to develop a school of art of its own, but did not even afford any indications that such a school was rising in the near future. It lay under the unhealthy influence, and, to some extent, carried on the traditions, of the Restoration period. What it possessed of taste and refinement was chiefly devoted to the cultivation of polite letters ; and literature and politics absorbed almost all that it had of intellectual force and vigour. Literature advanced with rapid strides ; Art stood still, if it did not retrograde. Great writers began to seek an audience among the people ; and the people exhibited an ever-increasing interest in what they had to say. With the artist it was otherwise. He still hugged the chains of dependence upon titled patrons ; and the result was to cramp his energies and extinguish his aspirations. He became before all things a portrait-painter; or he covered domes and ceilings and staircases with sprawling allegories, like those of Verrio and Laguerre. For the masses he did nothing ; he neither taught them sweet lessons of humanity, nor gratified them with dreams of beauty. In Art was perceptible that deficiency of the ideal element which we note in the age's Literature; it copied—it did not invent. The Queen Anne writers are often sympathetic, tender, and genial—which is not to be affirmed, however, of the Queen Anne artist, supine in the frigid depths of mediocrity and commonplace. The age and country which gave birth to a Marlborough and a Swift, a Peterborough and a Bolingbroke, could produce in the world of art nothing better than a Kneller. This one fact speaks volumes. An artist is depressed or elevated by the conditions under which he pursues his art; and in Queen Anne's reign these were unfavourable, and, indeed hostile; for if there were no Turner to surprise and delight and inspire, so was there no public prepared to receive, applaud, and study Turner. The wretched, prosaic, realistic character of the time, which impressed itself so unhappily upon English poetry, upon English politics, upon English theology, impressed itself not less adversely upon English—or what passed for English—art. It made itself conspicuous in dull portraits of duller men and women. It was unpleasantly visible in the leaden and plaster urns and vases sprinkled about the eighteenth century garden, with its straight-cut walks and formal avenues. It stared you in the face in the plain monotonous exterior of the eighteenth century mansion. It pervaded the life, the education, and the manners of eighteenth century society. It was a wretched thing; but the country endured and survived it.

Taking imitativeness and realism as the two main notes of English art in the reign of Anne, let us glance at the career of GRINLING GIBBONS, the greatest artist in wood whose name is inscribed upon our roll of worthies. The praise which Walpole bestows he richly merited :—' There is no instance of a man before him who gave to wood the loose and airy lightness of flowers, and chained together the various productions of the elements with a free disorder natural to each species.' He imitated Nature with the faithfulness of a loving eye and the skill of a bold and ready hand. Whatever his material—stone or marble or wood—it seemed to become plastic beneath his touch. The petals of the flower, the plumage of the bird, the leaves of the tree, were reproduced with such exquisite exactness that one might almost wonder which was the original and which the copy. The tendrils of the ivy grew, the bird pruned its wings as you gazed. Decorative carving, in the hands of Grinling Gibbons, became what it had never been before, what it has never been since. He did not invent, it is true, he *copied*, but it was with a freedom and a grace which preserved all the characteristics of the original. There was a breadth of treatment about all he did, and a picturesqueness of effect, which raised his work into the region of high art. But it was in execution that he excelled. If in originality of composition and felicity of grouping, he did not approach those mediæval carvers whose labours have decorated our old minsters and cathedrals, in grace, fidelity, and refinement of workmanship he was more than their equal.

Grinling Gibbons was certainly of Dutch descent, and some authorities claim for him a Dutch birthplace, but the balance of testimony seems in favour of the received tradition, that he was born in London (1648). At all events, we find him at a comparatively early age residing in Belle Sauvage Court, Ludgate Hill, where, it is said, he exhibited a pot of flowers so delicately and cunningly carved that the leaves quivered and shook with the motion of passing vehicles. Removing to Deptford, a fortunate chance discovered him to John Evelyn (1671). 'As I was walking' says the author of *Sylva*, 'near a poor solitary thatched house in a field near Sayes Court, I found him shut in; but, looking in at the window, I perceived him carving the large cartoon (the Crucifixion) of Tintoret. I asked if I might enter; he opened the door civilly to me, and I saw him about such a work as, for curiosity of handling, drawing, and studious exactness, I had never before seen in all my travels. I asked him why he worked in such an obscure and lonesome place: he told me it was that he might apply himself to his profession without interruption, and wondered not a little how I had found him out. I asked him if he was unwilling to be made known to some great man, for that I believed it might turn to his profit: he answered that he was but as yet a beginner, but would not be sorry to sell off that piece: on demanding his price, he said, an hundred pounds. In good earnest, the very frame was worth the money, there being in nature nothing so tender and delicate as the flowers and festoons about it, and yet the work was very strong: in the piece were more than one hundred figures of men, etc. I found he was likewise musical: and very civil, sober, and discreet in his discourse.'

Through Evelyn the picture was sold for eighty pounds to Sir George Vyner; and, again through Evelyn, King Charles's patronage was bestowed on the skilful carver, who obtained a place in the Board of Works, and was largely employed in St George's Chapel at Windsor, where 'the simplicity of his foliage at once sets off and atones for the glare of Verrio's painting.' There, too, he lavished his skill on the fine marble pedestal which supports King Charles's equestrian statue. Soon afterwards he executed the pedestal of the Charing Cross statue; and, rising to bolder flights, executed a statue of Charles II. for the citizens of London, which long ornamented the old Exchange. The artist by this time had grown opulent and famous, and removed from his obscure cottage in the

Deptford wilds to a house in the Piazza, Covent Garden. The Solomonic saw that the diligent hand maketh rich, never had a more striking illustration. The industry of Gibbons is as conspicuous as his fertility; and his handiwork is scattered far and wide over England. Every Londoner knows the specimens of his skill to be seen at Windsor and at Hampton Court. At Sion House the stone vases on the garden terrace were wrought by his chisel. The magnificent carvings in the choir of St Paul's and the oaken throne at Canterbury are his; for the latter, by the way, he received only seventy pounds, for the former, one thousand three hundred and thirty-three pounds seven shillings and fivepence. The great hall of Bush Hill Park, Winchmore, is adorned by his famous carving in relief of St Stephen's Martyrdom. At Cassiobury, the portrait of young Viscount Malden is set in one of his wondrously carved frames. At Fulham Church the finest monument is that of Dorothy Clarke (1695), with its angels and festoons of flowers by Grinling Gibbons. Carvings by him are extant in a house called Valentines, at Great Ilford. Going further afield, we find at Exton, in Rutlandshire, the magnificent tomb which he erected for Baptist Noel, Viscount Camden. It cost a thousand pounds, and measures twenty-two feet in height by fourteen feet in width. There are two figures of the noble and his wife, and bas-reliefs of their children. At Burleigh is a splendid profusion of his carving in picture-frames, chimney-pieces, and door cases; and the Last Supper, in alto-relief, finely executed. At Chatsworth, where he was asisted by Watson, a Derbyshire carver, are many ornaments by Gibbons, particularly in the chapel. 'In the great ante-chamber are several dead fowl over the chimney finely executed, and over a closet door a pen not distinguishable from a real feather. When Gibbons had finished his works in that palace, he presented the Duke with a point cravat, a woodcock, and a medal with his own hand, all preserved in a glass case in the gallery.' Lastly, the genius of Gibbons is finely illustrated at Petworth, where a noble apartment, sixty feet long, twenty-four feet wide and twenty high, is prodigally decorated with carved panels, and corresponding festoons formed of fruits, flowers, shells, and birds, copied from nature with wonderfully realistic power. An antique vase, suspended among birds and flowers, is executed in the purest classic taste. While the work here was in progress, the house caught fire, and Seldon, a favourite pupil and assistant of Gibbons, lost his life in saving the festoon which contains that beautiful vase.

On the accession of George I., Gibbons was appointed Master Carver in Wood, with the not too handsome salary of eighteenpence a day. He died at his own house in Bow Street, Covent Garden, on the 3d of August 1721.

Of FRANCIS BUD, the sculptor, it is unnecessary to say more than that he executed the statue of Queen Anne, so long a melancholy object in St Paul's Churchyard, and the Conversion of St Paul, which fills in the pediment of the Cathedral. Imitation work, and by no means of the first quality.

The Enameller's is not a high form of art, but it was popular in Queen Anne's reign, and CHARLES BOIT, the Swedish enamel painter, obtained much royal and noble patronage for his miniatures, many of which are still preserved, and show considerable facility and minuteness of execution. On Queen Anne's death, being embarrassed by pecuniary difficulties, he crossed over to France, where his unquestionable skill procured him employment. He died in 1726. To one of his works a historical interest attaches. He was ordered to execute a large plate, twenty-four inches by eighteen inches, for which a design in oil was painted by Laguerre, to commemorate the victory of Blenheim. It was to include portraits of the Queen and Prince George, Sunderland, Godolphin, and others, with Victory introducing Marlborough and Prince Eugene, and France and Bavaria lying prostrate on the ground, the whole surrounded by standards and trophies of arms. He was entrusted with an advance of one thousand pounds, a considerable portion of which he expended in constructing furnaces of a sufficient size to fire so large a plate; and on beginning to apply the colours another advance was made of seven hundred pounds. But he was so long over his preparations that the wheel of fortune made a complete revolution, Marlborough fell into disgrace, and the Tory Ministers ordered the painter to substitute Ormonde for Marlborough, and the genius of Peace for that of Victory. But Prince Eugene resented this insult to his great companion in arms, and refused to sit. The picture came to a sudden termination, and, owing to the death of Queen Anne, was never resumed.

In his *Epistle to Mr Jervas*, Pope lavishes his poetical eulogiums on a painter of very ordinary merit. Referring to his portraits of the Duchess of Bridgewater, Lady Worsley, and others, he exclaims:—

> 'Yet still her charms in breathing paint engage,
> Her modest cheek shall warm a future age.
> Beauty, frail flower, that every season fears,
> Blooms in thy colours for a thousand years.
> Thus Churchill's race shall other hearts surprise,
> And other beauties envy Worsley's eyes;
> Each pleasing Blount shall endless smiles bestow,
> And soft Belinda's blush for ever glow.
> O, lasting as those colours, may they shine
> Free as thy stroke, yet faultless as thy line;
> New graces yearly like thy works display,
> Soft without weakness, without glaring gay!'

Language like this might, with justice, have been applied to the works of a Reynolds or a Gainsborough, it was simply extravagant when lavished on the conceited Irish painter, whose success among 'persons of quality' and marriage to a rich widow (worth twenty thousand pounds) completely turned his head. He was a good copyist, and having executed a copy of one of Titian's masterpieces, exclaimed, as he compared the copy with the original,—'Poor little Tit! how he would stare!' When the Duchess of Bridgewater sent to him for her portrait, he rudely observed that she had not a good ear. What, then, did he think *was* a handsome ear? In reply, he pointed to his own.

CHARLES JERVAS was born in Ireland about 1675. Having studied under Sir Godfrey Kneller in London, he visited Paris and Rome; and on his return secured a flattering introduction to the public from the good-natured Steele, who, alluding to two of his portraits—he calls them Chloe and Clarissa—says,—'Their different perfections are suitably represented by the last great painter Italy has sent us, Mr Jervas. Clarissa is by that skilful hand placed in a manner that looks artless, and innocent of the torments she gives; Chloe is drawn with a liveliness that shows she is conscious of, but not affected with, her perfections.' The deplorable condition of English art in Queen Anne's reign, and the low standard of the public taste, may be inferred from this one fact—that Steele could write of Jervas as a great painter. Painting common-place portraits, and making good copies of great pictures, Jervas flourished in London for some thirty years, and died in 1739.

Another of the mediocrities of the period was HUGH HOWARD, the portrait-painter, whose aristocratic connections secured his comfort in life by preferring him to the posts of keeper of the State Papers and Paymaster of His Majesty's Palaces. Prior addressed to him some lively verses, beginning—

> ' Dear Howard, from the soft assaults of love,
> Poets and painters never are secure.'

LUKE CRADOCK would furnish a paragraph for the ingenious writers of books upon *Self Help*, *The Secret of Success*, and *The Pursuit of Knowledge under Difficulties*. He began life as a house-painter; but he had patience, perseverance, and some natural gifts; and he became noted for the grace and truth with which he painted birds.

LEWIS CROWE was a tolerable miniature-painter, and dabbled in water-colours. He died in 1724.

One of the best portrait-painters of the time, and a very judicious, if not a brilliant writer upon art, whose writings have still a certain value for the student, was JONATHAN RICHARDSON. He was born in 1665, and had the good fortune to study under Riley (the successor to Lely), whose niece he married, and whose fortune he inherited. In the history of English art, he has a close connection with Reynolds, for Hudson, who taught Reynolds, had been Richardson's pupil. His portraits were distinguished by their faithfulness and their conscientious manipulation. After a long and prosperous life, he died at Westminster on the 28th of May 1745. His works include *An Essay on the Whole Art of Criticism as it relates to Paintings*, and *An Argument in behalf of the Science of a Connoisseur*.

In our chapter on the Musicians, we have reference

made to WOLLASTON, who played violin or flute at Britton's weekly concerts. By profession, he was a portrait-painter; but he was held in small esteem, and in his declining years was glad to seek the charitable asylum of the Charter House.

Among the foreign artists who found a home in Queen Anne's England, MICHAEL DAHL, the Swede (died 1742), is of course well known. As a portrait-painter, he was much patronised by Queen Anne and her consort, and by many of 'the nobility and gentry.'[1] LOUIS LAGUERRE, who in decorative art, was not without a certain facility, covered numerous ceilings in English palaces and mansions with his pseudo-classical compositions. He died in 1721. At Little Stanmore Church are eight specimens of his craft, illustrative of events in the Life of the Saviour. He is best remembered now by his association with Verrio, in Pope's well-known couplet,—

> 'On painted ceilings you devoutly stare,
> Where sprawl the saints of Verrio and Laguerre.'

At Hampton Court, in the Presence Chamber, are three large decorative works, in the manner of Paul Veronese, by SEBASTIAN RICCI, painted by him during his brief residence in England, and unusually good specimens of his style. The altar-piece in the chapel of Chelsea Hospital is also from his pencil. His pupil, ANTONIO PELLEGRINI, also visited England, where he embellished ceilings and staircases for several of the nobility, and made designs, which were paid for but not adopted, for painting the dome of St Paul's.

---

[1] His portraits of Admirals Sir George Rooke and Sir J. Wisharts are to be seen in the Painted Hall at Greenwich; and at Hampton Court is one of his heads of Prince George of Denmark.

JOHN CLOSTERMAN was born at Osnaburg, in 1656. In 1679 he went to Paris, where he resided for a couple of years. He crossed over to England in 1681, and was at first employed by Riley as an assistant. He gradually rose into repute as a portrait-painter; was employed by the Queen, whose full-length portrait from his pencil now 'adorns' the London Guildhall; by the Duke of Somerset, whose children he painted; and by the Duke and Duchess of Marlborough, for whom he executed several portraits. He got into a good deal of trouble with the Duchess, and the Duke declared that it had cost him more trouble to reconcile him and the Duchess than to fight a battle. He made an unfortunate marriage; his wife proved faithless, and left him, carrying off all he possessed; and he died, with a broken heart and a distraught brain, in 1710.

I turn now to an artist who claims a longer notice than I have accorded to any of his contemporaries. Sir GODFREY KNELLER was born at Lubeck, on the 8th of August 1646, and studied the art of painting in Holland, at first under Rembrandt, and afterwards under Ferdinand Boll. From Holland he went to Italy, to acquire a knowledge of the great masters. Thereafter he settled in Hamburgh; but in 1675 he acted on the recommendation of a merchant named Baules, and transferred himself to London, where he found a world of patrons prepared to favour and support a man with genuine artistic powers. His success was immediate; and, well pleased with his auspicious reception, he settled down in the metropolis, and speedily amassed a fortune. It is a mistake to undervalue Kneller as a portrait-painter. He had less vivacity than Lely, but he had more dignity; and if he has not the picturesqueness of Vandyck, he is distinguished by his accuracy of drawing. He often painted very badly, but his best works are admirable, both in conception and execution. His popularity never flagged during nearly half a century, and he painted many of the principal personages of his time—as, for instance, five English sovereigns in succession, from Charles II. to George I.; Louis XIV., Peter the Great, and Charles VI. of Spain. To his facile and pleasing brush we owe the Hampton Court Beauties, portraits of the ladies of the Court of William III. and Queen Mary,—namely, the Duchesses of St Albans and Grafton; the Countesses of Essex, Peterborough, Dorset, and Ranelagh; Lady Middleton, and Miss Pitt. Walpole tells a good story in connection with those famous portraits. The Gunnings, he says, went the other day to see Hampton Court. As they were going into the Beauty room, another company arrived. 'This way, ladies,' cried the housekeeper; 'here are the Beauties.' The Gunnings flew into a passion, and asked her what she meant: that they came to see the Palace, not to be shown as a sight themselves.

William III. knighted him; Anne patronised him; and George I. gave him a baronetcy—an honour not again conferred upon gentlemen of the brush until Mr Gladstone recommended for it Sir John Millais, and Lord Salisbury procured it for Sir Frederick Leighton. He painted the forty-six portraits known as the Kit-Cat Club, now preserved at Bayfordbury, near Hertford. Among the best are Jacob Tonson, the bookseller; the artist himself, wearing the massive chain and medal of gold given him by William III., in acknowledgment of the skill with which he had, at the royal command, painted portraits of the plenipotentiaries at Ryswick; John Dryden; Congreve, painted in 1709, with the easy and airy expression of a foppish man of the world; Vanbrugh; Addison, in a large wig, with large, clear, steel-grey eyes; Sir Richard Steele; William Walsh, poetaster and critic; Lord Mohun; Sir

Robert Walpole; Pulteney, Earl of Bath; Charles Sackville, Earl of Dorset; and Boyle, Earl of Burlington. The rest are of greater or less interest from historical or social associations, but artistically inferior, though the whole are remarkable as executed by a single artist.

Kneller also painted some portraits for the Admirals' Gallery at Greenwich; conscientious work on the whole, but not his best. Of his best, however, is the full-length of the Countess of Ranelagh[1] at Cassiobury; his Earl Stanhope at Chevening; the Grimston portraits at Gorhambury; the full-length of Queen Anne, in royal robes, and the Duchess of Marlborough, at Grove Park; William III., at Hatfield; the portraits of Lord Somers, Lord Backhurst, and Lady Mary Sackville, Charles, sixth Earl of Dorset, Pope's 'grace of courts, the Muses' pride,' Dryden, Sir Charles Sidley, Betterton the actor, Locke, and Sir Isaac Newton, at Kade; Lord Chancellor Cowper, at Panshanger; and, at Windsor, Mary, William, Anne, and George I. This imperfect list impresses us strongly with the resolute industry of the painter, as well as with his substantial merits. A Kneller collection, by the way, would furnish a tolerably complete gallery of the worthies, personages, persons of quality, and men of letters who made history or adorned society in England in the early years of the eighteenth century.

Kneller as a man was about equally remarkable for his wit and vanity. In town he occupied a house in Great Queen Street, next door to surly Dr Radcliffe. There was an entrance from one garden into the other, and the doctor's servants took advantage of it to steal the painter's flowers. Kneller, indignant, sent word that he would have the door shut up. Radcliffe replied that he might do anything with it but 'paint it;' to which Sir Godfrey merrily

[1] It is to this lady that Fielding in his *Tom Jones* compares Sophia Western.

answered, that he would take anything from him but his physic. An anonymous poetaster has versified this anecdote:—

> 'Sir Godfrey and Radcliffe had one common way
> Into one common garden—and each had a key.
> Quoth Kneller, "I'll certainly stop up that door,
> If ever I find it unlocked any more."
> "Your threats," replies Radcliffe, "disturb not my ease,
> And so you don't paint it, e'en do what you please."
> "You're smart," rejoins Kneller, "but say what you will,
> I'll take anything from you—but potion or pill."'

As a proof of his vanity, his answer to Pope is often quoted:—'Sir Godfrey,' said the poet, 'I believe if God Almighty had had your assistance in making the world, it would have been more perfect.' ''Fore God, sir, I believe so too.' But Kneller, a man of quick perception, may very well have detected the motive of his diminutive friend's saucy question, and have answered him, as Solomon recommends, according to his folly.

Kneller had a country-house at Whilton, in Twickenham parish, now known as Kneller Hall. He built it between 1709 and 1711, and spent there his last years; but died at his house in London on the 27th of October 1723. It was a stately red brick mansion, with spacious rooms and a handsome staircase, painted by Laguerre. He had intended to employ Sir James Thornhill; but hearing that he had undertaken to paint Sir Isaac Newton's portrait, he swore that no portrait-painter should paint *his* house, and gave the work to Laguerre. His wealth enabled him to live here in great pomp, and filled the *rôles* of country gentleman and Justice of the Peace in quite a John Bull-ish spirit. His magisterial decisions, it is said, were animated rather by equity than law. Pope has some lines in allusion to one of his judgments, when he dismissed a man who stole a joint of meat, and censured its owner for throwing temptation in the poor man's path :—

> 'I think Sir Godfrey should decide the suit,
> Who sent the thief that stole the cash, away,
> And punished him that put it in his way.'

Kneller was buried in Twickenham Church. His widow demanded from Pope the fulfilment of a promise which she said he had made to her husband on his deathbed, to remove his father's monument, that she might erect one, fourteen feet high by eight feet wide, to her husband, for it was the best place in the church to be seen at a distance.' 'This surprised me quite,' says Pope. 'I hesitated, and said, I feared it would be indecent, and that my mother must be asked as well as I.' She burst into tears, and Pope was constrained to say that he would do all he could do with decency. Upon consideration he naturally declined to interfere with the monument. Lady Kneller appealed to the parochial authorities, who, of course, could do nothing; and so it came to pass that no memorial marks the resting-place of the great painter.

A monument was erected to him in Westminster Abbey, for which Pope wrote the epitaph :—

> 'Kneller, by Heaven, and not a master taught,
> Whose art was nature, and whose pictures thought ;
> Now for two ages having snatched from Fate
> Whate'er was beauteous, or whate'er was great,
> Lies crowned with princes' honours, poets' bays,[1]
> True to his merit and brave thirst of praise
> Living, great Nature found he might outvie
> Her works, and, dying, fears herself may die.'

THORNHILL, who was to have decorated Kneller's house, belonged to the painter and glazier school of art. He was to some extent a follower in the steps of Verrio

---

[1] Kneller had the good fortune to be celebrated in verse by Dryden, Prior, Pope, Addison, Steele, and Tickell.

and Laguerre, and loved to cover ceilings and staircases with inane compositions, mythological or allegorical. Nothing more forcibly illustrates the degraded artistic taste of England than that this painter of common-places, with his defective drawing and his feeble colouring, should have secured such an amount of patronage. It is true that his patrons did not pay him very well. The South Sea Company gave him only twenty-five shillings per square yard for decorating their hall and staircase, and at Blenheim he was limited to the same rate. For his work on the dome of St Paul's and in the hall of Greenwich Hospital he received only forty shillings, but then there were a great many square yards, and Thornhill contrived to amass a handsome fortune. Greenwich Hospital shows him at his best. He began the task in 1708, and completed it in 1727, bringing to bear upon it a good deal of conscientious labour, and displaying much carefulness of execution along with an unfortunate feebleness of conception. In the Painted Hall ' the ceiling is covered with an amazing number and variety of allegorical personages and figures, the meaning or purpose of which it is hard to find out. The grand feature of the design is, however, the great oval frame in the centre of the ceiling, upheld by eight gigantic slaves, and surrounded by an interminable variety of maritime trophies and commercial emblems and objects, while in the centre, under a purple canopy, are William and Mary enthroned, and attended by the cardinal virtues. Apollo, Hercules, and other of the old gods and heroes; Truth and Liberty, Wisdom, Fame, Tyranny, Envy, Calumny, Covetousness, and other attributes, good and evil; Neptune and Amphitrite, and the river deities, Thames, Humber, Severn, and subject streams; Dryads and Hamadryads; Time, and the astronomers, from Tycho Brahe and Copernicus to Newton and Flamsteed: the Four Elements, the Hours, the signs of the Zodiac, and a multitude of other beings and symbols, find their place in this marvellous composition '—or chaos, for anything like a clear idea it is impossible to decipher.

But it was thought wonderful in good Queen Anne's days, and the sovereign, whose artistic standard was as low as that of her people, employed his facile brush to complete the decorations which Verrio had began at Windsor Castle. At Bromfield Park, Southgate, walls and ceilings bear witness to his industry; and at Roehampton House, the seat of the Earl of Devon, the ceiling of the saloon has been decorated by him with a curiously unclassic design of a Banquet of the Gods in Olympus, in which the divine attributes are conspicuous by their absence. At Moor Park he is painfully *en evidence*. He was commissioned to decorate the hall and saloon by a certain Benjamin Hoskins Styles, who had made a fortune by speculating in South Sea shares; but when he had finished Styles refused to pay the three thousand five hundred pounds agreed upon, professing that the work was improperly executed. Thornhill sued him for the amount, and the claim was referred to Richardson, Dahl, and other artists, who reported in his favour, and awarded him an extra five hundred pounds for decorations about the house, and for his services as surveyor.

James Thornhill was descended from an old and decayed Dorsetshire family, and was born at Weymouth in 1676. His father was compelled to dispose of the family lands, and young Thornhill was sent into the world to carve a fortune for himself. Through the kindness of his uncle, Dr Sydenham, the celebrated physician, he was enabled to study painting in London, pursuing what we should now call the decorative branch, and coming into competition with Laguerre as an allegorical designer. His work at St Paul's, by an odd kind of non-sequence, obtained him the appointment of historical painter to Queen Anne. His historical pictures, like his portraits, are stamped with mediocrity—mediocrity the most hopeless.

In 1711 Thornhill journeyed through Holland and Flanders on artistic studies intent, and began to form a collection of drawings and pictures by old masters, which afterwards, when considerably enlarged, he threw open for the use of artists and students. On his return to England, perceiving that the great need of the day, at least in the world of art, was some provision for training young painters, he urged upon the Government a proposal for the establishment of a Royal Academy of Drawing and Painting. The British Government had not then learned that it was any part of a Government's duty to elevate the public taste and encourage a love of art, and rejected his scheme. Thornhill thereupon opened an academy, free of charge, for drawing and the study of the living model, at which William Hogarth was one of the earliest attendants. It was thus that he became acquainted with Thornhill's daughter, Jane. The two fell in love with each other, and as it was certain that Sir James, the member for Melcombe Regis, the favourite of monarchs, the wealthy 'grandee of easeldom,' would not look complacently upon their attachment, Jane ran away, and married her lover clandestinely, in March 1729, at old Paddington Church. It is satisfactory to know that Sir James afterwards forgave the offending couple.

Sir James, who was knighted by George I., in acknowledgment of the angels he had suspended on carved ceilings, and the Fames blowing trumpets he had sprawled upon spacious staircases, died at his seat, Thornhill, near Weymouth—he had been able to buy back the family estate—on the 4th of May 1734.

· · · · · · · · · · ·

We pass on to the architecture of England in the reign of Anna Augusta. The typical Queen Anne house, with its red brick exterior, its flat façade free of all attempt at decoration, its numerous long windows, its hideous portico, and the long flight of steps which form the approach to its heavy door, is pretty well known even in these days, for specimens of it are still extant. Inside, it had its merits: the rooms were usually ample and lofty, the staircases broad and massive, and adequate space was provided for the employment of decorative art. But there is nothing in it to call for special notice, nor have we any motive to speak respectfully of its builders. Our attention must be given to architecture on a more extended scale, in which England had at least one recognised master, Sir CHRISTOPHER WREN.

'*Si monumentum quæris circumspice.*' . . . And I think that no sublimer or more impressive monument of his genius could man desire or contrive than that massive pile of St Paul's Cathedral, with the swelling dome which lifts itself in such marvellous dignity and grace above the misty roofs of the crowded city. He who could conceive and execute so sublime an idea—such an epic in stone— could have been of no ordinary mould. If it be true that a great opportunity fell to his lot, it is not less true that he proved worthy of it. The man was equal to the hour and the work. What an ill-fortune might have been ours if the task that Wren so nobly undertook and accomplished—the task of creating a new London—had devolved upon a lower mind—upon one of those timid mediocrities who tread the servile path of imitation with tottering feet, now dwarfing some fine Gothic conception, and now mutilating some sweet Italian design! Wren was by no means insensible to the traditions and examples of the Past. He was profoundly versed in the principles of the ancient architecture, but he applied them with the boldness and independence of an original intellect. And hence it is that London is able to boast of a cathedral second only in grandeur to St Peter's, superior to it, perhaps, in its exquisite unity of design and harmony of proportion.

St Paul's, however, is but one, if the greatest, of the monuments which the genius of Wren created. The stately edifice of Greenwich Hospital, the beautiful church of St Stephen's, Walbrook, and some fifty other churches, not all of them without defects, but none of them without distinctive merits, as well as the stately column of the Monument, bear enduring witness to the fertility of his resource and the comprehensiveness of his knowledge. The various character of his works is remarkable: he seldom repeats himself, and he shows a singular felicity in utilising aspect and situation. He very rarely touches the commonplace: in his least successful buildings may be found some happy stroke, some ingenious adaptation, some bold flight of fancy, which shows the force and vigour of the master-mind, and justifies us in affirming that modern England has produced no greater architect than Sir Christopher Wren.

Wren belongs to Queen Anne's reign, not only in virtue of the generous support which he received at her hands, but because in her reign he set the crown on the head of his grandest work. For upwards of thirty years he had watched over the progress of the great cathedral which rose upon the ruins of the old metropolitan church; and in 1710 he had the happiness of laying, by the hands of his son, the topmost stone of the lantern on its cupola. The devout architect, then in the seventy-ninth year of his age, performed this final ceremony with humility and in prayerful gratitude, and all London poured out its vast population to witness it and rejoice in it—to admire the magnificent structure and do homage to its creator.

Wren had a great deal of trouble while building St Paul's. Just as Marlborough in his campaigns was harassed by the Dutch field-deputies, so was Wren badgered and bullied by the clerical and lay commissioners who had been appointed to the general superintendence of the work. They offered him throughout its erection a vexatious and ignorant opposition ; and when it was almost completed, they procured his dismissal—in 1728, when he was eighty-six years of age, and had held office nearly forty-nine years, as surveyor-general of the royal buildings. 'The length of his life,' says Walpole caustically, 'enriched the reign of several princes, and disgraced the last of them.' Wren bore this unjust treatment with his usual dignity. 'He betook himself to a country retirement, saying only with the Stoic—" *Nunc me jubet fortuna expeditius philosophari*": in which recess, free from worldly affairs, he passed the greatest part of the five last years of his life in contemplation and studies, and principally in the consolation of the Holy Scriptures; cheerful in solitude, and as well pleased to die in the shade as in the light.' His place of retirement was Hampton Court, where he enjoyed a happy and serene leisure, and with undecayed faculties made the most of life. His physical powers, however, began to decline, until, in journeying between London and Hampton Court, he caught cold, and on returning home felt slightly indisposed. His attendants were not alarmed, and he retired, as was his wont, to slumber a little after dinner, in his easy chair. From that slumber he never awoke, passing away so quietly that his death was unobserved, on the 25th of February 1723, in the ninety-first year of his age. A fitting resting-place was found for him in the vault of St Paul's Cathedral, under the south aisle of the choir.

Wren was of low stature, with active and well-built

limbs, and a certain natural seriousness of air and dignity of bearing. His face was that of a man of high intellect—the forehead broad and high, the mouth firm, the eyes large and expressive. 'He had such wonderful sweetness of temper, such a steady tranquillity of mind, and such pious fortitude, that no injurious incidents or inquietudes of human life could ever ruffle or discompose.' This is the language of filial eulogy; but it is confirmed by abundant evidence. Bishop Sprat says of him:—'His knowledge had a right influence on the temper of his mind, which had all the humility, graceful modesty, goodness, calmness, strength and sincerity of a sound and unaffected philosopher—to his merits his country is further indebted than has been acknowledged.' His intellect was not confined within the strict limits of his profession; his scientific researches were by no means despicable; he was a sound geometrician; he had some skill in drawing landscapes, and he had in him that strain of poetry which is essential, I suppose, to every great architect. Could a man create the Duomo of Florence or the West front of Exeter Cathedral unless he were a poet? He introduced some improvement in etching, and was the inventor of drawing pictures by microscopic glasses. That there was no empiricism in his science we gather from his declaration that 'Experiment and Reason is the only way of prophesying natural events.'

Wren was born on the 20th of October 1636, at East Knoyle Rectory, in Wiltshire. He was educated at home under a private tutor; spent a few months at Westminster School, under Dr Busby; and was entered as a gentleman commoner at Wadham College, Oxford, in 1646. His scientific precocity had already attracted notice. He had invented (in 1645) an astronomical instrument, resembling an orrery, and dedicated it to his father in a Latin poem;

and soon after his location at Oxford, he invented another instrument of use in gnomonic and pneumatic experiments, as well as a machine for sowing corn 'equally and without waste.' No wonder that he was welcomed with open arms by the *savants* of Oxford—by Dr Wilkins, Dr Hooke, Seth Ward, and other members of the Philosophical Society. He gave much attention to the study of anatomy, and invented some new processes for facilitating its progress; and as, meanwhile, he was foremost in the usual curriculum of the University, I feel no surprise that Mr Evelyn should mention in his Diary 'that miracle of a youth, Christopher Wren.' He was a B.A. at nineteen years of age; an M.A. at twenty-two, and a D.C.L. at thirty.

Arriving in London with a high reputation, he was appointed Professor of Astronomy at Gresham College. Among the members of the Royal Society he was one of the earliest and most active, as the reader may see by reference to Mr Wild's excellent history of that learned body, or to its Transactions. In 1660, the young prodigy —he was only twenty-nine—was chosen Savilian Professor of Astronomy. Happily he did not remain in a position which would never have educed his real powers; for in the following year his friends procured him the post of Assistant Surveyor-General under Sir John Denham, the poet, and turning his attention to architecture, he discovered, no doubt to his own surprise, that it was the pursuit most congenial to him. One of his first tasks was the survey of old St Paul's, which, during the Commonwealth, had fallen into a ruinous condition. He also built the Sheldon Theatre and portions of Trinity College, Oxford. The Great Plague drove him to the Continent in 1665, and he spent many weeks in studying the immense works then being carried on at the Louvre, under the celebrated Bernini. In the following year came Wren's great opportunity. 'I have named St Paul's,' wrote Evelyn to the architect, at a later period, 'and truly not without admiration, as oft as I recal to mind, as frequently I do, the sad and deplorable condition it was in; when, after it had been made a stable of horses and a den of thieves, you, with other gentlemen and myself, were by King Charles named commissioners to survey the dilapidations, in order to a speedy reparation. You will not, I am sure, forget the struggle we had with some who were for patching it up anyhow, so that the steeple might stand, instead of new building, which it altogether needed; when, to put an end to the contest, five days after, that dreadful conflagration happened, out of whose ashes this phœnix, now St Paul's, is risen, and was by Providence designed for you.'

Yes, the Great Fire was Wren's opportunity. To rebuild the ruined city became his official duty, and he devised a plan which would have made the new London one of the stateliest capitals in the world. 'He proposed,' says a contemporary, 'to have laid out one spacious street from Aldgate to Temple Bar, in the middle of which was to have been a large square, capable of containing the new church of St Paul's, with a proper distance for the view all round it, whereby that huge building would not have been cooped up, as it is at present, in such a manner as nowhere to be seen to advantage, but would have had a long and ample vista at each end, to have reconciled it to a proper point of view, and give it one great benefit which. in all probability, it must now want for ever. He further proposed to rebuild all the parish churches in such a manner as to be seen at the end of every vista of houses, and dispersed at such distances from each other as to appear neither too thick nor thin in prospect, but give a proper heightening to the whole bulk of the city as it filled the landscape. Lastly, he proposed to build all the houses uniform. and supported on a piazza like that of Covent

Garden; and by the waterside, from the bridge to the Temple, he had planned a long and broad wharf or quay, where he designed to have arranged all the halls that belong to the several companies of the city, with proper warehouses for merchants between, to vary the edifices and make it at once one of the most beautiful and useful ranges of structure in the world.'[1]

Wren was in advance of his age. The authorities shrank in alarm from the adoption of a scheme so bold and comprehensive, and it was left for a later time to adopt some of its features, imperfectly, and at a heavy expenditure. 'The chief difficulty,' says Wren's son, 'arose from the obstinate perverseness of great part of the citizens to alter their old properties, and recede from building their houses again on the old ground and foundations; as also the distrust in many and unwillingness to give up their properties, though for a time only, into the hands of public trustees or commissioners, till they might be dispensed to them again with more advantage to themselves than could otherwise have been effected. By these means, the opportunity, in a great degree, was lost of making the new city the most magnificent as well as commodious for health and trade of any upon earth; and the surveyor being thus confined and cramped in his designs, it required no small labour and skill to mould the city in the manner it has since appeared.'

Wren's design for the new St Paul's was similarly affected, though from a different cause. The architect would have adapted it strictly to the worship and ritual of the Anglican Church; but the Duke of York and his partisans, believing in the restoration of the ancient faith, were resolved that in its construction the precedents of the

---

[1] The main streets were to have measured ninety feet in width, the second-rate streets sixty, and even the minor thoroughfares were not to have been less than thirty feet.

mediæval cathedrals should be observed. Wren was forced to yield. In building the one-and-fifty churches which are connected with his name, he seems, on the whole, to have been left very much to his own judgment, and nothing is more remarkable than the skill with which he conquered or evaded the difficulties of site. They are not all of the same standard of merit; but the admirable convenience of the interiors, and the frequent beauty of spire or steeple, must not escape comment. The best, I suppose, are those of St Mary-le-Bow, St Bride's, St Stephen's (Walbrook), and St Magnus.

From Wren we must pass on to a lesser man, Sir JOHN VANBRUGH, inferior to his contemporary in elevation and purity of character as well as in architectural genius. Perhaps the only circumstance which connects the two is, that neither was educated as an architect : for the tradition that Vanbrugh studied architecture in France seems without any solid basis. It was probably through Court interest that he was appointed, in 1695, one of the commission for completing Greenwich Hospital, as Wren had obtained, some years before, the post of Surveyor-General, and in each case the knowledge of architecture came *after* the appointment. But Vanbrugh never became, like Wren, a *practical* architect. I have already sketched his career and dwelt upon the plays by which he is best known ; a few words may here be given to the massive piles with which, according to Dr Evans's epigram, he 'loaded earth.' Castle Howard, designed in 1702, is unquestionably an imposing structure, with its lofty central portico, its advancing wings, and its stately cupola. 'The number of roofs, cupolas, statues, vases, and many-clustered chimneys give to the horizontal profile of the structure a richness of effect' not often surpassed in British art. Meritorious features, combined with grave defects, are visible in Dalton Hall, Cheshire; Seaton Delaval, Northumberland; Easton Neston, Northamptonshire; and King's Weston, near Bristol. He also built, in 1706, the Queen's Theatre in the Haymarket; but, like later architects, he succeeded in constructing a fine house in which the audience could not hear the actors. Blenheim remains the worthiest monument of his architectural skill, but its erection brought him neither pleasure nor profit. He was harassed by a long controversy with the Duchess of Marlborough, and eventually sustained a severe pecuniary loss. It was the last of his buildings; and no doubt the memories connected with it were sufficiently disagreeable to its unfortunate architect.

Vanbrugh erected for his own behoof a small but comfortable residence at Whitehall, which was irreverently compared to a goose-pie, and furnished Swift with a fertile theme for his satire. Sir John had just been rewarded with the post of Clarencieux King of Arms, and the satirist represents him, in his double capacity of architect and poet, as engaged in the twofold work of writing a farce and building a house; and as he employed old materials in the one, and old scenes in the other, the 'experienced bricks' took their places readily, and—

> 'The building, as the poet writ,
> Rose in proportion to his wit.
> Now poets from all quarters ran
> To see the house of brother Van;
> Looked high and low, walked often round,
> But no such house was to be found.
> At length they in the rubbish spy
> A thing resembling a goose-pie!
> And one in raptures thus began
> To praise the pile and builder Van;
> "Thrice happy poet, who mayest trail
> Thy house about thee like a snail."'

The supposition that Vanbrugh had received no professional training is confirmed by Swift's remark that—

> 'Van's genius, *without thought or lecture*,
> Is hugely turned to architecture;'

and the satirist hints that he sought designs for his future buildings from the card houses built by children—

> 'From such deep rudiments as these,
> Van is become, by due degrees,
> For building famed, and justly reckoned
> At court Vitruvius the Second.'

But against Swift's satire and much general depreciation of our dramatist-architect may be put the eulogium of Sir Joshua Reynolds:—'I pretend,' said that eminent man, 'to no skill in architecture. I judge of the art now merely as a painter. When I speak of Vanbrugh, I speak of him merely on our art. To speak then of Vanbrugh in the language of a painter, he had originality of invention; he understood light and shadow, and had great skill in composition. To support his principal object he produced his second and third groups of masses—he perfectly understood in *his* art what is most difficult in *ours*, the conduct of the background, by which the design and invention are set off to the greatest advantage. What the background is in painting, is the real ground upon which the building is erected; and no architect took greater care that his work should not appear crude and hard; that is, it did not abruptly start out of the ground without expectation or preparation. This is the tribute which a painter owes to an architect who composed like a painter.'

Very little of JAMES GIBBS'S career belongs to the reign of Anne. He was an Aberdonian, and born about 1674; took his degree of M.A. at Marischal College; and passed over to Holland in 1694, and resided there some years. In 1700 he made the acquaintance of the Earl of Mar, who had some taste and skill in architecture, and was well disposed to further the interests of a clever young countryman. He assisted him with money and letters of recommendation, and sent him on a visit to Italy, where he studied under the architect Garroli, and examined with care the chief memorials of ancient and modern art. After ten years thus pleasantly and profitably occupied, he came to England, and in 1709-10 set up in London for the practice of his profession. Obtaining an introduction to the Ecclesiastical Commissioners, he was employed to design and erect some of the fifty additional churches in the metropolis which had been authorised by Act of Parliament. It was in this way that London came to boast of the really beautiful church of St Martin's, Trafalgar Square, which almost justifies the apostrophe in Savage's *Wanderer*,—

> ' O Gibbs ! whose art the solemn fane can raise,
> Where God delights to dwell and man to praise !'

Its main feature of attraction is its classic portico—an imitation, say the critics, of the Pantheon at Rome, as if a fine imitation were not better than a sorry original! He also designed St Mary's-in-the-Strand, and among his other works are the Ratcliffe Library at Oxford, the King's College and Royal Library at Cambridge; and the cumbrous monument to Holles, Duke of Newcastle, in Westminster Abbey. Gibbs died on the 5th of August 1754.

WILLIAM KENT, architect and landscape gardener, belongs as little as Gibbs to *the reign* of Anne, but he belongs at all events to *the age*. He came of a Yorkshire family, was born in 1684, and apprenticed to a coach painter at the age of fourteen. In 1710 some gentlemen of his own county sent him to Rome, after he had spent six or seven years in London, vainly attempting to establish himself as a painter of portraits and historical subjects. Lord Burlington carried him back to England in 1716, and he painted more bad portraits and covered ceilings with vile designs in chiaroscuro, until he discovered that if he had no skill in painting, and but little taste in architecture, he had some talent for landscape gardening. In this direction he undoubtedly did much good.

Mr Sala, in his book upon William Hogarth, alludes with severity to William Kent, 'the architect, painter, decorator, upholsterer, friend of the great, and a hundred things besides.' 'This artistic jack-of-all-trades,' he says, 'became so outrageously popular, and gained such a reputation for taste—if a man have strong lungs, and persists in crying out that he is a genius, the public are sure to believe him at last—that he was consulted on almost every tasteful topic, and was teased to furnish designs for the most incongruous objects. He was consulted for picture-frames, drinking-glasses, barges, dining-room tables, garden chairs, cradles, and birthday gowns. One lady he dressed in a petticoat ornamented with columns of the five orders; to another he prescribed a copper-coloured skirt, with gold ornaments. The man was at best but a wretched sciolist; but he for a long period directed the "taste of the town."' For St Clement Danes he painted an altar so outrageously bad that it was caricatured by Hogarth, excited general derision and horror, was removed by order of the Bishop of London, and sank eventually into an ornament for a tavern room.

Landscape gardening in England may be said to date from the reign of Anne. One of the earliest illustrations of the art was the garden at Blenheim, laid out by 'Capability' Brown. But its first great apostle and teacher was ORLANDO BRIDGMAN, who banished from his gardens the artificially trained and sculptured greenery previously in vogue, and discarded the mathematical forms and rectilineal designs of the preceding age. There was breadth, there was vigour in his plans. He had no love for symmetrical compartments; and though he attached too much value to straight avenues bordered by tall hedges, he used them only for his main lines; the remainder was varied by clumps of sylvan shade, and irregular clusters of oaks. What Walpole considered Bridgman's greatest achievement—the decisive step that led to all which followed—was the abolition of walled enclosures and the invention of the sunk fence; a novelty so bold and so surprising, that it was popularly described by the exclamation 'ha—ha,' to express the pleased astonishment caused by this ingenious method of marking a boundary or breaking a monotonous promenade. This simple innovation was universally accepted; everybody began to level and mow and roll their lawns; and the outlying portions of a park were made to harmonise with its inner area.

So much had been done when Kent appeared.

Though a wretched painter, he was sufficiently an artist, as Walpole says, to appreciate the charms of a landscape. He had confidence enough in the correctness of his opinions to venture upon the enunciation of new principles; and his talents were adequate to discern in the glimmering twilight of the efforts of his predecessors the possibilities of a great system. He felt the delightful contrast of hills and vales blending with one another almost imperceptibly. He marked the graceful effect of a gently undulating surface, and the picturesque landmark afforded by a gentle eminence when crowned with leafy trees. The skilful touch of his imagination communicated all these characteristics of a fine landscape to the grounds which he laid out. The three great elements of his art were perspective, light, and shade; his material—

besides the soil which he modified according to the conditions of his work—trees, which sometimes he distributed singly, sometimes in groups or masses, so as incessantly to vary the aspect, and diversify the vistas, and break spaces of too great an extent. Occasionally, buildings were employed to animate the landscape—pavilions, small classic temples, Chinese pagodas, Gothic towers. It was not until some years later that tombs, ruins, pyramids, even miniature fortresses, and other hideous objects, came into fashion.

'But of all the beauties he added to the face of this beautiful country,' says Walpole, 'none surpassed his management of water. Adieu to canals, circular basins, and cascades tumbling down marble steps, that last absurd magnificence of Italian and French villas. The forced elevation of cataracts was no more. The gentle stream was taught to serpentine seemingly at its pleasure, and where discontinued by different levels, its course appeared to be concealed by thickets properly interspersed, and glittered again at a distance where it might be supposed naturally to arrive. Its borders were smoothed; but preserved their waving irregularity. A few trees, scattered here and there on its edges, sprinkled the tame bank that accompanied its meanders; and when it disappeared among the hills, shades descending from the heights leaned towards its progress, and framed the distant point of light under which it was lost as it turned aside to either hand of the blue horizon.'

On the whole, I think it must be admitted that the harm Kent did to his fellow-creatures by his execrable portraits and pictures, was more than counterbalanced by the good effects of his expansion of the art of landscape gardening, and the encouragement thus given to the study of Nature.

CHAPTER V.

QUEEN ANNE'S SOLDIERS.

John, Duke of Marlborough—Early Life—Military Services—In Ireland—William III.-Campaigns of the Great War—Blenheim—Ramillies—Oudenarde—Malplaquet—Old Age and Death—Charles Mordaunt, Earl of Peterborough—His Romantic Career—His Exploits in Spain—His Last Years—James Richmond Webb—Earl Cadogan—Lord Cutts.

JOHN CHURCHILL, afterwards Duke of Marlborough, was born at Ashe, in Devonshire, on the 24th of June 1650. At that time Marshal Turenne was thirty-nine years of age, Montecuculi forty-two, and the great Condé twenty-nine. It was the year in which Cromwell completed the subjugation of Ireland, defeated the Scotch at Dunbar, and won the crowning victory of Worcester. John was the second son of Sir Winston Churchill, an old Cavalier, impoverished by his devotion to the royal cause, and of his wife Elizabeth Drake, who came of the Devonshire family of that name. An honourable lineage was all or almost all his parents could give him, for they were very poor. He received some slight teaching from a Devonshire clergyman, and was afterwards removed to St Paul's School, London. At the age of sixteen he was presented with a pair of colours and entered on his illustrious career ; this first step in life being due, it is said, to the influence of his sister Arabella, who was first the Duchess of York's maid of honour, and afterwards the Duke of York's mistress. There are fair grounds for believing, however, that he gained his ensigncy before his sister rose to her wanton elevation. At Court his personal advantages, for he had a handsome countenance and a well-proportioned figure, and still more, his rare charm of manner, recommended him to the favour of its easy beauties; and, on the authority of Chesterfield, it is recorded that Barbara Palmer, Duchess of Cleveland, presented him with the liberal love-gift of five thousand pounds, which, with a prudence remarkable in so young a man, he invested in an annuity of five hundred pounds secured on the estates of the Earl of Halifax. This transaction, however, did not occur until 1674, when he had already seen some service.

For in 1667, or thereabouts, he was sent for a short time to do garrison work at Tangiers. On his return he was promoted to a captaincy; and in 1672 he accompanied the *corps d'armée*, under the Duke of Monmouth, which joined the French forces against the Dutch. It was his good fortune (according to some authorities) to serve under Turenne himself, and so to learn the art of war under one of its most approved masters. In the campaigns of 1672 and 1673 he gained the approval of the great Marshal by his brilliant courage, and the firm discipline which he maintained. A lieutenant-colonel having abandoned a post which he had been ordered to hold to the last, Turenne exclaimed, 'I will bet a supper and a dozen of claret that my handsome Englishman will recover it with half the number of men that the officer commanded who lost it.' The wager was accepted, and, of course, was won.

At Maestricht he saved the life of Monmouth, led a forlorn hope with success, and received the public acknowledgments of Louis XIV. Promoted to a lieutenant-colonelcy, he continued in France — probably with occasional visits to England—until his regiment was recalled in 1677. These few years of service constituted Churchill's only military education; but we may say of a great general as of a great poet that he must be 'born' not 'made.' On his return home he renewed his attendance at Court as James's Gentleman of the Bedchamber, and afterwards Master of the Robes. Evelyn, who saw him then, says,—' He is a very handsome person, well spoken and affable, and supports his want of acquired knowledge by keeping good company.' He had leisure at this time to fall in love with Mistress Sarah Jennings, the younger daughter of a well-to-do Hertfordshire gentleman; and his passionate attachment to her touches the record of his busy life with the picturesque hues of romance. She was two years his junior; a woman of stately beauty, of a quick and strong intelligence, an ambitious spirit, and an imperious will. I have no doubt the courtship was somewhat stormy. Difficulties were interposed, moreover, by the parents on both sides; but the Duchess of York intervened, like a *dea ex machinâ*, and early in 1678 the couple were privately married. In the following summer, all obstacles having been removed, the marriage was publicly announced. I may say at once that though Sarah was a termagant, she proved a faithful wife and helpmate to the man who loved her so devotedly, and the vigorous guardian of his interests.

In 1679 Colonel Churchill was engaged in the private negotiations between Charles II. and Louis XIV.; in 1680 he accompanied the Duke of York to Edinburgh. Returning with him from Scotland in 1682, he was on board the *Gloucester* when it was wrecked, and was one of the few who escaped. In the same year he was created Baron Churchill of Eyemouth, in the Scotch peerage, and made colonel of the new Royal Dragoons (the 1st Royals). About the same time his wife was appointed Lady of the Bedchamber to the Princess Anne, over whom she soon acquired a remarkable ascendancy. When the Duke of York, in 1685, ascended the throne as James II., he bestowed further distinctions on his fortunate servant, who was promoted to the rank of brigadier-general, and made an English peer by the title of Baron Churchill of Sandridge. Yet it soon became evident that differences of opinion were springing up between them. Churchill was not without his failings, and, I fear, without his crimes; yet no impartial mind can doubt that he was, according to his lights, religious, and a devoted member of the Church of England. Politically he was a Tory, or, if the word be better liked, a Constitutionalist; and I believe he was thoroughly in earnest when he told Lord Galway that 'if the King should attempt to change our religion and constitution, I would instantly quit his service.' This declaration should be remembered; for it furnishes the key to much that is dubious in his conduct.

There was no reason, however, why he should not do his duty as a soldier when Monmouth's mad rebellion broke out. In the brief campaign which so completely crushed it, he practically commanded the King's troops, though ostensibly acting as Major-General under the Earl of Feversham; and it was his self-possession which won the Battle of Sedgemoor. The massacres which followed it he had neither instigated nor approved. His services obtained no other recognition than the gift of a colonelcy of a regiment of dragoons; and for three years he almost disappears from the historian's view. In May 1687, we find him writing to William of Orange that his 'places and the King's favour' he set at nought in comparison of being true to his religion. 'In all things but this,' he adds, 'the King may command me, and I call God to witness that even with joy I should expose my life for his service, so sensible am I of his favours.' The trial of the Seven

Bishops may be held to have finally determined Churchill in his desertion of James; and on the 4th of August he wrote an important letter to William of Orange:—' Mr Sidney will let you know how I intend to behave myself; I think it is what I owe to God and my country. My honour I take leave to put into your Highness's hands, in which I think it safe. If you think there is anything else that I ought to do, you have but to command me; I shall pay an entire obedience to it, being resolved to die in that religion that it has pleased God to give you both the will and power to protect.' When James refused to call a Parliament, Churchill finally broke with him; and during the night of the 24th of November, he fled, accompanied by the Duke of Grafton, to William's quarters at Exeter. On the following Sunday, the Princess Anne and Lady Churchill escaped from Whitehall, and attended by Compton, Bishop of London, made their way to Nottingham. Then James felt that the game was played out. 'God help me,' he exclaimed, 'for my own children have forsaken me!' Soon afterwards he quitted London, and, unmolested, embarked for France.

A good deal of obloquy has been cast upon Marlborough for his share in these transactions; and if we are to judge him by the moral standard of the present day, it will not be easy to pass a verdict of acquittal. But, in politics at all events, a much lower standard was in his age accepted, and I do not see that we can demand of him a virtue which none, or few, of his contemporaries exhibited. It would have been better and nobler if he had retired from James's service as soon as he found that James was deliberately bent upon the destruction of all that in Church and State he most revered; but this was an elevation of conduct of which the men of the Revolution were mostly incapable, and it may be said in apology for Marlborough that he did not disguise his opinions from the King, who, he may fairly have hoped, would in time have recognised the folly of his course of action, and have listened to his advice. On the whole, I think that if his conduct were not such as to merit admiration, it does not call for the severe censure that Macaulay, and the writers who follow Macaulay, have pronounced upon it. I am not at all sure but that a very good case might be made out in his defence. The events which had chequered the course of English history during the preceding half-century, had confused men's ideas of allegiance and personal loyalty. Churchill, it is possible, argued to himself that James II. had violated the Constitution, and broken his coronation oath; that every honest Englishman was bound to assist in delivering the country from the oppression of arbitrary government; but that, in accomplishing that deliverance, he might reasonably take thought for his own liberty and life and personal interests. And it may be assumed that, having received much special kindness at the hands of James II., he struggled long with a natural reluctance to abandon him. The rigid loyalist will, of course, condemn Churchill for having 'rebelled' at all; the constitutionalist will argue that he ought to have 'rebelled' much earlier; the impartial historian will, I think, make generous allowances for the difficult circumstances in which he and the public men of his day were placed, and remember the lax political morality which then prevailed.

William hastened to acknowledge the value of Churchill's adhesion. He was made a Privy Councillor and Lord of the Bedchamber, and afterwards raised a step in the peerage. Assuming the title by which he is known in the records of fame, he attended the coronation of William and Mary as Earl of Marlborough. In the first campaign of the new war against France he commanded the English brigade attached to the Dutch army on the Sambre, under the Prince of Waldeck, and won distinction by his brilliant share in the action fought at Walcourt on the 5th of August 1689. 'It is to you,' wrote King William, 'that this advantage is principally owing.' In 1690 he was not employed on the Continent, nor did he serve in the Irish campaign which was illustrated by the victory of the Boyne. He had probably offended William by his activity in pressing Parliament to increase the income settled upon the Princess Anne. But he was appointed on the Council of Nine left to assist Queen Mary in William's absence, and in the autumn proposed a military manœuvre which exhibited the combined boldness and prudence of his genius—namely, the despatch of an English fleet with 5000 men to reduce the great southern seaports of Ireland, which were occupied by French garrisons, and formed the channels of communication with France. The council opposed the plan as too hazardous, but William approved of it, and entrusted its execution to Marlborough, who in thirty-seven days captured Cork and Kinsale, and achieved the objects of his expedition. 'No one,' remarked William, 'who had seen so little service as Marlborough, was so fit for command.' He took him with him to the Continent in 1691, where, however, he had no opportunity of doing anything illustrious; but he drew a remarkable compliment from the Dutch General, the Prince of Vandemont, who, after acknowledging the respective merits of the English generals, went on to say that in Marlborough there was 'something inexpressible,' and that he could not fail to perform great actions. 'I really believe, my cousin,' replied King William, 'that my lord will make good everything you have said of him.'

On the 10th of January 1692, Marlborough was dismissed from all his offices. This sudden stroke excited general astonishment; the King's reasons for it were not very clear, and even now the historian is perplexed by the mystery surrounding it. What is known is that Marlborough, in common with other leading noblemen, had begun to doubt the security of William's position, and had opened communications with the exiled James; while it is suspected that he also contemplated the possibility of setting aside James, and raising to the throne, if it became vacant, the Princess Anne. At all events, Marlborough was disgraced, and an attempt was made to coerce the Princess into dismissing his wife. On her refusal, Mary sent a message by the Lord Chamberlain ordering Lady Marlborough to quit the palace, whereupon the Princess also quitted the palace, and established herself at Berkeley House.

Towards the end of the year Marlborough was arrested on a charge of high treason, in connection with Young's plot, and consigned to the Tower. But it was soon discovered that the man on whose information he had been arrested had forged his documentary evidence, and Marlborough was released with quite a halo of innocence about him. This was in April 1692. In the following August, on his way between London and his seat at Holywell, near St Albans, he was beset by highwaymen, and robbed of five hundred guineas. We pass on to 1694, when his resentment against William, and his desire to stand well with James, led him into the most inexcusable—or, rather, indefensible—action of his career. The English Government secretly fitted out an expedition against Brest. Particulars of its strength and destination were, however, supplied to James—that is, to the French Court—with the result that Brest was rapidly fortified, and such preparations made that the English attack failed, with a great slaughter of soldiers and seamen in the Bay of Camaret. Among the unpatriotic Englishmen whom a strange moral obliquity seduced into this betrayal of their country, Marlborough, it is said, must be included ; though it is urged, in partial extenuation of his offence, that the information on which the French authorities acted was really forwarded by others, and that he was careful not to send his own communication until it was too late to be made use of. The reader must accept the excuse *quantum valeat*. It must still appear that Marlborough's conduct in this affair was marked by political turpitude of a very base kind.

After the death of Queen Mary, more amicable relations came to be established between William and the Earl,—partly as a consequence of the more amicable relations which sprang up between William and the Princess Anne. Two years later, he was made governor to the young Duke of Gloucester,—Anne's son, and the heir presumptive to the throne,—William paying him a truly kingly compliment :—' My lord, make my nephew to resemble yourself, and he will be everything which I can desire.' The death of his pupil in 1710 did not shake his position; and his parliamentary influence was strengthened by the marriage of his second daughter, Anne, to the eldest son of Lord Sunderland, one of the great Whig leaders.

In June 1701 broke out the War of the Succession ; a war in defence of the liberties of Europe, which were openly threatened by the bold schemes of Louis XIV. for the aggrandisement of the House of Bourbon. England had long clung to the hope of peace, though her commercial interests were endangered by the restless aggressive spirit of France ; but the temper of her people took fire when Louis entered the bedchamber of the dying James, and promised at his death to recognise his son as King of England, Scotland, and Ireland. ' The promise which was thus made was in fact a declaration of war, and in a moment all England was at one in accepting the challenge. The issue Louis had raised was no longer a matter of

European politics, but a question whether the work of the Revolution should be undone, and whether Catholicism and despotism should be replaced on the throne of England by the arms of France.' Whig and Tory were agreed in their determination to punish the insolence of the French monarch. The Grand Alliance,—a league between England, the Empire, and the United Provinces,—renewed by the tact and patience of William; who saw himself on the point of realising the dream of his life,—a European confederacy against France. On the 7th of June 1701, the three Powers issued their formal declarations of war. But before hostilities actually began, William III. was no more. Disease and hard work had prematurely worn out his feeble frame, though with indomitable will he struggled to keep himself alive. 'You know,' he said to a friend, 'that I never feared death : there have been times when I should have wished it ; but now that this great new prospect is opening before me, I do wish to stay here a little longer.' His desire was not fulfilled. Riding in Hampton Court Park, he was thrown by his favourite horse, Sorrel, and broke his collar-bone. His system sunk beneath the shock, and on the morning of Sunday, the 8th of March 1702, he died at Kensington Palace. Happily his policy survived him. In the words of Burke,—'The master-workman died, but the work was founded on true mechanical principles, and it was as truly wrought.' It passed into the hands of one more capable of consummating it than he who had first essayed it. Before his death, William had selected Marlborough to take the direction of the war, and the appointment was of course confirmed by Queen Anne. War was declared against France and Spain on the 4th of May, and on the 15th Marlborough departed for the Hague, where, through the influence of the Pensionary Heinsius, he obtained the command-in-chief of the Dutch forces. When he thus entered upon his brilliant career of generalship, he was fifty-two years old.

Here I must introduce a quotation from Mr Saintsbury, which very forcibly balances the advantages and disadvantages under which he began this career.

In no historical instance, perhaps, have circumstances combined to give a man of great genius, long cramped by want of opportunity, so perfect an occasion as was offered to Marlborough by the accession of Anne. His wife's dominion over the Queen's spirit [1] was, of course, the most important single factor in the problem of his success, but it was by no means the only important one. Had Anne had for husband any other man than George of Denmark, Marlborough would probably have been hampered with the annoyance, if not the actual interference, of a nominal superior in the field. But *Est it possible?* was contented, if not entirely contented, with the title of generalissimo and residence at home, leaving that of captain-general, with complete control abroad, to Marlborough. No English soldier (for Ginkel's experience and merit were not likely to make any Englishman forget that he was Dutch, or Ruvigny's that he was French) approached Marlborough in military reputation. But it was even more important that he had, after a long period of distrust, been completely restored to William's confidence before his death, had been intimately engaged in the literary and diplomatic preparations of the King's last days, and, so to speak, held all the threads already in his hand. Add to this the facts that the unwisdom or the chivalry of Louis had, by his recognition of the Prince of Wales, complicated the quarrel of the Spanish Succession with what was, or seemed, an irreconcilable provocation of England, and that consequently a war on the greatest scale was inevitable, that the French finances were approaching disorder, their best generals and administrators dead or not come to maturity, their people wearied of forty years of war and taxation, and their nobility disgusted by the Pharisaism of the Court ; add all these things, and some glimpse of the chances which Marlborough had in his favour must be obtained. Against him he had the almost unbroken prestige of the French arms ; their troops, more homogeneous,

---

[1] Everybody knows the familiar relations which existed between them, and the names under which they corresponded :—Mrs Morley for the Queen, Mrs Freeman for Lady Marlborough, and Mr Freeman for Marlborough himself.

better equipped, better officered, and under more complete and absolute control of the directing spirit than any army of Europe; the jealousies and intrigues of the Allies; the unquiet state of English parties; the inevitable drawbacks of parliamentary government.

I pass on to glance at the nature of the instrument with which Marlborough was to accomplish the task he had undertaken,—the composition of that gallant English force, probably never exceeding twelve thousand in numerical strength, which he was to pass to victory on so many battle-fields. Contemporary evidence does not represent the English private soldier in a very favourable light. Here is Ward's description, with a strain of caricature in it, no doubt, but in the main, I suppose, sufficiently correct :—

A foot-soldier is commonly a man who, for the sake of wearing a sword, and the honour of being termed a gentleman, is coaxed from a handicraft trade whereby he has the hopes of nothing but to live starvingly. His lodging is as near heaven as his quarters can raise him; and his soul generally is as near hell as a profligate life can sink him. To speak without swearing he thinks a scandal to his post; and makes many a meal upon tobacco, which keeps the inside of his carcase as nasty as his shirt. He's a champion for the Church, because he fights for Religion, though he never hears prayers except they be read upon a drum-head. He often leads a sober life against his will, but he never can pass by a brandy shop with twopence in his pocket, for he as naturally loves strong waters as a Turk loves coffee. . . .

He's one that loves fighting no more than other men; though perhaps a dozen of drink and an affront will make him draw his sword; yet a pint and a good word will make him put it up again. Let him be in never so many campaigns in Flanders, he contracts but few habits of a Dutchman, for you shall oftener see him with his fingers in his neck than his hands in his pockets. He has the pleasure once a week, when he receives his subsistence, of boasting he has money in his breeches; and for all he is a soldier owes no man a groat, which is likely enough to be true, because nobody will trust him. Hunger and lousiness are the two distempers that afflict him; and idleness and scratching the two medicines that palliate his miseries. If he spends twenty years in war, and lives to be forty, perhaps he may get a halbert; and if he survives threescore, an hospital. The best end he can expect to make is to die in the bed of honour; and the greatest living marks of his bravery, to recommend him at once to the world's praise and pity, are crippled limbs.

The system of recruiting then in vogue could not be expected to fill the ranks with a good class of men. A recruiting officer, generally of the rank of captain, took up his quarters in some country town, attended by a sergeant and drummer, and then proceeded to levy recruits. The sergeant a man capable of any amount of drink, went round the villages, attended the fairs and markets, and by a liberal application of strong liquors, and unbounded promises of plunder and promotion, ensnared the yokels, who, after they had once taken the Queen's shilling, and been attested, had no means of escape. A lively picture of this kind of recruiting is furnished by Farquhar in his comedy of 'The Recruiting Officer.' Sergeant Kite reports to Captain Plume, his superior, the success he has met with :—

Kite. I've been here a week, and I've recruited five.
Plume. Five! pray what are they?
Kite. I have listed the strong man of Kent, the king of the gipsies, a Scotch pedlar, a scoundrel attorney, and a Welsh parson.
Plume. An attorney! wert thou mad? List a lawyer! discharge him, discharge him, this minute!
Kite. Why, sir?
Plume. Because I will have nobody in my company that can write; a fellow that can write can draw petitions—I say, this minute discharge him!
Kite. And what shall I do with the parson?
Plume. Can he write?
Kite. Hum! he plays rarely upon the fiddle.
Plume. Keep him by all means. But how stands the country affected? were the people pleased with the news of my coming to town?
Kite. Sir, the mob are so pleased with your honour, and the jus-

tices and better sort of people are so delighted with me, that we shall soon do your business.'

In 1706, the recruiting-field was extended by an Act of Parliament, which empowered justices of the peace and others 'to raise and levy such able-bodied men as had not any lawful calling or employment or visible means for their maintenance and livelihood, to serve as soldiers.' Prisoners convicted of minor offences were also, very frequently, allowed to enlist, instead of undergoing imprisonment. Thus Kite, in Farquhar's comedy, is made to say,—'The butcher, sir, will have his hands full, for we have two sheep-stealers among us—I hear of a fellow, too, committed just now for stealing of horses.'

Of the rank and file got together by these means, the officers were not unworthy. Very few of them received any military education; and though they were mostly the scions of good families, their manners, like their oaths, were of the roughest, while their morality was the morality of the camp. The dramatists of the day put them on the stage as roystering, careless, dissolute fellows, much given to wine and women and the dice-box—swearing strange oaths—making love with an indescribable impudence—but brave enough, and filled with a fine scorn of the French, who were then our 'natural enemies.' Sometimes they drew a less agreeable portrait—that of the carpet-knight or feather-bed soldier, who through the influence of his friends, contrived to escape foreign service, and swaggered safely in the Mall or in the Park. To quote again from Farquhar:—'I'm called captain, sir,' he makes one of his characters say, 'by all the coffee men, drawers, and grown porters in London; for I wear a red coat, a sword, a hat *bien troussé*, a martial twist in my cravat, a fierce knot in my periwig, a cane upon my button, picquet in my head, and dice in my pocket . . . (my name is) Captain Pinch. I cock my hat with a pinch,

I take snuff with a pinch, pay my women with a pinch, in short, I can do anything at a pinch, but fight and fill my belly.'

Such was the composition of the English army in the reign of Queen Anne. But there was excellent stuff at the bottom of this unpromising material, as Europe was soon to learn.

The campaign of 1702 began with the capture of Venloo in September. Lord Cutts, a dashing soldier, was in command of the besieging party. 'He desired that the covered way should, if possible, be cleared, to save the working parties [in the trenches] from assault, and hinted to those told off for the duty, that if the enemy seemed to retire readily they might try an assault. The troops, as impatient as their commander, jumped into the covered way, ran with the garrison through it, and pushing some planks laid for the convenience of the garrison across the moat, climbed up the counterscarp by the aid of long grass. It was an effectual surprise, and the garrison surrendered. The assailing party lost only twenty-seven men in this first achievement of the war.' The town capitulated on the 23d of September. Roermond, twenty miles further up the Maas, Stevenswart, and the great fortress of Liège were taken in succession; with the result that the whole territory lying between Liège and the Rhine, the Maas and the Meuse, was swept clear of the French, and a valuable portion of the Dutch frontier relieved from all danger of attack. This success had naturally a considerable influence on the fortune of the war, for it infused a new spirit into the soldiers of the Allies, and proportionately depressed those of the French, whose proud boast of invincibility was rudely dispelled. In England it had a great effect; and the rise of that imperial temper (so to speak), which has extended the sway of two small islands over so vast a portion of the habitable world, may be dated from the time when Marlborough first taught our soldiers how to conquer.

On November 3d, having put his army into winter-quarters, Marlborough left Maestricht, and, accompanied by the Dutch field-deputies, dropped down the Meuse with an escort of only twenty-five men. Below Venloo, the boat was surprised by a company of French marauders, who had made an incursion from Guelder, and the tow-rope being cut, they leaped on board, and overpowered the guard. The Dutch commissioners were provided with French passes; but Marlborough had thought it inconsistent with his dignity to ask for one. He was saved from capture, however, by the quick wit of his servant, who slipped into his hand an old passport that had once belonged to his brother, General Churchill. He presented it with so much coolness, that the plunderers did not minutely examine it, nor observe that the date had expired; and, retaining the escort as prisoners, they allowed Marlborough and his companions to proceed. A rumour of his supposed capture had got abroad, and the Dutch, who, with true popular instinct, had already learned to confide in his generalship, were greatly rejoiced when he reached the Hague in safety.

On his return to London he received an address of thanks from both Houses of Parliament, and was created Marquis of Blandford and Duke of Marlborough. 'When the services he had performed,' says Burton, 'substantial as they were, are estimated along with his late achievements, his elevation to the highest rank obtainable in his own country might look like the reward not of an accomplished but of anticipated service. It was the policy of the Government, however, to strengthen his hand for the exercise of his high command, by giving him whatever could be bestowed in rank on a subject of the British crown, and to cherish his authority in an army where persons who claimed the attributes of royalty had to obey him.' His consciousness of work well done—his forecast of good work to be done in the future—his enjoyment of the gratitude of a proud nation—were darkened in the spring of 1703 by the death, in his seventeenth year, of his only son, the Marquis of Blandford, a youth of great promise and many gifts.[1] He felt the blow very keenly; and it was long before he recovered his usual cheerfulness. Those enemies of the great duke who have loved to bespatter his memory with the mud of their savage criticism, and have accused him of 'having no heart,' are careful to ignore the fact of his strong domestic affections. No father ever loved his children more dearly; no husband ever loved his wife more passionately. And, again, in his friendship he was supremely loyal and generous. How, then, can it be pretended that he was without heart! As a commander, I believe it can easily be proved that he was very careful of the lives of his men; and Turenne himself was not more solicitous for the comfort and relief of the wounded. We may well wonder why writer after writer repeats the gross and groundless charges which the hired slanderers of Queen Anne's reign concocted in the excess of their party malignity, and the prejudices of Macaulay and Thackeray revived and sanctioned.

I must here attempt to indicate the principal features of Marlborough's character. It is specially noticeable that with him as with Cromwell, his genius was of slow development. There was nothing in Turenne's handsome Englishman' which could have justified the keenest observer in predicting that he would become one of the world's most consummate captains. This late maturity was owing, perhaps, to his imperfect education: he had to acquire his knowledge by experience and observation, which, though safe and sure teachers,

[1] He died at Cambridge, of smallpox, on the 20th of February.

are also slow. But by nature he had been endowed with the main qualities that go to make up a great commander; the intuition, the foresight, the promptitude, the power of combination, which we recognise in Cæsar and Hannibal, in Napoleon and Wellington,—in other words, the military genius. The virtue which distinguished him pre-eminently was, I think, his patience. 'Patience,' he wrote to Godolphin, 'will overcome all things.' And whether he was watching the operations of the enemy, or the disclosure of some political intrigue, or the execution of some carefully-conceived project of his own; whether he was concerned with the home Government or foreign cabinets, the Dutch field-deputies or the Allied Powers, this great virtue never failed him. He bided his time; he was never in a hurry, yet never too late. When Marlborough had once laid down the plan of a campaign, had once determined the object which he wished to accomplish, he put aside all uncertainty, all discouragement, all hesitation. He moved forward with a singular steadiness, with a persistency that bore down every obstacle. Such was his fertility of resource that the failure of any portion of his scheme never irritated or discouraged him; he simply set to work to replace it by some new and better idea. No general ever ventured upon enterprises of greater boldness, but then no general ever considered more elaborately how they might best be carried out. To the hasty observer his daring might seem at the outset an ill-judged rashness; but the prudence and tenacity which underlay it always achieved a most complete success.

His equability of temper must be acknowledged, for, it may be said of him—what can be said of few—that he never forgot himself. He was constantly harassed by foolish and impracticable colleagues; he was constantly assailed with the most atrocious calumnies; in the later years of the war he was embarrassed by the intrigues of faction; but his lofty composure never deserted him. As prosperity could not elate, so adversity could not depress. He preserved his tranquillity, his self-reliance, his well-balanced mind, under all conditions. He so carefully calculated every movement beforehand, with all its chances and possibilities, that it was not possible for him to be taken by surprise. In battle the victory goes to the general who makes the fewest mistakes and most promptly detects and profits by those of his opponent's. Military critics do not point to any errors of omission or commission on the part of this famous commander, but all agree that no general could commit any in his presence without immediate chastisement; and this because he was always so thoroughly prepared, so calm of mood, and so confident in his resources.

Voltaire said of him, in well-known words, that he never besieged a fortress which he did not take, nor fought a battle which he did not win, nor engaged in a negotiation which he did not bring to a successful issue. The full significance of this eulogium is best understood, as Earl Stanhope says, when we remember that to scarcely any other military commander could it be applied. Neither to the Black Prince nor Turenne, neither to Condé nor Prince Eugene, not even to Wellington, when we recall the siege of Burgos; nor to Napoleon, even if he died before the battle of Leipzig, when we recollect the disasters at Acre and Eylau.

Marlborough's physical gifts and charm of address were not without their influence in the peculiar position which he occupied. He was possessed of the finest manners imaginable; he could be deferential without servility to his superiors in rank; to an inferior he behaved with so exquisite a courtesy that he seemed to be receiving rather than conferring a favour. In the court, the council, or the camp he took the first place, but it was without any effort, and, by the consent of all, because he was so obviously the chief, the leader, the wariest soldier, the coolest statesman, the finest gentleman. It is not recorded that he ever did an ungraceful thing, or uttered a pettish or petulant speech. He moved everywhere with easy dignity, and nothing discordant or unbecoming could exist in his presence. It need hardly be said that his courage was of the highest order; but this, too, partook of the general equality of his character. He did not rush into peril like a knight-errant, but when in it appeared wholly unconscious of it. The hottest fire disturbed him no more than a levee at court, and he moved as calmly on the fiercest battle-field as on a parade. 'Without fear of danger,' it is said, ' or in the least hurry, he gave his orders with all the coolness imaginable.'

As he had no weakness either for wine or women, his enemies were hard put to it to asperse him with some low vice that might sully the bright metal of his character and impeach his superiority. They fixed upon that of avarice as one to which there was some ground for supposing that his nature inclined. He had known the pressure of straitened means in his early youth, and had learned the value of money. He was unquestionably thrifty; and the English people at one time looked upon thriftiness with disfavour. But it is not less true that he was capable of acts of splendid generosity. As for avarice, in its usual sense, I do not think he is fairly chargeable with it. There is no authentic evidence that way; the accusation was originally made by libellers who, to gratify their political hate, resorted to the foulest weapons. Modern writers when repeating it make a good deal of the old jest of Peterborough, who, being mistaken for Marlborough in the time of the great general's unpopularity, diverted the rage of the crowd by a sorry sarcasm :—' I will easily convince you that I am not my Lord Marlborough. In the first place, I have only two guineas about me, and in the second, they are very much at your service.'

This reputed avarice is one of the chief counts of the indictment which Macaulay, and after him Thackeray, have laid against Marlborough with an almost personal bitterness of feeling. But in opposition to their strangely venomous criticism may be put the fine tribute to his merits paid by the brilliant Bolingbroke, when his judgment was no longer obscured by the clouds of party warfare :—' I take with pleasure,' he said, ' this opportunity of doing justice to that great man, whose faults I knew, whose virtues I admired ; and whose memory, as the greatest general and as the greatest minister that our country, or perhaps any other, has produced, I honour.'

No great blow was struck on either side in the campaign of 1703 ; but Louis XIV., perceiving the dangers with which the European coalition threatened him, resolved, by a mighty effort, in the following year, to break it into pieces. The plan on which he decided is said to have been of his own conception, and was certainly marked by considerable military skill. He proposed that in the Netherlands his army should act only on the defensive, while, using Bavaria as a *point d'appui*, he launched an irresistible force into the very heart of the Empire, which he hoped at the same time to harass in the rear by fomenting an insurrection among the Hungarians. The capture of Vienna would make him master of Europe. In Bavaria he had already a large army, under Marshal Marsin, with a Bavarian contingent. The problem to be solved then, was the transport of another large army across the Rhine and through the Black Forest to effect a junction with it. The junction once accomplished, the march to Vienna would become a promenade. With patient labour and in profound secrecy—for in those days military strategists had not to take account of telegraphs and special correspondents—Louis and his war minister completed their preparations. 'A war of sieges,' says Alison, 'was to be turned into one of tactics, and 1704 promised the triumphs which were realised on the same ground, and by following the same plan, by Napoleon in 1805.' But Napoleon in 1805 had no Marlborough to divine and frustrate his strategy.

For the great duke quickly detected the secret object of the French preparations, and determined on a countermove, the splendid audacity of which has extorted the admiration of even the most prejudiced critics. He resolved to abandon Flanders and its fortresses, to carry his forces across the European watershed, and pour them down suddenly upon the armies collected by Louis in the valley of the Danube. Thus he would deliver Vienna, while at the same time he punished the Elector for his desertion of the Empire. If secrecy had been a necessary condition with Louis XIV., it was not less indispensable for Marlborough, who had to conceal his intentions not only from the enemy but from the Dutch Government, until the opposition of the latter, which might naturally be expected, could no longer be effective. He paid a visit to England, where he obtained an addition of ten thousand troops; and having settled the details of his scheme, returned to the Hague, where, through the influence of the Pensionary Heinsius, he obtained permission from the States to operate on the Moselle.

On May 16th he concentrated his forces, consisting of fifty-one battalions of foot and ninety-two squadrons of horse, at Bedberg, near Maestricht. On the 19th the march began, and on the 28th they were at Bonn. Advancing up the right bank of the Rhine, he met Prince Eugene of Savoy at Hippach, and established at once a cordial relation with the Imperialist leader. There, too, he met another Imperialist general, Louis, Margrave of Baden, a brave and experienced soldier of the school of Montecuculi. In virtue of his princely rank he claimed the chief command; but, eventually, it was agreed that he and the Duke should rule on alternate days.

Marlborough arranged with Eugene that the latter should cross the Rhine and endeavour to intercept Tallard on his route to join Marsin in Bavaria. He himself kept on his course towards the Moselle, until, after passing Mayence, he suddenly diverged towards the Upper Danube. For some days Europe lost sight of him, and the enemy were in complete perplexity as to his actual object. On the 13th of June he appeared at Gieslingen, and descending thence into the valley of the great river, interposed his army between the French and Vienna. To obtain command of the Danube, it was necessary to seize upon Donauwerth, a fortified town among the hills, which formed the key of Bavaria from the north. Above it rises the Schellenberg, a branch or spur of the rocky heights which here traverse the river plain. This eminence was strongly fortified, and garrisoned by a force of thirteen thousand men under Count D'Arco. Though his soldiers were fatigued with a long day's march, Marlborough resolved on an immediate attack, before the enemy could add to the strength of the position; and, forming a column of six thousand men, ordered an advance, while the Margrave co-operated by a flank movement. The fighting, which began at six o'clock, lasted through the late summer twilight; but, in spite of a desperate opposition, the Allies carried the height and drove the enemy into the Danube. The loss was heavy, one thousand five hundred killed and four thousand wounded; but of the garrison only three thousand escaped. Donauwerth was soon afterwards abandoned, and the Elector retired to Augsburg.

Meanwhile, Prince Eugene had held Villerny and

Tallard in check, with only fifteen thousand men, in the famous lines of Stollhoffen, on the Rhine; until the French generals received intelligence of the fight at the Schellenberg, and were compelled to decide upon some new plan of operations. Tallard resolved on marching to the assistance of the Elector, while Villeroy remained to watch Eugene. The Prince, however, broke up his camp, and hastened to reinforce Marlborough, who, detaching the Margrave with fifteen thousand men to invest Ingolstadt, hurried to meet him. A similar movement was undertaken by Marsin and the Elector, and eventually the French and Bavarian armies joined at Dettingen. Eugene and Marlborough at Donauwerth, about the 12th of August. Thus the two opposing hosts came into close contact—the French and Bavarians concentrating between Blenheim and Höchstadt, the Allies opposite to them along the Nobel. The former numbered about fifty-six thousand men (forty thousand French and twelve thousand Bavarians), with ninety guns; and the latter, fifty-two thousand men, with fifty-two guns. Not only was the numerical advantage with the enemy, but they had other and more important points in their favour. Four-fifths of them, as Alison remarks, were national troops, speaking the same language, animated by the same feelings, subjected to the same discipline, and accustomed to act together. They had, moreover, that confidence in themselves, and that contempt of their antagonists, which come from habitual victory. The Allies, on the other hand, were an assemblage as heterogeneous as Hannibal's army at Cannæ or Wellington's at Waterloo—a *colluvies gentium* of the troops of several nations, speaking different languages, trained on different systems, brought together but recently, and commanded by a foreign general. English, Dutch, Austrians, Danes, Wurtembergers, Hanoverians, and Hessians were blended in such nearly equal proportions that the army of no one State could be said to be entitled to predominance by its numerical superiority. They had had no long career of success to inspire them with that masterful hope which works out its own fulfilment. These diverse elements, however, were, for military purposes, fused into homogeneity by the genius of Marlborough; and it is certain that if the Allies had less reliance upon themselves than the French exhibited, they placed a greater faith in their leader. It is a testimony to the fine military qualities of the English regiments that they had already come to be recognised as the backbone of the army. The most important positions were given into their charge, and the most onerous enterprises confided to them to execute. Through their splendid discipline and unsurpassed intrepidity they attained so enduring and widespread a renown that even foreign historians characterise the victories won by Marlborough as English victories,—won by English valour.

On the north bank of the Danube lies the village of Blindheim or Blenheim. A short distance below it, a small stream, called the Nobel, flows into the great river. Its banks are marshy, and after heavy rains or sudden thaws, impassable. About three miles distant from the Danube, and parallel with it, a low range of thickly wooded hills connects with the Schellenberg at Donauwerth. Between those hills and the Nobel, but without carrying his lines down to the latter, Tallard deployed his columns. His right flank was protected by the Danube, and his left by the village of Blenheim, into which, with what proved to be a grave error of judgment, he crowded twenty-six battalions and twelve squadrons, who were so pent up that they could scarcely employ their arms. It is estimated that the village might properly have held about four thousand men: on the day of battle it contained no fewer than twelve thousand. This disposition seems to have been due to Tallard's conviction that Marlborough would strike to the right for Nordlingen.

To the left lay the village of Lützingen, where Marsin and the Elector were posted with twenty-two battalions and thirty-six squadrons. The centre, consisting of fourteen battalions, belonging chiefly to the famous Irish brigade, rested upon the hamlet of Oberglau. Thence extended to Blenheim a magnificent array of eighty squadrons, drawn up in two lines, and supported by seven battalions of foot. The artillery was ranged at intervals all along the line, which, strong on both wings, was dangerously weak in the centre.

The Allied right, opposed to Marsin and the Elector of Bavaria, was commanded by Prince Eugene. The left and centre were led by Marlborough in person. The composition of the force may be stated as follows:—Right wing— Prussians, eleven battalions and fifteen squadrons; Danes, seven battalions; Austrians, twenty-four squadrons; and Imperialists, thirty-five squadrons. Centre and left wing—English, fourteen battalions and fourteen squadrons; Dutch, fourteen battalions and twenty-two squadrons; Hessians, seven battalions and seven squadrons; Hanoverians, thirteen battalions and twenty-five squadrons; and Danes, twenty-two squadrons. Marlborough's plan of battle was bold and brilliant; it comprised a combined attack on right, left, and centre. Four brigades of infantry and one of cavalry, mainly English, under Lord Cutts, were directed against the village of Blenheim; on the left, Eugene was to attack and outflank Marsin and the Elector; while the main body of the Allies, including seventy squadrons of cavalry, whom Marlborough posted between his two lines of infantry, were to be hurled against the French centre.

At three o'clock on the morning of August 13th, the Allies began the advance in two divisions, each formed into two columns of infantry and two of cavalry, with the artillery between them. The weather was dull and dreary, with so thick a mist covering the plain that

Tallard was ignorant of their approach until they were within cannon shot. As the attack could not begin until Prince Eugene was in his appointed position, and the ground his troops had to cross was exceedingly difficult, the left and centre rested until midday, both sides cannonading with a good deal of impetuosity. The battle opened on the Allied left, where Major-General Wilkes, with the infantry, made a furious assault upon Blenheim, the vehement soldiers tearing with their hands at the palisades which protected it. But though Lord Cutts brought up reinforcements, and officers and men displayed the most vehement gallantry, the tremendous fire kept up by the force in Blenheim compelled them to fall back, though they did so in excellent order.

The attack on the centre, at first, was not more fortunate. The troops succeeded in crossing the marshy ground, but suffered severely from two assaults of the enemy. The second, by the famous Irish brigade, was pushed with so much determination that the Allies gave way; but Marlborough galloped to the spot, rallied his wavering regiments, and returned the attack. On the right, the first charge of Prince Eugene's cavalry was successful, so far as to break up the enemy's front line, and capture a battery in front of the village of Lützingen. The second line of the French, however, stood firm, and kept up such a rolling fire of musketry that, with great gaps torn in their ranks, the Imperialist horsemen withdrew. To their support Eugene immediately brought up his Prussian infantry, who now for the first time showed of what splendid soldierly stuff they were made, and meeting with composed steadiness the wild charges of the enemy, securely held their ground.

On the right centre the Prince of Holstein, with eleven Hanoverian battalions, attacked and carried the village of Oberglau, but the Irish brigade being let loose at them, they were driven into the marshes of the Nobel, with the loss of their commander. For a moment Marlborough's communications with Eugene were interrupted; until the Duke rode to the spot, strengthened his line with some English battalions, and flung upon the Irish a body of Imperialist cavalry, which crushed them like an avalanche.

In these various movements—these ebbs and flows of battle—the day was spent; dense clouds of smoke hanging over the hotly-contested field, and partly concealing the disorder into which the enemy's lines had been thrown by the energy of the Allied attack. At about five o'clock Marlborough struck home at Tallard's centre. Eight thousand splendid horsemen, under Major-General Lumley, fell upon the reeling ranks with a storm of steel; so heavy was the shock that they perforce recoiled some sixty paces. But the great guns renewed their crashing discharges; the trumpets again blared forth the stern command; and to the second charge the foemen offered but a faint-hearted resistance. Firing off their carbines aimlessly, they turned their horses' heads, smote their reeking flanks with hasty spurs, and tore full gallop from the field. The infantry, thus uncovered, were overwhelmed by the Allied battalions, and cut to pieces or taken prisoners. The battle was won. From right to left the French array was irretrievably shattered; on one side the fugitives seeking shelter in Höchstadt; on the other, attempting to swim the Danube, in the broad deep waters of which they perished by scores and hundreds. Tallard, with his chief officers and a squadron or two, took refuge in the village of Sonderheim, where they were surrounded by the Hessian cavalry, and compelled to surrender.

But there was still Blenheim, with eleven thousand men shut up in it, to be disposed of. Clerembault, their commander, had made fruitless efforts to obtain instructions from his superior officers; and at last, it is supposed, he crept out of the village to make his way for this purpose to headquarters, got entangled in the rush of fugitives from the main army, was swept into the Danube, and drowned. What constituted the main defence of the position against the enemy, now served to keep its defenders in a trap, while they were surrounded by the bulk of the Allied army. They showed a good deal of vigour and energy, but without result. It was a period, as Burton says, of awful suspense to the assailants as well as the assailed, for the solemn question arose—Were the victors, according to the hard law of a soldier's duty, to do their worst against the enemy if he persisted obstinately in a useless defence? Must they point all their guns against the doomed village, and crush its garrison under its shattered houses? Happily the French came to a wise resolution, and yielded, without dishonour, to the preponderant force that threatened to annihilate them if its general let it loose.

Blenheim (or Höchstadt, as the French call it) cost the victors four thousand five hundred killed and seven thousand five hundred wounded; and the defeated enemy upwards of twenty thousand killed, wounded, and missing, and between thirteen thousand and fourteen thousand prisoners. Marsin was unable to collect more than sixteen thousand dispirited troops with which to retreat towards the Rhine.

The victory of Blenheim proved a turning-point in the history of Europe. The change which it wrought in the aspect of affairs was almost magical. It prostrated at one blow the imposing structure raised by the ambition of Louis XIV.; swept away his dream of European domination; relieved Germany from the pressure of his armies. England it placed in the front rank of military nations; thenceforward our country became an important factor in every European combination. In some well-known stanzas Southey, from the humanitarian point of view, affects to depreciate this famous battle; but the student of political history knows that it accomplished a good deal for the cause of enlightenment and freedom, and that the blood was not wasted which mingled on that day with the waters of the Nobel and the Danube.

At the rewards which a grateful nation showered upon its great general I must briefly glance. He received the thanks of both Houses of Parliament. The royal manor of Woodstock was granted to him and his heirs; and a large sum of money was voted for the erection of that stately palace which still perpetuates the name of the great Bavarian battlefield. The poets joined in the national chorus of applause and gratitude; though of the strains of Prior, Philips, and Addison posterity remembers little except the elaborate simile in which the last-named compares the great chief to an angel sent to guide the rising tempest.

> ' Calm and serene he drives the furious blast :
> And, pleased the Almighty's orders to perform,
> Rides in the whirlwind and directs the storm.'

The war was now transferred from the German to the French side of the Rhine, and Bavaria having been reduced, Marlborough, early in September, concentrated his forces at Philipsburg, preparatory to the investment of Landau, the great fortress which commands the road between Germany and France. He thought it possible that Villeroy might fight in order to rescue it, and made his arrangements accordingly; but the French were not disposed to challenge conclusions with him in the field, and Villeroy fell back towards the frontier. The garrison of Landau, however, made a brave resistance, and it was late in November before the besiegers could make any impression upon it. While Eugene covered the siege, Marlborough, with twelve thousand men, struck across the hilly Hochwald to Trier, which he took by surprise, and made his winter quarters. The march was an extraordinarily bold one; as bold as Napoleon ever attempted.

Having thus rolled back the tide of French aggression, Marlborough was free to prepare for the execution of his cherished project, which, however, an untoward fortune prevented him from realising—namely, after the French had been expelled from their fortified positions in the Netherlands, to invade France, and dictate the terms of peace under the roof of the Tuileries. His first object, in the campaign of 1705, was to move along the valley of the Moselle, but owing to the supineness of the Imperial authorities, and the ill-faith of the Margrave of Baden, he found his moveable force reduced to about thirty thousand men, and was unable to act against the strong position which Villars, the ablest of the French generals, occupied among the wooded hills of Sirk. News soon reached him of the movements of Villeroy on the Meuse; that he had captured Sluy and the town of Liège, had invested the citadel, and compelled Auverquerque and the Dutch to retire. Suddenly and silently Marlborough broke up his camp, and, leaving his heavy stores at Trier, rapidly pushed forward to Auverquerque's assistance. At his approach Villeroy abandoned his trenches before Liège, and took shelter behind the formidable lines which the French had constructed on the Meuse, between Namur and Antwerp. Marlborough resolved to attack them between Leuwe and Hedelsheim, where they were covered by the small but deep stream of the Little Ghent. In spite of the objection of the Dutch field-officers, he made the attempt on the 17th of July; and so skilful were his dispositions, and so strenuous was the valour of his fighting men, that the lines were carried with little loss to the Allies. When Villeroy fell back to a new post upon the Dyle, supported by Louvain and Tirlemont, Marlborough would have followed him, but was prevented by the jealousy or timidity of the Dutch, who again interfered on the 10th of August, when the great Englishman counted upon a brilliant victory which would have immortalised the plain of Waterloo a century earlier. His mortification was so great that he threatened to resign his command,

and would have done so but for the pressure brought to bear upon him by his friends. The remainder of the campaign was unmarked by any event of importance, and he dismissed his troops early into winter-quarters.

Soon afterwards the Emperor conferred upon him the small Principality of Mindelheim—a state situated on the western frontier of Bavaria, about fifteen miles by twelve miles, which yielded an annual revenue of two thousand pounds. No doubt Marlborough's chief inducement to accept the gift was the circumstance that it raised him to an equality with the German princes in rank, and thus removed some of the embarrassments that had hampered him in his command.

Party politics detained him in England during the opening months of 1706, and it was late in April when he landed at the Hague. His idea was to operate with Prince Eugene in Italy, and carry out his projected invasion of France from the south-east; but the renewed activity of the French recalled him to the relief of the Netherlands, and he assembled his army, which reinforcements had brought up to a total of sixty thousand men of all arms, at Tongres. Villeroy, with sixty-two thousand men, still clung to his camp on the Dyle, and with him was Marlborough's old antagonist, the Elector of Bavaria, prepared, according to his silly vaunt, 'since the wine was abroad, to drink it to the lees.' A movement of the Allies which seemed to threaten Namur called Villeroy into the open field; and the two armies came into collision at Ramillies.

. . . .

Ramillies is a village on the high ground of Brabant, about eighteen miles south of Louvain. In the immediate neighbourhood rise three streams, of which the Great and the Little Gheet flow northward until they unite in a single channel which debouches into a tributary of the Scheldt. To the south, with an easterly sweep, runs the broader and deeper current of the Mehaigne. Among the uplands which overhang the last-named river in a kind of semi-circle, Villeroy, on Whit Sunday, the 23d of May 1706, drew up his forces. His right wing touched the village of Tavières, and thence, in two lines, his crescent-like formation swept round, past the village of Offuz, to that of Anderkirk, on the extreme left. Both Offuz and Anderkirk were covered by a morass. In the centre lay the village of Ramillies, which was occupied by twenty battalions ; and behind it, on the crest of the ridge, rose a burrow or tumulus of stone and turf, known as the Tomb of Ottomond, close to which, running upward from the Allied left, was the *chaussée*, or causeway, named after Queen Brunehault.

Marlborough disposed his army in a convex line, with his right thrown back from the Little Gheet, near the village of Foulz, and his left resting on the Mehaigne. This arrangement secured him at the outset a considerable advantage, as he could shift his troops from one flank to the other more quickly than the enemy. His plan of battle contemplated an attack on Tavières, in order to turn the flank of the French cavalry and push forward to the Tomb of Ottomond. With this in his hands, he could strike at the French rear, and enfilade their entire position. At the outset, therefore, he engaged Villeroy's attention by a formidable though false attack on his left, which induced him to draw reinforcements from his right to strengthen it. Marlborough, to continue the deception, kept his first line conspicuously before the enemy, while he withdrew his second under cover of the hilly ground, and massed it on the left. Then with a rush he carried the villages of Tavières and Ramillies. At the latter point the fighting was most desperate. The *Maison du Roi*, or Household Brigade, composed of the best blood of France, met Auverquerque's charge with a brilliant resistance, and drove back the Dutch infantry in great disorder. Marlborough, with seventeen squadrons, hastened to restore the fight. His person was recognised by some French dragoons, who, breaking from their ranks, closed swiftly around him. Fighting his way through the ring of sabres, he attempted to escape by leaping his horse across a ditch; but it fell and flung him. His aide-de-camp brought him another; while he was mounting, a cannon-ball struck off the head of Colonel Bingham, his equerry, who held the stirrups. The Duke, however, received no injury; and his soldiers, greatly excited by the peril to which he had been exposed, increased the impetuosity of their attack.

At this moment twenty squadrons which he had sent for came up from the right. Having formed in splendid order, in three lines, they dashed forward with a shout victorious, fell in a storm of spear and sabre on the French battalions, which scattered and fled. Sweeping through them, the horsemen soon occupied the height of Ottomond, and the Allies pressing their attack in front, the whole of the French army, taken between two fires, broke in confusion. An attempt to check the *débâcle* was made by the Spanish and Bavarian horse-guards; but they were charged through and through by the English cavalry and literally cut to pieces. The army which had made so splendid a show that morning on the breezy uplands of the Mehaigne, was broken up into disorganised fragments, and in grievous confusion, with the fatal cry of '*Sauve qui peut!*' fled from the lost field. With a few squadrons Lord Orkney pursued them as far as Louvain, a distance of eighteen miles. Marlborough and Auverquerque, with the main army, halted at Moldert, five miles from Louvain.

The loss of the French and Bavarians was between seven thousand and eight thousand in killed and wounded, and about as many in prisoners and deserters. They left behind them fifty-two guns and eighty standards; all their treasure, ammunition, and provisions, and even their soup kettles. The Allies, being the attacking force, also suffered heavily; one thousand and sixty-six killed and two thousand five hundred and sixty-seven wounded.

Though Ramillies has not made so deep an impression on the national mind as Blenheim, it was a more complete victory, and fought, I think, with even greater skill and determination. Its results were very important. Nearly the whole of Austrian Flanders was delivered from the yoke of French dominion. Brussels, Mechlin, Alost, Leuwe, Ghent, Bruges, Daum, and Oudenarde surrendered in rapid succession. 'So many towns have submitted since the battle,' wrote Marlborough, 'that it really looks more like a dream than truth.' Only Dunkirk, Nieuport, Ostend, and Antwerp remained in the hands of the French, and these were reduced before the end of the campaign. 'It is not to be expressed,' wrote the Duke to his colleague Godolphin, 'the great success it has pleased God to give us by putting a consternation in the enemy's army, for they had not only a greater number than we, but all the best troops of France.'

To consolidate his conquests and secure the line of the Lys, Marlborough, in the latter days of July, laid siege to the important town of Menin, which was not only strongly fortified and amply garrisoned, but provided with facilities for inundating the country roundabout. Louis XIV. was fully aware of the strategical value of the position, and Vendôme, who had succeeded Villeroy in the command of the French army in the Netherlands, was ordered to attempt its relief. On reaching the scene of action he found the troops too demoralised for any battle to be ventured on. 'Every one here,' he wrote, 'turns pale when the name of Marlborough is mentioned.' Menin succumbed, and Marlborough proceeded to invest Oudenarde, a fortress on the Scheldt, the waters of which could at once be let loose to cover it on the approach of an enemy. 'They will want an army of ducks,' exclaimed Louis, 'to capture Oudenarde!' But the capture nevertheless was effected; and Marlborough, with the deep religious humility characteristic of the man, wrote to Godolphin:—'It could never have been taken but by the hand of God, which gave us seven weeks without rain: rain began the day after we had taken possession, and continued without intermission.' The capture of Dendermond and Ath completed the Ramillies campaign; but Mons would have been taken had not the Dutch deputies renewed their policy of obstruction.

No military movement of importance marked the campaign of 1707. The Dutch Government embarrassed Marlborough by their constant objections to his plans for carrying the war into France. The Continental Powers, by their jealousy of one another, involved him in an endless embroglio of negotiation; while at home he had to detect and foil the intrigues set on foot by Harley and conducted by Mrs Masham, who was rising rapidly in the Queen's favour, while the Duchess was as rapidly declining. While he was in England his personal influence was still sufficient to defeat their conspiracies. and to procure the dismissal from office of Harley and St John. But he could not fail to see that the Queen had gone over to the Tory party, and that the country at large was beginning to weary of the war, in which it had no longer any direct interest. Having supped full of glory, it was counting the cost. This public opinion found expression in the House of Commons, where some of the extreme Tories even ventured to affirm that the war was prolonged by Marlborough to further his own ends—an offensive, and certainly an unfounded, accusation. But the fresh services which at this juncture he rendered to the cause of the Protestant Succession renewed for a brief interval his authority and popularity. France had prepared a formidable expedition for the object of invading Scotland and placing 'the Pretender' on the throne. Marlborough's energy anticipated the danger. He collected a strong

body of troops, which he despatched to the North. A
large garrison was stationed in Edinburgh Castle. Considerable reinforcements were brought over from Holland. A powerful squadron swept the North Sea, and the
invasion flotilla was compelled to return to Dunkirk without landing a soldier or firing a gun.

   .   .   .   .

In the spring of 1708 Marlborough rejoined his army ;
but owing to a severe drought, it was the end of May
before his troops were concentrated. A survey of the
theatre of operations convinced him that Vendôme, the
French commander, with whom was associated the Duke
of Burgundy, a prince of the royal blood, was at the head
of a superior force, and intended to recover the line of
the Dyle. He thereupon summoned Prince Eugene
to his assistance ; but before he could arrive, Vendôme,
with the help of confederates within the two cities, recaptured Ghent and Bruges, and had advanced upon the
town of Oudenarde. As this position commanded the
passage of the Scheldt, and was the key of Brabant,
Marlborough, rather than lose it, prepared to fight a
battle, even without Eugene's reinforcements. The prince
himself responded to Marlborough's appeal without delay,
riding forward with such impetuosity that he outstripped
not only his infantry but his cavalry, and arrived in the
Allied camp on the 7th of July, with none but the officers
of his staff in attendance.

Apprised that the Duke of Berwick was rapidly
hastening to effect a junction with Vendôme, Marlborough
set his troops in motion. A rapid march carried him to
Lessines, and secured the passage of the Dender. On his
approach Vendôme raised the siege of Oudenarde, and
fell back towards Gavre, with the intention of crossing
the Scheldt, and putting that river in his front. But
the Duke anticipated his design, and swiftly passing the
Scheldt, succeeded in getting between the French army

and France, between reinforcements and retreat (July 12th). A march of about fifteen miles brought him in front of the enemy's position. The French Marshal, perceiving that an engagement could not be avoided, had drawn up his troops behind the small river Norken, with his right upon Warreghem and his left upon the hill of Asper. They numbered a hundred and twenty one battalions of infantry, and one hundred and ninety-eight squadrons, or about seventy-five thousand men. As the Allies crossed the Scheldt, Vendôme gave orders to attack,—but those were immediately countermanded by the Duke of Burgundy, who ordered a different disposition. Of the delay thus caused by the dissensions of the French commanders, Marlborough took advantage to draw up his troops on a ridge of rising ground between Bevere and Moreghem. He then threw forward his cavalry under Earl Cadogan to attack Vendôme's advanced guard, which they did with such effect as almost to annihilate it. In this brilliant prelude to the main action the Electoral Prince of Hanover, afterwards George II., distinguished himself by his dogged courage.

Alarmed by this heavy blow, Vendôme would fain have retired his army, but was again thwarted by the Duke of Burgundy, and compelled to hold his ground. The battle was opened by the Duke, who, desirous apparently of ascertaining whether an advance of his right wing would be safe, ordered sixteen squadrons to cross the river; but observing the solid formation of the Prussian cavalry, and the steady, solid march of the British infantry, they were contented to maintain their post. Vendôme, who disapproved of the movement, had meanwhile ordered his left wing to the front; but Burgundy countermanded the order, alleging that an impassable morass separated the two armies on that side, though Vendôme himself had crossed the ground scarcely an hour before. Thus, for upwards of an hour, the French army remained in position; placing in Marlborough's hands an opportunity of which that great commander was not slow to avail himself. Convinced that the enemy's attack would be directed against his left, in front of the castle of Bevere, he strengthened it with twelve battalions; while skirmishers were thrown into the woods which lined the Norken; and strong guards posted to defend its bridges. Then, with the Prussian squadrons, he rode forward by the plain of Heurne, and deployed them in front of the French. A reserve of twenty English battalions, with a few guns, was stationed near Schaerken, under the Duke of Argyll.

The French of the right wing, comprising the picked soldiers of their army, the very flower of the military strength of France, were pushed forward, as Marlborough had foreseen; and after skirmishing with our advanced posts, gradually extended their line until they had outflanked the Allied left, and made themselves masters of a couple of villages which the Allies had garrisoned. This success was laboriously won. Each hedge blazed with an incessant fire. Men fought hand to hand in every enclosure; sternly disputed every stream and water-course. About six o'clock, when the battle had been raging a couple of hours, Count Lottum brought up a column of Prussians and Hanoverians, who not only checked the forward movement of the French, but compelled them to draw back, and recovered the ground that had been lost.

Marlborough and Eugene had hitherto watched together the currents and counter-currents of the battle. They now separated: the latter to take command of the right wing, which was composed almost entirely of English troops, and the former hurrying to the left, where lay the chief danger to the fortune of the Allies. Calling upon his Dutch and Hanoverian battalions, he completed the work which Count Lottum had so well begun; and forced the French right to some distance from their original position. Perceiving that the steep hill of Oycke, which commanded the field in that direction, had been left unoccupied, he concluded that it would be easy to turn the right flank of the enemy, and, to accomplish this, selected the veteran Auverquerque, with a strong body of infantry and cavalry. The veteran general executed this manœuvre with his wonted energy: seized the hill of Oycke; then changed front to the right, and, wheeling inwards, drew round the enemy in a kind of semi-circle, stormed in upon their centre, and cut their array completely in twain. Almost simultaneously Prince Eugene came up from the left, and so close was the contact of the Allied wings that, in the obscurity of battle, the Prince of Orange's advanced guard exchanged several volleys with the front ranks of Prince Eugene's before the error was discovered. To prevent a renewal of this useless slaughter, a general halt was commanded; an indispensable precaution, though it proved the deliverance of the French in the centre and left wing, who, in the darkness, escaped unobserved.

The loss of the Allies at Ramillies is estimated at three thousand killed, wounded, and missing. The French acknowledged to six thousand killed and wounded, and nine thousand taken prisoners; it was the darkness only which saved them from destruction. 'If we had been so happy,' wrote Marlborough, 'as to have had two more hours of daylight, I believe we should have made an end of this war.'

To check the Duke of Berwick, of whose movements we have already spoken, Marlborough ordered a division to seize the lines which the French had constructed from Ypres to Warneton, in order to protect the villages of the Lys and the Scheldt. He then crossed the Lys, and took up a position between Comines and Menin, which opened up to him the road to France. By the arrival of Prince Eugene's divisions, his army had been brought up to its average strength. On the other hand, when the Duke of

Berwick succeeded in effecting a junction with Vendôme (August 30), the losses of Oudenarde were repaired, and the French reached a total of one hundred thousand men. But Marlborough determined immediately on the siege of Lille, the vast fortress which, with so invincible an air, guarded the frontier of France. The curiosity of all Europe was excited by this colossal effort; for the fortifications of Lille, which had been designed by Vauban, were of immense strength and complexity, while the garrison consisted of sixteen thousand picked soldiers, under Marshal Boufflers, who was deservedly reckoned among the great French captains of the day. It was certain that Louis would exhaust his resources in its defence. The waterways in this quarter were commanded by the French, and Marlborough was compelled to collect his siege-guns, mortars, and ammunition at Brussels, and bring them thence by land—along almost impassable roads—a distance of twenty-five leagues, in the teeth of an army of one hundred thousand men. The convoy, it is said, consisted of sixteen thousand horses, and extended fifteen miles in length. Yet so admirable were his combinations, that, in spite of the Duke of Berwick's persevering exertions, it reached the Allied camp in safety on the 14th of August. Not a gun was lost—not a barrel of powder—not a keg of salted herrings. The French military historian, Fouquières, his admiration of consummate generalship prevailing over his patriotic prejudices, exclaims,—'Posterity will scarcely believe that it was in the power of the enemy to convey to Lille all that was necessary for the siege, and all the supplies of the army; to conduct thither the artillery and implements essential for such an undertaking, and that these immense burdens should be transported by land over a line of twenty-five leagues, under the eyes of an army of eighty thousand [one hundred thousand] men. Yet it is an undoubted truth; and never was a great enterprise conducted with more skill and circumspection.'

The operations of the siege, which began on the 13th, were superintended by Prince Eugene, with forty thousand men; Marlborough commanded the covering army, about fifty thousand strong, which he posted south of Lille in a strongly-fortified camp. Vendôme and Berwick approached the beleaguered city on the 2d of September. Louis, through Chamillart, his Minister of War, had sent them repeated orders to fight the Allies; but the two generals, after careful consideration, decided on disobeying them. To have attacked Marlborough in the position he had taken up, would have been to invite certain and inevitable disaster. As for Marlborough, he was dissatisfied with the slow progress made by the engineers. 'It is impossible for me,' he writes to Godolphin, 'to express the uneasiness I suffer for the ill-conduct of my engineers at the siege, where I think everything goes very wrong. It would be a cruel thing if after we have obliged the enemy to quit all thoughts of relieving the place by force, which they have done by repassing the Scheldt, we should fail of taking it by the ignorance of our engineers and the want of stores; for we have already found very near as much as was demanded for the taking of the town and citadel, and as yet we are not entire masters of the counterscarp.' During an assault in the night of the 20th of September, Prince Eugene was wounded in the head, and Marlborough thenceforward took the conduct of the siege, which he pressed with so much decision that Boufflers gave up the town, after a defence of sixty days, on the 22d of October. With five thousand men, the remainder of his garrison, he retired into the citadel, which he was forced to surrender on the 11th of December.

'The incident most striking to the imagination in the whole siege, was perhaps the desperate attempt made by the French to get powder through to the besieged by packing it in bags on men's backs. It would be, of course,

probable at any time, and most probable in those days of
flintlocks, that the powder would in a fight explode, with
certain destruction to the bearer, and this actually happened in many cases. The besieged had suffered greatly
for want of provisions and ammunition, but the besiegers
themselves were not much better off, and one crowning
attempt to cut off their supplies, led to a miniature
battle which, both for the gallantry displayed in it, the
decisive effect it had on the siege, and the curious suspicions which have been excited by its circumstances,
deserves detailed notice.'

This was the battle of Wynendael, of which Marlborough's enemies availed themselves to fling the blackest
aspersions on his character.

A large convoy of provisions and stores for the relief
of the besiegers had been assembled at Ostend ; and the
French were as desirous that it should not reach them, as
Marlborough was anxious to secure its passage. The
former, therefore, despatched Count de la Mothe with
thirty-four battalions and sixty-three squadrons, according
to the French account, or forty battalions and forty-six
squadrons, according to the English, to intercept it. Marlborough sent out for its protection a body of foot and
horse under two German brigadiers, which was followed
up by General Webb, with twelve battalions—after whom
went Cadogan with another twelve battalions, and twenty-
six squadrons (September 27th). Webb, with a force of
twenty battalions and three squadrons, came up with La
Mothe's advanced guard on the plain of Turout, and in
front of the little wood and castle of Wynendael, behind
which the convoy was marching. He drew up his little
army in two lines ; M. de la Mothe formed in eight lines, four
of infantry in front, and dragoons and cavalry in the rear.

I know not where to find a more picturesque description of the action that ensued, than is given by Thackeray
in his *Esmond*.

The French began the action, as usual, with a cannonade which lasted three hours, when they made their attack, advancing in eight lines, four of foot and four of horse, upon the Allied troops in the wood where we were posted. Their infantry behaved ill: they were ordered to charge with the bayonet, but, instead, began to fire, and almost at the very first discharge from our men, broke and fled. The cavalry behaved better: with these alone, who were three or four times as numerous as our whole force, Monsieur de la Mothe might have won victory: but only two of our battalions were shaken in the least, and these speedily rallied: nor could the repeated attacks of the French horse cause our troops to budge an inch from the position in the wood in which our general had placed them.

After attacking for two hours, the French retired at nightfall entirely foiled. With al the loss we had inflicted upon him, the enemy was still three times stronger than we: and it could not be supposed that our general could pursue M. de la Mothe, or do much more than hold our ground about the wood, from which the Frenchman had in vain attempted to dislodge us. La Mothe retired behind his forty guns, his cavalry protecting them better than it had been enabled to annoy us; and meanwhile the convoy, which was of more importance than all our little force, and the safe passage of which we would have dropped to the last man to accomplish, marched away in perfect safety during the action, and joyfully reached the besieging camp before Lille.

Major-General Cadogan, my Lord Duke's Quarter-Master General (and between whom and Mr Webb there was no love lost), accompanied the convoy, and joined Mr Webb with a couple of hundred horse just as the battle was over, and the enemy in full retreat. He offered, readily enough, to charge with his horse upon the French as they fell back; but his force was too weak to inflict any damage upon them; and Mr Webb, commanding as Cadogan's senior, thought enough was done in holding our ground before an enemy that might still have overwhelmed us, had we engaged him in the open territory, and in securing the safe passage of the convoy. Accordingly the horse brought up by Cadogan did not draw a sword, and only prevented, by the good countenance they showed, any disposition the French might have had to renew the attack on us.

This brilliant little action the Tories in England endeavoured to turn to political advantage. They extolled it as if it had been another Blenheim, and panegyrised Webb as the equal, if not the superior, of Marlborough.

Webb himself, a man of some merit, but addicted to gasconading and consumed with vanity, declared that he had been ill-used by the Commander-in-Chief, whom he accused of jealousy, and of neglecting to do him justice in the *Gazette*, and of giving the credit of the victory to his favourite, Cadogan. The account in the *Gazette* was not drawn up by the Duke, who, in his letters to Godolphin, speaks of Webb in the highest terms, and suggests that the Queen should make him some special acknowledgment. It is certainly true that in his first account of the affair he gives to Cadogan a larger share of praise than he really deserved. He was probably influenced by the character of the information which reached him; and, moreover, it was, after all, the presence of Cadogan and his cavalry which prevented the French from attempting to renew the battle. On the whole, there does not seem the slightest justification for accusing Marlborough of any intentional unfairness towards Webb. There is certainly as little ground for the silly charge in which the malignity of his enemies found further expression; that he had been bribed by the French throughout the compaign, and therefore had declined battle when he might have fought with advantage, and had sent Webb with an inadequate force, in the hope that he would be defeated, the convoy cut off, and consequently the prosecution of the siege rendered impossible. To state the calumny is to confute it. We need not attribute to Marlborough any splendid qualities of patriotism and heroism; but it is folly to deny his anxiety for his military reputation, or his political sagacity, and we may be sure that he would not have committed a crime which would also have been a blunder, which must have irretrievably ruined his fame, and disgraced him before Europe.

The reduction of Lille was accomplished by Marlborough's skill and perseverance. On the 3d of October the besiegers carried the outworks, and effected a lodgment directly opposite the breaches in the ramparts. Vendôme made a fresh effort to raise the siege, by opening the sluices and flooding the country, so as to interrupt the Allied communications with their depôt at Ostend. But the great Duke's resources were inexhaustible. The ammunition was packed in stout skins, and carried in flat-bottomed boats from Ostend to Leffinghen, whence it was conveyed to the camp in waggons mounted on very high wheels. In the conduct and defence of these novel convoys Cadogan greatly distinguished himself, and justified the confidence which Marlborough had always placed in him. It was about this time that General Auverquerque (or Overkirk) died : a veteran in arms, old in fame and years, and worn out with incessant fatigues and the trials of a score of battles. Marlborough regretted deeply the loss of so able and loyal a lieutenant. But the siege was prosecuted with unabated vigour ; and Boufflers, perceiving that no relief could be expected from Vendôme's army, and knowing himself too weak to resist the assault of the Allies, which might hourly be attempted, beat a parley on the 22d of October, and capitulated. The Allies, in recognition of his resolute defence, granted him favourable terms. Prisoners were exchanged ; the sick and wounded sent to Douay ; and the remainder of the garrison, five thousand strong, retired into the citadel, which Boufflers defended for six weeks longer.

To save the citadel, Vendôme executed a diversion against Brussels, despatching the Elector of Bavaria with fifteen thousand men. But Marlborough soon compelled him to retreat by attacking the French posts on the Scheldt at Oudenarde, which the enemy had been fortifying ever since the battle, and carrying them on the 26th of November. The passage of the Scheldt was triumphantly effected, and Marlborough, leaving Eugene in command at Lille, marched upon Brussels, where, on the 29th, he was received with a notable demonstration of welcome.

The citadel of Lille surrendered on the 11th of December; and the French army abandoned the campaign, retiring into winter quarters. Marlborough, however, suddenly concentrated his troops, and advanced against Ghent, which was invested on the 18th. 'The garrison was very strong, consisting of no less than thirty battalions and nineteen squadrons, mustering eighteen thousand combatants. The governor had been instructed by Vendôme to defend this important stronghold to the last extremity; but he was inadequately supplied with provisions and forage, and the result signally belied the expectations formed of his resistance. The approaches were vigorously pushed. On the 24th the trenches were opened; on the 25th, a sortie was repulsed; on the 28th December the fire began with great vigour from the breaching and mortar batteries; and at noon the governor sent a flag of truce, offering to capitulate if not relieved before the 2d of January. This was agreed to; and on the latter day, as no friendly force approached, the garrison opened their gates, and marched out in such strength that they were defiling incessantly from ten in the morning till seven at night.'

Bruges, and the smaller towns of Plassendail and Leffinghen, quickly fell into the hands of the Allies. Their capture completed the most brilliant of Marlborough's campaigns; the one in which he showed the greatest resource and the most consummate skill.

. . . .

The early spring of 1709 was occupied by the negotiations for peace which Marlborough's successes had forced upon France and her sovereign. On the part of England they were conducted by the Duke, who, however, was not personally responsible for the severity of the terms on which the Allies insisted. The instructions with which the Ministry furnished him were:—'That no negotiation for peace should be concluded with France, until the preliminaries were adjusted between England and the States.

That no peace could be safe or honourable, unless the whole Spanish monarchy were restored to the House of Austria. That the French King should be obliged to acknowledge the Queen's title and the Protestant succession to the crown; the Pretender to be removed from France; and the fortifications and harbour of Dunkirk destroyed. That a barrier should be provided for the security of the States against the attacks of France.' This barrier was to be formed by the cession of the fortified towns or fortresses of Furnes, Ypres, Menin, Lille, Tournai, Condé, Valenciennes, and Maubeuge. France, weakened by a long series of defeats, was really anxious for peace, and though unable to agree to such rigorous terms, offered very large concessions. 'M. de Torcy' (the French ambassador), said Marlborough, 'has offered so much, that I have no doubt it will end in a good peace.' That the Duke longed for the repose which his age and services might seem to merit, his private letters to the Duchess abundantly prove. 'Everything goes on so well here,' he writes, 'that there is no doubt of its ending in a good peace; but for some little time it must not be spoken of. You must have in readiness the sideboard of plate, and you must let the Lord Treasurer know, that since the Queen came to the crown, I have not had either a canopy or chair of state, which, now, of necessity, I must have; so the wardrobe should have immediate orders; and I beg you will take care to have it made so as that it may serve for part of a bed when I have done with it here, which, I hope, will be by the end of this summer, so that I may enjoy your dear company in quiet, which is the greatest satisfaction I am capable of having.'

The Dutch, however, increased their demands when they saw that France was disposed to yield. Contrary to the advice of Marlborough and Eugene, they insisted that Ghent and Dendermonde should be included among the barrier fortresses; and when England opposed this, they refused to join in demanding the demolition of Dunkirk. The moment seemed favourable to the French ambassador for an attempt to bribe Marlborough to throw his vast influence on the side of France. He was offered two million livres if he secured Naples and Sicily, or even Naples alone, for Louis XIV.'s grandson; and forty million livres extra, if, in addition, he saved to France the fortresses of Landau, Dunkirk, and Strasburg. Marlborough contemptuously rejected the bribe, and earnestly advised the French King to accept the proffered conditions, if he desired to save his kingdom from destruction.

The ultimatum of the Allies was finally delivered to Louis XIV. by the Pensionary Heinsius. Among other stipulations it provided that his grandson, the Duke of Anjou, was to surrender the kingdoms of Spain and Sicily in two months, and that, if he neglected to comply, Louis was to join the Allies in expelling him. This humiliating condition the King of France refused to accept. It was rejected with not less decision by France herself. Hitherto the war had not commanded the sympathies of the great body of the French people; but all at once it assumed a national and patriotic character, and the Allies were chagrined to find that they had exaggerated the exhaustion of France, and under-estimated her resources. How fertile these are, how capable of recuperation the energies of the nation when apparently at their lowest ebb, we have seen in our own time; and in 1709, after years of arduous warfare, after the loss of three mighty battles—of numerous smaller actions—of her recent conquests and most important fortresses—while suffering from poverty and famine and disease—she responded to her sovereign's appeal with wonderful alacrity. 'If I must wage war,' he exclaimed, and France endorsed his words, 'it is better to wage it against my enemies than against my children!' By summoning to the ranks the whole of the reserves, he was able to put into the field a force of one hundred and fifteen thousand men. Not such veteran soldiers as those who had contested Blenheim and Ramillies, but more formidable, perhaps, because they were inspired by the patriotic sentiment. At their head Louis placed Marshal Villars—the most fortunate of the French commanders—and soldiers like their leaders to be lucky men; and Boufflers, although his senior, offered to serve under him. Loaded with the hopes and prayers of their countrymen and their King, the two generals prepared to open the campaign of 1709.

Seeing that a renewal of the war was inevitable, Marlborough prepared for it with his characteristic foresight. He knew that the circumstances would stimulate France to a desperate effort, and therefore persuaded the English Ministry to increase the numerical strength of their contingent, while by the exercise of mingled tact and firmness he obtained reinforcements from the Allies. Immense exertions brought up his forces to a total of a hundred and ten thousand men. As for his plan of campaign, it was the same as in preceding years; to expel the French from the few fortresses they still held on the frontier, and then to invade France and march upon Paris.

To cover French Flanders and Hainault, Villars took up a very strong position, his right resting upon the canal of Douay, his left upon Bethune and its marshes, and his centre supported by the village of La Bassée. It was rendered impregnable by nature and science. The Allied commanders took the field on the 23d of June, with their forces massed in two great divisions; the right, under Eugene, consisting of Imperialists and Germans; and the left, under Marlborough, of British, Dutch, and auxiliaries. Finding the lines of La Bassée too strong to be carried, except with tremendous loss, Marlborough determined upon laying siege to Tournay. First, by a series of ingenious manœuvres he deceived Villars into a belief that the Allies had determined to attack him, and induced him to draw upon the garrison for reinforcements. Then, on the evening of the 27th, he suddenly broke up his camp, united with Eugene, and silently advanced for part of the night in the enemy's direction; but about two in the morning he ordered his troops to form into two columns and wheel to the left, one advancing upon Tournay, by way of Pont à Bovines, the other by Pont à Tressin. By the following evening, so rapidly and skilfully conducted had been the movements of the Allies, the investment of Tournay was completed, while a portion of its garrison lay in the lines of La Bassée; and so little foreseen had been Marlborough's strategy, that the town was very indifferently supplied with provisions and forage. Marlborough undertook the direction of the siege, and fixed his headquarters at Villeneuve. The covering army, under Prince Eugene, extended from Pont à Tressin on the Marque, to St Amand on the Scarpe.

Tournay is advantageously situated on the frontier of France. Its circuit was extensive: the interior walls were of ancient construction, but formidable advanced works had recently been erected from the plans of Vauban; and its citadel, a regular pentagon, was regarded by the great Condé as the most perfect of its kind. It was further strengthened by a complex system of mines and subterranean galleries, so that the French looked upon it as almost impregnable. 'It is a great relief to me,' wrote Villars, 'that the army have fixed upon the siege of Tournay, which ought to occupy the whole of the campaign.'

On the 10th of July the battering-train of heavy guns and mortars arrived from Ghent. The siege thenceforward was prosecuted with immense vigour, and the Allies gradually pushed their approaches forward in the teeth of an obstinate resistance. But, as Villars made no sign of coming to his relief, the governor surrendered the town on the 29th, and with four thousand men, the survivors of the garrison, retired into the citadel. The difficulties attending its siege were much greater than those which had surrounded the siege of the town: for the garrison was numerically adequate to the defence of this more limited circuit, and the subterranean works were of unusual strength and extent. Some delay was caused by a proposal from the governor to surrender if not relieved within a month. Marlborough assented, and a courier was despatched to Versailles to obtain the King's consent, but Louis refused, unless the cessation of hostilities was extended throughout the Netherlands. As this obviously unfair condition could not be accepted by the Allied commanders, the work of destruction and death went on. But owing to the numerous mines and galleries which the besieged utilised in these operations, and the necessity of meeting them by countermines and traverses, the siege was in ill odour with the Allied soldiers. Many who were among the most daring in the open field shrank from subterranean warfare, with its obscurity and uncertainty. To revive the spirits of their fighting men, Marlborough and Eugene visited the trenches in person, and rewarded liberally every instance of heroic conduct. In carrying on their secret labours the miners sometimes mistook friends for foes, and comrades engaged in deadly combat with one another. Sudden explosions blew battalions into the air, or the galleries were flooded, and hundreds suffocated or drowned. An officer in command of a small detachment was ordered to occupy a lunette which had been taken from the enemy; but his superior privately warned him that the post was undermined, and that the whole party would probably be blown up. He proceeded, however, in discharge of his duty; and having entered the caisse, served out wine and food to his men. Then he pledged them, 'A health to those who die the death of the brave!' Soon afterwards the mine was sprung; but the explosion, fortunately, failed, and the officer lived to be rewarded for his courage.

At length the spirit of the besieged gave way before the resolution of the besiegers ; and the citadel capitulated on the 31st of August. On the 3d of September the gates were given up ; and on the 5th, the garrison was conducted to Condé, not to serve again until an exchange of prisoners took place.

The road to Paris was now guarded only by the fortifications of Mons and Valenciennes ; and Marlborough, without delay, resolved to attack the former. The important lines of the Trouille, which had been constructed as part of its system of defence, were surprised and occupied on the 6th of September by the Prince of Hesse-Cassel, whose troops accomplished a march of fifty-two miles in fifty-six successive hours. Villars, finding himself thus cut off from the town, which, as it was weakly garrisoned, would not, he knew, maintain a prolonged resistance, and perceiving that its capture meant the loss of Hainault and the uncovering of the road to France, resolved upon fighting to regain the lines of the Tuille. The enthusiasm of his soldiers had been inflamed to the extreme by the arrival of Marshal Boufflers to serve, as a volunteer, under Villars. They were confident of success ; confident in the skill of their leaders ; eager to vindicate the military fame of their country. A finer army France had scarcely ever put into the field. In its camp were collected the choicest troops in the French service—the Gardes du Corps, mousquetaires, light horse, horse-grenadiers, and gens-d'armes. Among the cavalry of the line were the Carbineers ; among the infantry, the French and Swiss Guards, the Bavarian and Cologne Guards, and the Irish Brigade. Villars was assisted by the matured experience of Marshal Boufflers, and under him served Lieutenant-Generals D'Artagnan, Legal, Chemerault, Puységur. Guébriant, with Comtes Villars, Albergotti and Palavicini. The names of St Hilaire and Tolard adorn the page of history and the annals of science. With these were young

Coigny, the Duke de Guiche, and, let us add, the youthful Pretender, under the name of the Chevalier de St George, combining the graces of person with the valour hereditary to the Stuart race.

The Allies on the other hand, if weakened and fatigued by a long siege and a succession of laborious marches, were encouraged by the recollection of a hundred victories, and reposed a just reliance on the surpassing abilities of their great leaders. It is true that they were drawn from different nations, but they were bound together by the ties of discipline, and by the memories of battles and successes in which they had had a common share. Marlborough was their captain, with Eugene as his lieutenant; and among their officers were men of heroic mould—the Princes of Orange and Hesse-Cassel, the able and accomplished Cadogan, the gallant Lumley, Stair, Oxenstiern, Spaar, Ratzaty, and the Duke of Argyll. Youthful but apt pupils in the science of war were Saxe, Munich, and Schwerin.

The relative strength of the two armies when preparing for battle may be estimated at—

THE ALLIES.

129 battalions.
252 squadrons.
105 guns.   In all, about 90,000 to 93,000 men.

THE FRENCH.

130 battalions.
260 squadrons.
80 guns.   In all, 98,000 men.

The battle ground may thus be described:—It was a wooded plateau, rising from one hundred to two hundred feet above the Trouille, with the wood of Lanière on the western side, and that of Taisnière on the eastern. Between these woods stretched an elevated plain or glade, about a quarter of a mile wide, called the Trouée of Antwerp, leading northward to the village of Malplaquet. To the south, covering this village and the road to France, lay the French army, with its front protected by a line of embankment and a ditch, and its flanks by the two woods, which were filled with *abattis* and redoubts. The heights bristled everywhere with redoubts and palisades, stockades and *abattis*. Access to them was possible only through two defiles or *trouée*—that of La Louvière on the west, and that of d'Aulnoit on the east; and these were flanked by cross batteries, which rendered them almost impassable.

Marlborough would have attacked immediately, but yielded to the opposition of the Dutch deputies, who were in favour of delaying until reinforcements came up from Tournay. This involved a loss of two days, which the French occupied in adding to their already formidable entrenchments. Despairing of openly forcing them, Marlborough resolved to combine his front attack with a powerful demonstration in the rear. For this purpose he sent orders to the force under General Withers, coming up from Tournay, to halt at Ghislain, cross the Haine, and traversing the wood of Blangris, to fall upon the enemy's extreme left when the attack in front had begun. Baron Schulemberg received orders to contest the wood of Taisnière with forty of Prince Eugene's battalions, supported by forty guns so placed that their fire reached every part of the wood. Simultaneously a dense column, under the Prince of Orange, was to press upon the French right; and other diversions were to be effected at various points along the whole line.

The night, in both camps, was spent in silence, and in grim anticipation of the dread battle that was imminent on the morrow. The French were fully conscious of the strength of their position; yet not without emotion could they contemplate the prospect of a struggle against Marlborough's famous veterans. The Allies did not doubt but that the laurels of victory would be theirs; yet the bristling fortifications in front forbade them to hope that they would easily be purchased. It was a misty night, and the vapours still hung over plain and woodland when, at three in the morning, Marlborough's regiments assembled to join in the performance of Divine service. They then moved with perfect regularity to their respective stations; maintaining a firm and grave demeanour, like that of men who know they have an important duty to discharge, and are resolved to discharge it to the utmost of their capability. The French, on the other hand, displayed all their characteristic vivacity, and fell quickly into their ranks with loud shouts and snatches of martial song. It was seven o'clock when their great captain mounted his horse, amid cries of '*Vive le Roi! Vive le Maréchal de Villars!*' and took up his post on the left wing, having gracefully ceded the right, the post of honour, to Boufflers. As the two generals rode along the front, the vehement national cries redoubled; officers waved their sabres and plumed hats; privates brandished their muskets, and desired to be led against the foe; in short, the whole scene was well calculated to fill the minds of the two commanders with thoughts of victory.

Half an hour later, and the sun rose through the heavy clouds which hung over the woody defiles of Malplaquet, enabling the gunners to point their pieces with precision. A roar of artillery broke forth that seemed to shake the earth. Not a corner of the plain but was raked by shot and shell. Under cover of the terrific cannonade, Marlborough directed Count Lottum and the Prince of Orange's columns against the French right and centre. After advancing a certain distance, the Dutch halted, according to instructions, and formed in line out of musketry range; while Lottum still pushed forward, until, closing with the enemy, he deployed into three lines, and directed his attack from the right on the wood of Taisnière. At the same time Schulemberg's battalions, covering the right flank of Lottum's column, advanced against the wood in front; while Lord Orkney's brigade, on the left of Lottum, poured their well-directed volleys into the defences of the Trouée de la Louvière. The wood of Sart was occupied by three battalions under Gauvain. Prince Eugene, joining Schulemberg's battalions, and advancing with them, crossed several brooks, and plunged into the recesses of the Taisnière. When within pistol-shot of the enemy they received his fire, and so heavy was it and so continuous, that several battalions, reduced to skeleton formations, began to waver and yield ground. But they soon recovered; and after a hot contention the enemy were driven into the wood, where they were taken in flank by Gauvain's three battalions, and the fighting again went on.

Meanwhile, Marlborough in person led up some squadrons of cavalry to the support of Count Lottum, whose infantry, coolly facing the destructive musketry of the brigade '*du Roi*,' waded across a laborious swamp, and in admirable array reached the foot of their defences, swarmed with gleaming steel upon the breastwork, and for a few minutes held possession of it, while a storm of bullets whirled around them, and the big cannon-shot ploughed fatal furrows through the heaving ranks. Villars brought up a second brigade in good order, and after a sharp struggle the Allies were forced to retire. The Duke of Argyll sent some battalions to their assistance, and the horsemen galloping up, a combined effort was made against the enemy, and their position carried. About this time General Withers completed his movement in the French rear, and the enemy, caught between a double fire, began sensibly to give way.

The Prince of Orange, to whom I have already referred, had been ordered by Marlborough to wait for half an hour until the French should be embarrassed by the attack of Withers in the rear. The impetuous Prince fumed and fretted through the appointed interval; and then, though Withers had not yet made his presence felt, ordered his trumpets to sound the advance. In three columns, commanded respectively by himself, Major-General Hamilton and the Marquis of Tullibardine, and Generals Spaar and Oxenstiern, with a reserve of cavalry led by the Prince of Hesse-Cassel, his division moved forward, but was confronted by a hurricane of deadly missiles. The veteran Oxenstiern fell dead by the side of the Prince, whose aides-de-camp were either killed or wounded. His own horse was shot under him; but he marched on afoot, and with a wild yell his men clambered up the works and carried them at the point of the bayonet. But before they could deploy Marshal Boufflers hurled upon them a mass of fresh fighting men; a powerful battery swept their flanks; Spaar was killed and Hamilton severely wounded; confusion and unsteadiness spread from rank to rank. In vain the Prince snatched his colours from the man who bore them, and waving them above his head, exclaimed :—' Follow me, follow me, my friends; here is your post!' In vain the gallant Tullibardine brought up his Highlanders to the charge. A ceaseless fire rolled along the French defences, and the few who struggled through it unhurt found themselves confronted by a stiff hedge of bayonets. After heroically hopeless exertions, the Prince was compelled to retire his force, with the loss of several colours and an advanced battery, with two thousand killed and twice that number wounded. The French, shouting exultantly, poured out of their works in eager pursuit; but just in time the Prince of Hesse-Cassel's dragoons thundered up, and slashing furiously in among them, with sabres that were soon blood-red, drove them back in their turn, sorely discomfited.

Detecting the critical position of affairs, Goslinga, one

of the Dutch deputies, who had borne himself chivalrously in the fight, rode in quest of the great Duke, and met him returning from the successful movement against Taisnière. As, accompanied by Goslinga, he hastened towards the left, he perceived, with mingled emotions of pity and admiration, the wounded Dutch and Hanoverians limping back from the hands of the surgeons, pale and bleeding, again to take their places in the ranks and support their gallant comrades. He was soon joined by Prince Eugene. The two commanders called up their reserves, and rallied and re-formed the disordered battalions of the Prince of Orange. Having restored the battle in this quarter, they rode once more to the left, where the French attack had been renewed. Villars had despatched messengers to Boufflers requesting reinforcements, but the Marshal was too closely pressed to spare them; and Villars was compelled to obtain the necessary assistance from his centre, and, by so doing, to weaken it seriously. The right, thus strengthened, was hurled upon the Allied infantry with a force which sent them reeling back a considerable distance. But Marlborough had detected the weakness of the French centre, and struck at it with Lord Orkney's unbroken battalions, supported by a mass of cavalry. At the same time, Withers' attack upon the French rear was telling heavily. While hurrying to meet this new danger, Villars was wounded above the knee, and removed in a state of unconsciousness from the field.

On the Allied left Eugene, with his usual composure, had rallied and re-formed Schulemberg's battalions, and led them again into the thick of the fight. As he galloped with them he received a wound in the head. His attendants entreated him to retire, but he replied :—'If I am fated to die here, to what purpose dress the wound? If I survive, it will be time enough in the evening.' With blood-bespattered face he pushed forward, and his soldiers, inspired by his example, charged with a fury that would not be denied. The battle then began to turn in favour of the Allies, who got their great 40-gun battery into position, and scattered death and wounds among the hostile ranks, which, already wavering, were finally put to the rout. Boufflers could no longer refuse to see that the battle was lost, and with much coolness he prepared to retreat in tolerable order. Calling upon the Household Cavalry of France he exhorted them, in a short but stirring speech, to save the honour of their fatherland, and hurled their two thousand sabres on the battle-worn Allies. They scattered with their onset the fatigued troopers, and rode straight at Lord Orkney's battalions. Here they were stayed by a steady, relentless fire, and while they hesitated, Prince Eugene's horsemen dashed up to the scene of conflict. There was a short, sharp struggle, and then the French squadrons were seen to be in swift retreat. The Princes of Orange and Hesse-Cassel seized the opportunity to renew the attack on the French right, and this time succeeded. All along the line the Allies were victorious. Boufflers, however, did not lose his composure, and, with great energy forming up his broken battalions into three great columns, and covering their rear with his cavalry, he slowly withdrew to Bavai. In his previous battles, Marlborough had had to deal, when the victory was won, with a shattered army, incapable of withstanding the pursuit, demoralised and disorganised,—but on this occasion he found the French soldiers stubborn in retreat—they were defeated but not panic-stricken—so that Malplaquet yielded no such trophies as Blenheim had yielded, or Ramillies, or Oudenarde. It was not a decisive victory; and the capture of Mons, which surrendered on the 26th of October, was but an indifferent compensation for a terrible expenditure of life.

Terrible, we may emphatically pronounce it. Of the Allied infantry, there were five thousand five hundred and forty-four killed, and twelve thousand seven hundred and six wounded or missing; making a total of eighteen thousand two hundred and fifty,—among whom were two hundred and eight-six officers killed and seven hundred and sixty-two wounded. Including the cavalry, the loss of the Allies cannot be estimated at less than twenty thousand men. The French gave out that they had lost between six thousand and eight thousand; but it is certain that twelve thousand is a more correct figure. As a display of brilliant courage on the part of the two armies engaged, Malplaquet will always attract the attention of the military critic. 'The Eugenes and Marlboroughs,' wrote a French officer of distinction, quoted by Archdeacon Coxe, 'ought to be well satisfied with us during that day; since till then they had not met with a resistance worthy of them. They may say, with justice, that nothing can stand before them; and, indeed, what shall be able to stem the rapid course of these two heroes, if even an army of one hundred thousand of the best troops, posted between two woods trebly entrenched, and performing their duty as well as any brave men could do, were not able to stop them one day? Will you not then own with me, that they surpass all the heroes of former ages'?

Marlborough seems to have been roused out of his usual tranquillity by the lamentable carnage at Malplaquet. To the Minister Godolphin he wrote of it as 'a very murdering battle.' To the Duchess, at the close of the fight:—' I am so tired that I have but strength enough to tell you that we have had this day a very bloody battle; the first part of the day we beat their foot, and afterwards their horse. God Almighty be praised, it is now in our power to have what peace we please, and I may be pretty well assured of never being in another battle; but that, nor nothing in this world, can make me happy if you are not kind.' On public opinion in England it produced a very painful effect; greatly intensifying the growing dislike to a war which had already been prolonged over eight years. Harley the statesman, who was in great favour with the Queen, boldly denounced it as 'wanton carnage.' The pamphleteers of the day did not scruple to assert that the Duke had fought it in the hope of restoring his decayed popularity by a fresh victory; and even hinted that he had purposely exposed the lives of his officers, in order to swell his gains by the sale of their commissions. To these and other hostile attacks he imprudently lent additional force by a procedure which even his warmest friends regretted. Aware that his influence at Court had completely been undermined, and conscious that the approaching triumph of the Tories would be signalised by his early, if not his immediate, dismissal from his command, he solicited the Queen to grant him a patent constituting him Captain-General for life. His wisest friends, and especially Lord Chancellor Cowper, advised him that such an appointment was not only unprecedented, but unconstitutional. He persisted in his application, and was humiliated by a curt refusal. He departed from his dignity also, though not without provocation, in complaining to the Queen of the favour which she bestowed upon Mrs Masham, the tool and agent of his most determined political opponents. But from these mean intrigues I turn with pleasure to the field upon which Marlborough always appeared in his true greatness.

With a parting compliment from the Queen, who, in addressing Parliament, spoke of him as 'the chief instrument of her glory and of her people's happiness,' he crossed to the Hague, and plunged into an imbroglio of diplomatic difficulties, with the view of reconciling the opposing pretensions of the French King and the Allied Powers. Neither party could agree upon terms of peace. It is frequently insinuated, and even boldly affirmed, that Marlborough was the chief means of the prolongation of the war; but I do not believe that this conclusion will be entertained by any person who carefully and impartially examines his correspondence. At the age of sixty he might well, and I think he did sincerely, desire rest; and if he resumed hostilities, it was because he saw no other solution of the problem. 'I hope God will bless this campaign,' he wrote to the Duchess, 'for I see nothing else that can give us peace, either at home or abroad.' The fact is, that the Allies still made stipulations which the pride of Louis and the patriotism of France refused to accept. Reasonable terms the French would gladly have accepted; but they were prepared to endure the worst extremities rather than submit to national degradation.

At Tournay, on the 28th of April, Marlborough and Prince Eugene met to decide their plan of campaign,—which was based on the Duke's old idea of reducing the few fortresses still held by the French on the frontiers, and then penetrating to Paris. The first shock of arms fell upon Douai,—a position of great importance in the second line of defence which covered Artois. Villars was ordered to march to its relief; and on the 30th of May, he crossed the river Scarpe, and encamped on the plain of Lens, with the view of throwing reinforcements into the besieged city. The Allied commanders prepared to receive him; but Villars, on reconnoitring their position, found it so little to his liking, that, after manœuvring in their front for four days, he fell back without any attempt at fighting. Marlborough's feelings at this time are vividly expressed in his letter to Lord Godolphin:—'You will have seen,' he writes, 'that the Marshal de Villars has not been able to keep his word to the King of France, in giving a battle. If their resolution holds of venturing one—this country being all plains—it must be very decisive. I long for an end of the war, so God's will be done. Whatever the event may be, I shall have nothing to reproach myself, having with all my heart done my duty, and being hitherto blessed with more success than was ever known before. ... The discourse of the Duke of Argyll is, that when I please there will then be peace. I suppose his friends speak the same language in England; so that I must every summer venture my life in a battle, and be found fault with in winter for not bringing home peace, though I wish for it with all my heart and soul.'

On the 26th of June, Douai capitulated. Arras, 'the *last* of the triple line of fortresses which on that side covered France, and between which and Paris no fortified place remained to arrest the march of an invader,' became the next object of attack. An army of ninety thousand men was wheeled round towards it, but halted before the formidable entrenchments which Villars had rapidly and skilfully constructed on a line stretching from Arras to the Somme,—entrenchments which were defended by nearly one hundred thousand bayonets and sabres, and armed by one hundred and thirty pieces of cannon. When thus obliged to abandon the direct route to Paris—for it was impossible to besiege Arras with such an enemy on their flank—the Allied generals suddenly struck towards the coast, and invested the strong town of Bethune, which, taken by surprise, surrendered on the 28th of August.

During the siege of Bethune, Villars had broken up his cantonments at Arras, and, by a series of able manœuvres, concentrated his forces upon Avesnes le Comte, where he threw up a system of works not less formidable than that which had already defeated the advance of the Allies. Thus he had again contrived new and powerful defences for his country, when she was apparently lying at the invader's mercy. 'By simply holding them, the interior of France was covered from incursion; time was gained not only for raising fresh armaments in the interior, but what was of more importance to Louis, for waiting the issue of the intrigues in England, which were soon expected to overthrow the

Whig Cabinet.' These intrigues were on the point of culminating. As M. de Torcy, the French Ambassador, declared:—'What the French lost in Flanders, they gained in England.' The Tories, who, at this period, were the pacific party, because peace with France was an indispensable preliminary to the projected restoration of the Stuart dynasty, had at last succeeded in overthrowing the famous administration of which Godolphin had so long been the Parliamentary leader, and Marlborough the powerful adviser. Harley became Prime Minister, and St John Secretary of State; and the effect of this change of Ministers upon the conduct of the war soon became apparent. The Duke naturally hesitated to commit himself to any great enterprise, when he could no longer depend upon the Home Government for support. 'I am of opinion,' he wrote to Godolphin, in August 1710, 'that, after the siege of Aire, I shall have it in my power to attack Calais. This is a conquest which would very much prejudice France; and ought to have a good effect for the Queen's service in England; but I see so much malice levelled at me, that I am afraid it is not safe for me to make any proposition, lest, if it should not succeed, my enemies should turn it to my disadvantage.'

The siege of Aire began simultaneously with that of St Venant on the 6th of September. St Venant was taken on the 29th; Aire held out until the 12th of November; and thus, in one campaign, our great general captured four strong fortresses, with garrisons amounting to thirty thousand men. This was not an inadequate result; but as no decisive battle-field figured in the record, the feeling in England against the war was bitterly intensified. The elections for a new Parliament went in favour of the Tories, and the Duke, on his return home, was informed by the Queen that her Ministers would actively oppose his friends if they moved a vote of thanks for the late campaign. Three officers were deprived of their commissions for publicly drinking his health. Libels against his conduct, his capacity, even his courage,—coarse invectives against the Duchess, issued daily from the Press: unchecked, or rather encouraged, and sometimes suggested by the Ministry. No doubt this was gross ingratitude, but political parties are never grateful to their opponents, however illustrious may have been their services to their common country. And it had been the misfortune of Marlborough to have taken a conspicuous share in the partisan politics of the day. There were other causes which conduced to his unpopularity. The war had for some time, as I have already noted, been distasteful to the people, and specially so since it had dragged its slow length along unrelieved by any of those striking episodes which the multitude know how to appreciate. When the huzzas cease, the voice of complaint—of reproach, can make itself heard. The popular imagination refuses to be touched by the monotonous details of long sieges; and Malplaquet was won at too heavy a cost to rekindle John Bull's bellicose ardour. Again, those important results in the modification of European history which we now gladly and gratefully acknowledge to have been due to the genius of Marlborough, were not visible to or forecasted by his contemporaries, who, when they counted up the vast expenditure of blood and treasure occasioned by his campaigns, judged it necessarily by the immediate consequences.

It was a grave error of Marlborough to cling so long to office,—not to have retired when as yet retirement was possible with dignity. By doing so, he would have deprived his enemies of one of their stock invectives, and, in all probability, would have provoked a reaction in his favour. It is true that when the Duchess, in 1710, was compelled to surrender her appointments of Keeper of the Privy Purse and Mistress of the Robes, he inclined at first to throw up his own commands and withdraw from public life. But his resolution, which, perhaps, had not definitely been

formed, yielded before the arguments of Godolphin and
the Whigs, the influence of Eugene and the Dutch statesman Heinsius, and, probably, his own secret inclination,—
for it is not difficult to understand that he might desire to
conduct the war to a successful issue, and we must, I fear,
admit that he was fond of power and of the emoluments
of power. We regret, for Marlborough's fame, that he
did so yield. Libelled, vilified, humiliated, he should have
sought the shelter of private life, though, mayhap, his
enemies would not have allowed him to enjoy it, until his
country's mood had changed, and she could and would do
justice to his services. Meanwhile, bitter as must have
been the contempt, and fierce as must have been the
indignation that rankled in his heart at this juncture,
he preserved the impassible countenance and unruffled
address of his greatest power and prosperity. Says Archdeacon Coxe :—' Notwithstanding his multiplied causes
of disgust and disquietude, he took leave of the Queen
with every testimony of respect and duty, and of the
Ministers with every external mark of courtesy and
complacency.'

He arrived at the Hague on the 4th of March 1711.
But he was no longer the statesman and general who,
with supreme authority, held in his hands the issues of
war and peace. It was only through secret channels that
he obtained any knowledge of the private negotiations
which Harley and his Government were carrying on with
the Court of France. He had ceased to enjoy the regard
and confidence of his Sovereign ; he was hated and feared
by her Ministers, who lost no opportunity of discrediting
him. Nor had he the counterbalancing consolation of
possessing the affection of his countrymen, with whom the
hired emissaries of the Press had done their utmost to
render him unpopular and suspected. His avarice, his
disregard of the lives of his soldiers, his anxiety to prolong
the war, his pride, his ambition—on these themes the

journalists and pamphleteers, subsidised by the Ministry, were never weary of dilating, with a violence of invective and a licence of language which, I think, have never been equalled, certainly never surpassed, not even in our own time. Before all things, they laboured to instil into the public mind apprehensions of the part which the great captain might play in the future settlement of the kingdom. According to Mr Lecky, in this object they succeeded. 'The profound horror of military despotism which,' he says, 'is one of the strongest and most salutary of English sentiments, has been, perhaps, the most valuable legacy of the Commonwealth. In Marlborough, for the first time since the Restoration, men saw a possible Cromwell, and they looked forward with alarm to the death of the Queen as a period peculiarly propitious to military occupation. Bolingbroke never represented more happily the feelings of the people than in the well-known scene at the first representation of the "Cato" of Addison.

Placemen and place-hunters, political aspirants, the rank and file of the Tory party, Tory peers and Tory commoners, all joined in the dishonourable clamour which the spirit of faction had evoked. It is pleasant in these circumstances to come upon conduct of a very different description, and to observe how so able and virtuous a nobleman as the Earl of Orrery conceived it to be his duty to treat the great Duke. Writing from Brussels in September 1711, he says [1]:—'I have never had any hint from any of our Ministers of that kind of conduct which they think necessary in relation to my Lord Marlborough, but I have upon all occasions endeavoured to show him, I think I may say, at least, as much complaisance and respect as is either due to him from his station and character, or as the good of the public service exacts,

---

[1] His letter is preserved in the Blair-Drummond correspondence. See Report of the Historical MS. Commission (1885).

and I don't think he will pretend to complain of me upon this head. I am rather apt to believe that some people may think I ought to have shown him more coldness, but without regard to one or the other, I do assure you I have prescribed no other rule to myself for my behaviour towards this great man, than the interest of the public.'

. . . .

Supreme above all adverse conditions, Marlborough's genius, in this, his last campaign, shone forth with all its native vigour. His effective force in the field numbered eighty thousand men; but he had sustained a severe loss in the removal of his old friend and colleague, Prince Eugene, whom the new Emperor of Germany, Charles VI., recalled to Ratisbon to take command of the imperial army. He began the concentration of his troops in the neighbourhood of Douay upon the 1st of May; and Villars, in like manner, assembled his host between Bouchain and Moncy le Preux. The French Marshal had constructed, during the winter, a new and ingenious system of defences, extending from Namur on the Meuse to the coast of Picardy, which he called Marlborough's '*Non Plus Ultra.*' Traversing the swamps of the Cunche, it rested upon the posts of Montreuil, Hesdin, and Fervenrt, while it was protected in front by the celebrated fortresses of Ypres, Calais, Gravelines, and St Omer, from the walls of which still waved the *fleur-de-lis*. A series of redans crossed the plain which lies between the Canche and the Gy, while the Gy, to its junction with the Scarpe, and the Scarpe as far as Biache, were dammed up so as to overflow the surrounding country, and defended also by outworks and *têtes-du-pont*. Every elevation bristled with a battery; every open space was commanded by formidable redoubts. From the Scarpe to Bouchain, and thence to Valenciennes, was the line continued—from Valenciennes a fresh series of entrenchments swept onward to the Sambre, supported by Quesnoy and Landrécies; and along the Sambre, Maubeuge and Charleroi were the chief points until Namur was reached. Behind these extraordinary fortifications, which seem to have suggested to Wellington the famous lines of Torres Vedras, were distributed one hundred and fifty-six battalions and two hundred and twenty-seven squadrons; that is, about seventy thousand infantry and twenty thousand horse. The artillery numbered ninety heavy guns and twelve howitzers.

Marlborough recognised the immense strength of this position, and devised a masterly plan by which he hoped to turn it, and compel Villars either to fight a decisive battle, or lose his last great frontier fortress. On the 14th of June, with his army divided into six columns, and comprising about seventy-five thousand troops of all arms, he débouched on the open plain of Lens, and endeavoured to bring Villars to an engagement. He would have accepted the challenge gladly, but Louis had sent him positive instructions to decline fighting, as he expected to arrange with the English Government a speedy and advantageous conclusion of the war. Marlborough, finding that his adversary would not fight, prepared to break through the French lines and invest Bouchain; after which he proposed to winter on the French frontier, and, when rejoined by Prince Eugene in the following spring, to move upon Paris.

By a series of ingenious manœuvres, the Duke completely baffled Villars as to his intentions. He then despatched his heavy baggage to Douai, and his artillery to the rear; and having supplied his army with six days rations of bread, he raised his camp on the 4th of August, and wheeling his army to the left, swept through the woods of Villers, Neuville, and Gaverelle. Cadogan, with twenty-three battalions and seventeen squadrons, drawn from the garrisons of Lille, Tournai, and other fortresses in the rear, had already been sent ahead, and had succeeded in penetrating, unmolested, the French lines at Aubanchoil, about three in the morning. When Marlborough's columns reached the bank of the Scarpe, near Vitry, two hours later, they found the pontoons in readiness for their passage. There, too, the field artillery came up. Cadogan's success being known, Marlborough pushed forward with the utmost rapidity, and his troops, comprehending the splendid strategy by which their leader had masked his movements from the enemy, advanced with an ardour and enthusiasm that recalled the days of Blenheim, and Ramillies, and Oudenarde. By two o'clock the next morning, Marlborough's whole army had passed the French lines at Aubanchoil, without firing a single shot, having marched thirty-six miles in sixteen hours, over a country of considerable difficulty; and before evening, on the 5th, the Allied forces were massed in the plain which extends from Diog to Abancourt towards the Scheldt.

Villars had received information of Marlborough's march at eleven at night, but was unable to divine its object. Apprehending that an attack would be delivered against some point or other, he kept his troops under arms in readiness to meet it. About two in the morning, when fuller intelligence had reached him, he drew out the household brigade, and ordering his lieutenants to bring up the infantry without delay, galloped towards the scene of Marlborough's brilliant movements. His impatience outstripped the speed of the main body of his cavalry, and, with an escort of some hundred troopers, he rode into the defile of Saulchy, where he was nearly surrounded and made prisoner by an Allied outpost. His forces gradually coming up, he halted them in the rear of the defile; and, on the morning of the 6th, he turned off towards Bourlong, and arranged them in order of battle under cover of the guns of Cambrai, desirous — now that his '*Non Plus Ultra*' had been turned and taken in the rear—to risk the chances of a general action. Marlborough, however,

VOL. I. U

having gained his object, saw no reason for gratifying the French Marshal's wish.

The Duke's unsurpassed strategy—worthy of Napoleon in his palmiest days—excited the admiration of all Europe, and even in England temporarily silenced the voice of detraction. It is due to Bolingbroke to state that he was frank and hearty in his expressions of applause. 'My Lord Stair opened to us,' he said, 'the general steps which your Grace intended to take, in order to pass the lines in one part or another. It was, however, hard to imagine, and too much to hope, that a plan which consisted of so many parts, wherein so many different corps were to co-operate personally together, should entirely succeed, and no one article fail of what your Grace had projected. I most heartily congratulate your Grace on this great event, of which I think no more needs be said, than that you have obtained, without losing a man, such an advantage as we should have been glad to have purchased with the loss of several thousand lives.' On another occasion he writes,—'I look upon the progress which the Duke of Marlborough has lately made to be really honourable to him, and mortifying to the enemy. The event cannot be ascribed to superior numbers, or to any accident; it is owing to genius and conduct.'

At length the Duke undertook the siege of Bouchain,[1] amidst local obstacles of no ordinary kind, and in face of an army superior in force. The investment began on the 7th of August, and the trenches were opened on the 21st. On the 12th of September the place capitulated. The two armies remained in their respective positions—the Allies in their lines, supported by Bouchain, and the French encamped under the guns of Cambrai. The lands of the illustrious Fénélon, Archbishop of Cambrai, lying

---

[1] Some letters from a Mr Henry Watkins, preserved among the Blair-Drummond correspondence, give a vivid picture of this siege, and of the difficulties with which the Duke had to deal.

exposed to the foraging incursions of the Allied troops, Marlborough, with the regard he always showed for men of piety and virtue, posted a detachment for their protection, and to escort the convoys of grain which passed to the Archbishop's residence. So—

> 'The great Emathian conqueror bid spare
> The house of Pindarus, when temple and tower
> Went to the ground.'[1]

The reader must for a moment turn his attention to the struggle of parties at home; for it was to the council-chamber at St James's that the field of action had been transferred. Harley and St John, with marvellous adroitness, had detached Marlborough from the Whigs, and by flattering him with hopes of a cordial support, had secured his temporary co-operation with the Tory party. He had thus been led to sanction the despatch of the troops which should have reinforced his army in Flanders, on a fruitless expedition against Canada; though by so doing he was left too weak to carry out his plan for the invasion of France. Meanwhile, Harley and his cabinet pushed forward the secret negotiations with the Court of France, in flagrant violation of an article of the Grand Alliance, which pledged its members not to conclude peace separately. The Duke at length discovered this perfidious transaction, and the discovery brought on a rupture with the Tory Ministry. Hastily disposing of his troops in winter quarters, he returned to England, landing at Greenwich on the 17th of November.

A storm of obloquy threatened to blow the Duke's fame to the winds. The Tory Ministers had the meanness to attack him indirectly, even in the Queen's Speech:—'I am glad to tell you,' said Anne, who, like many dull women, had a vein of spitefulness in her nature, and doubtless rejoiced at the insult thrown on her old and famous servant,

[1] Milton, *Sonnets*.

'I am glad to tell you that, notwithstanding the acts of those who delight in war, both place and time are appointed for opening the treaty of a general peace.' In the debate which followed, Lord Anglesea declared that the country might have enjoyed the blessings of peace soon after the battle of Ramillies if they had not been delayed by some person whose interest it was to prolong the war. In reply to this open attack, the Duke rose, and, bowing towards the throne where the Queen was seated, spoke with a dignity and a sincerity which deeply impressed his audience:—

'I appeal to the Queen,' he said, 'whether I did not constantly, while I was Plenipotentiary, give her Majesty and her Council an account of all the propositions that were made; and whether I did not desire instructions for my conduct on this subject. I can declare, with a good conscience, in the presence of her Majesty, of this illustrious assembly, and of God Himself, who is infinitely superior to all the powers of this earth, and before whom, by the ordinary course of nature, I shall soon appear to render an account of my actions, that I was very desirous of a safe, lasting, and honourable peace; and was always very free from prolonging the war for my own private advantage, as several libels and discourses have most falsely insinuated. My great age,[1] and my numerous fatigues in war, make me ardently wish for the power to enjoy a quiet repose, in order to think of eternity. As to other matters, I had not the least inducement, on any account, to desire the continuance of the war for my own particular interest, since my services have been so generously rewarded by her Majesty and her Parliament; but I think myself obliged to make such an acknowledgment to her Majesty and my country, that I am always ready to serve them, whenever my duty may require, to obtain an honourable and a lasting peace. Yet I can by no means acquiesce in the measures that have been taken to enter into a negotiation of peace with France, upon the footing of some pretended preliminaries, which are now circulated; since my opinion is the same as that of most of the Allies, that to leave Spain and the West Indies to the House of Bourbon, will be the entire ruin of Europe, which I have, with all fidelity and humility, declared to her Majesty when I had the honour to wait on her after my arrival from Holland.'

---

[1] In the present day statesmen and generals would not talk of sixty-two as 'a great age.'

In the House of Lords the Duke's opinion prevailed, and an address embodying it was carried against the Ministers by a majority of twelve. But in the Commons, on the other hand, an address approving of the proposed peace, and indirectly censuring Marlborough, obtained a majority of two hundred and thirty-two against one hundred and six.

Thereupon the Government resolved upon open hostilities against the Duke, whose influence in the Upper House was still strong enough to endanger their position. They swamped the Whig majority by the creation of twelve Tory peers. The Duke was dismissed from all his offices; and in order to discredit him effectually with the public, he was accused of fraud and peculation in the distribution of the public moneys entrusted to him during the Flemish campaign; of having appropriated to his personal advantage sixty-three thousand three hundred and nineteen pounds three shillings and seven pence out of the sums set apart for the use of the British army, and two hundred and eighty-two thousand three hundred and sixty-six pounds, as a percentage of two per cent. on the sums paid to foreign ambassadors during the ten years of the war. There was great rejoicing in France when the news of the great General's fall arrived; and Louis emphatically exclaimed, 'The dismissal of Marlborough will do all we can desire.'

To the charges brought against him Marlborough returned a satisfactory answer. He showed that the percentage on which his enemies laid such stress was a voluntary gift from the foreign princes who had furnished auxiliary troops; that it had never exceeded thirty thousand pounds per annum, and had been expended in obtaining secret intelligence—a service on which William III. had annually expended fifty thousand pounds. He also proved that the perquisite received from the bread contractors had always been allowed to the commander of the British forces in the Netherlands, and that the same privilege was accorded to the Dutch Generalissimo. The malice of party, however, is deaf to reason and inaccessible to argument. The majority in the Commons passed a resolution of censure upon the Duke for illegal appropriation of the public moneys; but the Government were afraid to hazard an impeachment, and the country in general seems to have been convinced of his innocence. And it may be added that the very perquisite which in Marlborough's case was pronounced illegal, his successor, the Duke of Ormond, received without scruple.

The Treaty of Utrecht, between England, France, and Holland, was signed on the 6th of June 1713; and on the 16th of July the English troops separated from the Allied army—from the comrades with whom they had shared the lustre of so many memorable achievements. It was a remarkable scene, and a contemporary historian describes it with much vividness:—'The British soldiers were so enraged that they were observed tearing their hair and rending their clothes, with furious exclamations and execrable curses against the Duke of Ormond as a stupid tool and general of straw. The colonels, captains, and other brave officers were so overwhelmed with vexation that they sat apart in their tents, looking on the ground through very shame, with downcast eyes, and for several days shrank from the sight even of their fellow-soldiers. For it grieved them to the heart to submit to the disgrace of laying down their arms after so many splendid victories. Some left their colours to serve among the Allies, and others afterwards withdrew; and whenever they recollected the Duke of Marlborough and the late glorious times their eyes flowed with tears.'

The death of Godolphin severed one of the most powerful ties which had bound Marlborough to England, and he hastened to quit a scene which was associated with so much humiliation and disgrace. His reception at Brill, on the 24th of November 1713, was enthusiastic enough to have consoled him for the neglect he had experienced at the hands of his countrymen. 'At Maestricht he was welcomed with the honours usually reserved for foreign princes; and although he did his utmost, on the journey to Aix-la-Chapelle, to avoid attracting the public attention, and to slip unobserved through bye-ways, yet the eagerness of the public or the gratitude of his old soldiers discovered him wherever he went. . . . All were struck with his noble air and demeanour, softened, though not weakened, by the approach of age. They declared that his appearance was not less overpowering than his sword. Many burst into tears when they recollected what he had been and what he was, and how unaccountably the great nation to which he belonged had fallen from the height of glory to such degradation.' He abode for some time at Aix-la-Chapelle, and then returned to Maestricht, where, in February 1713, he was joined by the Duchess. Afterwards they took up their residence at Frankfort.

'It was from Frankfort,' says one of his latest biographers, 'that, new charges of malversation being brought against him, he wrote an answer to be laid before both Houses, which his partisans regard as final, and which certainly seems to have stopped all further proceedings. This new and last charge was connected with a rather intricate detail of military administration, Marlborough being charged with giving instructions to enter complete musters of the English troops when they were in reality defective, and with obtaining perquisities or fees on the strength of such musters. He pleaded in return (and, as has been said, no reply seems to have been made to the plea)— first, that he had acted under distinct statutory authority; secondly, that (at least this seems to be the drift of his very technical defence) the muster-money was applied to recruiting, and that the public was saved expense by the proceeding. To finish with this question of malversation, it cannot be too much impressed upon the reader that the frequent rhetorical allusions to Marlborough in all sorts of books as having "starved the soldiers," "cheated them of their pay," and so forth, are rhetoric and nothing more. The only two charges which an investigation, carried out with full powers and certainly in no friendly spirit, could establish, were the reception of the bread money and the deduction of the sixpence a pound on the pay of the foreign troops. The evidence as to custom in the former case, and the royal warrants in the latter, must be allowed to exonerate Marlborough of anything like direct peculation, though the system of perquisites, gratuities, *pots-de-vin*, and the like, is one, of course, very dangerous in itself, and very liable to further abuse.'

The day after Queen Anne's death, Marlborough returned to England (August 2d, 1714), but, owing to the enmity of the Dukes of Shrewsbury and Argyll, his name was omitted from the list of Lords Justices who held the Regency, until the arrival of the Elector. Some compensation was made for this slight, by his restoration to his offices of Captain-General and Master of the Ordnance. He planned the details of the campaign of 1715 against the Pretender, but did not in person take the field. The death of his daughters, Lady Bridgewater, and the beautiful Countess of Sunderland, greatly affected him; and the vehemence of his grief, acting on a mind oppressed by the great strain of his work as diplomatist, politician, and commander through ten years of arduous war, induced a severe paralytic stroke on the 28th of May 1716, from which he never wholly recovered. Through the skill and care of Dr Garth, he regained so much of his health as to be able to pay occasional visits to the House of Lords, and to enjoy the society of his grand-children. It is said that, on one occasion, he was observed to pause awhile before a portrait of himself in his brilliant manhood, and, turning aside, to murmur, with a sigh, 'Something then; but now—!'

In the June of 1722, he was again stricken with paralysis; and on the 16th of the month, at four in the morning, he passed away. He possessed his faculties almost to the last. On the evening of his decease, he listened attentively while prayers were read; and to a question of the Duchess whether he had heard them, replied, 'Yes; and I joined in them;' and we can well believe that he joined in them with faith and fervour.

His death took place at Windsor Lodge, which for some years had been his favourite place of residence. Thence his body was removed to Marlborough House, and afterwards to Blenheim.

To what I have said respecting the character and conduct of this great man—the most consummate captain that England, and perhaps even Europe, has seen—I will add only a few words from Mr Saintsbury, with which I heartily agree :—

'There is,' he says, 'what some accomplished cosmopolitans of our time doubtless regard as a vulgar side to the attraction of his life, and I for one have no hesitation in saying that it does not seem to me vulgar at all. It is that expressed by the old and not very exquisite rhyme—

"Jack of Marlborough,
Who beat the Frenchmen through and through."

When Marlborough took up the supreme command, it was nearly three hundred years since England had fought on land, and against foes not of her own blood, any but insignificant battles ; and over the French, in particular, no success of any importance had been gained. The advent of William the Deliverer had, indeed, set France and England once more thoroughly by the ears, but the result had hitherto been little but some more or less honourable beatings. With Marlborough's appearance things at once were changed. The force of native English soldiers under his command was at no time very great, but it was sufficient to give the country something more than a share in the mere fighting part of his victories ; and in point of generalship the most prejudiced enemy could not deny that Europe did not hold the Englishman's superior, while not merely friends, but impartial judges, would have been unanimous in agreeing that it did not hold his equal. A slight, if not a reproach, of centuries was rolled away from the nation in the course of those ten years. It is for this, first of all, that Englishmen ought to reverence the memory, stained as it is, and even if it were more stained than it is, of Jack of Marlborough.'

A ballad, which seems to have been popular with the people about 1713 or 1714, recounts 'Jack of Marlborough's' achievements in patriotic stanzas, and furnishes quite a history of his military career. It is entitled, *The*

Soldiers' Lamentations for the Loss of their General, in a Letter from the Recruiters in London to their Friends in Flanders, and consists of twenty six-lined verses. Considerations of space limit me to a brief quotation:—

> 'Brave leader, with such vast success
>   By bounteous Heaven crowned,
> Who can your valiant acts rehearse,
>   Or praises justly sound?
> Who ne'er your back turned to your foes,
>   Nor from a town untaken rose.
>
> But who for British honour will,
>   Or safety more take heed,
> Since he who goes French blood to spill,
>   Himself at home must bleed?
> Who Popish Louis has undone,
>   By Jews and Turks is overthrown.
>
> Ungrateful England, saved from harm
>   By heroes most renowned,
> Who for their matchless deeds of arms
>   Have with affronts been crowned:
> So fared it once with great Nassau,
> So fares it now with Marlboro'!
>
> 'Tis true, his foes have gained their ends,
>   It cannot be denied;
> But neither France's slaves nor friends
>   His name can lay aside;
> True English hearts will still proclaim,
> Great Marlbro's with Eugene's fame.'[1]

THE EARL OF PETERBOROUGH.

One of Macaulay's most brilliant bits of character painting is that which he devotes to the famous Earl of Peterborough. And as no political prejudices interfered to warp his judgment, to tempt him to heighten the colours and deepen the shadows, I think it may be accepted as in the main a likeness of the original not less

---

[1] WILKINS' *Poetical Ballads of the Seventeenth and Eighteenth Centuries,* ii. 124-130.

faithful than brilliant. It is just such a portrait of this eighteenth century Paladin as, I believe, most of us would attempt to draw after a study of his career. 'Peterborough, he says, 'may be described as a polite, learned, and amorous Charles the Twelfth.' But I must submit that he was a man of much greater capacity than the King of Sweden. 'His courage had all the French impetuosity, and all the English steadiness. His fertility and activity of mind were almost beyond belief. They appeared in everything that he did; in his campaigns, in his negotiations, in his familiar correspondence, in his lightest and most unstudied conversation. He was a kind friend, a generous enemy, and in deportment a thorough gentleman. But his splendid talents and virtues were rendered almost useless to his country by his levity, his restlessness, his irritability, his morbid craving for novelty and excitement. His weaknesses had not only brought him, on more than one occasion, into serious trouble; but had impelled him to some actions altogether unworthy of his humane and noble nature. Repose was insupportable to him. . . . His figure was that of a skeleton. But his elastic mind supported him under fatigues and sufferings which seemed sufficient to bring the most robust man to the grave. . . . Those who had to transact business with him complained that though he talked with great ability on any subject, he could never be kept to the point. "Lord Peterborough," said Pope, "would say very pretty and lively things in his letters, but they would be rather too gay and wandering; whereas, were Lord Bolingbroke to write to an emperor, or to a statesman, he would fix on that point which was the most material, would set it in the strongest and finest light, and manage it so as to make it the most serviceable to his purpose." What Peterborough was to Bolingbroke as a writer, he was to Marlborough as a general. He was, in truth, the last of the knights-errant, brave to temerity, liberal to profusion, courteous in his dealings with enemies, the protector of the oppressed, the adorer of women.'

Hookham Frere, in his poetic extravaganza of *Monks and Giants*, seems to have taken this splendidly erratic man of genius as the model of his ' Sir Tristram.' In the following passage every line is happily appropriate:—

> ' His birth, it seems, by Merlin's calculation,
> Was under Venus, Mercury, and Mars :
> His mind with all their attributes was mixed,
> And, like those planets, wandering and unfixed.
>
> From realm to realm he ran, and never staid :
> Kingdoms and crowns he won, and gave away :
> It seemed as if his labours were repaid
> By the mere noise and movement of the fray :
> No conquests nor acquirements had he made ;
> His chief delight was, on some festive day,
> To ride triumphant, prodigal, and proud,
> And shower his wealth amidst the shouting crowd.
>
> His schemes of war were sudden, unforeseen,
> Inexplicable both to friend and foe ;
> It seemed as if some momentary spleen
> Inspired the project and impelled the blow ;
> And most his fortune and success were seen
> With means the most inadequate and low ;
> Most master of himself, and least encumbered,
> When overmatched, entangled, and outnumbered.'

The Earldom of Peterborough was created by Charles I. in 1627. The first wearer of the title, nevertheless, sided with the Puritan party during the Civil War, though his sons Henry and John adhered to the King's cause, and fought in the Royalist ranks at Newbury. Under the Protectorate, the father acted as Master-General of the Ordnance ; his sons were proclaimed as traitors, and compelled to seek an asylum in France.

The younger of these sons, Lord John Mordaunt, was the father of Charles Mordaunt, afterwards Earl of Peterborough, who was born in 1658 or 1659. At the Restoration, Henry and John returned to England, and received many favours at the hands of Charles II., who did not always forget those who had suffered for loyal service. Their estates were restored. Henry, who had succeeded to the earldom, was made Governor of Tangiers; John was raised to the peerage by the title of Baron Mordaunt and Viscount Avalon. So it came to pass that his son was brought up under the evil influences of the most dissolute of courts. It may have been his intimate acquaintance with the 'seamy side' of loyalty, as typified by the Stuarts, that nurtured in him a strong antagonism to both Charles II. and James II. At least he doubtless learned to be an unbeliever and a libertine; nothing good could flourish in so unholy an atmosphere, and it was fortunate that, before his fine nature was utterly corrupted, he plunged into the more wholesome excitement of active life.

He was a lad of sixteen or seventeen when he joined, as a volunteer, the fleet, under Sir John Narborough, despatched to punished the Algerine pirates who preyed upon trading-ships in the Mediterranean. In an action fought under the guns of Tripoli in 1675, he distinguished himself by his gallantry, and gave excellent promise of the martial qualities which in due time he was to develop. He returned to England in 1677. During his absence his father had died, and Charles, at the age of nineteen, succeeded to the title. With characteristic impetuosity he fell in love and married, his bride being the daughter of Sir Alexander Fraser of Mearns. Domestic life, however, palled upon him quickly; and in 1678 he again volunteered to serve on the Algerine coast, and sailed on board the forty-two gun-ship *Bristol*. From the remarkable diary of its chaplain, Teonge, we learn that when he was lying ill in his berth, while his ship was tossed 'in the Bay of Biscay O!' Lord Mordaunt asked Captain Langston to permit him to take the chaplain's place on the following Sunday. Teonge, who overheard the request, supposed it was intended as a joke, knowing Lord Mordaunt's sceptical views on religious matters; but when he found that the young nobleman sat up all night zealously engaged in the composition of a sermon for the morrow, that he intended to read prayers, and had appointed his secretary to act as clerk and sing the psalms, he thought it time to interfere. He broke in upon the would-be preacher, who was in the great cabin conversing with the captain, and so handled him 'in a small and short discourse, that he went out of the cabin in a great wrath.' In his disappointment 'the irreverent Lord borrowed the carpenter's tools, and worked all day, himself, in nailing up his hangings. Being done on the Sabbath,' adds the chaplain. 'and no necessity, I do hope the work will not be long lived.'

My space is too limited for me to dwell on Mordaunt's several voyages to the Mediterranean, in the course of which he taught the corsairs to fear his restless activity and dauntless courage. In the intervals he occupied himself in the study of the masterpieces of English and foreign literature, and in extending his acquaintance with the old classic writers. He frequently appeared in his place in the House of Lords—always as a member of the patriotic party, and to the arbitrary policy of James II. he gave the most uncompromising opposition. On the 9th of November 1685 he spoke with all the fire and boldness of his nature against the King's expressed intention of maintaining and increasing the standing army. The most rigid constitutionalist could not have argued with greater vigour and lucidity. 'A standing army exists,' he cried, 'and it is officered by Papists. We have no foreign enemy; we have no rebellion in the land. For what, then, is this force maintained, except for the purpose of subverting our laws and establishing that arbitrary power so justly abhorred by Englishmen?' His attitude gave so much offence to the Court that, in the following year, he thought it advisable to leave England, and, crossing over to the Hague, he openly engaged himself to the service of William of Orange.

It was the policy of William to play 'a waiting game ;' to watch with patient vigilance the strife of English parties until the necessity of a ruler became apparent to all sensible minds, and he could ascend the throne of England with an undisputed title. A bolder course was urged upon him by the impetuous Mordaunt, for whom no enterprise was too daring, and whose interest in it was in exact proportion to its hazardousness. He recommended to William an immediate descent upon England. But the Prince, after due consideration, rejected the bold counsel, the ultimate result of which, if adoped, would probably have been a desperate civil war. Mordaunt continued, however, to attend his Court ; and when the time came for William to land in England as a Deliverer, welcomed by the voice of a large majority of the nation, Mordaunt was one of the first to offer his services. He sailed with the expedition from Brill on the 20th of October 1688. After passing unscathed through a severe storm, the fleet arrived off the Isle of Wight on the 4th of November. Mordaunt immediately landed on the Dorsetshire coast to raise troops in the name of the Liberator. The task exactly fitted his powers, and in an incredibly short time he had raised a considerable armed force, with which, on the 8th of November, he appeared before Exeter, and easily obtained its surrender. What followed is matter of history, familiar to every schoolboy. James fled from the kingdom which had abandoned him, and William and Mary occupied the vacated throne. They hastened to reward with a liberal hand Lord Mordaunt's valuable services : he was created Earl of Monmouth— the title borne by his maternal grandfather—a Lord of the Bedchamber, Custos Rotulorum of Northampton, and captain of a regiment of horse, of which William himself was colonel. He had already been placed at the head of the Treasury, though for what reason it is difficult to determine, since 'his romantic courage, his flighty wit, his eccentric invention, his love of desperate risks and startling effects, were not qualities likely to be of much use to him in financial calculations and negotiations.' He gave a proof both of his independence and his Protestantism when the King's first speech, prepared by himself, for the opening of Parliament, was submitted to the Privy Council. He objected to the phrase—'The Church of England is one of the greatest supports of the Protestant religion,' and procured its alteration to 'is *the chief support*.' William was not offended by the Earl's outspokenness, and when he crossed to Ireland, included him among the Council of Nine who were to assist Queen Mary in the administration of affairs.

Implicit confidence the Queen was unable to place in any one of her advisers, but she seems to have regarded the volatile and vehement Monmouth with special distrust. His love of intrigue was as insatiable as his love of enterprise ; and, in order to produce a sensation, he placed before her, as the work of some traitor in her household, a correspondence, known as 'the Lemon Letters,' which he professed to have intercepted. This correspondence recorded all the secret intentions of the Council for the benefit of James II. Mary, however, detected the fraud, and declared at once that Monmouth had invented them, and that they had been written in lemon juice by his private secretary, the notorious Major Wildman.

The details of financial business were little to his taste, and in 1690 he threw up his position at the Treasury. He then had greater leisure for political skirmishing, and he gave himself up with much enjoyment to a guerilla warfare against the Tories. These occupations not sufficing for his busy brain, he amused himself with making love, in which pursuit he was more ardent than fastidious—in rhyming, an art in which he did not attain to excellence— and in flying journeys between Whitehall and his Fulham residence. His regiment being quartered at Portsmouth, he applied for the command of a ship-of-war, with the view of joining Admiral Torrington's fleet in the Channel, but he was too late to play any part in the disastrous action off Beachy Head. In the following year he served under King William in Flanders, and extorted admiration by his military skill and fiery courage. At the end of the campaign he suddenly retired from public life, and for the next three years his time was chiefly spent at Parson's Green, where he had 'a large house with stately gardens.' Gardening was one of his hobbies; and his grounds, which covered upwards of twenty acres, were laid out from his own designs with great taste and at a lavish outlay. The fruit and flowers which he raised were noted for their perfection.

In 1696, when Sir John Fenwick's conspiracy against King William's life was discovered, Monmouth suddenly emerged from his horticultural seclusion, and courted public attention by an audacious intrigue. 'He had now reached a time of life,' says Macaulay, 'at which youth could no longer be pleaded as an excuse for his faults; but he was more wayward and eccentric than ever. Both in his intellectual and in his moral character there was an abundance of those fine qualities which may be called luxuries, and a lamentable deficiency of those solid qualities which are of the first necessity. He had brilliant wit and ready invention without common sense, and chivalrous generosity and delicacy without common honesty. He was capable of rising to the part of the Black Prince; and yet he was capable of sinking to the part of Fuller. His political life was blemished by some most dishonourable actions: yet he was not under the influence of those motives to which most of the dishonourable actions of politicians are to be ascribed. He valued power little, and money less. Of fear he was utterly insensible. If he sometimes stooped to be a knave—for no milder word will come up to the truth—it was merely to amuse himself and astonish other people. In civil, as in military affairs, he loved ambuscades, surprises, night attacks. He now imagined that he had a glorious opportunity of making a sensation, of producing a great commotion; and the temptation was irresistible to a spirit so restless as his.'

After prolonged and heated debates, the House of Commons passed a bill of attainder against Sir John Fenwick by twenty-three votes. It was carried up to the Lords on the 26th of November. Meanwhile, Monmouth had prepared an unscrupulous manœuvre. Fenwick had made statements inculpating the good faith of many eminent men of both parties; but King William had wisely resolved to treat them as calumnies. Monmouth's plan was to prove their truth. This could not be done without the help of the prisoner, and it was impossible to communicate with the prisoner except through female agency. Monmouth selected his first cousin, the Duchess of Norfolk, a woman notorious for her gallantries—whom her husband had vainly endeavoured to divorce, in consequence of the skill and ardour with which Monmouth had defended her. Through the Duchess's instrumentality several papers of suggestions ingeniously framed by the Earl with the view of inducing Sir John to reaffirm his charges, were conveyed to him in his prison; but for various reasons he decided not to adopt them.

On the 1st of December the bill of attainder passed the first reading. Sir John Fenwick's confession, which inculpated Marlborough, Godolphin, and other Whig peers in a charge of treasonable correspondence with King James, was then put before the House. They strenuously denied it, and the House accepted their denial. Fenwick was brought in, and asked if he had any other statement to make. He answered in the negative; and Monmouth, perceiving that his project had failed, immediately turned round, and became more zealous for the bill than any other peer. Long and heated debates continued for several days—sometimes for fourteen or fifteen hours a day, and the wayward nobleman spoke continually, and almost always in a strain of bitter invective. The bill at last passed its second reading, and Fenwick was again interrogated, but nothing could be extracted either from his fears or his hopes. After further debates, less prolonged but not less acrimonious than the preceding, the bill was read a third time by a majority of seven.

It was then that Lady Fenwick sought to revenge herself upon Monmouth, who, after professing an anxiety to save her husband, had become the most vehement of his persecutors, simply because he would not play the part of a tool in the Earl's wild and mischievous device. She showed to Lord Carlisle the papers which Monmouth had forwarded through the Duchess of Norfolk, and Carlisle laid them before the peers. Whigs and Tories combined to pour their wrath on the detected plotter's head; the Whigs, because he had been secretly conspiring to ruin the reputation of their two great leaders, Marlborough and Godolphin; the Tories, because he had dealt cruelly and treacherously with the prisoner and his wife. Monmouth replied to their attacks in a speech of nearly three hours' duration, which Macaulay describes as 'confused' and 'rambling,' though it seems to have glowed with eloquent invective and pungent sarcasm. He was a sublime egotist, and it was natural that he should speak in laudation of his sacrifices and services. With more truth he boasted of his disinterestedness; for it is certain that he cared neither for money nor power. Turning his piercing glance upon Nottingham, he exclaimed,—' I have bought no great estates, I have built no palaces, and I am twenty thousand pounds poorer than when I began public life. My old hereditary mansion is ready to fall about my ears. Who that remembers what I have done and suffered for His Majesty would believe that I would speak disrespectfully of him?'—(one of the accusations made against the Earl). He solemnly declared—and some persons accept the declaration, though the adverse evidence is absolutely overwhelming—that he had had nothing to do with the papers sent to Fenwick; and he accused the Papists of having concocted a scheme to ruin him.

At the conclusion of his speech it was moved, and unanimously resolved, that these papers were scandalous, and that the author had been guilty of a high crime and misdemeanour. Then came the question of their authorship. The Duchess of Norfolk adhered to her testimony, which was confirmed by several witnesses, that they came from Monmouth and were in his handwriting. Her character was violently assailed; she was denounced as untrustworthy; but her husband sarcastically replied,—' My Lord Monmouth thought her good enough to be wife to me; and, if she is good enough to be wife to me, I am sure that she is good enough to be witness against him.' By a nearly unanimous vote he was declared guilty of the act of which he had solemnly declared himself innocent. He was deprived of all his offices; his name was struck out of the Council Book; and he was sent to the Tower.

So complete and so absolute was his fall that scarcely any one could have believed in the possibility of his recovering his ground. But his self-reliance, his confidence in himself, was so boundless—his elasticity of spirit so inexhaustible—his energy so abundant, that he could at any time triumph over the most contrary fortune. ' Violent as a caged falcon,' and with no other solace than the invention of schemes for extricating himself from his difficulties, and obtaining revenge on his enemies, he would have fretted his heart out if he had long been detained in prison. On his release he found himself alone—

as hateful to the Tories as to the Whigs—and so poor that he talked of retiring to the country, living like a farmer, and putting his Countess into the dairy to churn and make cheeses. 'Yet, even after this fall, that mounting spirit rose again, and rose higher than ever. When he next appeared before the world, he had inherited the earldom of the head of his family; he had ceased to be called by the tarnished name of Monmouth; and he soon added new lustre to the name of Peterborough. He was still all air and fire. His ready wit and his dauntless courage made him formidable: some amiable qualities which contrasted strongly with his vices, and some great exploits of which the effect was heightened by the careless levity with which they were performed, made him popular; and his countrymen were willing to forget that a hero of whose achievements they were proud, and who was not more distinguished by parts and valour than by courtesy and generosity, had stooped to tricks worthy of the pillory.'

. . . .

For some years after his liberation he wisely withdrew from the public stage, that the follies and vices of the Earl of Monmouth might be forgotten, and a fresh page turned over for the record of the Earl of Peterborough. While travelling through France he visited Cambrai, and was entertained by its archbishop, the saintly Fénélon, who impressed him greatly by the charm of his conversation and the elevation of his character. 'If I remain with him another week,' he wrote, in his epigrammatic way, 'I shall be a Christian in spite of myself,'—which we may take to be Peterborough's version of a certain celebrated saying by the Roman Festus.

It was about 1701 when he renewed his normal activity. King William had been induced to pardon him, and knowing his wide range of capacity, he employed him to negotiate the Grand Alliance, as it was called, of

England, Holland, and Austria against France. Peterborough had secured the friendship of Lady Marlborough; and when, on the accession of Queen Anne, Marlborough became the most powerful man in England, his influence gave a new impulse to the fortunes of the erratic Earl, who was appointed to the command-in-chief of a naval and military expedition despatched to support the claim of the Archduke Charles to the throne of Spain. 'The English,' says Voltaire, 'were led by one of the most extraordinary men his country ever produced, the Earl of Peterborough, a man who in all respects resembled those heroes with whose exploits the Spanish imagination has contrived to fill so many volumes. He had wasted, given away, and more than once regained a fortune. The Spanish war he waged partly at his own expense, and he defrayed the charges of the Archduke and all his retinue.'

Hitherto he had been known chiefly by his amorous adventures and wild escapades; but Marlborough discovered the finer qualities of the man, and in placing him at the head of this expedition, entrusted him with almost unlimited powers. His sagacity was not at fault: the responsibility devolved upon the Earl called out his intellectual strength and tested his inexhaustible resources. He had a singular talent for command, but none for obedience: he could lead, but he could not follow. His capacity was great, but so was his egotism, and unless he could be first, he cared not if he had no place at all. Control or advice irritated him. 'As a subaltern,' says Lord Stanhope, 'he was heedless of orders. As a colleague he was ever discontented, ever railing. As a chief, on the contrary, he achieved some splendid successes. The same impetuosity of temper which made him overlook an obstacle, enabled him also in many cases to overleap it'

With five thousand English and Dutch soldiers—two-thirds English and one-third Dutch—Peterborough arrived at Lisbon on the 20th of June. He took on board the

Archduke and a numerous suite, and sailed for Gibraltar, where he was joined by the Prince of Hesse-Darmstadt and some veterans from the garrison, while his naval force was increased by the junction of a squadron under the gallant Sir Cloudesley Shovel. His little army then numbered seven thousand men.

From Gibraltar he proceeded to Alten in Valencia, where the oppressed inhabitants received the invaders with a hearty welcome, and the peasantry saluted the Archduke with cries of 'Long live Charles the Third!' The neighbouring fortress of Duria at once surrendered; and Peterborough, with his imagination excited by visions of conquest, suggested to the Archduke the possibility of finishing the war at a blow. He proposed to march at once upon Madrid, and establish the Archduke in the centre of Castille. There was only one fortified place between the coast and the capital; and the troops of King Philip were either in Catalonia or on the Portuguese frontier. The scheme was startlingly bold, but it was of that boldness which commands success. Unfortunately the Archduke was much influenced by the Prince of Darmstadt, and the latter, who had been Governor of Catalonia, and overrated his influence among the Catalans, urged that they should attack Barcelona. Peterborough reluctantly gave way; and the Archduke lost his fairest chance of winning the Spanish crown.

The invaders appeared before the Catalonian seaport, to find it a much harder nut to crack than they had anticipated. On one side it was protected by the sea; on the other by the strong fortress of Monjuich—the *Mons Jovis* of the Romans, the *Mons Judaicus* of the period when it was occupied by the Jews. It was held by a garrison whose numerical strength equalled, if it did not surpass, the besieging force. Week after week was spent in vain before it. The besiegers suffered severely from the summer heat, and their generals quarrelled among themselves, until

at length Darmstadt and Peterborough refused to speak t
each other. After nearly a month's compulsory inaction,
Peterborough announced his intention of raising the siege,
and carrying his army to the theatre of war in Italy. The
heavy cannon were sent on board the ships, and preparations were made for embarking the soldiers. Elated with
the prospect of speedy deliverance from the presence of
the enemy, on the 12th of September the citizens of Barcelona held high revel. Yet, on the following morning,
the English flag waved in the breeze from the ramparts of
Monjuich.

For at midnight Peterborough had suddenly presented
himself at the quarters of the Prince of Hesse. 'I have
resolved, sir,' he said, 'to attempt an assault. You may, if
you think fit, accompany me, and see whether I and my
men deserve the reproach of inactivity you have levelled at
us.' The Prince thought the attempt hopeless; but he
was no coward, and, calling for his horse, he mounted and
accompanied the Earl, who, having carefully surveyed the
defences of Barcelona, had convinced himself that its
garrison had ceased their vigilance. Twelve hundred
English foot and two hundred English horse were under
his personal direction. A thousand men were posted at a
neighbouring convent, as a reserve, under General Stanhope. By a winding march along the foot of the hills,
Peterborough and his men advanced until they were within
a quarter of a mile of Monjuich. At daybreak they
marched to the assault under a heavy fire which the
Spaniards opened upon them. Calm and unmoved they
pressed forward, and the Spaniards ran down to meet them
in the outer ditch. This movement Peterborough had
anticipated, and had instructed his men, when they
defeated the enemy, to follow close upon them, pell-mell,
and enter the works together. Carrying all before them,
the assailants reached the summit of the bastion, and
threw up a breastwork of loose stones to protect them-

selves, before the garrison had recovered from their surprise.

The Earl then sent for his reserve, so as to secure what he had gained. The enemy, however, still kept possession of the inner works, or citadel, whence they began to deliver a hot musketry fire, and, among other victims, struck down the Prince of Hesse by the side of his comrade in arms. About the same time a rumour ran through the ranks that the Spanish Viceroy was sending three thousand men from the town to recover Monjuich, and Peterborough rode off to reconnoitre. In his absence the small force he commanded began to reflect on their exposed position, and their small numbers, were seized with a panic, and prepared to evacuate the fort. Information of the incident was conveyed to the general, who rode back full speed to arrest the retreat, and by the sight of his ardent countenance and the sound of his trumpet-like voice, restored the spirits of his men. 'Face about and follow me,' he cried, 'or you shall have the scandal and eternal infamy upon you of having deserted your posts and abandoned your general.' Soon afterwards Stanhope came up with the reserve, and Peterborough made good his occupation of the fortress.

He next proceeded to invest the city; and his brilliant exploit had inspired his men with so martial an ardour that they made light of every obstacle, and pressed forward the siege with a determination which the Spanish garrison were unable to resist. On the 9th of October, a parley took place at the gates between Peterborough and the Viceroy, Don Francisco de Velasco, who agreed to capitulate. 'The articles were not yet signed,' says Voltaire, with his usual dramatic power of narrative, 'when suddenly cries of terror rent the air, and flames were seen to ascend from one part of the city. "You are betraying us," exclaimed the Viceroy; "we capitulated in good faith, while your English troops have entered by the ramparts, and are now slaying our people, and burning or plundering our houses!" "You mistake," cried Peterborough, "they are Darmstadt's Germans, not Englishmen ; and I see but one way of saving your city. Allow me and the officers of my staff, with an English escort, to enter immediately ; I will at once put a stop to these outrages, and return here to conclude with you the terms of capitulation." His air of truth, and the lofty tone of his address, together with the urgent need of the moment, induced the Viceroy to accept his proposition. The gates were thrown open, and Peterborough, followed by his staff, galloped through the streets of Barcelona. The German and Catalan soldiery, joined by some of the rabble, were sacking the houses of the principal citizens. Rushing upon them he compelled them to desist, and to restore the plunder with which they were about to make off. Having, as he had promised, put a stop to the outrages, and restored order amongst the troops, he returned to the city gates to sign with the Viceroy the articles of capitulation.'

Thus was his the glory of capturing, with a handful of men, one of the largest and strongest sea fortresses of Europe. His was the glory also of saving the life and honour of the fair Duchess of Popoli, whom he met flying with dishevelled hair from the brutality of some Catalan soldiers. With his ready sword he cut down two or three of her assailants, and, taking her on his horse, rode off, to restore her, uninjured, to the arms of her husband.

A chivalrous people like the Spaniards were deeply impressed by the splendid chivalry of this last of the knights-errant, whose adventures in love and war rivalled those of their own Cid. They made haste on all sides to give in their adhesion to the cause he represented. Of the five or six thousand troops who capitulated at Barcelona, four-fifths at least took service with Charles as rightful King of Spain, and when he made his public entry into the city, on the 23d of October, he was received with every mark of enthusiastic loyalty. Meanwhile Peterborough, by a sagacious step, hastened to confirm and strengthen these favourable sentiments, by a public declaration that the Queen of England would undertake to secure to the province the enjoyment of its ancient *fueros* —the rights and liberties of which the Crown of Castile had deprived it. This assurance won over, at all events for the time, the whole of Catalonia, and the contagion extended into the province of Valencia, where Charles was proclaimed king in its old and prosperous capital.

In spite of this sudden success, Peterborough's position was beset with difficulties. He was in want of reinforcements, of supplies, and of money. His letters home were full of the most pressing entreaties, and, at the same time, of denunciations of everybody with whom he had to act. 'In the beggarly circumstances of our princes and generals,' he writes, ' it is certain that nothing can be greater than the affection of all sorts of people to the king; and nothing greater than the contempt and aversion they have to the whole Vienna crew. . . . Never prince was accompanied by such wretches for ministers; they have spent their whole time in selling places; they have neither money, sense, nor honour.' But he was called to the field, and in the excitement of continuous action forgot to rail. The Spanish Government despatched the Count of Las Torres with seven thousand men to reduce San Mateo, which had gone over to the Archduke Charles. Peterborough had only one thousand two hundred men at his command, but even with this small force he resolved to raise the siege. On the first days of January he wrote to Colonel Jones, whom he had appointed its governor :—' Be sure, upon the first appearance of our troops and the first discharge of our artillery, you answer with an English halloo, and take to the mountains on your right with all your men. It is no matter what becomes of the town; leave it to your mistresses! Dear Jones, prove a true dragoon; preach this welcome doctrine to your Miguelets; plunder without danger.' Another letter, containing false intelligence, was designedly allowed to fall into the hands of Las Torres; and Peterborough played his game so skilfully that the Spanish general became convinced he was surrounded by superior forces, and raised the siege with such precipitation as to leave all his artillery behind him.

Peterborough's officers advised him to be content with this success, and to return to Barcelona; but his impetuous spirit could not endure repose. It was mid-winter; the roads were almost impassable; his soldiers badly fed and clothed; the retreating army greatly outnumbered their pursuers; but the indomitable energy of the man triumphed over every obstacle, and he went on his way victorious. At his appearance town after town surrendered, and on the 4th of February he entered in triumph Valencia, which his partisans already held. There he learned—for, as the priests and the ladies were on his side, he was always provided with intelligence—that a body of six thousand Spaniards, slowly advancing to the support of Las Torres, had encamped 'in listless security' at Fuente de Higuera. He at once resolved on surprising them. Sending forward his troops by a night march, he passed the Xucar unperceived; fell upon the enemy's camp like a bolt from the blue; and slaughtered, dispersed, or captured the entire detachment. Then he returned to Valencia, took upon himself the duties of the Government, and made love to the Spanish beauties, with the energy and success that he carried into his operations of war.

Brief was the leisure allowed him. The Courts of Versailles and Madrid were determined on a great effort to recover Barcelona. Philip called back the greater portion of his troops from the Portuguese frontier, and took the field in person. Louis sent a fleet from Toulon under his son, the Comte de Thoulouse; and despatched some veteran battalions, under the Marshal Tessé, who was to act as Philip's adviser, and take the chief direction of the campaign. At the beginning of April the Archduke was shut up in Barcelona, which was closely invested. The Earl hurried immediately to his relief, at the head of three thousand men. With so small a force it was impossible to give battle to the French army. He adopted, therefore, the tactics of the guerillas, and posting himself on the neighbouring mountains, harassed the enemy by incessant attacks on their outposts, cut off their stragglers, intercepted their communications with the interior, and threw supplies, both of men and provisions, into the beleaguered town. But he soon discovered that the only hope of relieving it was from the sea. The commission which he held from the British Government gave him supreme authority, not only over the army, but, whenever he was actually on board ship, over the navy also. Without making his design known to any, he put out to sea at night in an open boat, fell in with an English man-of-war, the *Leopard*, hoisted the Union Flag, and sent a pinnace to the Admiral, Sir John Leake, with orders to sail straight on Barcelona, and make ready to attack the French. Could these orders have been given a few hours earlier, it is probable that the whole French fleet would have been taken; but the Count of Thoulouse, apprised of the proximity of the English, put out to sea. On the 9th of May, when Peterborough and Leake arrived before Barcelona, they found that the enemy had disappeared. Unopposed, they entered the harbour, and amidst the acclamations of the people, landed reinforcements. On the following day Marshal Tessé raised the siege, and returned to Roussillon. 'I must not complain,' wrote Peterborough to the Queen, 'where there is so much occasion for joy; but when I spent two nights in a boat at sea to get on board the fleet, I was in hopes I might have given your Majesty some account of the other trust you have been pleased to honour me with: but a discreet retreat prevented these flattering hopes.'

Barcelona being relieved, Peterborough returned to Valencia, the city in Spain which he most affected. He was anxious to march upon Madrid, but the Archduke Charles did not share his adventurous spirit, and lingered irresolute in Catalonia. The Earl, indignant, shut himself up in his sunny city, on the shores of the bright Mediterranean, 'reading Don Quixote, giving balls and suppers, trying in vain to get some good sport out of the Valencian bulls, and making love, not in vain, to the Valencian women.'

After a long and disastrous delay, the Archduke advanced into Castile, and ordered Peterborough to join him. But the opportunity had been lost. The Duke of Berwick had occupied Madrid; and when the whole of the Allied forces were assembled at Guadelaxara, they were found to be considerably inferior in strength to the enemy. Peterborough devised a plan for the recovery of Madrid, with five thousand men, by a *coup de main*. The Archduke rejected it. The Earl's proud spirit flamed up at this indignity, and he demanded permission to leave the army. Permission was readily granted; and he set out for Italy, on the pretext that he was commissioned by the Archduke to raise a loan in Genoa on the credit of the revenues of Spain. In the following January (1707) he returned—not with an official character, but as a volunteer. His advice was asked and given, but of course not acted upon. The plan of campaign he suggested was admirably conceived, but the Archduke's counsellors could not appreciate it. The Earl, therefore, took his final departure.[1] He embarked in the *Resolution*, commanded by his younger son, intending to land in Italy, and to travel

---

[1] 'With him,' says Macaulay, 'departed the good fortune of the Allies. Scarcely any general had ever done so much with means so small. Scarcely any general had ever displayed equal originality and boldness. He possessed, in the highest degree, the art of conciliating those whom he had subdued.

on to Vienna. Off Leghorn they fell in with a French squadron, and after a vigorous action, in which the *Resolution* was much damaged, and her captain severely wounded, the vessel was run ashore, and they succeeded in escaping to Turin. The Earl was compelled to leave his son there, to recover from his wounds; but he himself, having changed his plans, rapidly crossed the Continent, and paid a visit to Marlborough in his camp at Jenappe. Thence he proceeded to the Swedish camp at Alt Rastadt, to see Charles the Twelfth, between whom and himself were many points of resemblance. This, however, did not prevent him from writing to a friend:—' It is undecided whether he is very wise or very foolhardy; but he has fifty thousand men mad enough to obey readily all his commands.' In August he re-appeared in London, where he received a hearty welcome from the multitude, and a welcome scarcely less hearty from wits and men-of-letters, and the leaders of society. At St Paul's, in the presence of the Queen, who ordered its publication, the Dean of Canterbury preached a warm panegyric on his genius and exploits. ' By command,' also, was printed an elaborate eulogium, entitled, *The Triumph of Her Majesty's Arms, both by Sea and Land, under the direction of His Excellency, Charles, Earl of Peterborough and Monmouth.* In acknowledgment of his services he was created a Knight of the Garter. He naturally expected also a vote of thanks from Parliament; but this was long delayed by political prejudice. The Government was almost as much

But he was not equally successful in winning the attachment of those with whom he acted. He was adored by the Catalonians and Valencians; but he was hated by the prince whom he had all but made a great king, and by the generals whose fortune and reputation were staked on the same venture as his own. The English Government could not understand him. He was so eccentric that they gave him no credit for the judgment which he really possessed. One day he took towns with horse-soldiers; then again he turned some hundreds of infantry into cavalry at a minute's notice. He obtained his political intelligence chiefly by means of love affairs, and filled his despatches with epigrams.'

disturbed by his merits as by his faults, and was influenced against him by the secret representations of the Archduke Charles, who resented his independent action. Coldly treated by the Whig Ministers, Peterborough, with his usual impetuosity, went over to the side of the Tories. He employed his physician, Dr Friend, to compile a book in his praise; and he solicited his new allies to bring his case before the Lords.

Accordingly, on December 19, the Earl of Rochester stood forth as his champion. First, he enumerated the great deeds of his brother earl, 'equalling, if not exceeding in importance, those of Marlborough,'—an absurd exaggeration. Next he argued that it had been the constant practice, when a person of rank, who had been employed abroad in an eminent post, returned home, he should either have thanks given him or else be called to an account.' Lord Halifax warmly praised Peterborough's skill and courage; but thought a vote of thanks to him should be postponed until, as he had requested, the whole of his conduct had been examined. No decision, however, was arrived at; and it was not until January 1711, that the vote of thanks was finally accorded.

'This hero,' says his biographer, 'was small in person and singularly spare, but had great capability of endurance. Hardship and fatigue told not upon him; and unusual, indeed, must have been the powers of the slender frame that fulfilled the behests of so indomitable a spirit.' He gave a striking illustration both of his physical and intellectual capacity in 1709,—the year in which he lost his wife, his two gallant sons, and other members of his family, by the ravages of small-pox. Entrusted with a special mission to Vienna, to arrange terms of agreement between the Emperor and the Archduke, he thought fit to set aside his instructions, and to act on his own views of policy. The Ministry, not unnaturally, sent him a letter of recall. This he sent back with his despatches, ignoring it entirely. But when he had brought his task to a satisfactory conclusion, he sent home by an express a full and graphic account; and afterwards, without servants or baggage, posted across the Continent, passed the Channel, and actually arrived in London before his despatches.

An admirable portrait of this extraordinary man is furnished by Swift in some doggerel stanzas, which, however careless in their rhymes, abound with incisive touches of character:—

> ' Mordanto fills the trump of fame,
> The Christian world his deeds proclaim,
> And prints are crowded with his name.
>
> In journeys he outrides the post,
> Sits up till midnight with his host,
> Talks politics, and gives the toast.
>
> Knows every prince in Europe's face,
> Flies like a squib from place to place,
> And travels not, but runs a race.
>
> From Paris, gazette à-la-main,
> This day's arrived without his train,
> Mordanto in a week from Spain.
>
> A messenger comes all a-reek
> Mordanto at Madrid to seek;
> He left the town above a week.
>
> Next day the post-boy winds his horn,
> And rides through Dover in the morn:
> Mordanto's landed from Leghorn.
>
> Mordanto gallops on alone,
> The roads are with his followers strewn
> This breaks a girth, and that a bone;
>
> His body, active as his mind,
> Returning sound in limb and wind,
> Except some leather lost behind.
>
> A skeleton in outward figure,
> His meagre corpse though full of vigour,
> Would halt behind him, were it bigger.

> So wonderful his expedition,
> When you have not the least suspicion,
> He's with you like an apparition.
>
> Shines in all climates like a star ;
> In senates bold, and fierce in war ;
> A land commander and a tar :
>
> Heroic actions early bred in,
> Ne'er to be matched in modern reading,
> But by his namesake, Charles of Sweden.'

Early in 1714, Lord Peterborough married the *prima donna* of the time, Mistress Anastasia Robinson. He induced her to consent to a private marriage, at which Lady Oxford attended as friend and witness ; but as he persisted in deferring the public announcement, Mrs Robinson long laboured under the reproach of an immoral connection. She continued on the stage until 1722, when an unpleasant incident caused her withdrawal from a profession with which she had never been in sympathy. Lord Peterborough always escorted her to and from the opera, and his public attentions not seldom exposed her to unpleasant misconstruction. At last, Senesino, an Italian singer, acted as if he believed her to be a woman of easy morality. Mrs Robinson hastened to complain of his insolence to Lord Peterborough, who, at the time, was in the theatre. He rushed upon the stage, seized the astonished singer, dragged him off, and compelled him on his knees to apologise to the offended lady. This public *esclandre* naturally produced a great sensation, and Mrs Robinson retired from the stage, of which for ten years she had been the acknowledged ornament.

The wits and men about town did not fail to profit by this affair, and General Lord Stanhope, who had served with Peterborough in Spain, venturing to indulge in a jesting allusion to 'the irrepressible spirit of the old Quixote,' was immediately challenged by him. Lord Delamere consented to act as his second ; but by some means the quarrel got noised abroad. Peterborough and Stanhope were both put under arrest; and their release was refused until they gave their word that hostile proceedings should be dropped.

Mrs Robinson for some time lived with her mother in a charming cottage at Fulham, close by the residence of her eccentric husband. She frequently assisted at his musical entertainments, and was always treated by the guests with the courtesy due to her well-known though unacknowledged position. Thither came Swift and Pope, Prior and Gay, and other men of light and leading; and witty, if not always wise, was the conversation to which these choice spirits contributed. Their host, who had a high and not altogether unreasonable belief in his culinary skill, sometimes assumed the garb of a *chef de cusine*, and prepared some special *plat* for the refreshment of his friends; and though he had reached the age of sixty-five, he preserved so much of the energy and vivacity of his earlier manhood, that the youngest of his guests did not surpass him in gaiety and high spirits. At intervals he made hurried visits to the Continent, dashing from place to place with his old impetuosity. Once, while travelling in Italy, he was arrested at Bologna, by order of Pope Clement XI., whom he had offended by his indiscreet utterances. His papers were seized, and for a month he was confined in Fort Urbain. But the English Government interfered to procure his release, and the Pope apologised.

In 1723, at an age when he was 'old enough to know better,' he began an amatory correspondence with Mrs Howard, afterwards Countess of Suffolk—the fair favourite of George II., whom Pope has celebrated with so much eulogistic fervour. She is described as 'remarkably young-looking, and charmingly dressed; neither brilliant nor witty, incapable of any keen feeling, and the type of a moral system whose morality is expediency, and whose religion is good breeding.' For nearly twelve years the aged inamorato continued to address her in impassioned verse and prose, the lady in her replies being assisted by the poet Gay; but it is only fair to admit that the intimacy between the two never went beyond the bounds of a decorous Platonism.

Peterborough had reached the age of seventy when he retired to Bevis Mount, a small but pleasantly-situated villa, which overlooked the bright expanse of Southampton Water. In 1732 he called his wife to his side, permitting her to wear her wedding-ring, and welcoming the patient tenderness which smoothed the path of his declining years. Under her vigilant care he seemed to renew his vigour and regain his health. But in 1735 he was seized with an illness to which no other than a fatal termination could be possible. To defer the end for a few months the physicians ordered him to Lisbon. He was unwilling to go without his wife, whose society he had learned to delight in, and whose attentions had become indispensable; while she, on her part, refused to accompany him unless he acknowledged her true position publicly. It is difficult to understand why he should have hesitated to do an act of the most obvious justice; but for some days he delayed his decision. One evening, however, he requested her to meet him next day at the apartment of his kinsman, Mr Poyntz, in St James's Palace. 'She went, not knowing for what purpose, and found all the Mordaunt family assembled there, as she, and they too, supposed, to bid him a last farewell. Presently he began to address them with much feeling, and, as he proceeded, with some slight return of the old animation. He told them of a lady, accomplished, talented, of spotless purity of life, endowed with exemplary patience and enduring affection, to whom he owed his best and happiest hours; his comfort in suffering and sorrow. His heart had always done her the justice which his weakness and vanity, he said, had refused her, and that he had loved her with a true and abiding love. That lady, he continued had been always his best friend, and for twenty-one years his affectionate and devoted wife. He then rose from his seat, took Anastasia by the hand, and presented her to his relations as Lady Peterborough.'

It is said that the scene so overpowered the lady whose claims were recognised in this theatric fashion that she fainted. One cannot help feeling that the Earl was not worthy of her. Before leaving England they were re-married, at Peterborough's desire, the clergyman who had performed the first ceremony being dead. On the voyage he endured severe suffering; and on the 25th of October, a few days after his arrival at Lisbon, passed away, very quietly, attended to the last by the affectionate devotion of his 'best friend.'

'He lived,' says Walpole, 'a romance, but was capable of making it a history.' I am not sure, however, that his life contains very much of the romantic element, unless the word 'romantic' is used as a synonym for 'eccentric,' 'wayward,' 'extravagant.' Aimless journeys performed with reckless impetuosity—undignified amours with women of every class—ostentatious profligacy—wild escapades, impelled apparently by some mental and moral 'twist'— what is there 'romantic' in all this? It is true, perhaps, that he was capable of making it a history, for he was unquestionably endowed with rare intellectual gifts; but except during his brilliant Spanish campaign, he scarcely made use of those gifts for any noble or worthy purpose. In a great degree, his life was a wasted life. An unhappy eccentricity of temper, and a superabundant egotism, led him to throw away his opportunities. He cared only to astonish, to surprise, to make men wonder; he never seems to have sought or desired their respect or esteem. But as he was the intimate friend of Swift and Pope and Prior, we must suppose that, after all, he possessed some generous and amiable qualities which were revealed in the

intimacy of social life. For myself, I do not profess any
particular admiration for a hero who had nothing in him of
the heroic.

. . . .

The Military History of the time records a few other
names which seem to merit a passing allusion. The
readers of Thackeray's *Esmond* will remember the pro-
minence he gives to the services of General WEBB, whom
he elevates upon a colossal pedestal of laudation. Webb
was a good, but not a great soldier, whose chief claim to
remembrance is that a political faction thought him
capable of being put forward as a rival in military fame to
John, Duke of Marlborough. It is seldom that even party
spirit ventures on so audacious an endeavour to ignore the
difference in stature between an ordinary man and a giant;
and posterity has not failed to detect and punish the folly
of the attempt. Webb distinguished himself as an efficient
lieutenant, and on one occasion, when he was in sole
command, showed that on a limited field he could handle
small bodies of men with address—but this is all. He was
brave as a lion, and understood his duties thoroughly; but
he had none of the intuitions, the foresight, the intellectual
grasp, the faculty of combination, the boldness of conception, which constitute a great commander.

From 1710 to 1715 John Richmond Webb held the
governorship of the Isle of Wight; a sinecure which in
those days was frequently the reward of military services.
From 1693 to 1706 it had been held by another of Marlborough's lieutenants—JOHN, LORD CUTTS, who, from his
coolness under fire, was popularly known as 'the Sala-
mander.' He came of an ancient Cambridgeshire family;
received a liberal education; entered the army at an early
age, and, as a 'born soldier,' soon rose to distinction. In
King William's campaigns in Ireland and Flanders his
extraordinary courage earned him speedy promotion, and

a brilliant military career was crowned by his appointment to be Commander of the Forces in Ireland, where he died in 1706.

His fine qualities as a soldier were notably displayed at the siege of Namur, and, again, on the field of Blenheim. His moral character does not seem to have been beyond reproach, and from contemporary allusions he would seem to have been excessively vain, irritable, and imperious. As Governor of the Isle of Wight he contrived to involve himself in a succession of petty quarrels. He interfered in the management of the corporations, disfranchised several burgesses of Newtown, threw a clergyman into the dungeon of Cowes Castle, and raised a feud between himself and the island gentry that threatened a serious result. But if he had some of the vices, he had also some of the virtues of the soldier; and perceiving that he had put forward inadmissible pretensions, he frankly acknowledged his error. A treaty of peace, in March 1697, was concluded between him and his 'subjects'; and thereafter Lord Cutts, who maintained a splendid hospitality, grew very popular in the island. It is recorded to his credit that he repaired and refitted the governor's apartments in Carisbrooke Castle at his own expense.

From 1725 to 1726, the Governorship of the island was held by the ablest and most accomplished of the captains trained in Marlborough's school.—WILLIAM, EARL CADOGAN. The son of an Irish barrister, he entered the army at an early age, and became quartermaster of the forces in 1701. Having joined Marlborough in the Low Countries, he quickly gained his good opinion by his energy, skill, courage, and efficiency. At the passage of the Danube his services were conspicuous; and at Blenheim he contributed in no small measure to the success of the day. He continued with Marlborough until the latter's overthrow, when he promptly resigned all his offices, and shared the adversity of his chief as he had shared his prosperity. On the accession of George I., he was reinstated in the public employment, and in 1716 raised to the peerage. He was sent in 1720 as ambassador to the Hague, and, as representing Great Britain, signed the historic treaty which constituted the Quadruple Alliance. Earl Cadogan, on the death of Marlborough, in 1722, succeeded him as Commander-in-Chief and Master-General of the Ordnance. He died in August 1726. It will be seen that he had no opportunity of distinguishing himself in independent command; but the important part he played at Oudenarde and Malplaquet proved him to be possessed of a fine soldierly capacity. He thoroughly understood the art of making war; on the battle-field was as cool as Marlborough himself; and, like him, combined a vigilant caution with the most daring courage. I take him to have been next to Marlborough, and, of course, *longo intervallo*, the most capable of the English generals of his time; and it is well known that he enjoyed the great Duke's special confidence, and was entrusted by him with the most delicate and difficult commissions.

CHAPTER VI.

QUEEN ANNE'S SEAMEN.

Condition of the Navy — Our Seamen — The Press-gang—Our Maritime Supremacy — Sir George Rooke—The Attack upon Vigo — Capture of Gibraltar—Off Malaga—Memoir of Rooke—Sir Cloudesley Shovel—His Career—His Shipwreck and Death -Strange Stories—His Monument—Alexander Selkirk—His Solitary Life in Juan Fernandez—Biographical Sketch.

IN speaking of the Military Commanders of Queen Anne's reign, I have briefly described the miserable material of which their armies was largely composed, and the unfavourable conditions under which men were enlisted to serve her Majesty. It cannot be said that a better state of things existed in the sister-service. The crews of our ships of war, like our battalions and squadrons, were recruited from the dregs of the population; and the recollection of this unfortunate circumstance will enable us to understand why, in those times, our actions at sea were so frequently indecisive. The splendid seamen of Drake and Frobisher, of Blake and Monk and Sandwich, had passed away—had passed away along with their ardent religious and patriotic feelings; and their successors, though perhaps not less physically brave, were greatly inferior in moral tone,—had no enthusiasm or sense of duty,—were reckless, insubordinate, addicted to drink, and almost as keen to turn against their own officers as to fight the national enemy. This is little to be wondered at, when we think of the treatment they received at the hands of the Government and from almost all in authority over them. To begin with, they were badly paid and wretchedly fed; they were herded between decks without any provision being made for health or decency; and for the lightest offences were punished with such severity that they soon became hardened into criminals. The men of good family who had formerly sought an active career upon the sea had been attracted towards a military life by the campaigns of William III., and their successors having risen from the forecastle, or volunteered from merchant vessels, were of an inferior stamp,—of a coarser nature and more violent temper,—and, conscious of their deficiencies, endeavoured to secure obedience by the brutality of their rule. A man-of-war in Queen Anne's age was too frequently a floating prison, with two-thirds of the crew, perhaps, prepared, on the first favourable opportunity, to mutiny against the tyrants who inflicted upon them hourly wrong; or it was a floating hospital, in which the fell disease of scurvy claimed its tens and scores of unhappy victims. Smollett wrote some thirty or forty years later, but no considerable change had taken place in the treatment of our seamen or the sanitation of our ships; and the lurid pictures which darken the pages of *Roderick Random* are as true of ships and men in the reign of Anne as in the reign of George II.

There was one important distinction between the two services. In spite of the recruiting officer, no man could be enlisted into the army against his will; but the Navy was to a great extent manned by impressment. In all the principal harbours press-ketches were stationed, and press-gangs paraded through the highways and byways of our coast-towns. They beat up the public houses and the grog-shops and the stews; they lay in wait by night to surprise the unsuspicious wayfarer; they crept along the main roads; they did not scruple to break into houses where they thought a likely fellow might be concealed.

But the horrors of the pressgang have been made familiar to every reader by our novelists, and I pass from the subject with the remark that the temptation to make light of individual liberty was very strong, when officers of press-gangs received 'twenty shillings for each seaman, and sixpence per man for each mile he shall be brought, if under twenty miles, and ten shillings for each seaman that shall be brought above twenty miles, over and above the said twenty shillings.'

Few of us recollect—what is nevertheless a fact—that our maritime supremacy is, after all, not more than a century and a half old. We beat the Dutch badly in the times of Cromwell and Charles II., but they also beat *us*; and the struggle between the two nations was not so easily or entirely decided in our favour as popular writers represent. In our later encounters with the French we were generally successful, but it must be remembered that at La Hogue we had a largely superior force. Indeed, it was not so much in our great battles that the higher qualities of our sailors were conspicuous as in the combats between single ships, where the pluck and endurance of the race could not be neutralised by the blunders or misconduct of our commanders. The French navy, at the beginning of the eighteenth century, was, I think, more formidable than our own in the number of its ships, in equipment, and in discipline. Their ships of the line were larger and better armed; their officers were better trained. There is ample evidence as to the wretched condition of our fleets at the outset of the great War of the Succession. Nor, up to this time, had England produced, with two or three exceptions, such as Penn and Monson, any distinguished admiral of the modern type—that is, any admiral who could manœuvre as well as fight his ships. Blake and Monk left the details of navigation to their subordinate officers; their experience had been gained in sieges and land battles, and they drew up their fleets and fought them as they drew up and fought their battalions and squadrons. A change began to take place with the coming in of the eighteenth century. Though it is true that Russel was a good seaman, and trained in naval affairs, at La Hogue he showed no conspicuous ability as a commander; and I am inclined to look upon the reign of Anne as the commencement of our modern naval system: to date from that reign — so important in our history — the glorious record of our supremacy at sea. And I am also inclined to point to Sir GEORGE ROOKE as the first in the long succession of great admirals who have made the naval fame of England. He was not a Rodney, a Hawke, or a St Vincent, much less a Nelson; but those illustrious chiefs were born to more fortunate times, when the true English seaman was rapidly maturing, and our country had come to understand the wealth of her maritime resources, and to appreciate the extent to which, both for conquest and defence, she would have to rely upon her navy. In his generation, and with the limited means at his disposal he did good service; and Vigo and Malaga are two names blazoned with honour upon his scutcheon.

The first year of Queen Anne's reign was illustrated by a naval success. Vice-Admiral Sir GEORGE ROOKE — then in his fifty-third year, and a seaman of great experience — was appointed to the command of a large fleet intended to act against Cadiz. On the 18th of August 1702, he arrived in Cadiz Bay, escorting a large number of transports, which had on board a combined English and Dutch force, under the Duke of Ormond. The Duke was a respectable soldier of the old school—afraid of responsibility—afraid of the initiative, and his caution was intensified by the obstructiveness of the Dutch commanders. All agreed to differ; no plan of action was projected; and as there was an entire ignorance of the strength of the enemy and the nature of the country, the troops, who had been disembarked, were re-embarked after a month's delay, and the expedition prepared to return home. This failure was a great mortification to Rooke, and hearing that a Spanish treasure-fleet, laden with the spoils of the Indies, had run into Vigo, he resolved to make an attack upon it, and, if possible, to retrieve the previous miscarriage of the expedition.

He arrived off the port on the 11th of October. Its defences had been greatly strengthened. The entrance, which does not exceed three-quarters of a mile in width, was commanded by the fire of seventy heavy guns; while from one side of the harbour to the other was carried a massive boom, composed of ships' yards and top-masts, fastened together with three-inch rope, and underneath with cables and hawsers. The top-chain was moored at either end to a seventy-gun ship; and within the boom were anchored five French men-of-war, of between sixty and seventy guns each, with their broadsides directed towards the harbour mouth. Undaunted by these formidable preparations, the English admiral and his lieutenants shifted their flags from their flag-ships to third-rates, which drew less water, and could get in nearer shore; and Rooke despatched Hopson, his second-in-command, with twenty-five English and Dutch men-of-war, all his frigates, fire-ships, and bomb-vessels, to break the boom, and force the passage into the harbour.

To co-operate in this service, the Duke of Ormond landed two thousand troops, who attacked and captured a stone fort at the mouth of the harbour, and seized upon a battery of twenty guns. As soon as the English flag was seen flying from the ramparts, the ships moved forward; and Vice-Admiral Hopson, in the *Torbay*, bearing down with all his canvas spread, drove hard against the boom, and snapped it in twain. Through the opening thus made the rest of the fleet entered the harbour under a tremendous fire, which our ships returned very vigorously. Gradually the shore batteries were occupied by our troops. Meanwhile, one of the Spanish fire-ships ran aboard the *Torbay*, and would certainly have burned her, had she not happened to have had on board a great quantity of snuff which, when she blew up, put out the flames. The *Torbay*, however, did not escape without serious injury, and she had one hundred and fifteen of her crew killed or wounded. So shattered was she, that the Vice-Admiral was compelled to transfer his flag to the *Monmouth*.

When the batteries were captured, the Spanish galleons hastily retired up the bay, and attempted to land their cargoes. The English squadron pursued them, and the Spaniards then threw their wealth into the sea, and set their vessels on fire. Six galleons, however, fell into our hands, and seven French ships of war. The loss of life on the side of the enemy was very heavy, and the destruction of property exceeded in value eight millions of dollars. It is asserted that a good deal of the treasure taken was embezzled. 'The public was not much enriched,' says Bishop Burnet, ' by this extraordinary capture, yet the loss our enemies made by it was a vast one.' From the specie brought to England a special coinage was made, having the word 'Vigo' under the Queen's effigy.

All things considered, this was a dashing exploit, and worthy of our Navy even in its most palmy days. It showed that Rooke was a man of decision and resource; capable of conceiving a bold scheme, and carrying it out with energy and determination. He displayed the same qualities in his next achievement,—the consequences of which were infinitely more important than any resulting from the affair at Vigo. In 1704, the year of Blenheim, the English Government, for the purpose of supporting the claims of the Archduke Charles to the throne of Spain, despatched a joint naval and military expedition to the coast of Catalonia. A body of five thousand to six thousand troops, under the command of the Prince of Hesse-Darmstadt, was embarked on board a powerful English fleet, under Sir George Rooke. The troops landed at Barcelona, but were so coldly received by the population, that it was considered advisable to re-embark them; and Rooke, sailing down the Mediterranean, passed the Straits, where he effected a junction with Sir Cloudesley Shovel's squadron. The commanding position and strategic value of Gibraltar could not but be apparent to the English admiral; and ascertaining that though the fortress was of unquestionable strength, it was very feebly garrisoned—the Spanish Government believing that Nature had rendered it impregnable—he resolved to attack it, and secured the assistance of the Prince of Hesse-Darmstadt. Within the Spanish defences were not more than a hundred men, but their commander, a gallant veteran, refused all proposals of capitulation. Accordingly, the English and Dutch marines, to the number of about eighteen hundred, were landed on the Isthmus, now known as the Neutral Ground; and the garrison was thus cut off from its supplies. Sir George Rooke, on the 2d of August, gave orders for the attack to begin, and a heavy cannonade was hurled against the fortifications. In five or six hours no fewer than fifteen thousand shot were expended, and the enemy at length were driven from their guns. On the following day was held a great religious festival; and a part of the garrison desisted from 'watch and ward' to pray to their saints. The eastern side of the Rock was thus left open to attack, and the English sailors, with wonderful agility, scaled the rugged precipice. At the same time an assault was made upon the Mole head, and though the springing of a mine caused a heavy loss, it proved successful. No further resistance was attempted; and on a second summons being sent to the governor, he surrendered, on condition that the garrison were allowed to march out with all the honours of war, and that those inhabitants who chose to remain under the British flag were guaranteed in the enjoyment of their rights and privileges.

The Prince of Darmstadt would fain have hoisted the Spanish standard and proclaimed King Charles; but Sir George Rooke firmly insisted on taking possession of the Rock in the name of Queen Anne. He appointed the Prince governor, and leaving a garrison of two thousand men under his command, went in search of the Toulon fleet, under the High-admiral of France, the Comte de Thoulouse, which was known to be cruising in the Mediterranean. Rooke had been joined by some Dutch vessels, the Comte de Thoulouse by some Spanish, and the strength of the two fleets was as follows:—

> ENGLISH—Forty-one English, eleven Dutch, sail of the line, with three thousand seven hundred guns, and twenty-three thousand two hundred men, besides six frigates and seven fire-ships.
>
> FRENCH—Fifty sail of the line, with three thousand five-hundred and eighty-three guns, and twenty-four thousand two hundred and fifty-five men, besides nine fire-ships and twelve French and eleven Spanish galleys.

The two armaments were therefore nearly equal; but as the French ships were better built and better armed, the superiority—such as it was—rested with the French.

On Sunday, the 13th of August, the two great fleets came into collision off Malaga. They fought all day—'very sharp fighting,' says Sir Cloudesley Shovel—and on both sides the ships were terribly knocked about,—'There is hardly a ship,' says Shovel, 'that must not shift one mast, and some must shift all.' The loss of life was severe: six hundred and ninety-five killed and one thousand six hundred and thirty-three wounded among the English, and four hundred killed and wounded among the Dutch: a total of two thousand seven hundred and twenty-eight killed and wounded. The French—three thousand two hundred and eight. Yet was there not a ship sunk, burnt, or taken on either side—a result astonishing to those of us whose knowledge of naval history is limited to the decisive battles and great triumphs of Rodney, Jervis, and Nelson. But both France and England claimed the victory. *Te Deum* was chanted in Nôtre Dame; and a public thanksgiving offered up at St Paul's. As a matter of fact, it was a drawn battle; but as the French retired to Toulon, Rooke to a great extent obtained his object.

I have said that the superiority—such as it was—rested with the French. By one of our naval historians this superiority is clearly defined:—'First, their ships were bigger; they had seventeen three-deck ships, and we had but seven. Secondly, they had a great advantage in their weight of metal; for they had six hundred guns more than we had. Thirdly, they were clean ships just come out of port; whereas ours had been long at sea, and had done hard service. Fourthly, they had the assistance of their galleys; and how great an advantage this was will appear from hence, that about the middle of the fight the French admiral ordered a seventy-gun ship to board the *Monk*, a sixty-gun ship of ours; which she did, and was beaten off three times, and after every repulse she had her wounded men taken off, and her complement restored by the galleys. Fifthly, the French fleet was thoroughly provided with ammunition; which was so much wanted in ours that several ships were towed out of the line, because they had not had either powder or ball sufficient for a single broadside. But the skill of the admiral, and the bravery of the officers and seamen under his command, supplied all defects; and enabled them to give the French so clear a proof of their superiority over them in all respects at sea, that they not only declined renewing the fight at present, but avoided us ever after, and durst not venture a battle on that element during the remainder of the war.'

I have already noted the assistance rendered to the Earl of Peterborough's action in Spain by the fleet under Sir Cloudesley Shovel and Sir John Leake. In July 1707, a fleet under Sir Cloudesley Shovel co-operated with an army under the Duke of Savoy and Prince Eugene, in an ineffectual siege of Toulon. In the following year the islands of Corsica and Minorca were seized by an English fleet under Sir John Leake; and with this achievement finishes the naval record of Queen Anne's reign.

Sir George Rooke, the son of Sir William Rooke, came of an old and honourable Kentish family. He was born in 1650, and educated for the law; but his seafaring bias was not to be overruled, and, entering the royal navy, he rose from rank to rank with such rapidity, that he was a captain before he was thirty. In 1690, as Rear-Admiral of the Red, he was present in the disastrous battle off Beachy Head; and in 1692, his courage and skill were conspicuous in the victorious action of La Hogue. It was he who led the flotilla into the bay, and destroyed the French ships under the guns of their forts. I subjoin Macaulay's account of this memorable deed of daring:—

> On the afternoon of the 23d of May all was ready. A flotilla, consisting of sloops, of fire-ships, and of two hundred boats, was entrusted to the command of Rooke. The whole armament was in the highest spirits. The rowers, flushed by success, and animated by the thought that they were going to fight under the eyes of the French and Irish troops who had been assembled for the purpose of subjugating England, pulled manfully and with loud huzzas towards the six huge wooden castles which lay close to Fort Lisset. The French, though an eminently brave people, have always been more liable to sudden panics than their phlegmatic neighbours the English and

German. On this day there was a panic both in the fleet and in the army. Tourville ordered his sailors to man their boats, and would have led them to encounter the enemy in the bay. But his example and his exhortations were vain. His boats turned round and fled in confusion. The ships were abandoned. The cannonade from Fort Lisset was so feeble and ill-directed that it did no execution. The regiments on the beach, after wasting a few musket shots, drew off. The English boarded the men-of-war, set them on fire, and having performed this great service without the loss of a single life, retreated at a late hour with the retreating tide. The bay was in a blaze during the night; and now and then a loud explosion announced that the flames had reached a powder room or a tier of loaded guns. At eight the next morning the tide came back strong; and with the tide came back Rooke and his two hundred boats. The enemy made a faint attempt to defend the vessels which were near Fort St Vaast. During a few minutes the batteries did some execution among the crews of our skiffs; but the struggle was soon over. The French poured fast out of their ships on one side; the English poured in as fast on the other, and, with loud shouts, turned the captured guns against the shore. The batteries were speedily silenced. . . . The conquerors, leaving the ships of war in flames, made their way into an inner basin where many transports lay. Eight of these vessels were set on fire. Several were taken in tow. The rest would have been either destroyed or carried off, had not the sea again began to ebb. It was impossible to do more; and the victorious flotilla slowly retired, insulting the hostile camp with a thundering chant of 'God save the King.'[1]

In the following year Rooke was sent, with twenty-three ships of war, to convoy the great Smyrna fleet, consisting of four hundred English and Dutch merchant vessels, laden with cargoes for the Mediterranean markets. Admirals Killigrew and Delaval, with a fleet of fifty ships, escorted him about two hundred miles beyond Ushant, and then returned to the Channel to guard against a possible descent on the coast of Devonshire. But the French armada, instead of sailing into English waters, had slipped round from Brest to Toulon, and there joined the Toulon

---

[1] The most interesting narrative of the action at La Hogue is to be found in *An Account of the late Great Victory*, 1692.

fleet; so that Rooke, when he arrived off Cape Lagos, found his way blocked by the whole navy of France. To have engaged such a force in open battle would have been madness. Rooke's great object was to save the rich argosies entrusted to his care: and sacrificing two or three Dutch men-of-war which had fallen astern, he contrived, by the exercise of a splendid seamanship, to carry sixty-five merchantmen into Madeira, whence they made their way to Cork. The remainder of the convoy was scattered far and wide, and both England and Holland sustained a heavy loss; but very few ships fell into the hands of the enemy, and eventually the larger portion got into friendly ports.

The admirable qualities as a commander which Rooke had exhibited in this affair fully merited the applause which they received. The merchants tendered him a formal vote of thanks. The King made him Vice-Admiral of the Red, and a Lord Commissioner of the Admiralty; and before the close of 1694 he was raised to the rank of Admiral of the Blue.

Shortly after the battle of Malaga, which provoked a pitiable display of party feeling—the Whigs doing their best to diminish its importance, because it had been gained by a Tory seaman, just as the Tories depreciated Blenheim, because it was won by a Whig general—Rooke retired from active service. He withdrew into private life, and lived on a very modest and unostentatious scale at his Kentish seat, until his death on the 24th of January 1708.

Another of the Queen Anne admirals who deserves notice is Sir CLOUDESLEY SHOVEL, who was born in the same year as Rooke, and died only a few weeks before him. In his early life he drudged as a shoemaker's apprentice, but, being of an aspiring disposition, he ran away to sea, entering on board ship in the sufficiently humble position of a cabin-boy. His great natural capacity and his zealous attention to duty secured him, however, an unusually rapid promotion; and he found a kind and loyal patron in Sir John Narborough, who had begun his career in the same lowly manner. In 1674 he served under Sir John in an expedition against the pirates of Tripoli; and led a brilliant night attack upon their place of harbourage, destroying their fleet under the very guns of the Moorish batteries. For his brave and successful conduct of this enterprise he was promoted to the command of a ship of war. Blunt and rough, with little education, but much strong sense, he embraced the principles of the Revolution, and willingly gave his allegiance to William III., who afterwards knighted him for his share in the victory of Bantry Bay. In 1691 he commanded the fleet that carried King William and his army into Ireland; and William 'was so highly satisfied with his diligence and dexterity—for, without question, in matters of this nature, he was one of the ablest commanders [who] ever put to sea—that he was graciously pleased, not only to appoint him Rear-Admiral of the Blue, but did him also the honour with his own hands, to deliver him his commission.'

Sir Cloudesley was present at La Hogue, and, in 1694, in the action of Camaret Bay. In 1703 he had command of the fleet in the Mediterranean. In 1705 he held joint command, with the Earl of Peterborough, of the expedition to Spain, and devoted his best energies to its successful consummation. In the words of his biographer:—'He furnished guns for the batteries, and men to serve them; he landed, for the use of the army, almost all the military stores of the fleet; he not only gave prudent advice himself in all councils of war, but he moderated the heats and resentments of others; and, in short, was so useful, so ready, and so determined in the service, and took such good care that everything he promised should be fully and punctually performed, that his presence and counsels, in a manner, forced the land officers to continue the siege till the place was taken, to the surprise of all the world, and, perhaps most of all, to the surprise of those by whom it was taken: for, if we may guess at their sentiments by what they declared under their hands in several councils of war, they scarcely believed it practicable to reduce so strong a place with so small a force, and that so ill provided.'

In 1707, as we have seen, an expedition was despatched to co-operate with the army of Prince Eugene and the Duke of Savoy in an attack upon Toulon. The military force was inadequate to the greatness of the enterprise, and in less than a month abandoned it; but the work of the fleet was done with equal vigour and success, and eventually its guns covered and protected the retreat of the Imperialist troops. After stationing a strong squadron at Gibraltar, and distributing a few ships along the coast of Italy, Sir Cloudesley set sail for England, and, on the 22d of October, arrived off the Scilly Islands. About noon he lay by; but, at nightfall, made sail again and stood away under his courses, from a belief, it is thought, that he saw the light on the island of St Agnes. The disaster that followed is thus described by Bishop Burnet:—

'When Sir Cloudesley Shovel was sailing home with the great ships, by an unaccountable carelessness and security, he, and two other capital ships, ran foul upon those rocks beyond the Land's End, known by the name of the Bishop and his Clerks; and they were in a minute broke to pieces; so that not a man of them escaped. It was dark, but there was no wind, otherwise the whole fleet had perished with them; all the rest tacked in time, and so they were saved. Thus one of the greatest seamen of the age was lost, by an error in his own profession and a great misreckoning, for he had lain by all the day before and set sail at night, believing that next morning he would have time enough to guard against running on those rocks ; but he was swallowed up within three hours after.' The three ships which perished in this miserable manner were the *Association* (flag-ship), the *Romney*, and the *Eagle*.

Sir Cloudesley's body—or what was supposed to be, and was certainly identified as, his body—was found some days afterwards on the shore of St Mary's, and removed to Westminster Abbey, to be interred with all due honour. Many years later, however, an aged crone confessed to the parish minister on her death-bed that a survivor from the wreck, exhausted by his life-and-death struggle against contending waters, made his way to her hut ; and that, to secure the valuable property he carried on his person, she had murdered him while sleeping beneath her roof. The woman then produced a ring taken from her victim's finger, which was afterwards recognised as one presented to Sir Cloudesley Shovel by Lord Berkeley.

Another version of this romantic story says, that some fishermen found a dead body, which, after stripping, and taking from the finger a valuable emerald ring, they buried. As they showed the gem all about the island, news of it came to the purser of the *Arundel*, who tracked down the wreckers, obtained possession of their valuable prize, which he pronounced to be Sir Cloudesley's, disinterred the body, and removed it to Portsmouth.[1]

Mackay draws a pen-and-ink portrait of the worthy

---

[1] These stories are disproved by a letter of Addison's, written when he was Secretary of State, and dated October 31st, 1707 :—' Yesterday we had news that the body of Sir Cloudesley Shovell was found on the coast of Cornwall. The fishermen, who were searching among the wrecks, took a tin box out of the pocket of one of the carcasses, that was floating, and found in it the commission of an admiral ; upon which, examining the body more narrowly, they saw it was poor Sir Cloudesley. You may guess the condition of his unhappy wife, who lost, in the same ship with her husband, her two only sons by Sir J. Narborough.* We begin to despair of the two other men-of-war and the fire-ship that engaged among the same rocks.'

* Sir Cloudesley married his patron, Sir John's widow.

Admiral: 'No man understands the affairs of the navy better, or is beloved of the sailors so well as he. He hath very good natural parts; familiar and plain in his conversation: dresses without affectation; a very large, fat, fair man, turned of fifty years old.' This honest, unpretending seaman, was disguised, on the monument erected to his memory in Westminster Abbey, after a fashion which provoked the humorous censure of Addison (*Spectator*, No. 26). 'Sir Cloudesley Shovel's monument,' he says, 'has very often given me great offence: instead of the brave, rough English admiral, which was the distinguishing character of that plain, gallant man, he is represented on his tomb by the figure of a beau, dressed in a long perriwig, and reposing himself upon velvet cushions under a canopy of state. The inscription is answerable to the monument; for, instead of celebrating the many remarkable actions he had performed in the service of his country, it acquaints us only with the manner of his death, in which it was impossible for him to reap any honour.'

A more enduring fame than Sir Cloudesley Shovel's—in spite of his monument in the great Abbey—rests upon the name of one of the humblest of Queen Anne's seamen, ALEXANDER SELKIRK. Not, indeed, that it is of his own making: for the story of his adventures, strange and singular as it is, would probably have been forgotten, had it not been seized upon by the genius of Defoe, and developed into the deathless romance of *Robinson Crusoe*.

The story is delightfully told by Steele in *The Englishman* (No. 26, Dec. 3, 1713), where he speaks of having frequently conversed with Selkirk soon after his return to England in 1711:—

He was put ashore from a leaky vessel, with the captain of which he had had an irreconcileable difference. . . . . His portion were a sea-chest, his wearing clothes and bedding, a firelock, a pound of gunpowder, a large quantity of bullets, a flint and steel, a few pounds of tobacco, a hatchet, a knife, a kettle, a Bible, and other books of devotion, together with pieces that concerned navigation, and his mathematical instruments. Resentment against his officer, who had ill-used him, made him look forward on this change of life as the more eligible one, till the instant in which he saw the vessel put off; at which moment his heart yearned within him, and melted at the parting with his comrades and all human society at once. He had no provisions for the sustenance of life but the quantity of two meals, the island abounding only with wild goats, cats, and rats. He judged it most probable that he should find more immediate and easy relief by finding shell-fish on the shore than seeking game with his gun. He accordingly found great quantities of turtles, whose flesh is extremely delicious, and of which he frequently ate very plentifully on his first arrival, till it grew disagreeable to his stomach, except in jellies.

At first he felt strongly the want of society, and his yearning to see the face of man was almost insupportable. He grew dejected, languid, and melancholy; was scarcely able to refrain from putting an end to his life; until, by degrees, by the force of reason and the frequent perusal of the Scriptures, and by occupying his thoughts in the study of navigation, he became reconciled to his solitude. Thereafter, the vigour of his health, freedom from the world's anxieties, a cheerful and serene sky, and a temperate air, made his life one continual feast. In everything he took delight, and with ornaments cut down from a contiguous wood, converted his hut into a most delicious bower, fanned with continual breezes and gentle aspirations of the wind.

The precautions which he took against want, in case of sickness, was to lame kids when very young, so that they might recover their health, but never be capable of speed. These he had in great numbers about his hut; and when he was himself in full vigour he could take at full speed the swiftest goat running up a promontory, and never failed of catching them but on a descent.

His habitation was extremely pestered with rats, which gnawed his clothes and feet when sleeping. To defend him against them, he fed and tamed numbers of young kitlings, who lay about his bed and preserved him from the enemy. When his clothes were quite worn out, he dried and tacked together the skins of goats, with which he clothed himself, and was inured to pass through woods, bushes, and brambles with as much carelessness and precipitance as any other animal. It happened once to him that, running on the summit of a hill, he made a stretch to seize a goat, with which under him, he fell down a precipice, and lay helpless for the space of three days, the length of which time he measured by the moon's growth since his last observation. This manner of life grew so exquisitely pleasant that he never had a moment heavy upon his hands; his nights were untroubled, and his days joyous, from the practice of temperance and exercise. It was his manner to use stated hours and places for exercises of devotion, which he performed aloud, in order to keep up the faculties of speech, and to utter himself with greater energy.

Steele goes on to observe that when he first saw him he felt that, if he had known nothing of his character and story, he should have seen in him, from his aspect and gesture, a man who had long been divorced from society —such was the strong but cheerful seriousness in his look, such his indifference to the ordinary things about him, like that of one sunk in thought.

When the ship which brought him off the island came in, he received them with the greatest indifference with relation to the prospect of going off with them, but with great satisfaction in an opportunity to refresh and help them. The man more frequently bewailed his return to the world, which could not, he said, with all its enjoyments, restore him to the tranquillity of his solitude. Though I had frequently conversed with him, after a few months' absence he met me in the street, and though he spoke to me I could not recollect that I had seen him; familiar converse in this town had taken off the loneliness of his aspect, and quite altered the air of his face.

ALEXANDER SELKIRK, or SELCRAIG, was born in 1676, at Largo, a small seaport town on the coast of Fife. He first went to sea in 1695. After six years' wanderings he returned home; but his wild and wayward disposition could not be satisfied with the monotony of domestic life, and in the spring of 1702 he found his way south, where he made the acquaintance of Captain William Dampier, the well-known seaman, whose circumnavigation of the globe had secured him a wide and lasting reputation. England was then at war with Spain; and Dampier, who was well acquainted with the American coast, proposed the equipment of an expedition to act against the Spanish in a quarter of the world where they were necessarily weakest. He found some merchants adventurous enough to subscribe the money requisite for fitting out two ships—the *St George*, of twenty-six guns, on board of which he hoisted his own flag, and the *Fame*, also of twenty-six guns, commanded by Captain Pulling. And having obtained commissions from the Lord High Admiral (Prince George of Denmark), to act as privateers against the Queen's enemies, they sailed for the South Seas. At the outset, however, a quarrel arose between Dampier and Pulling, which led to the latter embarking on a venture of his own, and sailing for the Canary Islands. To supply his place, the *Cinque Ports* galley, of sixteen guns, and carrying sixty-three men, was equipped, with one Charles Pickering in command, and Alexander Selkirk as sailing master.

The two ships were at Madeira on the 25th of September. They crossed the line on the 2d of November. Soon afterwards fever broke out on board the ill-found and ill-ventilated vessels; and at La Granda, in lat. 30 N., where they put in for water and food, Captain Pickering died. His successor was a man of cruel and unbending temper; and Selkirk was not long in forming a resolution to desert at the first opportunity, and seek an asylum on some lonely, uninhabited island. Doubling Cape Horn, the expedition began to round the coast of the mainland, and make for the island of Juan Fernandez, where they arrived about the middle of February. In this pleasant ocean oasis, which abounds in green savannahs, leafy woods, and crystal streams, the wave-worn mariners rested and refreshed themselves for some time. They took in a supply of wood and water, and refitted their shattered vessels. To economise the stores of provisions aboard ship, they caught a number of the goats which abounded in the island, and ate them, boiled with the green tops of the delicious cabbage-palm. They also killed several sea-lions, melting their fat to serve as oil for the lamps. Young seals fell victims to their keen appetite for 'fresh meat;' and their fare was further diversified by the quantities of fish which they caught in the neighbouring waters.

While taking their pleasure in this island-Eden they were surprised, on the 29th of February, by the appearance of a strange sail. Immediately they rushed on board their vessels, and hoisted all sail in pursuit. It was close upon midnight when the *St George* came up with her, and found her to be a French frigate of four hundred tons, armed with thirty guns. At sunrise the action began, and was continued for some hours with little advantage on either side. At last the Frenchman began to slacken fire, and was on the point of surrendering, when a fresh breeze sprang up, and he made sail. Dampier was in too crippled a condition to follow. He had lost nine men killed, and a third of his crew were wounded.

On the 22d the two English privateers were off Lima; and furling their sails that they might not be seen from the shore, they lay-to for some hours, in the hope of surprising some of the Spanish barques as they quitted or entered the port. On the 24th they captured a Spanish trader, from which they took all that was valuable. Some other prizes were taken; after which, on the 20th of April, they made an unsuccessful attack on the town of Santa Martha. In the following month they navigated the Bay of Panama; but a bitter quarrel arose between Dampier and Stradling, and the two privateers parted company, nor did they ever meet again.

The *Cinque Ports*, on board of which was Alexander

Selkirk, cruised for some time along the Spanish coast, but without making any prizes. A disagreement sprang up between Selkirk and his commander, and the former resolved at all hazards to quit the ship. Being compelled by want of provisions to return to Juan Fernandez, Stradling recovered two of his crew who had been accidentally left there on the occasion of his earlier visit. They described their island life in such glowing terms that Selkirk felt more than ever determined to abandon the *Cinque Ports*. Accordingly, as soon as her refit was completed, he was landed, with all his effects, and he leaped on shore in a temporary transport of joy and freedom. He shook hands with his comrades, and bade them farewell in a hearty manner; but no sooner, says his biographer, did the sound of their oars, as they left the beach, fall on his ears, than the horror of a life-long solitude—for such it might be—rushed upon his mind. His heart sank within him, and all his resolution failed. Rushing into the water, he implored his departing companions to take him with them. Stradling laughed at his entreaties, and declared that his situation was the most befitting for an individual so discontented and rebellious.

Over the details of his four years' residence it is unnecessary to linger. I have put before the reader Steele's animated summary; Selkirk's fuller narrative, as given in Captain Woodes Rogers' *Cruising Voyage Round the World* (London, 1712), has frequently been repeated. It is needful here only to describe the circumstances of his rescue.

In 1708, an expedition against the French and Spanish traders in the South Seas was fitted out by several Bristol merchants. It consisted of *The Duke*, thirty guns, commanded by Captain Woodes Rogers, and *The Duchess*, twenty-five, commanded by Captain Courtney. Dampier accompanied the expedition as pilot. The two ships sailed from Bristol on the 1st of August, doubled Cape Horn in December, and on the 31st of January 1709 came in sight of Juan Fernandez.

'Slowly,' says Mr Howell, 'the vessels rose into view, and Selkirk could scarcely believe the sight real; for often had he been deceived before. They gradually approached the island, and he at length ascertained them to be English. Great was the tumult of passions that rose in his mind; but the love of home overpowered them all. It was late in the afternoon when they first came in sight; and lest they should sail again without knowing that there was a person on the island, he prepared a quantity of wood to burn as soon as it was dark. He kept his eye fixed upon them until night-fall, and then kindled his fire, and kept it up until morning dawned. His hopes and fears having banished all desire for sleep, he employed himself in killing several goats, and in preparing an entertainment for his expected guests, knowing how acceptable it would be to them after their long run, with nothing but salt provisions to live upon.'

About noon next day, Woodes Rogers sent a boat on shore. Imagine the delight with which the solitary watched its arrival, and the eagerness with which he welcomed his countrymen. He embraced each of them warmly; but at first his excess of joy deprived him of the faculty of speech. At the time, he was wearing his last shirt; his feet and legs were bare; his body and thighs partly covered with the skins of wild animals. His beard was massive, and a rough goat-skin cap covered his unkempt locks. The first transports of happiness over, his tongue was loosed; he overwhelmed his visitors with questions, and readily replied to all which they addressed to him. Curiosity on both sides having been satisfied, the boat returned to *The Duke*, taking Selkirk with them, who, being recommended to Captain Woodes Rogers by Dampier as an excellent seaman, was immediately engaged as mate. For ten days the two captains remained off shore, refitting their vessels and collecting supplies of water, fuel, and fresh meat. On the 12th Selkirk took leave of the island which had been his lonely home for upwards of four years, and of the lonely, self-reliant life which was to suggest to a man of genius one of the finest and most popular romances in the English language.

Selkirk served under Captain Woodes Rogers during the whole of the expedition, which was distinguished by many stirring incidents of battle and adventure, but does not come within the province of the present writer. He landed at Erith, on the Thames, October 14, 1711, after an absence of eight years, one month, and three days. In the following spring he repaired to Largo. Of his later life there is little to be told. He married twice; entered the Royal Navy, and rose to the rank of a lieutenant; and died sometime in 1723.

END OF VOL. I.

INDEX TO VOL. I.

ABELL, JOHN, singer, 161, 162.
Academy of Ancient Music, founded, 195.
Academy of Music, Royal, foundation of, 160.
Actors, fugitive fame of, 137, 139.
Addison, quoted, 3, 4, 359, 360. [*See Spectator, The.*]
Agricultural Classes in Queen Anne's reign, *see* Introduction.
Aldrich, Dean, 177, 178.
'Almahide,' opera of, 153.
'Amadige,' opera of, 160.
'Ambleto,' opera of, 157.
Anne, Queen, character of, *see* Introduction.
'Antiochus,' opera of, 157.
Archer, character of, 2, 32.
Architecture in Queen Anne's reign, 221.
Army, English, condition of, 246, 247.
Art in Queen Anne's reign, 203-205.
Ashton, quoted, 52, 125, 126.
Aston, Tony, quoted, 111, 123, 128, 135.

BAKER, quoted, 22, 48, 104, 109, 119.
Ballad on Marlborough's victories, 314.
Barbier, Mrs, 156.
Barcelona, siege of, 327, 330.
Barry, Mrs, memoir of, 135, 140.
Bartholomew Fair, 125.
'Beaux' Stratagem,' the play of, 31-42.
Beefsteak Club, 121.
Betterton, death of, 123.
Betterton, Mrs, 133, 134.
Blenheim, Battle of, 258-263.
Blow, Dr John, 176.

Boit, Charles, 209.
Bolingbroke, Lord, 255, 306.
Booth, Barton, memoir of, 104-109.
Boutell, Mrs, anecdote of, 139.
Bracegirdle, Mrs, memoir of, 130-133.
Britton, Thos., biography of, 190, 191.
Brute, Sir John, character of, 51.
Bud, Francis, 208.
Burnet, Bishop, quoted, 358.
Burney, Dr, quoted, 166, 169.
Burton, Dr J. Hill, quoted, 250, 251, 263.
'Busybody, The,' play of, 75.

CADOGAN, EARL, 343, 344.
'Calypso and Telemachus,' opera of, 157.
'Camilla,' opera of, 148, 149.
'Careless Husband, The,' play of, 14-26.
Carey, Harry, memoir of, 185, 189.
Centlivre, Mrs, memoir of, 70, 74.
    „   „ quoted, 53, 77.
    „   „ plays of, 74, 88.
Chetwood, quoted, 115, 117.
'Chrononotonthologos,' extravaganza, 187.
Cibber, Colley, memoir of, 5-23; quoted, 110, 113, 114, 115, 122, 128-130, 131, 133, 136, 138, 143, 149, 167, 169.
Cibber, his plays, 11, 23.
    „ his quarrel with Pope, 40.
Clark, Jeremiah, 181.
Closterman, John, 213.
'Clotilda,' opera of, 153.
Club, Anthem, The, 176, 201.
Concerts, weekly, 194.
Congreve, quoted, 162, 172, 173.

'Constant Couple, The,' play of, 26.
Corbett, William, 201.
Covent Garden Theatre, 172.
Coxe, Archdeacon, quoted, 295, 301.
Creighton, Dr Robert, 200, 201.
Croft, Dr, 179, 180.
Crowe, Lewis, 211.
Cutts, John, Lord, 249, 261, 342, 343.

DAHL, MICHAEL, 212.
Daily Courant, The, quoted, 103.
Davies, quoted, 106, 138.
Dennis, quoted, 150.
Devil Tavern, 182.
Dogget, Thomas, memoir of, 109, 112; his 'badge,' 112.
Downes, quoted, 111, 118, 123, 125.
'Dragon of Wantley,' burlesque, 189.
Drama of the Restoration, 23.
Drury Lane Theatre, opera at, 130, 182.
Dryden, quoted, 131, 136.
Duelling, Steele's protest against, 69.
Dunciad, The, 101.
D'Urfey, Tom, 149.

ECCLES, JOHN, 173, 174.
'Elfrid,' play of, 91.
England, social condition of, *see* Introduction.
Englishman, The, quoted, 360, 361, 362.
Epigram on Vanbrugh, 54; on Mrs Tofts, 168; on Nicolini, 170; on Kneller and Dr Radcliffe, 216.
'Esop,' play of, 53.
Estcourt, Richard, 117-121.
Evelyn, quoted, 161, 205, 220, 237.

FARQUHAR, memoir of, 24-32.
Fashion, woman of, her day's occupations, 51, 52.
Fenwick, Sir John, plot of, 321-323.
Finger, Godfrey, 175.
Freeholders, small, condition of,
Frere, J. Hookham, quoted, 316.
'Funeral, The,' play of, 56, 58.

GALLIARD, JOHN ERNEST, 197-199.

Gambling, a vice of women of quality, 52.
Gardens, English, in Queen Anne's reign, 232, 233.
George, Prince, of Denmark, *see* Introduction.
Gibbons, Grinling, 205, 208.
Gibbs, James, 230, 231.
Gibraltar, capture of, 351, 352.
'Gift, The Cruel,' play of, 77, 78.
Gildon, quoted, 117, 123.
Goldwin, John, 201.
Greene, Maurice, 181-183.

HANDEL, his opera of 'Rinaldo,' 91, 92; his operas, 156, 158, 159, 160.
Hawkins, Sir J., quoted, 177, 178, 186, 200.
Haym, Nicolo, 184, 185.
Hazlitt, quoted, 11, 16, 51.
Hearne, quoted, 190, 191.
Heidegger, references to, 152, 153.
Hill, Aaron, memoir of, 89-102; quoted, 107.
Hogarth, William, 220.
Howard, Hugh, 211.
Hughes, John, 157; quoted, 165. 191.
Hunt, Leigh, quoted, 47, 48.
'Husband, The Tender,' play of, 59-61.
'Hydaspes,' opera of, 154.

'INCONSTANT, THE,' play of, 27-30.
Isham, John, 201.

JERVAS, 209-211.
Johnson, Dr, quoted, 145.
'Judgment of Paris,' a masque, 172.

KENT, WILLIAM, 231, 234.
King, Charles, 183.
King, Richard, 184.
Kneller, Sir Godfrey, memoir of, 213-217.
Kynaston, Edward, reference to, 123, 124.

LAGUERRE, LOUIS, 212.
La Hogue, Battle of, 354, 355.
Lawrence, 164.

Index.

L'Epine, Margharita de, memoir of, 164-166.
Leveridge, Richard, 162, 163.
Lille, Siege of, 276-280.
London, social life of, *see* Introduction.
'Lovers, The Conscious,' play of, 61-70.
'Lying Lover, The,' play of, 58.

MACAULAY, quoted, 23, 132, 315, 321, 325, 334, 354.
Mackay, quoted, 360.
Malaga, sea-fight off, 352, 353.
Malplaquet, Battle of, 288-295.
Marlborough, Duke of, memoir of, 235-314.
Marlborough, character of, 251-255; by Saintsbury, 313.
Marlborough and James II., 239, 240.
Marlborough and William III., 241-243.
Marplot, character of, 76.
Marshall, Samuel, 200.
Melantha, quoted, 129, 130.
'Merope,' play of, 96.
Mirabel, character of, 27.
Modish, Lady Betty, character of, 141, 142.
Mountford, Assassination of, 127, 132.
Musical Composers, 172-202.
Musical Small-Coal Man, The, 192, 193.

NAVY, ENGLISH, in Queen Anne's reign, 345-348.
Nicolini, 154, 155; memoir of, 168-171.
'Nonjuror, The,' play of, 10, 17, 18.
Norris ('Jubilee Dicky'), 124.

'OLD BACHELOR, THE,' play of, 8.
Oldfield, Mrs, and Farquhar, 43, 44; memoir of, 140, 144.
Opera at the Haymarket, 91, 148, 149.
Operatic Composers, restrictions upon, 158, 159.
Opera in England, early history of, 147, 160.
Oudenarde, Battle of, 273, 275.

'PAPAL TYRANNY,' play of, 9.
Parson's Green, Peterborough's seat at, 321.
'Pastor Fido,' opera of, 158.
Paul's Cathedral, St, 221.
Pelegrini, Antonio, 212.
Pepusch, Dr, memoir of, 194-197.
Peterborough, Earl of, memoir of, 314-342.
Picture, The, 46, 47.
Pinkethman, notice of, 124-127.
Pope, quoted, 144, 209, 210, 212, 217, 315.
Population of England at Anne's accession, *see* Introduction.
Porter, Mrs. notice of, 144.
Powell, his Puppet-Show, 93; anecdotes of, 117.
Pressgang, The, 347.
'Provoked Husband, The,' play of, 19-21.
'Provoked Wife, The,' play of, 50-52.
Purcell, Daniel, 174, 175.
'Pyrrhus and Demetrius,' opera of, 152.

RAMILLIES, BATTLE OF, 266-269.
Ramondon, Lewis, 169.
'Recruiting Officer, The,' play of, 31, 247.
Recruiting, system of, 247, 248.
'Relapse, The,' play of, 9, 49.
Reynolds, Sir Joshua, quoted, 230.
Ricci, Sebastian, 212.
Richardson, Jonathan, 211, 212.
'Rinaldo,' opera of, 91, 92, 156.
Robinson, Mrs, married to Lord Peterborough, 338-341.
Rockstro, quoted, 159.
Rooke, Sir George, memoir of, 348-356.
'Rosamond,' opera of, 150, 151.

SAINTSBURY, MR, quoted, 245.
'Sally in our Alley,' ballad of, 186.
Scarlatti, reference to, 152.
Schellenberg, the, capture of, 257.
Selkirk, Alexander, the story of, 360-367.
'She Would and She Would Not,' play of, 12-14.
Shovel, Sir Cloudesley, 350-360.

Spectator, The, quoted, 3, 4, 93, 94, 119, 120, 124, 154-6, 157, 169.
Stanhope, Earl, quoted, 253, 326.
Steele, Sir Richard, plays of, 57-70.
Swift, quoted, 165, 229, 230, 337, 338.

'TATLER, THE,' quoted, 115, 123, 125, 134, 143, 153, 166, 168, 210.
'Tender Husband, The,' play of, 55.
'Tesco,' opera of, 159, 160.
Thackeray, quoted, 59, 278.
Theatres in London, 1, 2.
'Thomyris,' opera of, 152.
Thornhill, Sir James, memoir of, 218-221.
Tofts, Mrs, 166-168.
Tournay, siege of, 285, 286.
Tudway, Dr, 199-200.
Turner, Dr William, 201.

UNDERHILL, CAVE, notice of, 122.

VANBRUGH, SIR JOHN, memoir of, 48, 56, 228-230.

Vanbrugh, plays of, 49-55.
Verbruggen, notice of, 123.
Verbruggen, Mrs (Mrs Mountford), notice of, 117-121.
Victor, quoted, 107.
Vigo, Naval attack upon, 349, 350.

WALPOLE, HORACE, quoted, 130, 205, 234, 341.
Ward, Edward, quoted, 192, 193, 246, 247.
Webb, General, 277, 279, 342.
Weldon, John, 173.
Wilks, Robert, memoir of, 112.
'Wonder, A,' ballad opera, by H. Carey, 188-189.
'Wonder, The,' play of, by Mrs Centliver, 79, 88.
Woolaston, 194, 212.
Wool Manufacture,
Wren, Sir Christopher, memoir of, 226-228.
Wynendael, Battle of, 277-279

'ZARA,' play of, 98-100.

www.ingramcontent.com/pod-product-compliance
Lightning Source LLC
Chambersburg PA
CBHW032013220426
43664CB00006B/226